A Philosophy of Comparisons

Also available from Bloomsbury

Comparative Philosophy without Borders, edited by
Arindam Chakrabarti and Ralph Weber
Early Analytic Philosophy and the German Philosophical Tradition,
by Nikolay Milkov
Ethics after Wittgenstein, edited by Richard Amesbury and Hartmut von Sass
The Aesthetics and Ethics of Copying, edited by Darren Hudson Hick and
Reinold Schmücker
The Philosophy of Being in the Analytic, Continental, and Thomistic Traditions,
by Joseph P. Li Vecchi, Frank Scalambrino and David K. Kovacs

A Philosophy of Comparisons

Theory, Practice and the Limits of Ethics

Hartmut von Sass

BLOOMSBURY ACADEMIC
LONDON • NEW YORK • OXFORD • NEW DELHI • SYDNEY

BLOOMSBURY ACADEMIC
Bloomsbury Publishing Plc
50 Bedford Square, London, WC1B 3DP, UK
1385 Broadway, New York, NY 10018, USA
29 Earlsfort Terrace, Dublin 2, Ireland

BLOOMSBURY, BLOOMSBURY ACADEMIC and the Diana logo are trademarks of
Bloomsbury Publishing Plc

First published in Great Britain 2022
This paperback edition published in 2023

Copyright © Hartmut von Sass, 2022

Hartmut von Sass has asserted his right under the Copyright, Designs and Patents Act, 1988, to be identified as Author of this work.

Cover image: MirageC © Getty images

All rights reserved. No part of this publication may be reproduced or transmitted in any form or by any means, electronic or mechanical, including photocopying, recording, or any information storage or retrieval system, without prior permission in writing from the publishers.

Bloomsbury Publishing Plc does not have any control over, or responsibility for, any third-party websites referred to or in this book. All internet addresses given in this book were correct at the time of going to press. The author and publisher regret any inconvenience caused if addresses have changed or sites have ceased to exist, but can accept no responsibility for any such changes.

A catalogue record for this book is available from the British Library.

A catalog record for this book is available from the Library of Congress.

ISBN: HB: 978-1-3501-8438-1
PB: 978-1-3501-8551-7
ePDF: 978-1-3501-8439-8
eBook: 978-1-3501-8440-4

Typeset by RefineCatch Limited, Bungay, Suffolk

To find out more about our authors and books visit www.bloomsbury.com and sign up for our newsletters.

In Memoriam

Prof. Minouche (2011–17)

Contents

Introduction: Comparisons – A Marginalised Classic ... 1
   1. To Begin With: A Telling Imbalance ... 1
   2. Comparisons/Comparing: State of the Field ... 2
   3. Comparisons: A Historical Remainder ... 4
   4. Comparisons: Structure/Grammar/Limits ... 5
   5. On What Follows: An Overview ... 6

Part I Comparison as Structure and Comparing as Practice ... 13

1 Comparisons. A General Account ... 15
   1. Introduction: How to Approach the Topic? ... 15
   2. On the Architecture of Reasonable Comparisons ... 18
      2.1. *Conditions and Preconditions* ... 18
      2.2. *Comparisons as Complex Relations* ... 19
      2.3. *Who C(omp)ares?* ... 21
      2.4. *Comparative Relata* ... 22
      2.5. *The* tertium comparationis ... 24
      2.6. *Comparative Contextualism* ... 25
      2.7. *On Reasonable Comparisons. An Annotation* ... 28
   3. On the Differences of Similarity ... 30
   4. Two Demarcations ... 32
      4.1. *Comparisons and Analogies* ... 32
      4.2. *Comparisons and Metaphors* ... 34
   5. Comparisons and their Functions ... 39
   6. Comparative Limits ... 41

2 Comparisons. A Typology ... 45
   1. Introduction: Different Types – One Structure ... 45
   2. A Typology ... 46
      2.1. *Simple/Complex* ... 46
      2.2. *Result-Oriented/Experimental or Explorative* ... 47
      2.3. *Stable/Emergent* ... 48
      2.4. *Contrastive/Analogical or Similar* ... 49
      2.5. *Diachronic/Synchronic* ... 50

		2.6.	Genetic/Typological	51
		2.7.	Impartial or Pure/Asymmetrical	52
	3.	Coda: On Pointed Comparisons		55

3 On Comparative Injustice 59
   1. Introduction 59
   2. Injustice, Comparatively 60
      2.1. Comparative Injustice – Typologically Considered 60
      2.2. The Will to Compare. On Comparative Philosophy 63
      2.3. Peter Winch on Understanding an Alien Culture 66

Part II Three Studies in Comparativism 71

4 Orientation, Indexicality, and Comparisons: A Theme from Kant 73
   1. Introduction: A Philosophy of Orientation? 73
   2. Orienting Oneself: A Kantian Theme 75
   3. Orientation's Architecture. An Extended Analysis 78
      3.1. Defining Orientation 78
      3.2. Orientation in its Element 80
      3.3. Orientation, Subjectivity, and Indexicality 82
      3.4. Orientation as Twofold Comparison 84
      3.5. On Being Already Oriented 87
   4. Coda: The Perils and Treasures of Disorientation 89

5 Comparative/Descriptive: Wittgenstein and the Search for 'Objects of Comparison' 91
   1. Introduction: After Dogmatism 91
   2. The Assets of Description 93
   3. Language-Games as 'Objects of Comparison' 96
   4. Comparing as a Mode of Description 100
      4.1. 'Objects of Comparison': External and Internal Comparisons 102
      4.2. Pure and Intentional Comparisons 103
      4.3. Incompleteness: On the Dynamics of Comparing 104
   5. Comparative/Descriptive: A Concluding Note 106

6 Comparative Ironism: Richard Rorty on Plural Vocabularies and the Comparisons Between Them 109
   1. Introduction: Theories or Examples? 109
   2. Irony and the Plurality of our Vocabularies 111
      2.1. A Farewell to Truth? 111
      2.2. Irony and the Plurality of Descriptions 113

		2.3. Between Vocabularies, or: Philosophy as Comparativism	115
	3.	Nearing the End: Irony, Comparatively	122

Part III On Relocating Incomparability — 123

7 Against Structural Incomparability — 125
 1. Introduction: Incomparability as a Marginalized Classic — 125
 2. Choices and Comparisons — 127
 3. Incomparability: A First Sketch — 129
 4. A Traditional and a Less Traditional View: Raz and Broome — 132
 5. Ruth Chang on Being on a Par — 135
 6. On Explaining Structural Incomparability Away — 139
    6.1. *Three Forms of Non-Comparability* — 140
    6.2. *Vagueness: Predicates and Comparatives* — 142
    6.3. *Multidimensionality* — 143
    6.4. *Choices, Comparisons and Beyond* — 144

8 On Indexical Incomparability — 147

9 The Curious Case of Normative Incomparability:
 Comparisons, Animals and the Quest for Adequacy — 151
 1. Introduction: 'for all is vanity' — 151
 2. Meeting Elizabeth Costello — 154
 3. A Delicate Comparison and its Aftermath — 158
    3.1. *Costello, Kafka's Red Peter, and the Holocaust* — 159
    3.2. *Three Objections* — 162
    3.3. *Costello's (Un)Belief* — 165
 4. On Extending our Sense of Possibilities — 168
 5. Finally: The Curious Case of Normative Incomparability — 171

Epilogue: Living in an 'Age of Comparison'? An Interpretation
with Diagnostic Intent — 175
 1. In the 'Age of Comparison' — 175
 2. On Nietzsche's Assumption — 176
 3. The Dangers of Levelling Down — 177
 4. And Today: A 'Society of Singularities'? — 178
 5. A Hybrid Ending: On the Future of Comparison(s)/Comparing — 180

Bibliography — 223
Index — 241

Preface

This book has a rather long and ramified genesis. My interest in the topic leads back to a conference and the subsequent interdisciplinary volume on comparisons and their methodology I co-organized and co-edited, respectively, with Andreas Mauz in 2011 (under the title *Hermeneutics of Comparison*, originally in accent-free German).

Writing the first chapters of this book (which became part three) started during a visiting scholarship at UC Berkeley in 2018, generously financed by the Swiss National Foundation. I also have to thank R. Jay Wallace who was my mentor at Berkeley and with whom I had the chance to discuss some of the ethical topics addressed in these texts. Intriguing discussions with Hans Sluga and Barry Stroud (R.I.P.) led to other relevant areas and they corrected some of my views, especially on Wittgenstein and a descriptive approach in/to philosophy.

I would also like to express my gratitude to several friends and colleagues for good (and 'bad') advice along this intellectual trip: Marlene Block, Jonathan Campbell, Ingolf Dalferth, Lisa Heller, Patrick Horn, Andreas Kilcher, Ekkehard Knörer, Andreas Mauz, Olaf Müller, Raymond Perrier, Randy Ramal, Carlos Spoerhase, Werner Stegmeier, Jörg Volbers and Dave Youssef, as well as to the participants of workshops and conferences held in Bielefeld, Claremont and Zurich, where parts of the argument were tentatively presented and vividly debated. A special thanks goes to Michael Hampe. And – in a very different regard – to Hannah Zufall touching on a very specific form of incomparability.

I am very happy that Bloomsbury was interested in this project. In particular, I am grateful to Colleen Coalter and Becky Holland for their support in smoothly leading this manuscript through production and in bringing it to light. And I have to thank Wiley and Meiner for their permission to use the epigraphs in chapter 1 and 6. Bible quotations (as used in chapter 9) do not fall under the 'fair use' rule – interestingly!

This book is dedicated to the memory of my dear friend Prof. Minouche without whom the final chapter on our relation to animals and the limits of comparisons would have looked quite differently, if it existed at all.

Hartmut von Sass
Berlin, March 2021

Introduction: Comparisons – A Marginalized Classic

1 To begin with: a telling imbalance

You can furnish an entire library with books solely dedicated to *metaphors*; you will need to dedicate a good part of your library to sheltering the volumes on *analogies*, and yet it will still take a considerable amount of space to store your exegetical and philosophical literature on *parables*. But what about comparisons and the act of comparing? A mini-shelf might already be more than necessary. It is an interesting but hardly self-evident circumstance that tropes have traditionally gained significant attention through *rhetorics*, in theories of argumentation, as well as in semantics, and despite comparisons being the most prominent figure of speech given their permanent usage in our everyday dealings ('those who live, compare!'), academically speaking they are still lurking in the shadows. Therefore, this striking imbalance between factual prominence and intellectual neglect is telling. But what exactly does it tell us? That comparisons and the practice of comparing – as an exception to the rule among tropes – are just trivial?

As a matter of fact, it is not easy to find contributions to the topic in question from theoretical philosophy, particularly from the philosophy of science.[1] And to do this with a philosophical approach might already be based on an assumption that is highly disputed: namely, that it is fruitful, or at least makes sense, to speak of comparisons without an immediate reference to a practical or scientific context. In other words: one has to subscribe to the claim that there is (something like) a *general theory or hermeneutics of comparison* that foregrounds all the separated fields in which concrete comparisons are applied. If one repudiates the possibility of a general theory, which would be applicable or relevant to these divergent areas of usage while also focused on maintaining an academic interest in the practice of comparing, one might refer to the *disciplinary* work on comparisons and comparing. There are several comparatively-oriented subjects – some of them even have the term within their names – and here we find methodological reflections on what they are actually doing, yet always in relation to a specific field: literature, law, religion, etc. Hence, we are facing a simple and binary alternative: a general comparative structure actualized within different areas (*top-down*) or a variety of comparisons bound to particular arenas (*bottom-up*) – *a comparison or practices of comparing*? This is not a very satisfying alternative, but I will nonetheless focus on the former option.

However, there is important philosophical work on comparisons that focuses on more specific issues. In particular, there are two debates in which comparisons, as well as the problem of incomparability, play a significant role: the clash of *conflicting values* and the incommensurability of *rival scientific theories*. The one issue belongs to the debate on value and virtue theories challenged by intra-personal or, more importantly, social and cultural plurality. The fear in this case is that without being able to compare values, a rational choice between moral or existential options is up in the air. Comparability of divergent values is then considered to be part of moral rationality. The counter-position called *comparativism* that confronts this fear defends the all-encompassing possibility of comparatively weighing up values.[2] The other issue, the rivalry of scientific theories, is linked to the problem of incommensurability – a classical chapter within the philosophy of science since Ludwig Fleck, Thomas S. Kuhn and Paul Feyerabend.[3] Here, the general view is that theories are embedded in paradigms, and these paradigms are diachronically or synchronically separated in such a way that no translations from one paradigm into another are possible. Since there is also no metaparadigm, incommensurability not only entails untranslatability, but also incomparability.

Now, while these debates might bring us closer to structural and methodological questions connected to comparisons and comparative procedures, it is still acceptable to address the marked imbalance between the prominence of comparisons and their marginalization. It is not only surprising, but even bewildering that comparatists have systematically neglected one of their own key concepts. In a way, comparison may be regarded as the great unknown trope, despite its double life in science and ordinary contexts. Therefore, the basic aim of this study is to present a general account of comparisons and comparative procedures to confront this void. This not only implies giving a general theoretical account of comparisons and their structure, but also paying sufficient attention to the embeddedness of comparisons in a variety of practical contexts which inform the act of comparing and its concrete forms of application. The first element entails fighting the – so often bemoaned – 'theoretical poverty of comparative research';[4] the second element calls for dedicating our awareness to the modes of practically and theoretically *securing comparability* and, hence, for contemplating the *limits of comparison as structure* and *comparing as a practice*.

2 Comparisons/comparing: state of the field

The imbalance sketched out in the previous section does not mean, as was already stated, that there are no methodological accounts within disciplinary contexts. The lack of a philosophical account of comparisons – a potential account that would parallel the hugely ramified debates on metaphors, their structure and their semantics – does not imply that there are no important contributions from other fields that are essentially based on comparative procedures.[5] This is particularly true for sociology, literature studies and criticism, and historiography. These approaches are highly relevant for the following project, first by providing theoretical considerations embedded in a concrete scientific context and secondly by creating a test field for a general account that is supposed to be relevant for these separate fields. However, a crucial gap remains between discipline-bound approaches and interdisciplinary collaborations on the one hand, and a general account of comparisons as a trope and the act of comparing on the other.

An influential example of *interdisciplinary work* on comparisons comes from a Berlin-based research group at Humboldt-University, led by Jürgen Schriewer and Hartmut Kaelble. The volumes edited in the course of this project beginning in the late 1990s bring together contributions from history and historical methodology,[6] macrosociology[7] and international political sciences.[8] Especially important and fruitful were those papers that connected comparisons with pertinent issues, such as complexity, transfer-studies, as well as the problem of causality.[9] However, it is fair to say that the focus of most of these contributions does not lie directly on comparison's structure but, rather, is concerned with the methodological difficulties in determining, or even constructing, the comparative *relata*. Therefore, the question is how to avoid incomparability by securing a meaningful structure of comparative procedures.

A second and more recent interdisciplinary research project called 'Practices of Comparing: Ordering and Changing the World' was started at the University of Bielefeld, Germany, in 2017.[10] This is a collaboration encompassing diverse projects especially from the humanities that are all bound together by a praxeological approach to the topic: neither structural questions abstracted from concrete scenarios in which comparisons are at work, nor comparative agents, individuals or collectives are the primary interest. Rather, as the title suggests, comparing as a practice is the focus. This 'third way'[11] – beyond mere structures of comparisons and simple comparative actions – concentrates on comparisons in relation to conflict, valuation, perception, digitalization and communication. Therefore, the question of *how comparisons work* is flanked by the related issue of *what agents do when they compare*. This entails historical accounts, as well as investigating more recent modes and forms of comparing in multiple contexts.

If comparisons have received philosophical attention, it has generally taken three particular forms. First, comparisons – their forms and limits – are dealt with in the context of comparative philosophy, i.e. a cross-cultural endeavour bridging the gap between the Western and Eastern traditions, which (re)gains a sense of the richness of neglected branches of philosophy, as well as of the limitedness of one's own intellectual perspective.[12] Secondly, and connected to the first aspect, the problem of what might be called 'comparative injustice' is a topic that became significant in (post)colonial studies and then in (post)structuralist and deconstructivist philosophy as well (for both topics, see chapter 3).[13] These limits of comparisons are amplified within a third area of research in which the problem of incomparability looms large. As mentioned above, this is mostly dealt with in practical and moral philosophy to process the tension, conflict or even clash between different values (often enough in the context of a pluralistic society). Considerations, such as those by Ruth Chang,[14] concerning attempts to choose rationally between incompatible options have led to a widespread debate about the (im)possibility of incomparability, the notion of 'parity' and, based on this specific issue, the dynamics of comparisons in general (chapter 7 and 8 are dedicated to these topics in greater detail).

Although all these more particular issues have informed this study, this last debate on incomparability is the aspect of philosophical comparativism that comes closest to the ambition of the following chapters: namely to help to overcome the imbalance between the ubiquity of comparisons in science and everyday life on the one hand and a philosophical attitude of neglect on the other.

3 Comparisons: a historical remainder

There is another empty space, however, that won't be addressed in this inquiry. A history of comparisons is an intriguing field of study in its own right and, indeed, it gives access to other highly relevant aspects within the history of science.[15] Here, I can and shall restrict myself only to three comments which revolve around turning points for comparisons and their intellectual contextualization in the sciences and beyond.

After Similarity. It was Michel Foucault who had stressed a crucial turning point for comparisons and their status.[16] Foucault claims that there had been a similarity between thought and world, between language and reality – a similarity in the mode of correspondence securing the possibility of truth (or, Truth). There had been, as the assumption goes, a specific connection between signs and signified things that was later coined as the 'readability of the world'.[17] This late medieval ontology did not survive, and the traditional correspondence built on it had to disappear at the same point. Where once was *similitudo*, there is now silence; where once was stable meaning, there is now semantic fluidity.[18]

This has an impact on comparisons and their relevance. The traditional relation between thought and world, between language and reality, was a non-comparative correspondence based on an *ontologically-a priori match*. After the age of similarity, comparisons had been gaining significance because the link between two ontologically different categories was substituted by a comparison between tokens of the same ontological category. Instead of relating units of language to units of reality, from now on one could compare different ways of articulation with alternative modes of expression (for more detail, see chapter 6 on Richard Rorty and his 'Comparative Ironism'). Therefore, 'the order of things'' is *not internal* to things anymore, but rather, that order is fabricated by classifications ranging from identity to difference by means of comparative methods.

Comparison as Method. This ontological shift contributes one decisive component to a development that takes place much later. The transformation from thinking in terms of invariant substances to thinking analogically and comparatively turned out to be a necessary condition for the establishment of natural sciences based on comparative methods. It has often been emphasized how important it was that the sciences, and later on the humanities, entailed comparative procedures, but also the other way around, namely that the scientific character of particular disciplines was secured by their comparative orientation. This was a complicated and ramified process in the intellectual history of 'Western' societies marked by divergent traditions and background assumptions. For the career of comparative methods, empiricism as 'standard philosophy' in the English-speaking world was crucial. In sharp contrast to this former tradition, the romantic-idealistic idea of individuality created many hindrances for accepting the comparability within the 'order of things'. In this sense, there was, arguably, a long-lasting ambivalence between the 'incomparable' individuality on the one hand, and the unavoidability of comparisons – facing the increasing number of scientific results, the ethnological knowledge and taxonomical alternatives – on the other.[19]

The nineteenth century, however, witnessed the rise of comparative procedures as well-received and acknowledged methods, leading either to the export of comparisons to turn disciplines into comparative enterprises, or to the creation of new comparative subjects essentially connected to and based on that very method.[20] Part of the scientific canon of our present day reaches back to this twofold extension of comparisons that, however, was complemented by other methods such as experiments, case-by-case-studies, statistics,[21] etc. Or comparisons simply remained disputed, for instance by Gadamer, as a mere 'subordinate tool'.[22]

Comparison's Late Modernity. After the *ontological shift* from *the order in things* to *ordering things* in early modernity, as well as the *scientific establishment of comparisons as method increasingly securing the status of being scientific*, we already entered comparison's flipside. It has often been observed that comparisons amplified the internal differentiation of social systems and that they helped to enable orientation between these systems, nationally and internationally.[23] However, there is also the more recent danger of 'comparative totalization'.[24] *Globalization and digitalization* have the troubling effect of a literally all-encompassing 'world traffic' that is in danger of failing to recognize and appreciate bigger differences as a result of levelling them down in the mode of comparison. Everything can now be the object of comparative exercises due to an extensive availability of all *relata*; this exercise then turns into a digitally legitimized valuation of everything in lists, likes and eventually rankings.[25]

This *dialectics of leveling down for the sake of comparability and of establishing new differences as a result of comparative measurements and scalability* is the main source of what Friedrich Nietzsche characterized as the 'age of comparison' (see the epilogue for a diagnostic reading of that assertion). While Nietzsche thought that leaving that epoch behind was something that would happen in a not too distant future, rather it seems today that we are just living in a new, yet intensified, version of that very age.

4 Comparisons: Structure/Grammar/Limits

In one of the very first philosophical papers exclusively dedicated to comparisons, the English writer, philosopher and psychologist James Sully stated back in 1885: 'The term Comparison may be roughly defined as that act of the mind by which it concentrates attention on two mental contents in such a way as to ascertain their relation of similarity or dissimilarity.'[26] A few pages later, he added: 'To compare is to view two things as like or unlike in some definite respect, and unless this common ground or *fundamentum* of the relational act is distinctly seized, the whole process remains indistinct and imperfect' (495). First, what we have in Sully's comment is a marked oscillation between a structural account of comparisons and a characterization of the act of comparing as an 'act of the mind'. This latter account is the rather traditional one and is to be found in the work of Locke, Montesquieu, Rousseau and Hume, among others.[27] Here, comparisons are not primarily regarded as a particular relation between items, but as a cognitive activity constituting that constructed relation. In more recent studies on comparisons and the act of comparing, this oscillation is dissolved in favour of a structural reading that is, as we saw in the second section, itself challenged by a praxeological account with its critique of *comparative cognitivism*, as well as *structuralism*. Then, comparisons as instruments for drawing on relations must be considered as embedded in practical contexts and environments. The structure of comparisons is then merely a secondary abstraction.[28]

The second element that is already touched on by Sully is the distinction between comparison's structure and the ways of securing comparability by stabilizing its '*fundamentum*'. Therefore, we are confronted with what one might call *comparative constructivism*, which deals with modes of avoiding in- and noncomparability and ways of producing comparability by creating the comparative *relata* (that are not just 'out there', but products of stipulation) and by seizing the comparative regard (i.e. the *tertium* that is dependent on the concrete demands on the comparative act). It is important to appreciate the extent to which comparisons are themselves the results of construction and not based on or secured by some variety of ontological underpinnings. Comparability is not an intrinsic feature of things 'in themselves', but the result of categorization, stipulation and applied taxonomies.[29]

And finally, Sully also reminds us of the danger of 'indistinct and imperfect' comparisons. This touches on various forms of *comparison's limits* – the idea of the incomparable sublime, to borrow Kant's term, or the notion that particular items cannot principally be compared with one another (see part III on this topic). As already mentioned, the attempts to circumvent these limits and to secure meaningful comparisons are acts of construction based on specific decisions, particular interests and necessary or possible stipulations. Comparisons access their material in a particular way. Thinking about comparisons, then, also implies an awareness of what might be called *comparative perspectivism*. Comparative acts structure their *relata* in a particular way, and they never do this without alternatives. Given the fact that comparative constructivism accompanied by its perspectivist sibling confronts us not only with the limits, but also with the power, of comparisons and the potential influence of their results: the duty – not to say, virtue – of comparing with mindfulness, fairness, carefulness is of eminent significance. The possibility of 'comparative injustice' forces us, therefore, to pay attention to the *politics of comparison* and to contemplate an *ethics of comparing*.[30]

5 On what follows: an overview

As indicated, the overall thematic ambition and the central argument running through all three major parts of this book is *developing, specifying and defending the claim that there is a general structure of comparisons as trope and act, without being, therefore,* forced to turn insensitive when it comes to the contextual embeddedness of comparative practices.

This claim is all but self-evident, since the more prominent counter-voices in recent debates concerning comparativism suggest that theoretical generality and practical contextualism rule each other out (see section 2 again). More concretely, there are two versions of that critical take: the more modest one assumes that it is *methodologically required* to give the conceptual priority to contexts in which comparisons are applied while being unable to draw more general claims from these settings; the stronger version implies that the comparison's structure changes according to changing applications of comparative procedures. Although there is a highly important *particula veri* in a context-sensitive attention to particulars, both versions – the modest and the more ambitious one – I hold in chapter 1, have not been substantiated. Put constructively and very bluntly, you can have it both ways: sticking to an *encompassing theory of comparisons* as well as *contextualizing comparisons* in concrete, and yet divergent arrangements, ordinary and scientific ones.

This is precisely the *leitmotif* informing this book's three-part setup. Its *context-sensitive generality* is presented in part I whereas the element of generality has here the priority over contextual issues; this is, then, inverted in the following part II by referring to three exemplary while philosophically intriguing constellations, to show in which sense concrete contexts can inform applied comparisons (and the other way around); it is this mutual dependence between structure and context that can be confronted with comparative constraints which leads, in the final part III, to distinguishing between three basic forms of incomparability – structural, indexical and normative – as well as the inter-relations between these theoretically and morally essential forms of limited comparisons and, eventually, their breakdown.

Hence, this threefold structure of the book reflects what the subtitle promises: a work that is dedicated to the architecture, practices and ethical implications of comparative acts.

Part I: comparisons as structure and comparing as practice

It was stated above that a profound philosophical analysis of comparative procedures is still missing (see section 1). This opening part meets that very desideratum. Chapter 1 elaborates on the general structure of comparisons with special regard to the elements of which each comparison consists; chapter 2 specifies this structural analysis by suggesting a typology capturing different emphases within comparative procedures without undermining the general comparative formula; drawing on these considerations between unified structure and divergent applications, chapter 3 focuses on the person performing comparative acts which amounts to integrating the intention, but also a potential preoccupation 'behind' that act up to the danger of what I should call 'comparative injustice'.

In more detail: the first chapter clarifies the ramified architecture of comparisons while defending the basic claim that there is a general structure relevant to every comparative act. Comparing will be presented as a multi-digit relation with special emphasis on the contextual aspects of the comparative elements (i.e. of the *relata*, the *tertium*, the comparative subject). Moreover, it relates comparisons to and demarcates them from relative tropes, such as metaphors and analogies, as well as touching on the problem of similarity while ending with a critique of comparisons.

The second chapter is the counterpart to the preceding one: while chapter 1 gives a general account, this chapter presents important distinctions between comparisons by suggesting a heuristic and, thus, a heuristically helpful, but necessarily expandable typology. This typology is itself comparative in nature; it compares comparisons by using certain *tertia comparationis*. It is important to note that the generalized architecture developed before is not questioned but rather presupposed and deepened in this typology.

One crucial element within comparison's structure that is especially relevant for some of the versions presented in the typology is the comparing subject. Chapter 3 is dedicated to this topic of comparative performances between enabling comparisons and undermining their validity. Recent epistemology has opened itself to (its) ethical implications concerning power, participation and manipulation. Miranda Fricker's 2007 seminal book *Epistemic Injustice* represents this trend in a significant way, but without particular interest in comparisons. However, comparisons too are located at the very interface between epistemic and ethical issues. Therefore, this part concludes with considerations concerning 'comparative (in)justice', a covering term for different forms of applying comparisons' general structure for recursively justifying results that are based on already predefined and, hence, potentially injust parameters.

Part II: three studies in comparativism

The specific interest in comparative performances in chapter 3 functions as an entrance door to the practical contexts in which comparisons are significant and applied. While the focus in the first part was on structural questions, this part integrates this structure into concrete practices without playing out that contextualism against the initial claim of a unified form of all comparisons. Now, practices are by no means isolated units; they are related to other practices informing each other. And this allows for refining the general structure by exposing it to the ramified network of related activities. A selection is, obviously, unavoidable, but will give the opportunity to contextualize comparisons in a sensitive and informative way. The second part will be dealing with comparing *and* . . .

- orienting oneself;
- describing;
- expressing oneself.

The surplus value of this procedure consists of the following aspects: first, the embeddedness of the act of comparing in a *wider conceptual and practical neighbourhood* can be clarified; second, the claim of a general structure can be tested and, eventually, substantiated while at the same time elaborating on comparing and its typologically classified forms by untangling the relation of comparisons to these other practices, *externally* (comparisons *and* . . .) or *internally* (comparisons *as part of* . . .); third and as a side-effect, we can learn more about spatial and logical orientation, the philosophical status of descriptions and the dynamics of self-expression and identity-formation when regarding them as related to comparative acts. On the basis of part I, it can be shown, in this part, *how a generalized account and context-sensitivity* can go hand-in-hand within a programmatic comparativism.

In more detail: the fourth chapter starts off by analysing the Kantian standard account of orientation in order to eventually amend that account by deepening and correcting it in three respects: the *indexical character* of orientation that is due to the particular standpoint of the subject who is oriented by a particular cluster of available reference points; the twofold *comparative procedure* of orientation in which a situation is assessed by virtue of a practically justified and indexically structured net of orientations; and the *receptive modes* of orientation, which mirror the 'existential' fact that the subject is already oriented to a situation through established institutions. The chapter ends by briefly considering the pitfalls and benefits of disorientation.

Chapter 5 jumps into twentieth century philosophy. Wittgenstein presents his later writings as purely descriptive philosophy. One tool for realizing the purity of descriptions is provided by the multifaceted language-game analogy. Less attention, however, is given to the fact that Wittgenstein is also a philosopher of comparison, which invokes the question of how description and comparison relate to one another. Starting from the fact that language-games are themselves structured comparatively, this chapter characterizes comparison as a specific mode of description in order to propose a classification of descriptive comparisons.

Chapter 6 draws on Richard Rorty's postmetaphysical hermeneutics and the role that comparisons – so far neglected – might play within that framework. It is well known that Rorty is critical of the traditional idea according to which true sentences are those that correspond to the reality 'mirrored' by them. If that idea itself does not correspond to 'truth', the vocabularies we rely on, try out or feel at home with are not justified by a non-linguistic authority, but can only be compared with one another. Comparisons provide, then, an intralinguistic orientation facing the plurality of sometimes incompatible ways of articulating oneself. This chapter deals with various versions of comparing vocabularies, as well as with the limits of these versions.

All three chapters in this middle part crucially rely on the grammatical and typological distinctions worked out in part I. Moreover, they testify to the assumption that elaborating on comparisons benefits from measuring their conceptual and practical environment represented here by three adjacent practices.

Part III: on relocating incomparability

While part II has the character of a threefold deep drilling, this final part takes up the line of argumentation set up in the opening part – by way of a seemingly simple question: how is incomparability possible? In other words, and in relation to structural and practical issues worked out in both previous parts, in which sense is it conceivable that comparisons turn structurally impossible or/and practically out of reach? For meeting this (double) question of comparison's flipside, the refined structure and typology create the backbone for the analysis of comparative breakdown: this will be particularly relevant for *structural* forms of in- and noncomparability (cf. again chapters 1 and 2); however, there is no comparison without a comparative agent, and with this personal (or formal, technical or digital) subject the problem of indexicality re-emerges here and, thus, creates an *indexical* form of incomparability (cf. also chapter 4); there are cases in which, structurally speaking, comparisons are in fact possible whereas a certain way of using and relying on them might seem to be dubious or even crossing normative borders, which enters the moral sphere and the ethically delicate topic of *normative* incomparability (cf. also chapters 3 and 6).

Accordingly, this final part deals with the limits of comparing by distinguishing between three forms of incomparability: structural, indexical, normative. Each of the three chapters is dedicated to one form of them, and given the fact that these forms are, to some extent, interrelated, this part will not only give an account of incomparability and its three variants, but clarifies at the same time in which sense they hang together.

In more detail: chapter 7 discusses recent attempts to make sense of the idea of incomparability and what is sometimes called 'parity' (esp. J. Broome, J. Raz, R. Chang). It distinguishes between in- and noncomparability, as well as different forms of vagueness and fuzziness. The upshot of this longer chapter – drawing heavily on part I – is the claim that there is no such thing as structural (or technical) incomparability, and this makes space for another, analytically suppressed version of incomparability presented in the final chapter.

Before elaborating on that alternative version, chapter 8 reactivates earlier discussions on the personal element in comparisons – *who* is comparing? with what kind of *intentions*? – in taking into account the 'subjective' scope and 'objectified' limits of a comparison. Indexicality is a technical tool for clarifying the complicated relation between the comparative act and the one which brings it about. In terms of this part's argumentation, this chapter serves as an interlude by considering additional aspects of structural incomparability while preparing its non-structural and, hence, normative counterpart.

What this means precisely will be clearer by way of a highly complicated example: is it adequate to compare our treatment of animals with the Holocaust? Or do we encounter here a case of normative incomparability? Given this backdrop, this last chapter has three goals: first, it gives a more elaborated account of the concept of normative incomparability; secondly, it refers to a scene from literature, namely J.M. Coetzee's novel *Elizabeth Costello*, to give a 'think description' of a particular case in which we are confronted with normative claims about the (in)adequacy of comparing; thirdly, it aims at producing a tentative outlook on the demands of dealing philosophically with these kinds of severely evaluative, yet particularly moral disagreements. Looking back at all three forms of incomparability, it will be argued that the normative form is an amplification of its indexical sibling while presupposing structural comparability – which leads back to and mirrors the generalized while context-sensitive account running through all three parts.

In sum, part I sets the stage by working out a unified account of comparisons; part II challenges this general approach by exposing comparisons as practices to related ones; and part III uses the refined structure and its contextuality for elaborating on instances of incomparability. The coherence of this argumentation is based on two different and yet essential aspects: the first could be coined *holistic*, insofar as all chapters complement each other by establishing or discovering various links between them that are made explicit; the second aspect is *consistence*, because the book's structure unfolds in a strictly argumentative way in which the results of one part are indicative of or become necessary for understanding and elaborating on the following part. However, holistic and consistent coherence does not secure to have covered up all (important) facets of the topic – I think here of themes such as the comparative media and the materiality of comparisons – but I hope the most relevant and interesting ones.

To these more significant and intriguing topics also belongs the fact that comparisons and comparative procedures benefit (or suffer) from social, political and scientific upsurges (or 'counter-booms'). This precarious dimension is dealt with in the epilogue not providing a traditional as well as comprehensive summary; instead, it presents a diagnostic essay drawing on Friedrich Nietzsche's famous assumption that we are living in an 'age of comparison' ('Zeitalter der Vergleichung'). This concluding piece attempts to interpret Nietzsche's influential diagnosis or premonition against the backdrop of more recent developments within our 'digital age', its promises of all-encompassing scalability and the ambivalent consequences for comparisons. And it also deals with their promising and, yet, menacing impact on our 'age'.

Part I

Comparison as Structure and Comparing as Practice

Is there a general architecture that is essential for every comparison? Does the heterogeneity of comparisons force us to give up the idea that a general account of comparisons is possible? Does not such a generality lead us straight to the reduction of complex phenomena? Usually, the answer to the first question is 'no', since the response to the other two questions is 'yes'. The simple claim of the following section is that we should give the opposite reply to each of these questions.

As we shall see, the notion that there is a general structure relevant to every comparison is often abandoned in favour of paying attention to comparison as a practice. Here, the object of philosophical analysis is not a particular structure but, rather, a performance and activity undertaken by someone, either individually or collectively. This important shift from comparison as a label for a particular structure to 'doing comparisons' within a web consisting of several practices is part of a broader methodological transformation in social (as well as other) sciences. However, as much as this *practical turn* is to be appreciated, this shift from structure to practice is a shift in emphasis; it does not justify the conclusion that the new attention to the practical embeddedness of comparisons replaces (the possibility of giving) a general account.

The first chapter tries to turn this possibility into reality. It suggests an architecture of comparisons without simplifying their structure. Traditional accounts are concentrated on the relation between the comparative objects and the comparative regard (*tertium comparationis*). All these elements, however, have a contextual aspect. According to what might be called comparative contextualism, this context-embeddedness is not a contingent part of comparisons, but rather, it belongs to their very structure. The allegedly simple structure of comparisons between x and y in regard to A then turns into a more ramified and interesting constellation as soon as the concrete contexts of x, y and A are also taken into consideration. Some of the ambitions behind the practical turn just sketched above are captured by this basic idea of comparative contextualism.

This chapter is not only concerned with structural questions, but also with elaborating on the distinction between reasonable and meaningless comparisons, the spectrum of comparative results between similarity and difference, the divergent tasks to be fulfilled by comparative acts and their limits, as well as the demarcations of comparisons from tropes to relative figures of speech (in particular, metaphors which themselves entail a comparative element).

Again, sticking to a general account does not exclude the appreciation of the variety of comparisons and their contexts. Therefore, chapter 2 presents a *heuristic typology* that takes on traditional distinctions between comparative practices in the sciences and humanities in order to significantly refine these differentiations. Although the refinement cannot lead to a complete typology (since there is no typological completeness in general), it might serve as a more exact and helpful overview of comparisons, including their conditions, function, and status.

Based on this typology, chapter 3 unpacks different forms of 'comparative injustice'. This widespread phenomenon ranges from predetermined results where the comparative procedure appears to be neutral, to unequal comparative regards where this imbalance is disguised by different subregards. Cases of comparative injustice are manifold, and they testify to the fact that comparisons are by no means self-sufficient tropes and are always integrated into argumentative contexts.

This chapter also applies these more abstract considerations to the work of philosophy itself. Initially, the methodological problems of a comparative – meaning cross-cultural – philosophy come to the fore. Subsequently, it will be shown how difficult it is to circumvent comparative injustice, even in cases where one has an awareness of and sensitivity to this very danger. Peter Winch's early paper on understanding different cultures will help us to discern this hermeneutically severe problem.

1

Comparisons. A General Account

Comparing as an activity, as an actively relating consideration, an active going back and forth of the conceiving view between the relata presupposes initially a 'sensory' equality or similarity, something that is effective in the sensuality before all particular recognition and correlation.

Edmund Husserl[1]

1 Introduction: how to approach the topic?

In the beginning was ... a simple alternative: either one approaches our topic by elaborating on a general structure that underlies all of its concrete applications or one pays attention to the different contexts in which this structure manifests itself and takes shape. Either one programmatically neglects the structure's embeddedness in the practical world to give priority to a structure that is allegedly not context-bound (to avoid the stronger term 'context-free') or one denies the validity of this methodological separation between a structure and its environment by claiming that a generalized structure may remain abstract, while this very abstraction is to be tempered by reference to particulars. Either one sticks to a top-down policy, regarding comparisons as homogeneous relations despite all contextual ramifications and potential differences, or rather, one opens oneself to the divergent practices of comparing by giving preference to a bottom-up approach that embraces the diversity among comparative procedures, in both the scientific sphere and that of everyday experience. In short, thus far it seems that either *comparison as structure* or *comparing as practice,* may serve as an analytical starting point.

To dispel the impression that this sketch merely presents us with an unsatisfying set of alternatives, let us take a closer look at both options and then at their relation to one another. The first alternative entails the claim according to which a comparison stands for a general structure that is independent of the context of its application. This is not to deny that one could distinguish several forms of comparison (cf. the typology in chapter 2), but these differences do not touch on structural aspects, as they are limited only to comparative adjustments to the divergent contexts and purposes of particular comparisons. The independence of the comparative structure from practical concerns means only that understanding and giving an account of comparisons does not, structurally speaking, necessarily include the reference to issues of applied comparisons. However, this does not entail that we could know something about comparisons and their structure without being exposed to concrete comparative activities. To use Hans Reichenbach's terminology, it is one thing to talk about the 'context of discovery', and it is quite another thing to refer to the 'context of justification'.[2] In this sense, we would be 'justified' in speaking of *the* comparison as a uniform structure while admitting that this has only been 'discovered' inductively by being acquainted with its particular applications.

This somehow *monolithic conception* can again be broken down into at least three historically influential subcategories. There is (1) comparison as (part of) a *scientific method,* accompanied by experimental, statistical and case-study approaches for establishing general, mostly empirical propositions.[3] Instead of a proper 'method', following Ian Hacking, one might also speak alternatively of a 'style of (scientific) reasoning', which includes postulations, experiments, hypothetical constructions, statistical analysis, among other methods and styles.[4] There is (2) also comparison as a *cognitive operation* both in scientific work, as well as in our everyday lives. Here, comparison stands for a procedure by which two or more elements are related to each other in order to ascertain their shared similarities and specific dissimilarities.[5] And finally (3), there is comparison as a *mental act and process* or as an important part of our imagination that links different objects to one another.[6] Hence, comparison is a faculty of the mind (Locke and others[7]), a part of our cognition and passions (Hume[8]), or a competence of the human mind beyond reflection and abstraction (Kant[9]). There are of course no clear divisions between (1), (2) and (3), but all three subversions suggest that when it comes to comparisons – despite their marked differences in characterization and status – we are always dealing with a stable structure to be found in divergent frameworks, whether scientific, operational or mental.

This monolithic account has recently become the target of severe criticism in two ways: one, the status ascribed to comparisons in (1), (2) and (3) is wrong-headed because comparisons are in fact *practically embedded activities*, which brings us to the programmatic transition from comparison to comparing. Secondly, comparative practices (or comparing as a practice) do not exhibit a generalized structure; rather, these practices host *manifold and nonreducible forms of comparing* in relation to the contexts in question. Both critiques are obviously independent of each other; one can subscribe to the first while refuting the second, and, to anticipate the course of my argument, this is what I will argue in this chapter.

Before doing this, one has to gain a deeper understanding of what one might call the *pragmatic account* of comparing. This account belongs to the more general 'practical turn' in the humanities, especially in literary and cultural studies, along with historiography. And in the course of this turn 'practices', i.e. ways of *doing* something, are considered to be the smallest units of analysis, description and reconstruction. Instead of isolating an agent from his or her practical environment – artefacts, objects, background conditions, the context in its materiality, but also the complicated network of interests, preferences and intentions – this whole web of interactions becomes the object of analysis in a theoretical account of practical engagement (while giving this theoretical account is itself nothing but its own practice).[10] The traditional tendency of dividing activities into subjects, objects, instruments and local context is now replaced by an account that integrates all these items and therefore conveys a different idea of agency, knowledge (from knowing that ..., to knowing how ...) and the latent or explicit background conditions of our 'being-in-the-world'. This 'praxeological' approach stresses the fundamental embeddedness of actors and actions within a ramified web of routines, customs, conventions and established habits beyond sovereign choices and well-defined ambitions. The post-Cartesian duality between agent and his or her nonsubjective context is then undermined in favour of a more fluid and rather heuristic distinction between embodied actions and their formative surroundings.[11]

This pragmatic (or praxeological) account is supposed to provide a critique of and a significant alternative to the monolithic approach sketched above. Hence, it is not primarily concerned with comparisons as exhibiting a particular structure – since there is, it is claimed, no such single and uniform structure. It is not primarily concerned with the use and potential misuse of comparisons as instruments of (de)valuation either – since the isolated subject (with its methods and styles, cognitive operations or mental acts) that could bring about such a (de)valuation is also itself a reduction. Hence, comparing as a practice provides us with a relatively holistic approach in order to integrate all aspects that are relevant to the act of comparing under particular conditions.[12] The basic question then is no longer 'what *is* a comparison?' but, rather, 'what are people *doing* when they compare?'

Monolithic vs. pragmatic – is this a real either/or distinction? One would likely answer in the affirmative when approaching this question from the monlithic standpoint. However, as soon as we are dealing with this binary opposition in a more pragmatic fashion, the strict either/or dimension starts to disappear. First, it is, I think, correct to be hesitant about accepting the traditional offers regarding the status of comparisons – as methods and styles, cognitive operations or mental acts. These offers do show facets but hardly provide an all-encompassing picture of comparisons. Secondly, it is also insightful to opt for a very different account of comparisons, characterizing them as activities embedded in concrete and complex surroundings, while leaving behind the problematic gap between the comparing subject and the objective material that is to be compared. But thirdly, the sensitivity to the contextual embeddedness and the readiness to adopt practices as the smallest units of significance (and meaning) does not, I maintain, preclude the initial question concerning a structure that is characteristic of all comparisons from being of decisive relevance. On the contrary, the different comparative practices lead precisely to the assumption of a general and structurally uniform comparison whose structure, conversely, helps to deepen our understanding of the differences within the range of applied comparisons.

I do not see how the attention given to the divergent acts of comparing supports the methodological and far-reaching claim that there is no structure common to all comparisons. This attention rather shows that this generality is clearly defensible, while allowing for significant differences in the practical embeddedness of comparisons. To sum up, we can – and should – have it both ways: a 'general account' of comparisons is not only possible, but by virtue of this account, we can better elaborate on the pragmatic concerns of *doing comparisons*.

The section to come is thus dedicated to offering a 'general account' of comparisons that treats the comparative practice as consisting of different elements worth considering in more detail. The subsequent sections are concerned with the embeddedness of this structure and how it may be used to clarify the level on which the differences among comparative activities are really located. This account will remain 'general' despite all details and might, therefore, be safeguarded against what the comparative sociologist Charles Tilly, following Alfred North Whitehead, coined the 'fallacy of misplaced concreteness'.[13]

2 On the architecture of reasonable comparisons

As this section's heading suggests, we are dealing here with two different topics: the structure of comparisons already circumscribed as 'monolithic' architecture, as well as the reasonableness of a comparison in contrast to its lack of significance and sense or, in more extreme cases, its impossibility. This juxtaposition is not accidental, since reconstructing comparisons as entailing a particular structure is, at the same time, part of demarcating and limiting the scope of reasonable comparisons.

A rather formal structural analysis will be offered now, and it proceeds as follows: the difference between conditions and preconditions for comparing A and B will briefly be introduced (2.1); then, the basic comparative structure requires a detailed elaboration (2.2) in order to illuminate the particular elements constituting a comparison. Here, the question of the comparatively constructed character of these elements will also be raised (2.3–2.5). After these steps, the contextuality of comparisons will become the focus (2.6), concluding with some suggestions concerning the reasonableness of comparisons (2.7).

2.1 Conditions and preconditions

To be able to compare A and B, several conditions must be fulfilled. One can distinguish between two kinds of conditions, namely those that have to be realized *before* the comparative act has begun and those that are based on the comparative act *itself*. Examples for the first group are mostly trivial, such as having at least more than one item to be compared, the stability of the items to be compared with one another, and, far less trivial, that A and B share an attribute or property that is the relevant comparative category (for details, see chapter 7, section 6.1 on the problem of categoriality). These conditions are in fact *pre*conditions and might, therefore, be called 'protocomparatistic'.[14] Examples for the second group are more complicated, such as determining a shared context for A and B, having well- or sufficiently-defined *relata* or finding a comparative regard for relating A and B to one another. These conditions might be called performative because of their emergence from the act of comparison itself (we will come back to this question of performance in 2.4 and 2.5). Accordingly, in the first case we are dealing with conditions which enable the comparison in question, meaning that they must be *already fulfilled* in order to compare A and B. In the second case, we are dealing with conditions that go back to the comparative act itself, meaning that the comparison as an activity is, in a way, *self-fulfilling* in that it realizes its own conditions in comparing *A* and *B*.

2.2 Comparisons as complex relations

As we have seen at the outset – take a look again at the chapter's epigraph – Husserl describes the comparative act as an activity that resembles a moving back and forth, similar to an intended oscillation between the objects of comparison in order to detect (precondition) or to create (performatively realized condition) 'sensory' equalities or similarities. Comparisons are not mere ways of putting *A* and *B* side by side, as the original term might suggest (Greek: *para-bole*; Latin: *com-parare*); they enable a more specific form of relating *A* and *B* to one another.

The structure of comparisons is, at first glance, very simple. Different items (*relata*) are compared by a subject performing the comparative act (*x*: an individual, a collective or a nonhuman mechanism, such as an algorithm) in relation to one respect (*tertium comparationis*). Since there is not and cannot be a comparison *simpliciter*, the comparative regard is a necessary element of every act of comparing items.[15] I suggest calling the items the *material* part, while the *tertium* serves as the *formal* aspect, of comparisons. And comparisons entail a result that is relational and dependent on the *tertium*.[16] According to the so-called trichotomy thesis, there are only three possible results when comparing *A* and *B*: better, worse or equal. This thesis is disputed, since there might be a fourth result which is termed 'being on a par', a kind of vague sameness between *A* and *B* that is not reducible to the three traditional results. Incomparability is then the claim that none of these three or four results can be substantiated (for details, see chapter 7).[17]

However, this analysis is insufficient, since both the material and the formal elements of the comparison have a *context* that is essential for comparisons not only to be meaningful, but also to be possible in the first place. This implies that the items do not exist in a void but within a concrete arrangement, which is the essential *particula veri* in the praxeological account. Take a very simple example: imagine a friend of yours has a birthday and you have two ideas for a present. Suppose now that it turns out (and you find out) that your friend already has present *B*. Comparing *A* and *B* without that particular context might have led to a very different decision than the one you will now make, namely choosing *A*. One could also claim that the connection between *A* and its context C_A (and the same goes for the contextualized *B* and C_B) entertain an internal relation. C_A is then only analytically separable from *A* but nevertheless intrinsically connected to it as long as the comparison between *A* and *B* has any relevance.

But the claim goes further, namely, to say that the comparison between *A* and *B* is not only meaningless (and not reliable) without taking the contexts C_A and C_B into account, but not possible either. Why that stronger claim? Because one cannot switch off the context that remains, often enough, latent or is taken to be self-evident. Assuming that your friend had not been given the gift *B* is itself part of an implicit context that was – here wrongly – presupposed, but that can nevertheless be made explicit. Hence, there are no *A*s and *B*s without Cs_A and Cs_B. These contexts may be tacit, but that does not mean that they are not there, at least latently; they might have just been 'blindly' or 'silently' taken for granted. This very simple example shows that the *relata*, as well as the comparative regard, can remain stable while contextual shifting produces a different comparative outcome. Putting the stress on the contextual aspect of objects to be compared is supposed to capture this significant, yet rather overlooked, difference.

There are not only the contexts of the material aspects of the comparison to consider. The formal aspect, the *tertium comparationis*, also has its specific context, which we may call C_T. Let us again refer to an example: it is an already-established complaint – typical of the discourse on comparisons – that one cannot compare apples with pears. This reservation is simply caused by the presupposition that A and B must already entertain a certain degree of resemblance (*similitudo*) (see section 3). Apples and pears, only connected to one another by means of a comparison would, then, not meet that condition. This claim is obviously confused, since it merges two problems into one: trying to find one appropriate regard T for A and B is not quite the same as having a comparative regard T and then asking whether A and B are comparable according to that already chosen *tertium*.

However, it is not wrong-headed to call for a specific similarity, but the question is how to understand this call correctly. One might say that the similarity between A and B is not an *ontological* one (the actual resemblance between apples and pears) but, rather, a *constructed* one, by way of already having or now choosing the formal respect (*tertium*) by virtue of which the relevant comparison will be made.

Now, this constructive regard, in a way, creates the kind of resemblance required even for comparing apples and pears, and that creation is based on the context of the comparative regard (C_T). For example, let's say you want to bake a cake (I am writing here as a non-expert), and the question is: which kinds of fruit better suit the taste that the cake should have. According to that regard, one might prefer pears over apples. By C_T – for example, the guests for whom the cake is baked, their tastes, the specific event, etc. – the fruits turn out to be similar enough, while determining, as well as contextualizing, the regard which enabled the comparison in question. Here again, 'enabled' is to be read not only in the sense of securing the meaning and significance of comparing A and B, but also in the sense of making that comparative act possible. A change in T's context (which should be distinguished from changing A's and B's contexts) here might also imply a different comparative result.

To complicate things a bit more, one should also take into account that both kinds of contexts – of the material items (A, B, ...) and of the formal regard (T) – are not independent from one another. Refer again to our example of the birthday present: take T to be the criteria of newness and surprise – not the worst idea when searching for a birthday gift. The context of a friend's birthday as a kind of institution informs the significance of T, or to put it more simply: usually, a birthday present should be surprising, which is the context T that establishes the criterion of newness. Hence, if you know that your friend already has present B, you will choose present A. Now, let's slightly alter the example: imagine that your friend possessed a beloved watch and then carelessly lost it somewhere. Given this background, you decide to buy him a new one that is exactly the same. Now, you will choose B, since the context of the items has changed in such a way that the criterion T (of newness and surprise) is now met in a different manner.

To sum up: a comparison between two items (obviously, more are also possible) is a relation made up of five elements:

- *performative*: the institution conducting the comparison (x);
- *material*: the items A and B;
- *formal*: the comparative regard T;
- *contextual 1*: the contexts of the *relata* (C_A, C_B);
- *contextual 2*: the context of the particular *tertium* (C_T).

These five elements are necessary and, thus far, they seem to be jointly sufficient features of every comparison (for the upgraded version, see 2.7). At this point, the claim that comparisons have a 'monolithic' architecture might have now gained a more precise shape. This claim says, on the one hand, that every comparison is constituted by these five elements, and on the other hand, that all actual differences between comparisons are not of structural nature but, rather, are derived from different constellations between these elements (x; A and B; T; C_A and C_B; C_T). Therefore, a comparison's structural unity does not rule out sensitivity to the contextual diversity of comparisons.

2.3 Who C(omp)ares?

Let's have a closer look at the list above and its elements. There are, as I already mentioned, different candidates that may function as the performative x in order to bring about a comparison. Trivially speaking, individuals or collectives usually serve as the comparison's subject. However, we are about to confirm Nietzsche's intriguing assumption that we are living in an 'age of comparisons' ('Zeitalter der Vergleichung') in which 'vertical' valuations are gradually disappearing and, instead, literally everything is turning out to be 'horizontally' comparable (the Epilogue will offer an interpretation of Nietzsche's diagnosis). The omnipresence of advanced search engines fed with inconceivable quantities of data and structured by inscrutable algorithms testify to this contemporary extension of the meaning of the 'agent' – or, rather, a digital pseudo-agent – behind comparative acts.

However, speaking of an 'agent' might already be misleading insofar as, in more complicated settings, the performative x is in many ways *involved* in the comparative procedure.[18] This involvement can take different forms: *epistemically*, since a point of view that is external to the objects of comparison, as well as the stability of that perspective, are disputable;[19] *relationally*, since the one who compares might not remain untouched by the comparative procedure (its comparative regard, its results) itself – what could change, adjust and supplement a particular comparison;[20] and *motivationally*, since comparisons are not free of explicit or latent preferences, as well as extracomparative purposes, interests or even pervasive agendas informing – and, eventually, distorting – comparative results.[21]

In this sense, comparisons are not necessarily sovereign acts because the (human or nonhuman) institution conducting the comparison is itself part of that very practice without standing 'outside' the act, at least in more ramified, and especially in more normatively-loaded, cases. Moreover, comparisons are by no means self-contained activities, but are integrated with pre- or noncomparative considerations – to the dangerous extent that comparisons are functionalized for giving evidence to an already-predefined result. Here, we are touching on one of the major topics of comparative research: the precarious implementation of a comparison within a network of power, interests and biased intentions, and hence the ambivalent question of who it is that c(omp)ares (on this issue, see chapter 3).

2.4 Comparative *relata*

Structurally speaking, anything can be compared with anything else.[22] It is therefore a confused notion to suggest that a comparative item, which may really be a cluster of several properties (for instance, an apple with colour, taste, etc.), could *per se* be excluded from a comparison with another item (a pear). Insofar as the idea of uniqueness (of *A*) is linked to the assumption of *A*'s incomparability, one can simply refute that linkage or deny that any item could instantiate that very idea. We should do the former, as every single item is, strictly speaking, unique, whereas this ontological fact does not support the claim that ascribes an incomparable character to literally all items.[23] The remaining problems of comparability can only be dealt with when referring to a *tertium* establishing a particular comparison (see 2.5).

There are nevertheless issues that primarily concern the comparative items and their relation to one another. First, a comparison presupposes at least two items. Either we have two different *relata* compared at a particular time *t* (e.g. the unemployment rate in California and Wyoming in September 2017; *synchronic*); or one item *A* is compared with itself by virtue of a developmental regard using t_1 and t_2 (e.g. the unemployment rate in Wyoming in September 2017 and September 2018; *diachronic*); or we have a combination of both options. In this case, we are dealing with two items *A* and *B*, but *A* at t_1 and *B* at t_2 (e.g. the unemployment rate in California in September 2017 and in Wyoming in September 2018; *diachronic**).

Secondly, these three cases hint at additional problems that one has to bear in mind methodologically (especially in historical studies, political science, ethnology and economics). (1) There has to be a synchronic stability within the *meaning* of the comparative regard, which means that what counts as 'being unemployed' in California and Wyoming has to be similar; otherwise comparing these rates is useless (*semantic stability*).[24] (2) There has to be a sufficient degree of stability within an item *A* between t_1 and t_2 (for example, compared in terms of unemployment); hence, if *A* is Wyoming and t_1 and t_2 are 1817 and 2017, this comparison is also useless simply because Wyoming as a US state did not yet exist at t_1 (*diachronic stability*).[25] (3) An additional difficulty stems from potential interactions among the objects of the comparison. It may be the case that California's unemployment rate increased considerably because every Wyomian searching for a job decided to leave for Los Angeles. This comparison is, however, not undermined, but rather, its explanatory power is diminished (*problem of independent relata*).[26] And finally, (4) when comparing *A* and *B* with regard to *T*, all other variables have to be stable. This is not the case when referring to the unemployment rate in California at t_1 and Wyoming t_2 – with negative consequences for the validity of this comparison (*problem of consistency*).

Now, (1)–(4) have more to do with the relation between comparative items. But what about these items themselves? It has often been stated that the more significant question concerns the ways of creating and stabilizing the *relata* – rather than the quest for a 'monolithic' structure for every comparison.[27] This statement reflects the constructivist (or nominalist) assumption that the comparative items are not just 'out there', but are in some way generated. One could present this claim in two different versions. The *weaker version* says that one compares items that are indeed 'real', while their comparative abstractions are constructed and, for the sake of their comparability, adjusted or even manipulated. When comparing the unemployment rates in California and Wyoming at a certain time *t*, it is, so the argument goes, not clear at all what 'California' and 'Wyoming' precisely stand for, due to a necessary lack of concreteness – as labels for highly complex political, social and economical systems – they might have as geographical terms. Insofar as California and Wyoming are adjustable to different comparative settings, they show a certain degree of 'plasticity',[28] due to their internal complexity. This complexity has to be reduced in order to make insightful comparisons, while this reduction itself is an act of construction. In contrast, the *stronger version* says that there is no 'real' California or Wyoming, since 'California' and 'Wyoming' are always only mere constructions brought about within a specific comparative framework in which several aspects – institutions conducting the comparison, the comparison's purpose, the chosen regard, etc. – influence each other and, hence, do not leave the constructed comparative *relata* untouched. In a Kantian fashion, Peter Zima claims that we have no access to the items 'themselves'; we are left with mere (re)constructions.[29]

On the one hand, it is important to pay attention to the possibility – and sometimes, necessity – of constructing comparative items for enabling the relevant comparison. Often enough, and in cases exceeding a particular degree of complexity, these constructions (through stipulations, definitions, reductions, adjustments, etc. concerning 'California' and 'Wyoming') belong to the set of comparative conditions or preconditions (see again 2.1). On the other hand, this generalized comparative constructivism – in both its stronger, as well as its weaker, forms – remains exaggerated. For one, Zima and other constructivists suggest that here we are dealing with an epistemological problem by relying on the dubious duality between the unaccessible 'real' and its 'mere' construction. It seems to be far more adequate to characterize the problem as one pertaining to the complexity of *A* and *B*, a complexity that has to be tentatively reduced in order to be able to compare both items in the first place. Hence, a decreasing complexity seems to be accompanied by a declining degree of comparative (re)construction. If we, for instance, leave 'California' and 'Wyoming' behind as labels for highly complex political, social and economical systems and, rather, take them as geographical entities to be compared in terms of size or population, the necessity to intervene constructively simultaneously decreases. If we, for instance, refer to everyday comparisons, such as comparing the top scorers in the English Premier League, the degree of construction necessary to find out who scored the most is – nearly, but not totally – zero. An all-encompassing comparative constructivism is, therefore, an inappropriate description for many cases, namely for those exhibiting a lower degree of complexity.

2.5 The tertium comparationis

As was already noted, there is no comparison *simpliciter*, which means that there is no comparison without a regard by which comparative items are comparable and are in fact compared. This *formal* element of every comparison serves as the necessary (and yet not solely sufficient) basis for putting two or more items into a comparative setting. The possibility of comparisons, as well as the problem of comparability, are always rooted in a *tertium comparationis*.[30] Or, hermeneutically speaking, it is the comparative 'whereupon' (*'woraufhin'*), as well as the point 'from where' (*'von woher'*), that makes it possible to compare in the first place.[31] In this sense, the comparative regard is either described as the focus and designation or as the starting point for the comparative act when characterizing this act in local or perspectival metaphors of orientation.

Not every *tertium* has to be *explicit*, but each one is open to being made explicit. Often enough, the comparative regard remains *latent* because it is self-evident, silently presupposed or just taken for granted. If asked where one prefers to live, in California or Wyoming, a straightforward reply has to postulate a regard according to which this oblique comparison may become significant. Making the regard explicit might imply a reference to different regards, such as cultural diversity, the landcape's beauty, the open-mindedness of the people, etc. This difference between latent and explicit regards leads then to another distinction, namely the one between *simple* and *multidimensional* comparisons in the framework of a single comparative setting. The former version means that A and B are compared by reference to one single *tertium*. This is the case when comparing both US states in terms of topographical size, the result of which is fairly clear. When putting both states into the more ambiguous framework of preferences (for instance, where to live), one has to deal with an equally ambiguous result. The general comparison supervenes on subcomparisons based on several comparative regards (diversity, beauty, the population's character, etc.). Obviously, the overall result will be far less distinct, due to three reasons: one, the question as to which regards were relevant for the general comparison is disputable; two, preferences are not quantifiable and, hence, harder to weigh up; and three, the combination of different results on the sublevel by virtue of the general result of comparing California and Wyoming as residences will necessarily remain inconclusive.

The constructivism we have already encountered in regard to the comparative items is also relevant, and even more so, in regard to the *tertium comparationis*. All comparative regards are not 'real', since these regards are necessarily stipulated, (pre)defined and determined. The fact that, in some way, every regard T_1 is constructed also means that there are always comparative alternatives $T_2, T_3, \ldots, T_n$ which could substitute for T_1. However, this last sentence entails an ambiguity concerning T's constructive character, an ambivalence that should be resolved: either (1) it means that T brings the constructive character into every comparative practice (comparisons as relations constructed by comparative regards); or (2) it means that T itself is a construction (comparative regards as constructed entities). (1) and (2) do not preclude each other, but rather go hand in hand.

(1) The comparability of items is, of course, not an intrinsic property of these items themselves but results from relating them comparatively in reference to a regard T.[32] By applying T, one presupposes a certain kind of similarity, as well as a certain degree of difference, between A and B. The similarity is based on at least one category applicable to both items: by introducing taste as a comparative regard, apples and pears turn out to be comparable; apples and the virtue of chastity are unfortunately not comparable in relation to that T. As long as A and B share the category introduced by $T_1, T_2, \ldots, T_n$, A and B are comparable in the range T_{1-n}. At the same time, a difference between A and B is necessary to avoid the analytic, yet empty, statement that A equals B in every regard.

(2) Every comparison is not only constructed by introducing a comparative regard, but this regard itself derives from a *pre-* or *intra*comparative determination.[33] In more complex comparisons between A and B, it is often the case that potential regards $T_1, T_2, \ldots, T_n$ share that complexity and, hence, have to be redefined, adjusted and manipulated in order to make a comparison transparent. When comparing California and Wyoming in terms of their unemployment rate, one must again define precisely what 'unemployment' means in a more concrete manner (given the political, social and economic contexts in both states).

In (1), the comparative act is enabled, i.e. constructed, by introducing a *tertium* (or several *tertia*); in (2), this *tertium* is itself *pre*comparatively constructed or developed *within* the course of a particular comparison, i.e. the context of a ramified practice of comparing.[34] These differences only partly cover the range of possible relations that the *relata* and the *tertia*, embedded in their particular contexts, can entertain in certain comparative settings. Again, these differences do not touch upon *structural* issues. Rather, they indicate different *constellations* within a comparative setting, such as: initially determining the *relata* A and B to eventually define a *tertium* T; having one comparative item A, as well as a relevant regard T_n, and then searching for additional comparable items B, C and D; or having several items A, B and C and adjusting their contexts C_A, C_B and C_C to be able to employ a particular regard T_n, etc. All these divergent constellations testify to the constructive, yet also constructivist (and experimental; see 2.7), dynamics *prior to,* as well as *within,* comparative procedures, which function by privileging particular elements and then relating them to the missing items required in order to make that very comparison. The typology submitted in chapter 2 aims to capture this range of comparative constellations.

2.6 Comparative contextualism

Up to this point, we have elaborated on the comparative structure, which consists of a comparing subject (human or nonhuman; x), at least two items (*relata*; $A, B, \ldots$), and a comparative regard (*tertium*; T). These performative, material and formal elements are *necessary* for every comparison. However, in section 2.2 it was claimed that they alone are *not sufficient*. Therefore, the positive proposition has to be defended that comparisons entail additional, yet equally necessary, items and that these items, I suggest, concern the context of the *relata* (C_A, C_B, ...), as well as the context of the *tertium* (C_T).

What does this less-trivial claim amount to in more detail? First, integrating contextual considerations into the structure of comparisons functions as a critical commentary on the traditional separation between an allegedly abstract formalism on the one hand, and its concrete, yet seemingly secondary, application in practice on the other. Secondly, this could be taken as a shared concern between the 'monolithic' account presented here and the pragmatic (or praxeological) accounts that are critical of a uniform structure. Thirdly, considering the contextual elements as indispensable to every comparison entails the claim that a particular comparison disappears as soon as C_A, C_B, ..., or C_T are missing – just as, for instance, the lack of a comparative regard T_n dismantles the comparative structure altogether. Fourthly, one has to, however, at least tentatively explain why the claim of necessity appears to be trivial when it comes to the material and formal elements, and yet, when addressing contextual aspects, it calls for justification.

This section is concerned precisely with this explanation that leads to a defence of what might be called 'comparative contextualism' (or, if you prefer, '-isms'). And it is based on a threefold conjecture: namely, that every *relatum A* and every *tertium T* already come with a context C_A and C_T (*A* and *T* are never completely context-free); that these items (*A* and *T*) are not identical with their contexts (because *A* and *T* can be combined with different contexts C_A and C_T); and that this close connection between *A* and *T*, as well as between C_A and C_T, obscures the fact that a particular comparison is already based on several background assumptions that are often just taken for granted, presupposed or blindly accepted. Hence, insisting on C_A and C_T as equally necessary comparative elements is about making these "tacit" assumptions explicit. To clarify this threefold conjecture, I will give a brief description of a more *general* contextualism in Husserl and Heidegger (1) and then demonstrate *comparative* contextualism by referring to concrete cases (2).

(1) *General contextualism*. The basic thesis of general contextualism is that every entity is primarily part of an environment and its surroundings. 'Entity' is an intentionally vague term, considering that it could entail very different things: objects, artefacts, persons, but also practices, values, convictions, etc. 'Primarily' means that these environments and surroundings are the contexts in which these entities have their place and with which we are more or less acquainted. We know these entities only by being practically exposed to them, not in an abstract void, but by confronting them in specific situations. The meaning and significance of these entities lead us back to these contexts, whereas the rupture and breakdown of a practice could, derivatively, serve as an occasion that enables us to consider an entity as detached from its usual context.

Heidegger captures this 'ontological' precedence of practical dealings over secondary abstractions by introducing the duality between 'ready-at-hand' (the range of usual contexts of an entity; '*zuhanden*') and 'present-at-hand' (abstracting the entity from concrete contexts; '*vorhanden*').[35] Heidegger himself claims that every present-at-hand status can only be a derivative inference from a precedent ready-at-hand status and that this inference usually stems from instances of disfunctionality.[36] The late

Husserl also subscribes to this claim of practical embeddedness, yet remains loyal to the methodological possibility, and even scientific obligation, to determine ways of 'bracketing' reality and to isolate the entity in question from its context(s).[37] Authors submitting strong pragmatist accounts may, in contrast, deny what Husserl has called '*epoché*' by stating that this isolation of an entity merely resembles the creation of an alternative context. Here, contextualism is transformed into a stricter holistic doctrine.[38] In any case, in all three readings, the essential message is that an entity A has a context C_A and that only through C_A, can the entity A have meaning and significance. Insofar as the entity A is a human being or a *Dasein*, the context C is its 'being-in-the-world' or, with a slightly different emphasis, its 'lifeworld'. Accordingly, a comparative structure which stipulates that its material and formal elements be completely detached from their contextual embeddedness seems to be at odds with this general contextualism in the wake of Husserl, Heidegger, and a particularly pragmatic interpretation of their work.[39]

(2) *Comparative contextualism*. This contextualist version is about employing the general claim of (1) within comparative settings. What has to be demonstrated to achieve this? First, as already noted, the connection between the *relata* ($A, B, \ldots$) and *tertia* (T) to their contexts ($C_A, C_B, \ldots$, and C_T) is an essential one – without claiming that a particular item (A) is necessarily linked to a particular context (C_A). Secondly, there are no completely context-free *relata* and *tertia*; hence (and thirdly), contexts can change and may intentionally be substituted by other contexts, with the consequence that the comparative arrangement changes as well. We will begin with the material elements of comparisons and then turn to the formal ones. For both the material and formal elements, it is easier to defend the contextualist claim in situations with a more complex comparative setting, and thus, this defence is more difficult to make when confronted with comparisons within an abstract framework (allegedly) devoid of any concrete surroundings. I will proceed by referring to examples in each case.

C_A – simple cases: here, one could recall the birthday-present scenario mentioned in section 2.2. Newness and surprise may serve as the comparative T when there are two presents in mind (A and B). All elements (A and B, as well as T) remain stable while the context of the material items (C_A, C_B) changes. Thus, if you heard about your friend already having present B, a watch, you might rather prefer A as something new. Imagine that your friend had lost his watch somewhere. Given these particular circumstances, you opt to buy him a new one that is exactly the same kind as the lost one. Now, you will prefer B, because the context of the relevant items has changed in such a way that the criterion T, newness and surprise, is better met by B than by A.[40]

C_A – more difficult cases: for the sake of the argument, we must refer to very simple examples as well, because they seem to have no necessary context, precisely due to their simplicity. 'Simple' could mean, for instance, dealing with a quantifiable regard, such as the question of who scored more goals, player A or B. This seems to allow for a straightforward answer, considering that A scored five times, while B scored seven times. However, here it is already presupposed that one could neglect the number of games A and B have played (apart from other contextual aspects, such as their position, scored points for assists, etc.). Hence, if one changes the context of both material items (the players A and B) by integrating the numbers of games they participated in into the calculation, the comparative result will be different, although all other elements remained stable.

C_T – simple cases: for this scenario we can again refer to the comparison of two complex systems, such as the states of California (A) and Wyoming (B) in terms of their unemployment rate T. Now, the unemployment rate T is such a complex item that it is not hard to imagine divergent contexts (C_T): is the meaning of 'unemployment' roughly the same in both states? (*semantic stability*); is there a (hidden) connection between the Californian and Wyomian unemployment rate? (*problem of independent relata*); what does governmental support for unemployed individuals look like in both states? (*problem of consistency*), etc.

C_T – more difficult cases: here, we have to turn to comparisons that are as simple as possible, for instance, comparing the height T of two geometrical forms A and B which are supposedly devoid of any concrete or real environment. What one can do, however, is make explicit that even such context-averse conditions do not lead to a completely context-free scenario. Even here, one would have to define the perspective from which A and B should be perceived, whether A and B are in a vacuum, etc. And in dealing with all these more precise issues, one is thus creating particular contexts $C_{T1}, C_{T2}, \ldots$ in such a way that one is entitled to claim that establishing a context without context is itself nothing but a context.

As we will see in more detail later (see chapter 9), there are cases of contextual embeddedness that do not support comparative arrangements but, instead, prohibit them. These cases belong to normative considerations in which the particular contexts of items to be compared with one another (C_A, C_B) are evaluatively or morally burdened in such a way that performing a comparison between A and B is taken to be normatively impossible. Comparing an event (A) with the Holocaust (B) is not impossible because of structural limitations; rather, for some, this comparison is morally unacceptable, while the 'impossibility' is only conceivable through certain contextual assumptions (C_B) that have to be made explicit in order to understand and appreciate this precarious debate.[41]

2.7 On reasonable comparisons. An annotation

Is there anything comparatively reasonable to say about reasonable comparisons? Since this topic has to do with a particular range of possible comparisons, one fruitful approach might be to demarcate reasonable comparisons by limiting their scope – instead of directly asking what precisely the comparative reasonableness consists of. There are two steps to this limitation:

(1) Structurally, there is the important distinction between comparability and *non*comparability (in contrast to *in*comparability; see chapter 7, section 6.1). Trivially speaking, all reasonable comparisons belong to the realm of comparability and represent a subset of that very domain. However, this domain – which entails the *structural possibility* of all comparisons – is again limited by another one of its subsets, namely the subset of all *normatively incomparable* relations. These comparisons are structurally possible but are disputed or even excluded due to evaluative or moral considerations (cf. chapter 9). Hence, reasonable comparisons belong to a particular

range that consists of all structurally possible comparisons and yet excludes those comparative acts that are taken to be normatively – evaluatively or morally – unacceptable. Since this latter clause is itself not a mere given and, rather, is subject to ramified debates, the limits of reasonable comparisons can be part of that dispute as well.

(2) With the second step we must leave merely structural considerations behind. When translating 'reasonable' as 'useful', we can ask what kind of aim comparative acts are connected to.[42] For this purpose, it might be suggested to distinguish between *result-oriented* and *experimental* comparisons (see also the typology in chapter 2). Result-oriented comparison simply means that comparing A and B in regard to T is part of a search for getting more insight about A and B within a rather well-defined arrangement. Now, this straightforward outcome is not always of primary interest when comparing A and B. What one can also do by comparing these items is try out and test different constellations between all the comparative elements characterized above. In these cases, one determines, for example, the material and contextual items, as well as a particular result, in order to uncover the effect that this determination has for potential *tertia comparationis*. Then, one might again change this conditional arrangement by redefining the comparative assumptions to achieve an equally conditional conclusion.

To sum up: in step one, reasonable comparisons are a subset of those structurally possible comparisons that are normatively taken to be adequate and permissable (hence, there are no clear cuts here); in step two, the difference between this domain of structurally and normatively possible comparisons, as well as their reasonable subset, could be established by elaborating on the different purposes implied by comparative acts. These acts are reasonable insofar as they either lead to an outcome sought within a concrete comparative arrangement or they are reasonable insofar as they can uncover the relations between all comparative items by conditionally determining some of them to uncover relevant effects on other items. Result-oriented comparison is focused on '*clear and distinct*' *outcomes*; comparative experimentation, in contrast, is interested in *clarifying relations* between the performative, material, formal and contextual elements of a particular comparison. Both types together constitute the range of reasonable comparisons, while demarcating where the realm of comparative unreasonableness is to be found.

Both types show also that we have to upgrade the 'monolithic' definition of comparisons a little. The *comparative result* is itself a necessary item of every comparison. When it comes to result-oriented comparisons, this claim might sound rather unpretentious; there is no comparison without some sort of result, either a clear, ambivalent or even fuzzy, one. In experimental comparisons, however, comparative results gain more prominence as proper and independent elements of every comparison. In these latter cases, as we have just seen, one might start by using a predefined outcome in order to test different consequences regarding the choices for other comparative items. In such an experimental setting, the usual arrangement of comparisons is placed upside down by stipulating a potential outcome and on the basis of that conditional assumption, contemplating and trying out potential performative, material, formal and contextual aspects that amount to that preferred 'result'.[43]

And now, I submit, the list of necessary elements for every comparison is complete; all additional aspects – for instance, tools for comparing or a comparison's medium and 'materiality' – are beneath the status of necessity.

3 On the differences of similarity

Comparison and similarity belong, in some sense, together. This is at least a common and widespread conviction which claims that a too strong dissimilarity between *A* (apples) and *B* (pears) undermines the possibility of comparing *A* and *B*. Hence, similarity (and relative terms such as 'resemblance' and 'likeness') has served as a comparison's (pre)condition (see section 2.1).[44] According to this view, comparative procedures not only produce results that range from a certain degree of similarity on the one hand, to marked differences on the other, but are themselves already based on a *similitudo* between comparative items.

It was Michel Foucault who first claimed that there has been a paradigmatic transition from *thinking in similarities* to an *age of representation*, with the gradual loss of an ontologically underwritten analogical connection between Being and thinking, as well as between the world 'outside' and our ways of representing this world. Since the Baroque period, Foucault believes, the 'murmuring resemblance of things'[45] has disappeared, and the act of comparing these things is now a far cry from that initial world order.[46]

In recent years, however, the concept of similarity has celebrated a modest revival – not in the anachronistic sense of returning to pre-Baroque times but, rather, in a pragmatic fashion whereby similarities signify a useful middle ground between two stricter extremes, namely the identification of *A* and *B* and their absolute contrast. Therefore, similarity serves either as a 'cognitive' term meant to create a relation between similar entities or as part of an 'ontology of similarity' that mirrors features factually shared by *A* and *B*. This concept, as scholars in literary studies claim in particular, entails an 'uncertainty principle'. Hence, its advantage is also what is usually taken to be its problem: similarity as a fuzzy, vague and diffuse notion.[47] As Albrecht Koschorke states, it has a 'de-dramatizing' effect, allowing for partial inclusions, networks or overlapping features and fluid relations instead of the 'diacritical energy' of concepts like 'alterity', the 'other' and the 'alien' as expressions of total dissimilarity.[48] Similarity, then, invites a conceptual disarming and a philosophical 'cooling-down'.[49]

Edmund Husserl was one such 'cool' philosopher in measuring this middle ground of similarity. He defined heterogeneity as the total negation of similarity and then refuted the idea that there is anything truly heterogeneous; partial (in contrast to 'pure' or 'total') similarity and likeness is always there. However, comparing *A* and *B* does more than simply juxtapose these items; there has to be an intention behind putting these items into a comparative setting or, as Husserl says, a 'similarity-in-terms-of'. Insofar as this relating of an item *A* to other items *B*, *C*, *D* … is always possible, all items are, to some degree – i.e. with regard to particular and shared features – homogeneous.[50]

Traditionally, similarity is dealt with on the level of properties. Insofar as the identity between A and B entails the complete sharing of all properties between A and B, similarity is the partial sharing of some of them. This Leibnizian (and mathematical) notion has been criticized by Nelson Goodman, who argued that this notion (and, therefore, 'similarity' as a philosophically significant term *tout court*) remains useless because any two items share at least one property, such that similarity is a 'global' relation – literally everything is then similar to everything else – and similarity claims are therefore at best uninformative.[51]

Moreover, similarity functions symmetrically: if A is similar to B, then B has to be similar to A as well. However, similarity does not work in a transitive manner: if A is similar to B, and B is similar to C, A does not have to be similar to C. If in fact it is, then C is – due to the symmetry principle – similar to A as well.

Genuine similarity might mean something more substantial than 'mere sharedness', which brings us back to comparative relations. As already noted, two items A and B can be similar in two ways: by A and B sharing features (*categorical*), as well as by doing this to particular degrees (*gradual* or *phenomenological*). Furthermore, one might say, that this sharedness is *ontologically given* or *comparatively constructed*. For instance, some apples and pears share the property of being green, and they might share this colour to the same degree; both aspects are not constructed. In contrast, California and Wyoming share the property of having unemployment (rates), and they might share this to the same extent as well. But due to the complexity of California and Wyoming as political systems and for the sake of their comparability, it has to be constructed (predefined, stipulated, adjusted, etc.) what 'unemployment' means in both states.

Therefore, similarity between A and B can obviously be the result of a comparison, but can only be its (pre)condition to a limited extent. First, A and B have to share a property (i.e. have to have a categorial similarity); this condition is synonymous with the aforementioned problem of categoriality: A and B are comparable with regard to T if and only if they share the category expressed by T. In this weak sense, A and B are always partially similar since there is always a T_n categorially shared by both items or, to put it in Husserl's terms: A and B are never totally heterogeneous. Secondly, the comparability of A and B is not dependent on any degree of an instantiated property; if A is very green while B is red, this does not undermine their comparative setting. Thirdly, the comparability of A and B, however, presupposes a similarity in another sense: not only on the level of properties but, rather, on the level of contexts. Comparing California and Wyoming in terms of unemployment is, as noted, based on similar (ideally, identical) background assumptions, such as the meaning of 'unemployment', a similar system of social and political support for unemployed people, similar insurance systems combined with incentives for re-entering the job market, etc.

To conclude, comparisons and similarity do belong together, but in a manner different from usual conjectures. Trivially, similarity is one of the possible outcomes of comparing A and B. Conversely, A and B have to be similar in a categorial sense of sharing at least one property (identical with the category expressed by a particular *tertium comparationis* T). Here, the quest for similarity as a comparative (pre)condition is reducible to the problem of categoriality. Moreover, A's and B's contextual elements (C_A and C_B) have to be similar; if they are not, their comparability becomes severely threatened or even undermined, as the comparison between A and B turns into an unreasonable one (again, see 2.7).

4 Two demarcations

Thus far, structural questions have been at the heart of our approach to comparisons. A complementary way to better understand how comparisons function might be to clarify the relations that comparisons entertain with other figures of speech and thought. To do this, the following section is dedicated to providing (at least) a sketch of how to demarcate comparisons from analogies (4.1) and metaphors (4.2). Analogies and metaphors belong to what has traditionally been called the category of tropes; distinguishing them from comparisons is exemplary and heuristic in nature.

4.1 Comparisons and analogies

There are two basic forms of analogies. The *analogia attributionis* expresses the similarity between different *relata* in regard to one or more properties. Hence, a property T is attributed to different entities $(A, B, C, \ldots)$ that could be different (but do not have to be) in all other regards from one another $[T: A, B, C, \ldots]$. This kind of analogy between $A, B, C, \ldots$ articulates their similarity in terms of T. In contrast, the *analogia proportionalitatis* entails a more complex structure in relating two relations to one another. Here, two *relata* (A and B) entertain a relation (in one or more ways) similar to the relation between two other *relata* (C and D) $[A:B \approx C:D]$.[52]

The *analogia attributionis* is based on the comparative structure presented above; thus, *analogiae attributionis* presupposes conventional comparisons by referring only to those items $A, B, C, \ldots$ that instantiate the property T within a particular range of similarity. Hence, this type of analogy integrates those items that are the comparative results on the basis of T.

Things are slightly different when it comes to the other kind of analogy, which is often characterized as incomplete induction. For clarification, let us take a closer look at a prominent example, namely David Hume's *Dialogues Concerning Natural Religion*, published posthumously – hence, '*post*-Hume' – in 1779. The *Dialogues* are a seminal work on the philosophy of religion, and arguably, they represent the proper beginning of this philosophical discipline in its modern shape and form in general.[53] In these dialogues – that are rather trialogues – we meet the following protagonists: Philo, the sceptic and critic of religion, Cleanthes, the natural theologian and defender of rationally-justified religious belief, and finally, Demea, the (allegedly) orthodox and 'true' believer. For large sections, the *Dialogues* are concerned with critically assessing a classical analogical argument presented by Cleanthes – who is addressing Demea – in the following form:

> Look round the world: Contemplate the whole and every part of it: You will find it to be nothing but one great machine, subdivided into an infinite number of lesser machines, which again admit of subdivisions, to a degree beyond what human

senses and faculties can trace and explain. All these various machines, and even their most minute parts, are adjusted to each other with an accuracy, which ravishes into admiration all men, who have ever contemplated them. The curious adapting of means to ends, throughout all nature, resembles exactly, though it much exceeds, the productions of human contrivance; of human design, thought, wisdom, and intelligence. Since therefore the effects resemble each other, we are led to infer, by all the rules of analogy, that the causes also resemble; and that the author of nature is somewhat similar to the mind of man.[54]

Just as a watchmaker – the 'intelligent cause' and bearer of organized intentions (40) – constructs a reliable chronograph, God is thought of as *causa prima* whose effect is considered by Cleanthes to be as well ordered as a watch's motion. By a quasi-mathematical rule of three, one is now entitled to infer with great probability, from supposedly similar effects and the well-known causes in earthly matters, an equally similar cause on the transcendent level: God as the watchmaker and 'author' of all things (ibid.). In consequence, Cleanthes concludes with some sense of satisfaction: 'By this argument *a posteriori*, and by this argument alone, do we prove at once the existence of a deity, and his similarity to human mind and intelligence' (20).

It is interesting, but not surprising, to observe that Cleanthes' analogical argument – also known as the 'argument from design' – does not include some sort of theological amendment expressing a categorical difference between God and world; rather, it underlines the almost perfect earthly order to integrate this disputable assumption into the inference (from known things) of a first cause 'behind' everything. The highly optimistic empiricist Cleanthes is convinced of being able to go beyond a merely deistic framework limited to an Aristotelian prime mover; he presents a theistic conclusion claiming that there is not only something meaningful to say concerning God's existence (the *fact* that He exists), but also in regard to His nature (the *way* He exists). Taking the analogy literally implies then that God indeed took care of His creation by having tuned it perfectly, just as the watchmaker did, and nonetheless, he still has the ability to intervene when a repair turns to be necessary (cf. 47). For Cleanthes, however, it is obvious that this theistic version is the exclusive explanation of our universe, its existence and nature, whereas for him, relinquishing this analogical argument is tantamount to saying goodbye to religion altogether (see 78 and 91).

Philo emphatically repudiates this comparative procedure by exhausting the dynamics of Cleanthes's *analogia proportionalitatis* to its limits. An analogy gains strength with an increasing similarity between both relations $A:B$ and $C:D$, whereas its explanatory value decreases correlatively. At this pole of Cleanthes's analogy, the problem of anthropomorphism looms large (cf. 44 and 47). In contrast, an analogy loses validity if both relations $A:B$ and $C:D$ are dissimilar, whereas its explanatory value increases correlatively.[55] At this analogical pole, the danger lies in God's unrecognizability (cf. 35). In the first case, few things can safely be explained; in the second case, a lot of things can be expounded upon, but with less certainty.[56]

What does all this have to do with comparing? First, and trivially, what Cleanthes is presenting here is a comparison of two relations. Secondly, an *analogia proportionalitatis* is a special comparative form, insofar as the number of its material elements is fixed:

two relations where each relation again possesses two items. If this analogy is used as an analogical argument, the similarity of both material elements is decisive for the argumentive validity. This is an exception since usually the similarity between *A* and *B* is obviously not crucial for comparing *A* and *B*. Similarity between material items is a possible comparative result, but not a condition for being able to compare these items. Thirdly, Philo does not share Cleanthes's optimism about inferring God from the world – an optimism that is at the heart of 'natural theology'. One of Philo's critical remarks concerns the search for a comparative (or analogical) regard *T*. Here, in some respects, the analogy seems to work successfully (for instance, regarding intentions and the structure of divine and human agency; T_1). In other respects, however, the analogy is in danger of failing miserably (for instance, regarding the problem of evil: it is not possible to infer a prime mover with all the predicates of perfectibility from the world as a 'mixed bag'; T_2).[57]

Therefore, both kinds of analogy, *attributionis et proportionalitatis*, entertain a twofold relation to comparative procedures. On the one hand, they are themselves comparisons by virtue of putting different items, as well as relations, into a comparative setting in regard to a *tertium T*. On the other hand, they are already based on a pre-analogical comparison, insofar as both analogies only entail those items *A, B, C,* . . ., as well as relations *A:B* and *C:D,* that are in fact similar in regard to a particular *tertium* T_1. In both cases, this comparative regard T_1 is determined, and one item *A* or one relation *A:B* is already chosen as well – and only in view of these conditions, one searches for further items and relations sufficiently similar to *A* or *A:B*. As soon as additional items *B, C,* . . . and relations *C:D,* . . . are found, one might, conversely, try to find alternative regards $T_2, T_3,$ . . . that could support the initial assumption that *A, B, C,* . . ., as well as *A:B, C:D,* . . ., are similar (while excluding those regards T_n that do not support that premise). The bigger this similarity (categorically and gradually; see section 3) is, the sooner one might be inclined to accept the analogy as one form of an *argumentative justification*, as Cleanthes did; the smaller the similarity is, the more likely it turns out to be applicable to that analogy in a *merely heuristic manner*, an olive branch that Philo and Demea, for very different reasons, were not ready to offer or accept.[58]

4.2 Comparisons and metaphors

The relation between comparisons and metaphors is, needless to say, a highly complicated one. Not because of the nature of that relation itself but, rather, because of the divergence within theories of metaphors. It is not possible here to give more than a rough overview regarding the semantic and structural problems connected to comparisons and metaphors. And I will proceed in four steps: a. metaphors *as* comparisons; b. the interaction theory of metaphors; c. the refutation that a proper theory of metaphors is required or even possible; d. finally, the topic of 'absolute' metaphors. All four steps focus on the question as to which impact different theoretical frameworks have on the comparative element in/for metaphors.

a. *Metaphors as comparisons*. According to the classical approach since Aristotle and Quintilian, metaphors are shortened (or abbreviated or condensed) comparisons.[59]

Metaphors then constitute a subclass of comparisons. It is this picture against which modern theories of metaphors have been formulated in order to claim a separation between metaphors and comparisons.

However, starting off with similarities between metaphors and comparisons is an obvious option. Characterizing metaphors *as* comparisons already has important implications: first, it entails the claim that every metaphor could be replaced by a comparison; hence, the term 'substitution theory'. Secondly, it follows that metaphors, due to their possible substitution, are ornamental in character; they serve then as mere decoration for rhetorical purposes. Thirdly, one has to explain why the identification between the two is slightly disguised and, therefore, why metaphors are described as 'implicit' or 'elliptic' comparatives.

To give a simple example:

1. Richard is a lion.
2. Richard is *like* a lion.
3. Richard is strong and brave and ...
4. Richard is as strong and brave and ... *as* a lion.

The substitution theory of metaphors, or what might also be called the comparativist account of metaphors, which claims that sentences such as (1) are not only replacable by sentences such as (2), but also that what (1) is *really* saying is expressed in (2). Moreover, the extent of the (alleged) likeness or similarity are aspects that readers or listeners have to infer from the concrete communicative setting in which the metaphor is used. Most importantly, when one adheres to this theory, one is committed to subscribing to the (semantic) equivalence between (2), (3) and (4), since 'substitution' does not refer primarily to replacing a metaphor by an explicit comparison but, rather, to substituting metaphorical (and comparative) sentences by nonmetaphorical (and noncomparative) sentences.[60]

And it is precisely this last claim that creates difficulties and, eventually, reasons to refute the substitution 'theory'. The open, yet justified, question is simply in which way (3) has to be completed (i.e. what else comes after 'strong' and 'brave'?) to capture the meaning of (2). It might be the essential point of a metaphor *not* to clarify that question, thus creating an open space that involves the reader and listener to find further connotations that s/he takes to be adequate in a particular context. Then, metaphors do not only stand for a general structure but, more importantly, for a linguistic dynamics that allows the audience to participate. The easy transition from (1) and (2) to (3) and (4) is, thus, in danger, which gives rise to the need to approach metaphors in an alternative way.

b. *The interaction theory of metaphors*. Let us refer to a telling statement put forward by one of the guiding lights of a new philosophical interest in metaphors in the 1950s. Max Black states in a later paper: 'To think of God *as* love and to take the further step of identifying the two is emphatically to do something more than to *compare* them as merely being alike in certain respects. But what that "something more" is remains tantalizingly elusive: we lack an adequate account of metaphorical thought.'[61] First, Black's statement is a critical note on the comparativist account that puts the stress on the aforementioned vagueness regarding how to fill the gap in sentences such as (3) to mirror what sentences such as (2) express. This problem is met by what has been coined as the 'interaction theory' of metaphors that changes the relation between metaphors and comparisons as well. And it is itself framed in a metaphorical manner. According to Black's version of this theory, 'God is love' consists of 'God' as *frame* and 'love' as *focus*, while Ivor Richards prefers to express a similar thought by employing *tenor* and *vehicle* as to describe the elements interacting with each other. For both authors, there is no comparison between God and love but, rather, an *asymmetrical* interaction occurring in such a way that connotations from the focus/vehicle inform the meaning of the frame/tenor.[62]

This characterization begs the question of how to clarify this interaction (as contrast, opposition, etc.), and it provokes a response as to whether the relation between focus/vehicle and frame/tenor is really asymmetrical. It was Monroe Beardsley who denied the importance of the second question to find new ways of answering the first.[63] For Beardsley there is a structural asymmetry between both elements of a metaphor, but for him it is not clear and in fact belongs to the metaphorical dynamics that it remains vague and ambivalent as to which part is the focus/vehicle and which serves as the frame/tenor. Accordingly, Beardsley speaks of a reciprocity between both poles and, thus, of a constant 'twist' and 'inversion' between them. However, he sticks to the traditional idea that there is a conflict or even a contradiction between two levels of meaning here interacting within a metaphorical setting. In other words, there is a metaphorical, as well as non-metaphorical and proper, meaning.

Of course, there are several uncertainties connected to these theoretical propositions: what does 'interaction' and 'twist' really mean?; do these characterizations apply to all metaphors (or just to a subgroup of them)?; what is the scope of frame and focus (words, concepts, sentences, systems, etc.)?; and, does this theory stand the test of self-application given the fact that its versions are themselves put in a highly metaphorical language?

Max Black called metaphors that cannot be explicated by comparisons 'emphatic'.[64] For our purposes, the question is: are there non-emphatic metaphors or is there any comparative element in metaphors when presupposing the interaction theory? First, to state that there is a contrast or opposition and eventually a twist between both elliptic poles of a metaphor might already be a comparative statement. Secondly, insofar as the reader or listener is involved – there is not only an 'interaction' between focus and frame, but also between a trope and an active audience – s/he has to contemplate and consider which attributes are possible, apt or intriguing when bringing focus and frame into mutual play. God as love obviously expresses intimacy, care, an emotional relation, trust. But what else? Confronting that question implies a comparative act between what is usually connected to love in inter- and intrapersonal relationships and the theological case. We are dealing here with what I shall call *explorative comparisons* (see chapter 2, section 2.2). Thirdly, Black does not deny that there is in fact a comparative element in metaphors; he only suggests that between focus and frame there is 'something more than to *compare* them as merely being alike in certain respects' (cf. above). This again could mean two different things: one, a metaphor does not merely amount to a comparison, but entails other practices as well, such as testing possible, or even absurd, connotations of a frame by relying on intriguing and surprising foci; and two, one has to compare when using a metaphor, but comparisons are not primarily or exclusively about a likeness between focus and frame or also, as we have seen, about contrasts, oppositions and, in the end, about extending the traditional meaning of the frame by challenging it with new focal elements. 'God is love' implies a comparison between the connotations of both but leaves space for probing new semantic links as well. It stresses the similarities between God and love, but also provokes resistance in a provocative and comparative way by suggesting God's dark sides, his revenge, remoteness, hiddenness; and by doing this, the meaning of 'God' (and 'love') may shift as well, as has happened when characterizing God in agapeistic terms in a religious context for which such an identification might have sounded unfamiliar, strange or even alien.

c. *Refuting a proper 'metaphorical' meaning*. In both cases, the comparativist account (a), as well as the interaction theory (b), it is presupposed that it is possible to present a general account of metaphors and, additionally, that metaphors have a proper metaphorical meaning. And both premises came under pressure. Concerning the first aspect, some authors deny that it is fruitful to invest in a general account, since there is no single answer to that question.[65] Concerning the second and more important aspect, some authors repudiate the common idea according to which there is a dualism between ordinary (or literal) and metaphorial (and non-literal) meaning. I will concentrate on this latter issue by calling to mind what Donald Davidson suggested critically in his 1978 paper 'What Metaphors Mean'. His general claim in that article reads as follows: 'metaphors mean what the words, in their most literal interpretation, mean, and nothing more'.[66] Hence, it is a major mistake to think that metaphors possess another additional meaning beyond their literal one. It is correct to say, Davidson claims, that metaphors cannot be paraphrased, but not because metaphors express something new or different, but rather, because there is nothing to be paraphrased in the first place (cf. 32).

The more constructive upshot of Davidson's 'monistic' (or antidualistic) account is this: a metaphorical statement does not say more than what is meant when the sentence is used in a literal way, and by using a metaphor, one draws attention to a resemblance between two or more things. Thus, for Davidson, there is no semantic dualism between two layers of meaning and, therefore, no need to translate the one into the other. Rather, there is a distinction between meaning and use (or effect), and metaphors do not belong to a separate realm of meaning, but stand for a particular usage (33, 45). Instead of speaking of different meanings, Davidson suggests dissolving the ambiguity of sentences by referring to different contexts of application (see 35). Metaphors might *extend* the initial meaning, but they do not create or constitute a new semantic realm. In this sense, metaphors are related to non-metaphorical usages as lies are: sentences conveying a lie do not have a different meaning either, but they stand for a particular context of application. The same goes, Davidson claims, for metaphors (cf. 42–3).

Accordingly, Davidson no longer relies on the metaphorical language – *frame*, *focus*, *tenor* and *vehicle* – to describe metaphors, and hence, the comparative element between frame/tenor and focus/vehicle has no place either.

However, in another respect Davidson is still interested in comparisons, namely in comparing metaphors to *similes*. He states: 'The simile says there is a likeness and leaves it to us to pick out some common feature or features; the metaphor does not explicitly assert a likeness, but if we accept it as a metaphor, we are again led to seek common features (not necessarily the same features the associated simile suggests; but that is another matter)' (40). Metaphors and similes are just two kinds of tools among countless others that serve to alert us to aspects of the world by inviting us to make (see above) explorative comparisons, whether the *tertium comparationis* is visible or is instead disguised. However, there is, Davidson adds, a crucial difference between metaphors and similes (and comparisons) when it comes to their truth values: 'If a sentence used metaphorically is true or false in the ordinary sense, then it is clear that it is usually false. The most obvious semantic difference between simile and metaphor is that all similes are true and most metaphors are false' (41). Or put in other words via an example: 'We use a simile ordinarily only when we know the corresponding metaphor to be false. We say Mr. S. is like a pig because we know he isn't one. If we had used a metaphor and said he was a pig, this would not be because we changed our mind about the facts but because we chose to get the idea across a different way' (ibid.). To sum up, only if sentences are considered to be false, do we take them as metaphors. And we might exploratively start to hunt for hidden implications. That is why metaphorical sentences are often enough '*patently* false' (42), and almost all similes are trivially true. The absurdity in the metaphorical sentence – (1) 'Richard is a lion' – creates an obstacle to believing it and urges us to regard this sentence in a metaphorical way. But in a Davidsonian (and Rortian)[67] framework there is no longer a comparative setting between 'Richard' as frame and 'lion' as focus. And in a strict sense, they do not compare two poles of an ellipsis but, rather, present an identification – 'Richard *is* a lion' – that is obviously false. Precisely insofar as a comparison is a trope, it must be in some (open or hidden) regards true, apt, intriguing or irritating, surprising, precarious.

d. '*Absolute*' *metaphors*. As we have seen, Davidson (and his followers) says farewell to a theory of metaphors. Without belonging to these followers, Hans Blumenberg implicitly agrees with this theoretical reservation, yet interestingly, there is, compared to the Davidsonian picture of metaphors, a telling inversion since Blumenberg reactivates the divide between literal meaning and its metaphorical counterpart. This is expressed by the duality between concepts and 'absolute metaphors'.[68] Their absoluteness stands for their resistance against terminological (and hence, conceptual) claims. Therefore, Blumenberg states, absolute metaphors are not translatable into conceptual speech. Blumenberg's program of a metaphorology based on this duality takes the following shape: 'Metaphorology attempts to reach the substructures of thinking, the ur-ground, the liquid solution of systematic crystallisation; but it also seeks to make graspable with which "courage" the mind is in its imagination ahead of itself and how its history designs itself in the courage of speculation.'[69]

Hence, a conceptual history finds its counterpart in a metaphorology that aims at detecting the background metaphors that inform, influence and eventually structure our thinking. It uncovers the 'meta-cinetics'[70] in our ways of thinking (and judging, seeing, feeling, etc.) based on a network of absolute metaphors. It is futile, Blumenberg claims, to find a non-metaphorical equivalent to important metaphors such as light for truth, horizon and paradigm for contexts, or nautical metaphors for existence and

Dasein.[71] Realists may be interested in getting rid of metaphors, but, as Blumenberg asks rhetorically, is what will be left then, reality?[72]

Blumenberg's metaphorology is not dedicated to simple and everyday metaphors, but to a metaphorical background that does not reveal a common and more general structure. Therefore, Blumenberg does not characterize metaphors in a metaphorical way, as Black and Beardsley did. A possible comparison between focus and frame is then not of relevance here. Does the entire topic of comparisons and comparability, one might ask, have any significance for this chapter devoted to working on metaphors? An allusion, at least, is conveyed by Blumenberg's claim that (all or only absolute?) metaphors are not translatable into non-metaphorical expressions. This might be taken as a sign of incomparability between metaphors and candidates for their literal equivalents. However, this will not do, since incomparability is not based on untranslatability, whereas the claim that a metaphor is not translatable into a non-figurative counterpart is itself a possible comparative result.

Therefore, one might conclude, the development of a theory of metaphor resembles a history of an increasing distance between metaphors and comparisons. This view, however, presupposes a rather linear theoretical evolution that has simply not taken place. It is true that the traditionally close relation between both tropes has increasingly vanished, but a general characterization of that relation remains beyond reach, as even this fragmentary overview has indicated. This is (and remains) rather a question of the specific and highly divergent contexts in which metaphors become a topic in their own right.

5 Comparisons and their functions

There is obviously no *singular* function of comparisons, but a wide range of different tasks that comparisons can and might fulfill. The question of 'how to do things with comparisons' could then be addressed in a more adequate manner by focusing on some of the most significant aspects of applying comparative procedures – some obvious and some marginal. The following list starts off by paying heed to more epistemic usages and leads eventually to more practical and hermeneutical settings – without feigning completeness.

1. *Comparing as gaining knowledge*. This epistemic or, as some have it, 'cognitive'[73] function of comparative procedures has been underlined within different disciplines. There is the creation of knowledge by comparison between *A* and *B*, especially by comparatively contrasting *A* and *B*. As John Locke already stated: gaining and extending knowledge goes back – and according to him, exclusively – to 'comparing clear and distinct ideas'.[74] However, this contrastively-gained knowledge is not identical with discovering new things that are surrounded by old ones. It is rather about uncovering new aspects of old things by relating them to other items in a new way. Either the material elements of a comparison are known before starting the comparison, and different *tertia* are tried out to better understand the *relata* (for example, using a comparison portal for flight connection in terms of price, duration, etc.); or the

comparative regard is determined, and some of the *relata* are known, while finding additional ones by way of comparison (for example, comparing flights, train connections, etc. to get from x to y in the shortest period of time). In both cases, comparisons lead only to relatively new insights, not to absolute new knowledge.[75]

2. *Comparing as inference/giving reason.* Speaking very generally, one might say that there are two types of inference: (i) a deductive kind of thinking, in which one grasps certain slightly evident premises and some rules of inference and then moves on from there to conclusions; and (ii) a comparative or analogical version, in which one proceeds from one aspect to the next, from one description to the next until a sort of resemblance is formed or comes to the fore. Obviously, comparisons cannot justify something in the stronger version (i),[76] but – as an incomplete sort of inference – they are able to provide reasons in the weaker version (ii). This could be done in an analogical way, especially by an *analogia proportionalitatis* (see section 4.1) or by what is called an *a maiore argument*: the general form p because q is modified into p because even q or, put stronger, *if even q, then a fortiori p*.[77] For instance, if one supports a law that forbid cars in cities to reduce pollution (q), one should all the more support a ban on SUVs in inner cities (p).

3. *Comparing as (de)generalizing.* Comparative methods belong to the most important vehicles for justifying generalizations – or for repudiating them. In the first case, this amounts to 'retrospective reconstructions'[78]; in the second case, it entails the critique of them. If A-like events are followed by B-like events, then one might be justified in inductively concluding that A is generally followed by B due to a causal relation or a correlation. However, historiography and sociology are full of very prominent examples in which such general connections had been presupposed or defended but, in the end, turn out to be falsely claimed.[79] By making additional and more exact comparisons, one could show that these connections were only alleged ones. One might think of the secularization theory claiming that "modern" societies go hand in hand with the decline of religious commitments. But specifying the meaning of 'modernity' and 'religiosity' only leads to the notion that their relation is a highly complicated one beyond tenable generalizations.[80] Here, we also see the critical flipside of comparisons.[81]

4. *Comparing as explanatory abbreviation.* Comparisons between A and B relate items in a particular way, but they do not explain this relation in any way. Nevertheless, comparative settings can take on explanatory tasks in an abbreviated or condensed manner. It is often the case that one shortens an explanation by referring to a similar, yet more obvious or familiar case to which the first one is compared. The (self)evidence of the latter scenario is used to clarify the more-obscure first case. For instance, if someone wants to understand the behavior of a stanger, one might try to explain it by referring to another, more well-known person behaving in a similar way, given that both contexts are also similar. Hence, a double similarity is presupposed here. And we are dealing with an abbreviated explanation insofar as the comparison itself does not explain anything at all but, nonetheless, is used to transfer the explanation of a slightly-evident case to a still-dubious one. In this sense, comparisons serve also to provide apt examples or to illustrate unfamiliar cases by presenting similarities to more familiar ones.

5. *Comparing as exploration.* In contrast to the usual presupposition of certain similarities between A and B in order to compare them, one could also benefit from an

irritating, yet intriguing, dissimilarity between different *relata* in order to illuminate new aspects of them and their relations. A recent example of this is Stanley Cavell's book *Cities of Words*, which has the telling subtitle 'Pedagogical Letters on a Register of the Moral Life'.[82] Cavell is interested in depicting several ways of living together, as well as community, intimacy and, in particular, marriage. He refers to authors like Kant, Emerson, Thoreau, Mill, Nietzsche and Wittgenstein, but also, and surprisingly, to Hollywood productions of the 1930s and 1940s, as well as more contemporary movies such as the Johnny Cash film *Walk the Line* (2007). Through this conversation between remote sources – a conversation that never took place before – Cavell creates an arrangement that suggests, tests and explores new facets of an old theme while the comparative regards are neither stable nor certain. Here again, these comparative examples and their fluid setting do not merely stand for theoretical claims formulated without any link to concrete cases. Rather, their status exceeds mere illustration. Introducing new *relata* that again mirror new facets of the topic in question makes Cavell go back to already-used examples on which new light is thrown by unfamiliar cases.

6. *Comparing as orientation/arranging/classifying*. This dynamic aspect of comparative procedures is accompanied by its 'Apollonian' counterpart. Comparing is then also (and foremost) an element of creating orientation, structure and order – of classification. There is no orientation without comparative elements that select, prioritize and establish a hierarchy (see also chapter 4). Often enough a particular structure is not unveiled, but created and produced, and classifications are generally based on comparing the materials to be classified. One might think of Carl von Linné's famous nomenclature in botany and zoology, i.e. an impressive enterprise to establish a precise overview by applying the Aristotelian distinction between *genus proximum* and *differentia specifica* (hence by stating, as well as stipulating, differences and similarities for fulfilling the needs of orientation, structure and a comprehensive overview).[83]

7. *Comparing as attracting attention*. Last, but not least, certain comparisons work as hyperboles in trying to express something adequate by using language or particular phrases, as well as by referring to comparative *relata* that do challenge the limits of adequacy. I shall coin these comparisons 'pointed' ones (and will come back to them in chapter 2, section 3). Other comparisons rhetorically generate attention by taking up rather positive, yet ambivalent functions as jokes and bits of irony or as decoration and linguistic ornaments: 'My mom always said life is like a box of chocolates – you never know what you're gonna get.' Or, as the German Enlightenment philosopher Alexander Baumgarten summed up: 'there are cases in which the comparative act is only there in an aesthetic regard, for instructing the imagination and for the amusement of the mind'.[84]

6 Comparative limits

As we saw in the previous section, there are comparisons that fulfill critical tasks. The following section, however, deals with comparative arrangements that are themselves the object of critical reflection. This critique ranges from internal weaknesses connected to comparative settings via a reservation concerning the possible outcome of comparisons, to the limitations of comparing as act and practice in a more general sense. I will proceed in nine steps that start with comparative difficulties touching on the status of comparisons.[85]

1. *Lacking self-sufficiency*. It has often been stated that comparisons only have a relative evidence. If one defined different comparative items and if one established a comparative regard, then, and only then, can this constructed arrangement lead to a comparative result. This is different in deductive contexts that entail two or more premises, and a particular conclusion necessarily follows; in this sense, deductions are logically self-sufficient.[86] In contrast, comparisons are *provisional* without being true or false but, instead, more-or-less useful in relation to the stipulated arrangement, as Niklas Luhmann states.[87]

2. *The advance towards simplicity*. There are simple and complex comparisons (see chapter 2, section 2.1). Simple comparisons only entail one single *tertium*, whereas their more complex counterparts have more than one. However, this creates the difficulty of multidimensionality, i.e. the problem of how to combine different comparative regards in order to provie one tenable result. For instance, one could compare different cars in relation to their power, acceleration, speed, yet also in regard to non-quantifiable aspects, such as design or contexts in which one needs a vehicle. How does one combine these aspects to make a decision? Scenarios like this one reveal a certain kind of dilemma: either one sticks to simpler forms of comparison for gaining more secure results or one turns a comparative setting into a more relevant, but complicated one, while accepting that the result's vagueness will increase accordingly.[88]

3. *Decontextualization*. It has often been criticized that comparative settings tend to imply an anti-hermeneutical drift.[89] Although comparisons have a context – i.e. the comparative items and regards are necessarily connected to a particular environment – comparing as a practice is tantamount to decontextualizing the material and formal elements. Comparing two historically very different accounts of marriage (see Cavell's work on remarriage above) tends to dim the cultural background assumptions informing these accounts in the first place. However, one could confront that critique not by refuting its justification, but by pointing out that, to some extent, every act of comprehension, including comparative arrangements, is accompanied by decontextualizing the elements of that arrangement. Accordingly, the initial critique merely expresses an obvious difficulty that cannot be circumvented that easily.

4. *Creating the comparative relata*. As already noted, comparisons are not built and cannot rely on 'natural' elements, but are dependent on the creation of their material items and formal regards. Here again, one might say that to think otherwise – hence to neglect comparative constructivism – is to stick to the 'myth of the given'. Insofar as this unavoidable constructive character is accepted or even appreciated, an awareness of the ways of forming, transforming or adjusting comparative elements is required as well. In other words, comparative settings are not *per se* protected against the constant danger of being integrated into an illustration of, or even justification for, predefined results. Manipulating the elements of comparisons is always an option and hence a serious danger.[90]

5. *Comparisons and the danger of being arbitrary.* This last aspect combined with the aforementioned problem of comparative insufficiency touches on the potentially arbitrary character of comparative results. The fact that, first of all, the material elements of comparisons are necessarily forms of construction, definition and stipulation, and the additional fact that, secondly, comparative regards are bound to and dependent upon particular interests, as well as explanatory or descriptive purposes, lead to the constant danger of (mis)constructing comparative settings. As we have already seen, comparing the unemployment rates between two states is a highly-complex matter, and its outcome as a tenable result presupposes an awareness for crucial differences when it comes to the meaning of the concepts involved and the divergent character of contexts on which one relies to compare the relevant *relata* in the first place. Otherwise, comparisons become obscured by noncomparative – political, historical, rhetorical, etc. – interferences (see section 2.4).

6. *The threat of circularity.* The potentially arbitrary character of comparisons hints towards the further danger of comparative circularity. This danger takes two different forms. One, comparisons are, as we have also already seen, based on relevant comparative regards; there is no comparison *simpliciter*, since every comparative act requires a particular *tertium*. However, their *tertia* are based on comparative acts themselves. Thus, a comparative setting makes another setting possible. Two, and more problematically, comparisons give the impression of leading to (and eventually justifying) a result that is not predefined. Often enough, however, comparative settings start off with such a predefinition in order to use a comparison to – allegedly – justify a particular result. One might, for instance, think of advertising a particular job while already having one applicant in mind. Hence, one could adjust the job description in such a way that the person one already has in mind fits best the requirements. Here again, we have to deal with a form of circularity (and, often enough, comparative injustice) insofar as one pretends to offer a job using an open procedure while, in reality, its outcome is already determined. This is then nothing but a simulation of a just comparison.

7. *The lack of creativity in comparisons.* Comparisons are not creative; they do not create something new, and they do not reveal something completely new.[91] The comparative mode is not the mode of discovery *A*, but of relating an already-known *A* to *B*; it does not explain anything but is an elaboration on particular constellations and arrangements.[92] If one wants to defend the cognitive status of comparisons – meaning that genuine knowledge can be based on comparative settings – then one might claim that we are dealing with *relational knowledge,* unfolding already-existing, yet potentially hidden, connections between *A* and *B* without discovering something ontologically new.

8. *Comparison's quantifying effect.* One of the major problems connected to comparisons is their inclination to level-down different things. Comparing scalable *relata* is not too difficult an endeavour, whereas the comparison between unquantified items meets various obstacles. Therefore, it does not come as a surprise that comparative settings are accompanied by the methodological pressure to reduce items that are not scalable (such as values, ideas, preferences, etc.) to scalable counterparts. There are in fact ways of providing – or rather of simulating – this reduction by not comparing *A*

and *B* directly, but by comparing the popularity of *A* and *B* through counting their 'likes'. Obviously, these methods of quantification have their justifications and advantages, but they can also lead to the general question as to whether it is possible and fertile to mirror qualities by exclusively relying on quantities.

9. *Comparative desingularization*. While the previous aspect touches on levelling-down differences by reduction, the problem of desingularization hints at losing sight of the particular, the special and the unique. This reservation is amplified by paying attention to certain dynamics within comparative settings. A particularly problematic form of desingularization is what has been coined as 'nostrification',[93] i.e. the neglect of the alien and unfamiliar by pretending to be able to classify it within the context of the familiar and the known. Here, the challenges of alterity and, hence, comparative injustice loom large and are the constant companions of comparative enterprises. And the serious possibility that certain things elude and escape the range of an allegedly all-encompassing comparability becomes here prominent and pressing again, whereas the plain proposition that something belongs to the realm of the incomparable might be based on a comparative act itself.

The list of comparative pitfalls is long and certainly longer than the one presented here. But when facing the unavoidability of comparisons and comparative procedures, the consequence cannot be to leave comparisons behind but, instead, to be careful with regard to comparative shortcomings or to use them in intriguing ways.

2

Comparisons. A Typology

1 Introduction: different types – one structure

Comparisons, ordinary as well as scientific ones, possess what I call 'monolithic' structure. This structure consists of performative (the subject), material (*relata*), formal (*tertia*), contextual (from the contexts of both the *relata* and *tertia*) items and finally the comparative result (see, for all details, chapter 1, section 2). While providing a typology does underline the differences between comparisons, it does not, however, undermine the monolithic claim. In other words: the differences captured typologically are not based on *structural differences* concerning the performative, material, formal and contextual items, as well as a comparison's result. Rather, they are grounded in *different relations* that these structurally invariant elements entertain. Thus, the comparative unity and the typological differences go hand in hand.

Referring to relational aspects to explain comparative differences, however, just postpones the problem in question. Now, we have to ask about the reasons 'behind' divergent relations between comparative items. Again, these reasons are not of a structural nature, but go back to different intentions connected to particular comparative practices and certain contextual restrictions and criteria informing divergent comparative acts. In short, we are led back to more concrete and practical background assumptions affecting the relations between the constitutive items of every comparison.[1] Accordingly, a *unique comparative structure* is compatible with *different relational constellations* within that structure, while these differences point to a *divergence among practices and their contexts*.

The section to come presents a typology that consists of seven pairs. It elaborates on these couples and, by doing so, aims at embracing the most relevant differences within comparative practices. The subsequent chapter will concentrate on just one of these types that is characteristic of what one might call comparative injustice. This kind of injustice – in contrast to comparative 'purity' – is rooted in using (or rather, misusing) a comparison to seemingly justify an already predefined result. In these cases, prejudgements, prejudices and preferences latently or explicitly inform a comparative act, which creates one of the most severe difficulties within comparativism and which is, with equal severity, criticized and deconstructed by post-colonial studies, comparative literature and religion, and comparative types of philosophy, to name a few. I will concentrate on this last example to clarify what it means to be comparatively unjust, as well as to be critical thereof.

2 A typology

The typology presented here consists of seven pairs, each of which points to one relevant aspect or problem within comparative precedures. Using binary pairs, characterized by their regard towards one aspect or problem, constitutes itself, of course, a comparative setting. This typological list, while meant to reflect on prominent difficulties and pertinent distinctions between different comparisons (and comparative practices), is necessarily incomplete; there can be no completeness here anyway, since there are always potentially additional regards according to which this list could be extended or by which subdistinctions could easily be established. Hence, the following list highlights and reflects upon aspects and problems that exert considerable influence on the process of conducting particular comparisons. Combining the list's incomplete, yet, to some extent, evident character demonstrates its heuristic status. Combinations between different pairs are possible, and towards the end of this section we will examine the more important examples of these crossovers.

2.1 Simple/complex

This first binary pair may itself be understood in two different ways. And both ways are usually interrelated. According to the first reading, 'simple' means one-dimentional: A and B are compared to one another with regard to a single *tertium comparationis* T. Hence, 'complex' means that A and B are in a multidimensional relationship because of being compared with regard to multiple *tertia*. In the first case, a Mercedes 230 SEL is compared to a Buick Century in terms of speed. In the complex case, both cars are compared with regard to speed (T_1), power (T_2), acceleration (T_3), etc. The 'complex' case is not merely complex due to its multidimensionality, but because of the problem of how to combine the results regarding $T_1, T_2, T_3, \ldots$ into one overall result in order to answer the simple question as to which car is the better one, the one from Stuttgart or the one from Detroit.

This already hints at the second reading of the simple-complex distinction, touching on the problem of (non)quantifiable *tertia*. Speed, power and acceleration are all quantifiable, i.e. scalable regards. And yet, their combination is not easily quantifiable, since it is not clear how to assess the impact of $T_1, T_2, T_3, \ldots$ upon the overall result. Personal preferences, contexts calling for practical or stylish cars, etc. will inform the divergent ways in which one weighs the value of each these regards (including the question as to which regards are considered relevant in the first place). Therefore, quantifiability on the sublevel does not imply quantifiability on the level supervening on these sublevel regards (see also chapter 7.2 and 7.3).[2] A comparison between A and B might, nevertheless, be possible, especially when the results on the sublevel are fairly unambiguous. If the Mercedes is better in terms of most of, or even all of, the Ts, then answering which car is the better one is not difficult.

The situation gets more complex when moving beyond cars, speed, power and acceleration to comparisons of A and B in relation to a nonquantifiable regard T. This regard will be expressed by a vague predicate denoting something that eludes scalable measurements.[3] Which band is better: Emerson, Lake and Palmer or Pink Floyd? We must first define the different regards according to which we compare both bands, for instance originality T_6, technique T_7, impact on other music T_8, etc.[4] Again, we will meet obvious problems here. For one, it is hard to decide which band is better in regard to T_6, T_7, T_8, ... even if these regards are considered separately, since they all are genuinely vague. 'Vague' does not only imply nonquantifiability, but also the fact that it is not clear at all what 'originality', 'technical skills' and 'musical impact' are supposed to mean at a greater level of detail. Then, restricting the comparison to T_6, T_7 and T_8, or extending it by taking T_9 into consideration, is a stipulation which heavily informs the comparison and its result. Thus, it is an open question which subpredicates (originality, technique, musical impact, etc.) the overall predicate (regarding which band is better) consists of. And, finally, the combination of vague predicates on the sublevel in favor of an overall result will – as in the scenario above – also be vague.

To sum up: either 'simple' is synonymous with 'one-dimensional' and 'complex' with 'multidimensional', or 'simple' refers to quantifiable regards and 'complex' to nonquantifiable ones. What we have seen is that multidimensional comparisons have mostly (but not always)[5] nonquantifiable (and complex) overall results – independent of quantifiability or nonquantifiability on their sublevels.[6] However, all these obstacles do not necessarily exclude the possibility of achieving a clear result. One can give due attention to all comparative difficulties while being convinced that Pink Floyd is the best band of all time. Nonquantifiability makes comparisons difficult, but it does not make them, *per se*, impossible.

2.2 Result-oriented/experimental or explorative

The binary pair 'simple/complex' pertains to different constellations between a *tertium (or tertia) comparationis*, quantifiable and nonquantifiable ones, as well as the relevant material items (A, B, ...) of the comparison. Turning now to the duality between result-oriented and experimental comparisons, we have to address the status of a comparative outcome; put more precisely, we have to address the question as to whether the result is to *be found comparatively* or is *already defined precomparatively* with consequences for the rest of the comparative setting.

This distinction – one could also speak of *closed* and *explorative* comparisons[7] – puts the stress on two very different aims and expectations connected to a comparison (see also chapter 1, section 2.7). In result-oriented comparisons one compares *A* and *B* in regard to *T* within the contexts of *A*, *B* and *T*, while searching for more insights about *A* and *B* within a well-defined comparative constellation. Think again of California and Wyoming: both states might be compared in terms of their unemployment rate. Under the premise that all contextual background assumptions are stable and allow for a comparable setting (for instance, that in both states what counts as being 'unemployed' is roughly the same), this comparative act between *A* and *B* is directed towards a particular outcome. Here, *comparing is merely conducting or implementing* a comparison within a stable (or stabilized) arrangement.

In contrast, searching for a result does not have to be the primary aim of comparing *A* and *B*. Comparing them also allows one to probe and test several constellations that inhere between all comparative elements. This procedure resembles a form of *free variation* and leads to a comparative dynamics. There is even something playful about it with its conditional determination of certain elements (which potentially include the outcome) that clarify the influences on the comparative variable (i.e. the items that were not defined). And then, one might again change the arrangement determining other comparative items in order to see the consequences for another comparative variable. For instance, university rankings present a highly competitive comparative setting. Usually, they have well-defined parameters according to which universities around the globe are compared with one another and, eventually, ranked. Now, one could turn the scenario upside down to determine that Oxford should defend its pole position; and given that premise, one could try to find the comparative regards T_n, T_{n+1}, … in order to secure Oxford's first place. Changing these regards T_n, T_{n+1}, … again or giving some of these *T*s less or more importance will threaten that particular ranking.

This example does not really demonstrate the 'playful' character of comparative surplus but, rather, a severe problem in rankings and the danger of their manipulation (see section 3). Nevertheless, it might allude to the conditional character of comparisons in starting from one defined setting to uncover its impact on other comparative items and then to change that constellation again by redefining the setting for uncovering the impact on other comparative elements. While a result-oriented approach is dedicated to producing *distinct outcomes*, experimental or explorative comparisons are focused on *clarifying relations* between the performative, material, formal and contextual elements of a particular comparison.

The first is a *shortcut* to get directly to a useful result, while taking its material, formal, contextual, etc. assumptions for granted. The latter is a *detour* to unveil the relations between all comparative items involved. Result-orientation protects against the mere conditionality of its counterpart, while comparative experimentation lets us see more clearly the constructive element in comparisons which may, eventually, protect us from comparative one-sidedness and the threat of manipulation.[8]

2.3 Stable/emergent

The difference between result-oriented and experimental comparisons is connected to another distinction: one between stable and emergent comparisons. This distinction concerns the comparative regard, and it leads to distinguishing between *tertia* within a comparative act that are stable and well defined and those that are emergent. In the first case, it seems to be clear which way to conduct a particular comparison because the context of the applied *tertium* T (hence: C_T) is so strongly linked to that *tertium* T that any potential vagueness concerning the concrete context and comparative regards on a sublevel is practically excluded or suspended. For example: automobile magazines compare different products according to certain criteria T_1, T_2, T_3, etc. And usually T_1, T_2, T_3, etc. stand for speed, power, cost-effectiveness, etc. A particular context C (consisting of sublevel regards T_1, T_2, T_3) 'silently' accompanies the overall *tertium* T when answering the question as to which car is better according to these standard criteria T_n.

This does not always have to be the case. Often enough, this link between an overall regard T and its context C_T, including different sublevel regards T_n, is only tenuous.

Consequently, one could exploit that vagueness by keeping the comparative regard systematically unstable. Then, this regard begins to oscillate in and out of focus due to the lack of clarity regarding its concrete character. Without a regard, however, there is no comparison. This tension between lack of clarity and the necessity of employing a *tertium comparationis* might amount to involving the reader or listener in the process of creating the comparison by searching for or tentatively stipulating a comparative regard. Given the variety of readers and listeners, that search, and its resulting stipulation, will not necessarily amount to the same thing. Accordingly, different *tertia* – and, thus, different comparisons – may be suggested, tried out, repudiated and again considered for application.

Again, an example might illustrate this abstraction.[9] This time, it is not taken from automobile magazines, but from the New Testament. Jesus portrays the Kingdom of God with different parables; one of them reads as follows: 'The kingdom of heaven is like a grain of mustard seed, which a man took, and sowed in his field: / Which indeed is the least of all seeds: but when it is grown, it is the greatest among herbs, and becometh a tree, so that the birds of the air come and lodge in the branches thereof' (Matthew 13:31–32).[10] It is obvious what is being compared here, but it is unclear according to which regard that comparison works. In this sense, the regard is unstable. The parable's *conciseness* is, one might say, precisely rooted in a particular *vagueness* that counteracts the tendency to make things unambiguous and objective. In tentatively relating the 'kingdom of heaven' to a 'grain of mustard seed', a possible *tertium* might appear, emerging from that comparative dynamic. And that emergence does not necessarily leave the *relata* untouched. Dependent on a particular regard T – strength, resilience, the relation to other creatures, etc. – the meaning of 'kingdom of heaven' and 'grain of mustard seed' may also change and shift.

The distinction between stability and emergence also has a relative counterpart, namely the distinction between *self-contained* and *involving* comparisons. In the first case, a comparative setting is already complete and waits simply to be activated by someone; however, it is not decisive about who this performing subject is, since the result is supposed to be independent of any concrete agent. This can be different in the second case because it is a concrete reader and listener who has to come up with the regard T enabling the comparison between A and B. And not everyone will cultivate exactly the same comparative regards when the *relata* A and B are 'kingdom of heaven' and 'grain of mustard seed'.[11] This latter comparative setting is thus not only *subject dependent*, but also *subject involving*. And it entails a twofold *productive effect* in creating or finding a possible regard T, as well as in turning the reader or listener into an active part of the comparison itself.[12]

2.4 Contrastive/analogical or similar

Obviously, comparisons expose or uncover differences or similarities between A and B (or their exact or fuzzy equivalence). 'Exposing' and 'uncovering' lead, however, in different directions insofar as differences or similarities may be *merely registered* or *intentionally highlighted*. This difference is reflected by the distinction between result-oriented (closed) and experimental (explorative) comparisons (see section 2.2). The former is the context of exposition; the latter the context of uncovering. And now, we can integrate the binary pair 'contrastive/analogical' into the binary pair 'result-oriented/experimental' – which itself results in four comparative constellations.

Within a result-oriented (and stable) comparative setting one can put the stress on differences between certain *relata* by treating them as separated units. This could be done by applying an *individualized* comparison focused on differences between, for example, societies, communities, organizations, etc. in regard to one feature (for instance, military budgets). In contrast, a *generalized* (or inclusive) comparison is interested in, for instance, rules, regulations, functions, etc. shared by different *relata* when treating them as part of a common context to which they all belong (for instance, countries as part of a union). In the first case, there is one regard (the military budget) according to which the different and mutually independent results $A, B, C, \ldots$ (usually countries) come to the fore. In the second and inclusive case, the *tertium* leads to observing shared clusters and effects partly as a result of constant interactions (within a political network, federation or union).[13]

Within an experimental (open) comparative setting one can, intentionally, put the stress on differences for marking strong contrasts or on significant similarities to underline the sharing of a regard T by very different relata A, B, C. In the first case, one might stipulate a regard T that brings the differences between A, B, C to the fore, although there are other Ts that could have shed light on their similarities as well. Comparing the USA and Germany in terms of their political system could lead to contemplating the immense differences between, say, the American presidency and the idea of chancellorship in Germany, instead of regarding both as two facets of Western democracy (which would be a different regard T). In the second case, one might concentrate on features shared by highly different *relata* while remaining fully aware of their differences. For example, one could contemplate the reasons for revolutions in several countries at different times to come up with a general notion of revolutionary causes and effects across different countries and centuries.

Is there any real difference between dealing with similarities and differences within result-oriented and experimental comparisons? For one, this distinction is only a gradual one without a clear separation.[14] And yet, in the first setting, similarities and differences are mere *results* that have to be accepted and recorded. Within the second arrangement, similarities and differences rather serve as premises and *starting points* for finding particular *relata* that fit the (correct or merely artificial) assumption that a regard T is instantiated differently or analogically by A, B, C.

Integrating the binary pair 'contrastive/analogical' into the pair 'result-oriented/ experimental' is itself a contrastive endeavor, precisely because there are several analogies between comparisons directed towards a result or performed as an experiment, respectively.

2.5 Diachronic/synchronic

Up to this point, we mostly dealt with comparative settings that relate several items $A, B, C \ldots$ to one another at a particular time t. It is often the case that this stable point in time t is silently presupposed while not taken to play a significant role in the comparison in question. One might neglect or even ignore this temporal aspect when comparing; and, to some extent, there is nothing wrong with that.

In contrast, there are many cases in which temporal aspects are of essential relevance when comparing A and B. One might think of, for example, political polls. In these polls one investigates different *relata* $A, B, C \ldots$ (usually, parties) at t_1 (usually, before elections), but more often one conducts a poll at different times $t_1, t_2, \ldots, t_n$ within a temporal range t_1–t_n. For the sake of the comparison's validity, to prevent excessive interference from other events, influences, developments, etc. this range should not be too long. What we can see here is a twofold comparability: the one between $A, B, C \ldots$ at t_1 or $t_2 \ldots$, or t_n (*synchronic*), as well as the one between A or B, or $\ldots$ at t_1 and $t_2, \ldots$, and t_n (*diachronic*).

In diachronic settings, it seems that we have only one single *relatum* accompanied by a comparative regard T. However, comparisons presuppose more than just one material item, but they do not presuppose the numerical discriminability of these items. Since diachronicity "duplicates" or "multiplies" the *relatum* A (at t_1 and $t_2, \ldots$, and t_n), a comparison is possible. For instance, the political performance of one party could obviously be compared to itself at different times, and this is sufficient for having more than one material item, although only one party is in play here. In contrast, synchronic comparisons do not call for this clarification because they only entail *relata* that are numerically discriminable $(A, B, C, \ldots)$.

Synchronic and diachronic comparisons can be independent of each other or can be combined together. They are separate if, for instance, two parties (A and B) in one poll at t_1 are synchronically compared, while one diachronically compares the results of one party (A or B) at different elections at t_1 and t_2. They are combined if, for example, one party A and its result at a past election (t_1) is compared with the results of other parties ($B, C, \ldots$) at a recent election (t_2). This crossover can be methodologically problematic, but there are contexts in which such a combination is instructive. Party B might find itself now (t_2) in a similar situation as party A did in the past (t_1). Here, the contextual elements of the material items (C_A and C_B) secure the validity of combining diachronicity with synchronicity. The similarity between C_A and C_B justifies the comparative result (see also chapter 1, section 3).

However, in most cases this contextual similarity is not there, and this absence calls for separating diachronic and synchronic comparisons again. Diachronic comparisons underline the similarities and differences of the similar (A at t_1 and t_2), whereas synchronic comparisons underline the similarities and differences of the different (A and B at t_n).

2.6 Genetic/typological

The binary pair 'genetic/typological' is the only one in the typology presented here whose usage is well established in the comparative sciences. It concerns the relation between the different material items of a comparison. Genetic comparisons presuppose contacts and influences between the *relata*, whereas the typological counterpart highlights only the analogies and similarities between them.[15] 'Contacts and influences' either mean direct causality between A and B or (this is the weaker form) indirect influences between *A* and *B* through a third element *C*. In both genetic cases, the mutual independence of *A* and *B* is excluded. In contrast, 'analogies and similarities' either refers to *A*'s and *B*'s sharing of one comparative regard T_1 or (this is the stonger form) *A*'s and *B*'s sharing of a range of comparative regards $T_1, T_2, ..., T_n$. In both typological cases, the mutual dependence of *A* and *B* is presupposed.

There is an affinity between genetic and diachronic comparisons but no significant affinity between typological and synchronic comparisons. Genetic comparisons are always diachronic due to the causal connection between the *relata*; the reverse implication, however, does not hold, since diachronicity does not necessarily imply direct or indirect 'contacts and influences'.

While genetic comparisons are of great importance, especially in historal cross-cultural studies,[16] they are connected to a methodologically severe problem. The direct or indirect causal link between *A* and *B* (for instance, two countries or cultures) could threaten and eventually undermine the comparison between *A* and *B*, since this connection – for instance, what may be called cultural 'transfer' between the 'West' (Europe) and the 'East' (China)[17] – creates a specific contextual environment for *A* and *B*, and these contexts C_A and C_B limit the comparative validity. In the end, these contexts give the priority to elaborating on the precise influence and 'transfer' between the 'West' (Europe) and the 'East' (China), instead of comparing *A* and *B* with contexts C_A and C_B independent of each other.[18]

A significant affinity between typological and synchronic comparisons is, however, not in sight, simply because the similarity expressed by typological arrangements can be found in diachronic, as well as in synchronic, settings. But genetic and typological comparisons can be combined insofar as genetic contacts and influences can create the typological similarity in question (these contacts and influences could, of course, have the opposite effect too). For instance, the legal institutions (such as courts) are typologically comparable between the US, Germany and France, but their similarity goes back to directly causal connections and indirectly effective circumstances. The first and stronger case points to the historical and political interrelatedness between American and European jurisprudence; the one genetically influenced the other and *vice versa*; the second and weaker case points to the fact that the very institution of legal power reacts to typologically similar difficulties in different societies, namely different ways of breaking the law.[19]

2.7 Impartial or pure/asymmetrical

By turning, finally, to the duality between impartial and asymmetrical comparisons, we turn, at the same time, to the problem of comparative normativity. What is meant by this term is an *intracomparative balance* or *asymmetry* between the material items within a particular comparison. Comparisons can be conducted impartially and, in this sense, neutrally and purely; there is, then, no privilege or priority given to one (or more) of these *relata* in contrast to the remaining items. However, comparisons can also be conducted partially and impurely; in this case, there is in fact a privilege or priority given to one (or more) of these *relata* that is normatively loaded. In the first case, we are dealing with a symmetrical relation without any preferences; in the latter case, we are dealing with an asymmetrically normative relation benefitting one side of the comparison while running the risk of devaluating its counterpart.[20]

This danger of devaluation on an everyday level, but on a scientific basis as well, transforms comparative acts between A and B into procedures which *align or adjust B to A*. This devaluation could take up an explicit and open, as well as a factual and latent, form – an alternative mirroring the duality between contrastive and analogical comparisons (see again 2.4). On the one hand, normative comparisons could be instrumentalized for depreciating a *relatum* or even for negating it; this is the contrastive aspect of underlining the differences between A and B. On the other hand, comparing normatively could also be applied to discern the already-known and familiar within the unknown and alien; this is the analogical aspect of underlining the merely alleged similarities. In the first case, differences are not neglected but, rather, are interpreted as expressions of divergent values and their relevance. In the latter case, differences are indeed ignored in refuting real alterity in the course of 'nostrifying' the 'other', as the sociologist Joachim Matthes claims.[21]

Normative comparisons, then, exhibit two complementary character traits: *devaluation* (and its extreme, *exclusion*) and *usurpation* (and its extreme, *levelling everything down*). Within this scheme, impartial or pure comparisons had to find a middle position between these extreme poles of comparative activity – a middle position resembling the Aristotelian definition of virtues as the *mesotes* of two vices.[22] This hint at ancient virtue ethics is not an accident, since finding intracomparative balances or allowing for asymmetries within a comparison leads again back to *moral implications* entailed by comparative practices (see, especially, chapter 9). And these implications go back either to factually conducting a comparison between A and B by referring to certain regards T, which leads to exclusion or usurpation, or to willfully aiming at these extremes by defining comparative regards T that allow for the normative result initially intended.

Three additional comments might now be in order. First, it is a reasonable concern as to whether the distinction between impartial and asymmetrical comparisons really holds, or if it is not rather the case that every impartiality is reducible to normative asymmetries. Without denying this danger, one should defend the difference between comparisons that are conducted without agenda or prejudgements and those that are led by precomparative premises. Talking about 'pure' comparisons does not necessarily mean to compare without intentions and interest, but it does mean to be open to any possible result and to potential revisions of these results. Purity in this sense should not be excluded. Secondly, latent or explicit precomparative judgements do not have to be problematic in every case and regard. This is obvious in trivial cases of personal preferences. Here, characterizing comparisons as asymmetrical could also be taken to be descriptive and not necessarily pejorative. But even in cases where this asymmetry is in fact inappropriate, it is not impossible that a devalued comparative item, as it were, claims its right to gain comparative fairness and caution. For instance, through a productive kind of unsettling, evidence might come to the fore that initiates a kind of comparative self-correction by allowing for alternative regards and contexts to emerge. Thirdly, something 'alien' and 'different' is only possible against the backdrop of something 'familiar' and 'known'. As much as the tendency toward exclusion and nostrification looms problematically large (socially, as well as scientifically), there is nevertheless an asymmetrical element on an epistemic level, namely that discerning the (contrastive) 'other' presupposes an acquaintance with one's own environment and context. This tension between problematic asymmetries within practices of comparing and the epistemic asymmetry between the familiar and the alien is particularly prominent in some of the most important comparative disciplines. We will come back this issue in the next chapter with regard to comparative philosophy.

This typology does not only aim at capturing essential distinctions within comparative settings and at reflecting upon important challenges within 'the operation called "comparing"'; it was also an attempt, at least, to sketch relevant crossovers between the comparative pairs characterized above. Not all, but some of these pairs entertain alliances, are interwoven and go hand in hand. Think again of the connection between result-orientation/comparative experiments and contrastive/analogical comparisons or recall the affinities between genetic and diachronic comparisons. Moreover, the status of defining pairs of comparisons is not always the same. In some cases, we are dealing with complementary kinds that are incompatible with each other (for instance, a comparison either is simple or complex); in other cases, overlap or combinations are possible (for instance, diachronicity and synchronicity are combinable; genetically linked items can be part of a typological arrangement). And finally, some types have additional subtypes that reflect important differences within the range of their application. These differences concern either semantic differences (for example, 'simple' comparisons could refer to one-dimensionality or to quantifiability), or they concern differences in the mode in which a comparison is conducted (for instance, stable comparisons are self-contained, while comparative emergence leads to the involvement of whomever is conducting the comparison).

The typology presented here is itself comparative in nature, i.e. it functions as a small comparative compendium. Therefore, in all seven pairs A and B are compared according to one particular regard T – an arrangement that results in the following overview:

(i)   dimensionality: *simple/complex*
                         one-/multi-dimentional
                         quantifiable/nonquantifiable
(ii) completeness: *result-oriented/experimental or explorative*
(iii) stability: *stable/emergent*
                         self-contained/involving
(iv) differentiality: *contrastive/analogical or similar*
(v)   temporality: *diachronic/synchronic*
(vi) causality: *genetic/typological*
(vii) normativity: *impartial or pure/asymmetrical*

(i) concerns the character and constitution of the *comparanda*; (ii) and (iii) reflect on different comparative framings that touch upon the relation between the *relata*, *tertia*, their specific contexts and the status of the comparative result; (iv), (v) and (vi) present divergent relations between different *relata*; (vii) also does this by integrating normative aspects into this relation. Despite all differences within and between (i)–(vii), the initial 'monolithic' claim, according to which comparisons entail one particular structure, is not undermined but, I hope, deepened, precisely by giving this comparative plurality its due.

3 Coda: on pointed comparisons

Let's start off by looking at three very different examples of a *pointed* comparison:

(i) It belongs to common football wisdom that: 'Football is religion and Franz Beckenbauer is the emperor.'
(ii) The Pope said recently: 'Abortion is like hiring a hitman.'[23]
(iii) Facing government pressure to support 'delivering Brexit' the British Tory MP Anna Soubry said as early as fall 2017: 'It's like the counter-revolutionary forces of Chairman Mao or Joe Stalin. It's not enough that you went against everything you ever believed in; you have to sign up *in blood*. It's like Orwell's thought police and the reign of terror combined.'[24]

All three examples need, of course, more elaboration on their specific meaning and they call for a more sensitive embeddedness in their cultural, religious and political context: (i) the fascination and excitement grounded in and accompanying sports might take the form of comparing it to the impact of spiritual devotion. As in religious veneration, this fascination and excitement is, often enough, personalized. Football, as other sports, is also a game of heroes, and one of them is the German Franz Beckenbauer, celebrated as the 'Kaiser', which stresses the fact that the former defender has played in a sovereign, and even aesthetic, fashion like no one else who played that position. (ii) Pope Francis compares abortion to contract-killing while several US states are attempting to restrict the procedure, as the state of Alabama did in July 2019. The Pope suggested even stronger – and more pointed – comparisons by alluding to the Holocaust. And he has reiterated his stance against abortion several times, by saying that the procedure should not be carried out even when the foetus is deformed or gravely ill. This is disappointing for people with a more 'liberal' stance insofar as the Pope seemed to be softening the Catholic church's strict position in 2016 by officially authorizing all priests to forgive the 'sin of abortion'.[25] (iii) In an early act of creating 'political discipline' or, at least, a coherent voting behaviour, it was felt that former British prime minister's (Theresa May's) handling of Tory members of the House of Commons had factually been an act of threatening democratically-elected representatives to vote in a predetermined way. After two years of trying to 'deliver Brexit', British Tory MP Anna Soubry stated more recently that even Stalin would have been surprised by the new prime minister Boris Johnson's decision to force the Tories to support his version of a hard Brexit on 31 October 2019 to leave parliament,[26] and he has realized that threat in the meantime.

Obviously, this is not the appropriate place to discuss the concrete contents of (i), (ii) and (iii). Rather, these three examples are supposed to provide a better understanding of pointed comparisons, as each of them may help to highlight one particular aspect to be found in this kind of comparative act. And we will proceed conversely by first consulting case (iii) for a general analysis of pointed comparisons.

To begin with, the pointed element of a comparison is part of its character and tone, but also functions as an implicit excuse, namely that the comparison is hyperbolic. There is something inappropriate about this comparison, whereas its pointed element also contains, if not a self-evident aspect, then at least an understandable, or even catchy, one. To put it in Adornian terms: there is something right within the wrong here. Or, to put it in a more epistemic way: the truth of pointed comparisons does not lie in the correspondence between what is said and how things 'are', but rather in a *deliberate and calculated inadequacy* that conveys a proposition in a trenchant, yet also openly exaggerated manner. Referring to Mao and the mass murderer Joseph Stalin or relying on Orwell's dystopian stance on society and power might underline the gravity Anna Soubry sees in the political developments in her home country. And yet, comparing the undeniably severe situation the UK finds itself in with the behaviour of past dictatorships is a bold, risky and, for some, even an irritating suggestion.

On a more technical note, pointed comparisons are multi-digit comparisons, meaning that they necessarily entail more than just one comparative regard. One *tertium comparationis* (sometimes, more than one) functions as the point – or focus[27] – of the comparison; all other possible regards, however, are not in focus, as they are dimmed out, marginalized or even neglected. When Soubry compares the action of the UK's government with Mao and Stalin, she concentrates latently on a form of political pressure that we know from antidemocratic leaders; Theresa May's behaviour then is not only characterized as equally antidemocratic, but also as inconsistent given the democratic framework of Great Britain's constitution and self-understanding. In contrast to this critical focus, other possible regards such as aspects of, for instance, Stalin's (pre)political career as agitator, revolutionary and ruthlessly despotic autocrat are not in focus or remain at the side-lines.

The hyperbolic character of pointed comparisons is therefore based on two elements. One, the focus is exaggerated – Mao's and Stalin's deeds are far more severe than what May has done; 'Orwell's thought police and the reign of terror' are far more serious than what UK politics is experiencing right now. This comparative exaggeration justifies – or tries to do so – its truth by hitting a point and being open about its auxesis. Two, all other regards that were meant to remain in the background undermine the justification of pointed comparisons since these *tertia* only reveal sub-comparisons that are hard to accept or are blatantly unacceptable. May is not the mass murderer that Stalin was; the UK is not a *1984*-esque empire despite the increasingly-problematic story of Brexit. Hence, pointed comparisons are *positively- or negatively-hyperbolic tropes*, while their evidence is based on an audacious ambivalence between adequacy and surplus: the first feeds the second, whereas the second undermines the former.

One might ask: evidence – for whom? Which brings us to the second case (ii). When the Pope claims that abortion – without any further restrictions or qualifications concerning future parents, divergent circumstances, conflicting moral and religious values, etc. – is *like* hiring a killer, then this might be taken as a traditional expression of 'the' Catholic standpoint or a reflection of doctrinal necessities. 'Evangelicals' and 'religious fundamentalists' will welcome such a statement by taking it as their theologically-underwritten duty to defend it against all odds. 'Conservatives' will also appreciate this stance, which, however, does not mean they will subscribe to it in every case. More moderate groups may try to find internal resources for offering alternatives to the Pope's dogmatic non-dogma (i.e. it does not fall under the purview of his infallibility). Other believers could attack the Pope's lack of sensitivity to the situation of parents and especially of women. And, again, others for whom the Pope or any other religious authority has no say in these (and other) matters will make a case for the irrelevance of, or even the dangerous impact on, combining religion with the issue of reproduction. Therefore, a wide spectrum of divergent standpoints is brought to the fore here, along with the significance of the question as to whether we are dealing in case (ii) with a (pointed) comparison or not.

The Pope or other highly-conservative voices in this debate could have said – instead of *comparing* abortion with allowing murder – that abortion *is nothing but* murder. Seen from their strict perspective, (ii) is not a comparison (or a metaphor or analogy) at all, but about establishing a mere, and nonfigurative, identification. This is different in regard to all middle- ground positions, namely those allowing moderate conservatives to appreciate alternatives, as well as Catholic critics of the Pope, other religious people and, of course, nonreligious opponents, including those actively fighting for the right to abortion as an expression of freedom over one's own body and life. For most of them, we are in fact dealing with a (pointed) comparison, and their 'reactive attitudes' might range from accepting the comparative evidence to positions being increasingly critical of the comparison's adequacy. At this other end of the spectrum, we eventually find those who repudiate the right to compare abortion with any form of killing, a repudiation which might in the end amount to a position that claims a normative incomparability between abortion and the comparative counterpart suggested by the Pope.

The upshot of this consideration in view of different reactions to a pointed comparison is this: whether we are dealing with a comparative act is not independent of evaluative background assumptions informing our relation to what is presented as comparison. For some, a comparison is an identification in disguise (hence, there is no comparison in the end); for some, a comparison, even if possible, is out of place (hence, we have incomparability in its evaluative form);[28] and for the rest, we are in fact dealing with comparisons – precarious, 'wild',[29] or hyperbolically-evident ones. Without touching the general structure of comparisons, their pointed version confronts us with the evaluatively-loaded question of whether we are dealing with comparisons at all, with a form of incomparability, or with different reactions to a scenario of comparability.

Not only is an audience acknowledging that a comparison *as* a possible comparison is in play here, but also that is the context of communication. Often enough, pointed comparisons are part of a joke; they might constitute a caricature or belong generally to a rhetorical move to apply a comparative setting between critique and appraisal. This brings us back to our first example (i). Celebrating football as religion and one of its most famous players as emperor – hence, mixing sports as an activity with religious and political concepts – is another instance of comparing items in a pointed way. However, there is also a dynamic element to the aforementioned question concerning (in)comparability, the comparative setting and its adequacy. Comparisons might *become* pointed ones – and they can also *lose* that status again. Calling Franz Beckenbauer the 'emperor' has turned, for some or even many, into a more dubious expression since he (and others) is accused of being involved in corrupt business practices in the course of financing the football World Cup in Germany in 2006. Again, whether these allegations are justified (or not) is not relevant here. What is relevant is that the classification of a comparison as pointed is not set in stone, nor merely structural or context-free. And here as well different reactions are possible. Some might say, an emperor stands in a realm beyond the everyday business of organizing an event – the pointed element of the comparison then serves as part of an implicit apology. Others might claim that an 'emperor' cannot afford to be involved in corruption and an alleged bribery affair – the pointed comparison here is taken to be literal, which itself allows for different reactions, from amplifying the comparison's pointed character due to its increased degree of dubiousness, to saying farewell to what that laudatory comparison initially sought to express. In sum, comparisons are embedded in contexts, and their contextuality informs their precise character as pointed, non-pointed or modest comparisons.

3

On Comparative Injustice

1 Introduction

It has become a methodological topic in its own right that *epistemic questions are questions of historical developments intertwined with questions of power*. This link between *knowledge, history and politics* – all terms to be taken broadly – not only touches on the possession of and access to knowledge, it also concerns the origin, genesis and formation of knowledge. The philosophy and history of science have hesitantly reacted to this emergent awareness of and sensitivity to historical contingencies in and political influences on knowledge-formation by establishing two interrelated fields of research: on the one hand, *historical epistemology* as reflection on the contingent conditions under which – as well as by means of which – knowledge is generated;[1] and on the other hand, a variety of analytic, therapeutic, discursive, deconstructivist and structuralist *tools* for detecting and *revealing power dynamics* that inform and interfere with genuinely epistemic (but also historical, political, social and scientific) problems.[2] And we have already reached the stage upon which both research fields not only have been brought together more closely, but during which they have themselves come to be regarded as subjected to historicity and power.[3]

A growing awareness of historical contingencies tends to strengthen constructivist and relativistic positions within epistemology. Insofar as comparative procedures are concerned, this places greater emphasis on the modes in which a comparison's *relata* and *tertia* have become products of construction and adjustments. In consequence, they are not 'given', and thus, they are not to be taken for granted, but to be reflected upon as results of stipulation, correction, adaptation and as manifestations of background assumptions – both past and present ones. When comparing Europe and the 'East', both material items have to be determined and sufficiently well predefined before a comparison between them is possible; hence, one has to constructively deal with the fact that the terms in play, 'Europe' and the 'East', are already loaded with premises, values and expectations.

A growing awareness of politics and power as factors influencing the search for knowledge exposes, in contrast, normative issues and leads to moral demands on those engaged in that search. Politics and power embody non-epistemic dynamics affecting, or even manipulating, epistemic results. This does not have to be unjust *per se*, but it is, in any case, dubious. This is also true for comparative settings that are – particularly in their experimental/explorative and emergent/involving versions – severely vulnerable to these kinds of influences. The above-mentioned moral demands on those conducting these comparisons are equally severe since they call for dealing carefully with the risk of succumbing to comparative injustice and for attempting to (re)gain that justice for the sake of the comparison's validity, but also, and more to the point, in the interest of those affected by possible comparative results.

Let us focus for the rest of this chapter on this latter aspect, namely the precarious relation between knowledge-formation and the question of power in regard to the threat of comparative injustice.[4] Instances of comparative injustice are, arguably, some of the most thoroughly discussed issues regarding comparisons and their general application. These methodological discussions are particularly present in postcolonial and cross-cultural studies, as well as research in global history, sociology and ethnology.[5] In contrast to these important (inter)disciplinary debates, I shall first concentrate exclusively on purely structural considerations, drawing on the typology laid out in the previous chapter to pin down which concrete forms of comparative injustice can be inferred from and identified by these typological distinctions (2.1). Afterwards, I will briefly turn to what is called comparative philosophy, focusing particularly on its critical intentions (2.2), which will then be followed up by a section recalling a very early expression of comparative philosophy, including its ambitions, problems and internal critique, by drawing on Peter Winch's seminal essay 'On Understanding a Primitive Society' (2.3). This provides an exemplary occasion for capturing what is at stake in cases of comparative injustice, in contrast to the methodological responsibility to safeguard that justice for the sake of comparisons and those affected by them.

2 Injustice, comparatively

2.1 Comparative injustice – typologically considered

One obvious way to elaborate on comparative injustice is to focus on the performative subject conducting the comparison in question. Here, we have a both weak and a strong version: either the comparison is *factually* conducted in a way that is one-sided or driven by unjustified prejudgments, or there is an explicitly *mal intention* behind that comparative procedure. In other words, a comparison may only be unjust when someone latently or wilfully (mis)uses it. However, in both cases, by way of the factual procedure and by intention, this injustice has to manifest itself structurally – which brings us from intentions back to our typology.

To begin with, there are pairs that are more relevant to our topic than others. The couples orbiting dimensionality (i: simple/complex), differentiality (iv: contrastive/analogical), temporality (v: diachronic/synchronic) and causality (vi: genetic/typological) are only indirectly, i.e. through the other three pairs, influential with regard to comparative justice and injustice. And even within that threefold group, there are crucial differences: in terms of completeness (ii: result-oriented/experimental) and stability (iii: stable/emergent), it is, for both types, only the second category that may have unjust effects, since result-orientation and stable comparisons were defined as consisting of all necessary – and not manipulated, but sufficiently well-defined – elements, allowing for a comparatively valid outcome. We have a similar situation concerning normativity (vii): trivial, impartial (or pure) comparisons belong, per definition, to the range of just comparisons, and thus, only the second term remains relevant here as well. The interesting cases are then those that allow for the comparative setting to be influenced in order to implicitly or intentionally integrate normative assumptions into a particular comparison.

Therefore, we are dealing with experimental, emergent and asymmetrical comparisons as responsible for comparative injustice. Again, they do not lead necessarily to instances of comparative injustice, but they do delimit the range in which these instances are possible. Hence, not every comparative experiment is problematic, but only those that are not open and truly explorative. Not every emergent *tertium* leads us off course, but the exclusive focus on one which 'silences' other possible *tertia* is inappropriate. And not every asymmetry in comparisons is unfair, since either these asymmetries are themselves comparative results, or there are extra-comparative and convincing reasons for bestowing the privilege to A over B.

Now, the three remaining types of comparative acts are not on the same level. Emergent comparisons are, in the end, a subclass of comparative experiments in trying out different *tertia*, while all other comparative elements remain stable (recall again the parable of heaven and the grain of mustard seed in chapter 2, section 2.3). And asymmetrical comparisons – if not referring to a comparative result – form a part of one possible constellation within a comparative exploration that end up giving the privilege to A over B. Therefore, we can concentrate on what have been labelled as experimental comparisons to give an account of comparative injustice. However, after this incremental limitation, we can open the scope of analysis again by differentiating between several constellations within comparisons that can make them unjust. This results in the following list (including examples):

(a) *The unjust construction of relata*. As mentioned before, the material elements are not just given, but are either taken for granted or are the results of stipulation, construction and adjustment. Returning to the example of comparing the unemployment rates between Wyoming and California, it is first essential to be aware of the political, social and economic situation in both states, including potential relations (and 'transfers') between them, in order to compare in a responsible way. Secondly, it is equally crucial to clarify what 'unemployment' means (which already touches on (b)), as well as what really counts as being unemployed in Wyoming and California. If there are different definitions of this complex term in play, a comparison is undermined at the outset because the extension of 'Wyoming' and 'California' relevant for 'unemployment' has become unclear.

(b) *The unjust construction of a tertium while silencing other tertia*. This refers again to emergent comparisons in which the comparative regard has to be found or defined intra-comparatively. Imagine an open employment position and different applicants who are applying for it. However, the employers already know who they want to hire, namely mister X, but are nonetheless obliged to advertise this position publicly. By simulating a transparent application process, while giving the job to that person X who was initially wanted, one has to define a *tertium* (or *tertia*) for justifying the choice in favour of X. Other *tertia* might have had different consequences, which is already a sufficient reason for "'silently' neglecting them.[6]

(c) *Ignoring/dimming the material and/or its formal context*. Contrary to standard accounts of comparative procedures, we have emphasized how the contexts of the material (C_A, C_B, ...) and the formal elements (C_T) of a comparison also belong to its basic structure (see chapter 1, section 2.6). A telling instance of interfering with both kinds of contextual elements at the same time, and in a fairly dubious way, can be seen in the process of is what is called 'gerrymandering': this is the politically motivated adjustment of election districts that legally increases the chances of a politician getting (re)elected by distributing potential voters in a politically expedient way. Under the disguise of rather technical and geographical questions, one deals, in fact, with highly political issues – *post*-democratically.[7] There are different sub-strategies of gerrymandering, but all of them entail this kind of manipulative politics, representing one of the most-discussed problems in the political sciences.[8]

(d) *Bestowing priorities*. This last case brings us back to comparative partiality that becomes unjust as soon as we are in contexts that require comparative purity. An example for ignoring this purity is shown in the following scene: someone, let's call him Max, goes to his bank asking for a loan. Max is thirty-eight, an unsuccessful former professional football player without any proper degree from a university. The bank assistant consults his system that relies on an algorithm which was programmed by someone who dislikes professional sports, thinks that football players have no future after thirty-eight, and is convinced that a life without a university degree is empty. Max does not get his loan, as the algorithm was fed with information provided by these (de)valuations – a scenario of an impure and asymmetrical comparison that is becoming more and more prominent under the conditions of a 'digital society'.[9]

Structurally speaking, (a) through (d) cover all basic forms of comparative injustice. First, they all belong to the realm of comparative experimentation which adjust certain elements within a comparative setting, including cases of emergent and asymmetrical comparison. Secondly, these forms are either built on the construction and adjustment of the material, formal and contextual elements driven by particular comparative interests, or they are based on precomparative or intracomparative (de)valuations concerning the items to be compared with one another. Finally, comparative injustice takes the form of experimenting with possible comparative constellations while giving one of them unwarranted privilege or it takes the form of prioritizing one *relatum* over all others without explicitly integrating this valuation into the comparison in question. The first form could be dubbed *simulated impartiality* (encompassing (a), (b) and (c)); the second could be called *short prioritizing* (consisting of (d)).

Both forms of comparative injustice, the simulated and the short form, may lead to two kinds of unjust results, based on the mechanisms elaborated on here. Drawing again on the binary pair 'contrastive/analogical' (see chapter 2, section 2.4), injustice, in the relevant sense here, could lead to or imply *comparative exclusions* as an extreme form of establishing unfair differences, or *comparative usurpations* as an extreme form of levelling down pertinent differences. Cases of simulated impartiality (a, b, c) are open both to exclusion or usurpation in constructing and adjusting the material, formal and contextual items in such a way that either equality or, at least, similarity is ignored in the name of alleged difference and, eventually, unjustified exclusion; or these differences are neglected in order to claim similarities between A and B that are not present. Even more prominent cases of comparative injustice – *short(ly) prioritizing A over B* (this is (d)) – entail both tendencies as well, but in a slightly different fashion: either by privileging A although B is equally good or in privileging A to make its difference to B disappear.

Comparisons are open to instrumentalization in the mode of devaluation/exclusion or levelling down/usurpation. Both forms together constitute the range of comparative injustice. On the other hand, all comparative acts that neither simply simulate impartiality, nor shortly prioritize, amount to just comparisons.

2.2 The will to compare. On comparative philosophy

After these structural considerations, we can now turn to a more concrete case of comparative injustice, which also exhibits a peculiar relation between knowledge-formation and power dynamics. It has often been emphasized that the period of colonialism and imperialism in particular strengthened comparative approaches in several sciences.[10] This is especially the case due to early 'intercontinental' experiences of cultural otherness and, along those lines, more frequent travel activities, which increased opportunities for comparison between the 'new continents' and 'worlds' and the European home countries and cultures.[11] In cultural studies, as well as in philosophy, the ambivalence between latent or explicit devaluation/exclusion and programmatic usurpation/levelling-down is – or has been? – particularly prominent for a long time.

Some authors claim that the very idea of living in one culture is itself the product of intercultural comparison. Hence, we are not dealing here with epistemic questions of generating and justifying knowledge, but rather with identity politics regarding how other cultures create their identity in the same way by comparing themselves to surrounding (counter)cultures. In this sense, the sociologist Dirk Baecker states that living in a culture is no longer a question of veneration (a *vertical relation* to a deity), but a question of comparing that very culture with its cultural context (a *horizontal relation* to other cultures).[12] 'Modern cultures', Baecker goes on, are the results of the intellectual practice of comparing to create and secure an identity by differentiation and, eventually, by exclusion. Comparisons lend themselves effectively to this task because they may mobilize a society more vividly and sustainably than any other cultural techniques. Baecker sums this up somewhat drastically: 'A nation is a culture's armament for the purposes of comparison.'[13]

This kind of comparative identity politics illustrates the aforementioned ambivalence between the tendency towards privileging differences, and thus operating with contrastive comparisons, and the tendency towards levelling-down real differences in a manner that may threaten cultural particularity. The opposing tendencies are often taken not only to be instances of comparative injustice and cultural single-mindedness, but also of 'epistemic violence' performed using the backdrop of comparative necessity.[14] The concern here seems to be that historical-political colonialism is now being repeated and reproduced through its methodological aftermath. Insofar as contrastive comparisons have gained more prominence than their analogical counterparts – and thus have placed more emphasis on alterity than the elaboration of similar and overlapping aspects – this asymmetry has itself become subjected to criticism. Here, the entire opposition between highlighting differences and alterity, on the one hand, as well as emphasizing similarities and modes of 'nostrification' on the other, has been placed into brackets so as to move beyond the overheated debate in favour of giving more 'relaxed' characterizations their due. According to the literary scholar Albrecht Koschorke, both poles in the opposition, alterity and nostrification of the other, still share the same logic of remaining within a merely negative interdependence. Therefore, he calls for what might be labelled a *post-post*-colonial discourse, open to the ways in which mutual influences are exchanged between two different cultures. Elaborating on 'similarities' is then supposed to lead to a middle ground both between and beyond the extremes of exclusion and usurpation.[15]

Turning now to philosophy, we initially encounter a very 'similar' situation of normatively loaded colonialism during the early stages of confrontation between different ways of thinking and then, later, a severe critique of that form of widespread eurocentrism and its exclusive focus on 'Western thought'. It was the late Edmund Husserl who put forth a short, yet comprehensive, diagnosis of what he took to be an all-encompassing 'crisis' in thinking.[16] For Husserl, it was the mathematization of the universe, starting off with the work of Galileo Galilei, as well as the 'self-misunderstanding' of Descartes when he established a duality between mind and world, and between significance and facticity, that was almost unbridgeable. For our purposes, it is not of central importance that Husserl fought against this duality by introducing the antipositivist notion of 'life-world' (*Lebenswelt*) to regain the essential connection between mind and world, as well as between significance and facticity. Rather, it is relevant that Husserl claimed that the only tradition possessing this kind of thinking – including this particular set of problems, such as materialism, naturalism, solipsism – was the European one. More explicitly, he believed that only Europe could have a proper philosophy. China and India, Husserl states, belong merely to the 'empirical anthropological type' (16), far away from the transcendental considerations that are essential for philosophy. Europe as a term is, of course, not primarily intended as a geographical category; rather, it represents the ancient Greek tradition: 'European mankind' has inherited Greek philosophy and stands within its 'teleology'. Hence, the positivist crisis of philosophy is, accordingly, not only a crisis within a particular philosophical tradition, but a crisis of philosophy in general, affecting all other sciences informed by the Greek legacy (12).

On the one hand, there are other prominent voices – for example, Schopenhauer's and Nietzsche's – in late-nineteenth-century philosophy refuting this kind of 'European' single-mindedness. On the other hand, Husserl is by far not the only one calling for contrastive comparisons in philosophy to be amplified to the level of total exclusion of other genuinely philosophical traditions. Heidegger's awkward claim that Greek and German were the only languages in which true philosophizing could be possible is rooted in a similar constriction of intellectual expression.[17]

Husserl's normatively loaded and burdened comparison remains, to a large extent, implicit. 'Europe' is related to non-European traditions, while constructing both *relata* in two divergent ways: 'Europe' is removed from the realm of geographical banalities – to which the rest of the world still belongs – without giving any reason for *not* equally considering 'China' and 'India' in a non-topographical, and thus also normative, manner (*a. the unjust construction of relata*). This makes it almost impossible to find a shared comparative regard, such as 'original thinking' or 'innovative ways of articulation', to place 'Europe' and 'China', along with 'India', into a comparable setting. Husserl might claim that 'thinking' in an empathetic sense is at home only in Europe, as other comparative regards are neglected or ignored (*b. the unjust construction of a tertium while silencing other tertia*). By exclusively referring to the Greek tradition, Husserl already creates a one-sided context that supports, in a circular manner, the initial claim regarding 'Europe' as the sole inheritor of that ancient tradition. Even if one agrees with the implicit assumption that China and India have remained untouched by Greek thought, it is still necessary to pay heed to what they have inherited (*c. ignoring/dimming the material and/or formal contexts*). Husserl's impure and asymmetrical comparison is unjust from the outset by its stipulation of the relevant concepts – 'philosophy', 'the Greek tradition', 'Europe' – in such a way that is already derived from a precomparative (de)valuation (*d. bestowing priorities*).

Husserl's philosophical colonialism and unacknowledged arrogance has become the target of a philosophical movement that critically counteracts the Eurocentrism, normative and geographical, that underpins this kind of exclusion of other or alien modes of philosophical articulation. For this purpose, one has to revise the normative construction of the *relata* by not allowing them to work on two different levels (against (a)); one has to appreciate different *tertia comparationis* that are not at home solely on one side of the comparative setting (against (b)). One must say farewell to the exclusiveness of the Greek influence on our thinking by extending the scope of 'our' and 'thinking' (against (c)); one has to be self-critical regarding precomparative valuations by upholding the methodological virtue of true openness, yet while acknowledging the difficulty of sticking to that virtue as a result of cultural and linguistic imprints by which we are deeply influenced (against (d)).

Therefore, the methodological demands on comparative philosophers are indeed ambitious. In the wake of Alexander von Humboldt and other early representatives of that tradition,[18] the goal is to extend and differentiate our concepts and sense of possibility within philosophy, without aiming at a new synthesis of divergent modes of philosophical expression.[19] However, in the end, comparative philosophy does not primarily compare but, rather, shows awareness of philosophical multilingualism and thus deserves the term 'cross-cultural philosophy', leaving the very idea of prioritizing 'Western' thinking behind, which might be itself a very 'Western' idea.

2.3 Peter Winch on understanding an alien culture

After methodological considerations of comparative injustice and a general characterization of 'the will to compare' in cross-cultural philosophy, we will turn now to one of its early practitioners. Peter Winch's influential 1964 paper 'On Understanding a Primitive Society' is, in the strictest sense, not itself a specimen of comparative philosophy. But it is a philosophically intriguing and methodologically critical commentary on the hermeneutic assumptions, as well as epistemic consequences, of ethnological research and its tendency to comparatively (de)valuate the 'other' or alien culture.

Winch, known for his work in social philosophy and ethics within a particular Wittgensteinian tradition, concentrates on the act of 'understanding', whereas his terms for the object of this understanding are, seen from today's standpoint, fairly problematic. Speaking about 'primitive society' draws on Wittgenstein's nonpejorative usage of 'primitive' in the sense of unreflected and basic.[20] The main reference point of Winch's paper is the research conducted by the British anthropologist Edward E. Evans-Pritchard on the central-African tribe of the Azande during the second half of the 1920s. One might prefer the concept of 'culture' to that of 'society', whereas Winch does not provide an account of these terms in his writing. His question is double: can we 'understand' the Azande and their practices (and also, what does 'understand' mean in this case)?; followed by the subsequent problem: are we entitled to claim that these practices – in our 'Western' vocabulary called 'magic' and 'witchcraft' – are confused and beyond rationality?[21] Winch's general suspicion is that even a careful author such as Evans-Pritchard is not immune from replying in problematic ways to both questions.

To begin with, Evans-Pritchard claims the Azande culture to be heavily influenced by the practice of consulting oracles and that without oracles they would be completely lost (18). Based on the relevant field research, one can state that the Azande engage in these consultations to their own satisfaction; the support and advice given by the oracles are taken to be reliable and helpful and function as an integral part of their *Lebenswelt*. However, Winch detects in Evans-Pritchard's reading of these practices 'a misleadingly close analogy with scientific hypotheses' (21). These oracle consultations – as part of their 'philosophy' – are misunderstood when regarded as hypotheses waiting for justification, Winch claims. Accordingly, the comparison between 'Western' and Azande hypotheses in relation to causality and prediction would be out of place. Winch fears that Evans-Pritchard (and others) are ultimately convinced that the Azande's 'mystical notions' and ritual patterns of behaviour are based on mistaken assumptions that can be explained by logic and science (17 and 26).

This brings Winch to considerations regarding the quest for a unified notion of rationality that is potentially shared by Africans and Europeans. Obviously, Winch is highly critical of such an endeavour. He refutes even the latent attempts in the work of Evans-Pritchard (as well as of Alasdair MacIntyre) to demonstrate that our causal and rational mode of thought is superior in comparison to that of the Azande. Winch reminds his readers of the embeddedness of rationality and causal thinking in different cultures and contexts. What it means to be rational is only answerable in reference to one's own culture (esp. 31). We might be dealing here with divergent 'patterns of thought', as culturally established usages of thinking, expectation and language, but this notion does not presuppose that there is a common reference with which to decide which system is the 'correct' one that should prevail in the intellectual competition (33–4). We are all born and 'thrown' into our cultures, Winch claims, and only within these cultures – not outside of them – is it possible to speak of 'getting it right' or 'making mistakes' in a way that has any sense (35). It was MacIntyre himself who assumed that invoking categories of rationality and causal thinking amounts to imposing our concepts of rationality and causality on the alien culture in question. But here, Winch indicates that MacIntyre, despite his own critique, is himself guilty of such an imposition (37).

Winch leads us to the very root of the difficulties we encounter when comparing cross-culturally by referring to the precarious notion of language as mirroring 'reality', for better or for worse. He states: 'Reality is not what gives language its sense. What is real and what is unreal shows itself *in* the sense that language has' (12). The claim that some languages are 'closer' to reality than others is, Winch adds, a confused notion. The duality between right/wrong is thus not applicable to cultures, but rather, it receives its meaning and significance only *within* different cultures. Accordingly, a comparison between European rationality and the allegedly irrationality within Azande culture would lead us astray. Apart from the obvious problem of dealing with different vocabularies – 'rationality', 'causality', etc. all belong only to one *relatum* of the comparison – one must not take for granted that there is a common ground which licenses such a comparative setting between the Azande and Europe in the first place. One has to concede that our understanding is, of course, based on what is available *to us*, but that does not mean that we are entitled to evaluate Azande 'magic' by our categories or that these categories are in any significant sense 'better' than the Azande's terms (or that our categories are in any way adequate for fully understanding Azande categories) (37). After these considerations, which exhibit an affinity for relativistic positions, Winch presents two different peace offerings:

(i) *A noncausal reading.* Winch contemplates the possibility that what we call 'magic', 'consulting oracles' and 'witchcraft' has to be removed from a causal framework. Rather, it has to be acknowledged that these practices seem to hold their weight within the Azande culture. Analogous to a so-called noncognitivist interpretation of petitionary prayers in our culture, one could suppose that what the Azande are performing is also beyond an instrumental understanding. Studying foreign cultures entails, for Winch, appreciating different ways of 'making sense' (40). A causal approach might turn out to be at odds with a true appreciation of that difference.[22]

(ii) *Limiting notions.* Drawing on other discussions in moral philosophy and reacting to the common charge of relativism, Winch recalls what he introduced as 'limiting notions', such as 'good' and 'evil', 'birth' and 'death' – hence, concepts he considers to be found, in one shape or form, in all cultures due to their existential basality (43–4). Starting tentatively from the domain of shared concepts or notions, one might find a common ground for relating one culture to another.[23]

Winch's provocative paper touches on several issues – realism, the concept of reality, hermeneutic questions, relativity and relativism – that are obviously of great philosophical importance.[24] Our concern, however, is his critical commentary on cross-cultural studies and their methodological difficulties in light of philosophical and comparative sensitivities. Winch's main interest is arguably the preference for explicitly or latently *contrastive* comparisons in early ethnology and empirical anthropology that, in the end, turn the heuristic status of comparative contrasts into non-heuristic evaluations. Even authors like Evans-Pritchard and MacIntyre who are aware of the danger of cultural usurpation by imposing our vocabulary and frame of mind on the Azande's culture still carry, at least in Winch's account, exactly these remnants of methodological colonialism.

Turning now to our list which surveys different modes of comparative injustice, one might generally detect the sometimes open, yet more often disguised, strategy of granting priority to *A* over *B*. The assumption that Western rationalism only shows the inferiority of Azande practices is an example of (d). It might be an additional problem that speaking of the 'West' and its 'culture' (or, as Winch does, 'society') already falls under the potentially unjust construction of certain *relata* (a). More importantly, however, we are dealing here with implementing particular *tertia* – rationality, causality, etc. – that are already derived from and are at home in one of the *comparanda* while 'silencing' other comparative regards (c).[25] Winch is particularly interested in showing how difficult it turns out to be to pay sufficient attention to the contextual elements within a comparison. The *Lebenswelt* of the Azande might show that 'rationality' (as C_T) is something that is not alien to the Azande, but simply has different connotations. This 'life-world' might also show (and for Winch it seems to do so) that particular practices, such as consulting oracles, are embedded in Western and in Azande culture in highly different, yet diachronically comparable, ways. Avoiding comparative injustice entails the unveiling of these divergent contexts (C_A and C_B), reinforcing the notion that 'witchcraft' does not have to be magical at all (d).

However, 'magical' for whom? Winch's first peace offering could itself be regarded as disempowering within the cultural clash between the West and the Azande by offering a reading of the oracle practice, which circumvents causal claims that are in severe contradiction with 'our' rational framework, while proposing an alternative reading that is not magical anymore – even according to *our* standards (i). Here, Winch claims to counteract comparative injustice by changing the context of rationality as one of the relevant comparative regards (C_T).

The second peace offering consists of encouraging a search for sufficiently similar concepts and ideas which stem from the sharedness of being members of humankind as limited by birth and death (ii). Here, Winch relies on comparative regards *T* that are applicable to both relata *A* and *B* in the same or in a similar way. These fundamental 'limiting concepts' are supposed to give license to tentatively transgress the borders of cultural compartmentalization. It is nevertheless a precarious assumption that these 'limiting concepts', though fundamental, do have a similar meaning and significance. 'Birth' and 'death' are, as is well known, connected to divergent ideas of pre-existence, resurrection and eternal life that do not allow for hasty generalizations and reductions to one common perception of these basic 'facts of life'.

Winch's contribution forces us to confront the dangers of comparing unjustly. This also pertains to cases in which there is already significant sensitivity to the constant simulation of result-oriented comparisons due to different modes of constructing the material, formal and contextual items when comparing *A* and *B*, as well as granting privilege to *A* over *B* (especially when these letters stand for entire cultures, our own and a remote one). In short, he calls for a 'hermeneutics of suspicion' that does not take comparative justice for granted, even in contexts in which comparative injustice is criticized and repudiated.

We started off with Winch's double question: can we 'understand' the Azande? His answer: there is only the constant attempt to understand 'other minds', an attempt that is relevant to approaching the world of other cultures (to which even our own culture might belong from time to time as well). And: are we entitled to claim that alien practices such as 'magic' and 'witchcraft' are confused? His answer: calling them 'irrational' might be nothing but the next terminological usurpation by the 'West', a usurpation against which philosophy can only warn. And this warning might be a constant reminder of the *methodological demands* placed on comparative *philosophy* that are, consequently, *moral demands* on the comparative *philosopher*.

Part II

Three Studies in Comparativism

Part I presented a general account of comparisons and comparative procedures for everyday contexts, as well as for scientific ones. Defending the possibility and fruitfulness of a general account encounters severe criticism – either that the alleged generality does not sufficiently allow for understanding the differences between types of comparisons (see chapter 2), or that the act of comparing as a particular practice is in danger of being neglected. The generality of the first part, however, does not aim to deny those differences or to downplay the praxeological character of comparing. To address the first concern, the intention had been to present a comprehensive structure that is complex enough to integrate the comparative plurality in question to circumvent the unhappy opposition between the structure of comparisons and comparative practices and, instead, to embrace the practical aspect structurally. Hence, one can have it both ways.

To address the second concern – the danger of marginalizing comparison as practice –part II is dedicated to this topic. The claim that there is a significant opposition between technical structure and practical context is repudiated – not primarily through argument, but rather through referring to concrete practices related to comparisons. What has shifted from the previous part is a change in perspective: from technique (*how does a comparison work?*) to '"doing comparisons' (*how to do it?*; *who is performing it?*). The so called 'practical turn' in social (and other) sciences is then, rather, misrepresented as a new paradigm of thinking about comparisons, yet this underlines the importance of developing a comparative structure that is not reductive regarding concrete applications of comparisons.

In this sense, the following section is supposed to deepen our understanding of comparative procedures by working out the connection between comparisons and relative practices as units of philosophical analysis. A general account might benefit from this contextualization, and the hope is that we gain, inversely, a better understanding of those other practices as well. The selection is, admittedly, idiosyncratic, but the exemplary character of the subsequent studies is neither avoidable nor to be regretted. Each of the three chapters also include an exegetical element, since all of them have a 'sparring partner' to discuss a general concern by reference to particular, representative texts embracing that concern. The focus lies on connections of these texts and their themes to comparative procedures, not on the interconnections among those relative practices.

The three studies concern:

- *the relation between comparisons and orientation*, which is a Kantian theme;
- *comparisons within a descriptive philosophy*, which goes back to the later Wittgenstein;
- *comparisons in the face of plural vocabularies*, which leads us to Richard Rorty's neo-pragmatist œuvre.

While Kant deals with orientation as specification of 'pure reason', chapter 4 dissolves this metaphorical usage in favour of a literal understanding: orienting oneself in a particular context, space, landscape. We then turn back from transcendental philosophy to a pragmatic and, hence, practical version of it. And it will become clearer in which sense comparative acts are involved in finding orientation (there are also links to indexicality elaborated on in chapter 8). Reservations against more general claims in the form of theories already make up a branch of philosophy in its own right. Wittgenstein's methodological restriction of philosophical work to 'pure description' in contrast to explanation and foundations leads to language-games as descriptive units, as well as to comparisons between and entailed by them (this double function of comparisons also touches on the themes in chapter 1.4). Finally, by Rorty's 'ironic stance' facing the plurality of what he calls 'vocabularies' (i.e. narratives, articulations, theories) we will become acquainted with a complicated crossover between epistemology and ethics. Rorty invites us to try out different vocabularies or at least to embrace their already existing plurality. This implies comparisons *between* vocabularies in the case of language's correspondence to reality being a confused idea. And it is, for Rorty. Thus, chapter 6 invokes topics of individual self-understanding and 'cultural politics'.

All three studies are, at the same time, concerned with the *limits of comparison and comparing as a practice*. And these limits are twofold: on the one hand, the *embeddedness of comparing* and relative practices – the fact that one is always already oriented somehow within a context; the concern that descriptions do not remain merely descriptive by having a normative impact; the experience that some vocabularies are alien to us in contrast to those contributing to our identity-formation. On the other hand, the *impossibility of comparisons*, the disorientation that is not solved by further comparisons; the nondescriptive elements in the plea for a descriptive (and comparative) philosophy; the illusion that we are truly able to endlessly try out new modes of (self-)description and to weigh up comparisons between them.

4

Orientation, Indexicality and Comparisons: A Theme from Kant

1 Introduction: a philosophy of orientation?

There are themes and topics in philosophy, and elsewhere, which are so inscribed into our existence that they warrant both an intellectual and a practical awareness. Orientation is definitely one of those topics. We all know the familiar scenario: trying to find one's way in a foreign city, having the map at hand or on display, locating oneself on the map by referring to prominent markers, buildings, street names, background knowledge or assumptions in order to tentatively move in one direction while repeatedly comparing the given surroundings to the necessarily reductive topology called a street map. 'Orientation' is used here to mean a diverse set of particular actions that remain, for the most part, latent and implicit. The term seems to serve as a wide-ranging concept encompassing several actions, including locating, adjusting, correcting, aligning and, especially, comparing what one encounters as reality to an instrument of orientation that is a sketch of, in one way or another, that very reality. What interests me in the following chapter is precisely this relation between a situation as a 'slice' of reality, as it were, and our orienting means and tools. In short, I want to explore the act of orienting oneself and its connection to the act of comparing that occurs in orientation – a connection that will bring to light additional features of the nature of comparison.

Let us linger, for a moment, over this scenario of travelling in a foreign city: a particular setting, a location and its environment on the one side of the comparison and the map or screen on the other. As already noted, the map is a necessarily reductive tool since a non-reductive map of the city would be nothing but – the city itself. That would not be of much help. Orientation is not primarily about the details, but about a more abstract structure within which one has to locate oneself. Now, the extent of topographical abstraction is itself relative to the needs and requirements of the person trying to find orientation. Hence, we find different scales of maps for the 'same' urban area. Finding one's way will remain a matter of luck unless one can locate oneself in that area and on the map; there must be an identifiable starting point; then, one selects reference points that create a net of relations and proportions. And eventually, the person finds directions – either *geographically* (north, west, etc.) or *indexically* (above, left, etc.) – by comparing the given situation to this created web which consists of one's own standpoint as well as the net of references. Usually, this procedure resembles an oscillation between the real location and the map, an implicit negotiation concerning which part of the comparison possesses the authority for orientation: the piece of reality that one does not really know yet or the map whose information is far from self-evident. Whether one achieves an overview, as the goal of local orientation, must be verified by referring to the map; and conversely, whether one is applying the map correctly might be determined by a 'reality check'. In the course of this back-and-forth exercise, the reference points – again, markers, buildings, street names, background knowledge or assumptions – are the *expedients of experiment*: they serve as pragmatic conjectures that must also be justified in the process; they give grounds for a person's orientation while also needing some sort of grounding.

However, this scenario, consisting of a starting point, several reference points and an orientation tool in need of corroboration, expresses only the *spatial* aspect of orientation. There is, obviously, an essentially *temporal* dimension to the act of orientation that can be differentiated into two features. Often enough, one is in dire need of orientation while under pressure and the restriction of time.[1] The pragmatic selection of suitable reference points is an important step towards the required orientation. However, this selection presupposes alternatives and implies that other orientations may have ensued under different conditions. Therefore, orientation is not simply temporal, but must be hastily achieved, not always, but often; and each orientation is a draft, a preliminary layout dissolving again as soon as the orienting requirements are sufficiently met. In this respect, orientation is fluid, stable in its instability, to be adjusted to the situation. It only 'exists' in action.

While orientation is a geographical metaphor – one might say an 'absolute' one[2] – it is not restricted to this obvious field of application. We not only speak of orientation in space and time, but also in politics, morality, religion, sexuality, divergent ways of finding or articulating, individually or collectively, our standpoint within a horizon of alternative options and in reference to salient markers. And we use comparisons in these non-geographical orientations, though perhaps in a more sophisticated or hidden fashion. The ubiquitous discussion of 'world views' illustrates both the widespread preoccupation with orientation and its transgression of the merely spatial-temporal application, appearing in the conceptual, attitudinal and emotional realms.[3] However, celebrating the omnipresence of orientation – in institutions, customs, religion, law, reason, and in various cultures, forms of life, contexts, practices, circumstances – leads directly to the danger of dissolving its concreteness.

Nevertheless, orientation as a philosophical topic entails intriguing questions of theoretical and practical impact: the necessity of orientation in a given situation under uncertain conditions and confronted with divergent, potentially incompatible alternatives (*plurality*); the instability of orientation given its provisional nature until certain practical requirements are fulfilled by a complicated interplay between a standpoint, references and a particular horizon (*performativity*); the uniqueness of each orientation means that it only has helpful significance *for someone* particular (*indexicality*); and finally, the relativeness of our orientation tools entails a comparative procedure between a slice of reality and an oversimplified sketch of reality (*comparability*).

However, what is the point of a general account of orientation? What problem does clarifying the concept solve? Why investing in this concept in the first place? These are fair questions that mirror the seemingly marginal character of the topic. However, the act and 'institution' of orientation is a pervasive phenomenon, as alluded to at the outset. And yet, there is a crucial misbalance between the topic's factual prominence and its philosophical neglect. This chapter responds to that problem. But there is more to it, there is a growing interest in what I would like to coin 'philosophy of existence'. While (analytic) philosophy usually does not show much interest in problems traditionally dealt with in the existentialist tradition, such as death, love or sense, a new thematic and methodological openness to these topics is developing in recent times.[4] Here, the modes of existence, i.e. the ways in which one exists, come into play. Obviously, orientation is such a mode. This chapter makes this existential mode explicit.

Now, orientation as a topic itself calls for an orientation. And insofar as orientation is considered to be a – or *the* – essential element of our 'being-in-the-world' and, more precisely, of 'care' (*Sorge*),[5] a philosophy of orientation might, then, fall under the designation of *prima philosophia*.[6] However, the traditional connotations that come with such a characterization are at odds with the basic features of orientation described above as a fluid practice. A philosophy of orientation – informed by Kant, Nietzsche and Niklas Luhmann[7] – is itself meant to be a critical response to the legacy of metaphysics by privileging the pragmatic and contextual dimension of orientation and by saying farewell to a line of thinking that looks for the ultimate ground, the absolute beginning or *arché*. Insofar as classical metaphysics is the attempt to transcend contextual embeddedness, a philosophy of orientation is, in contrast, a project to uncover the very conditions, structures and implications of that embeddedness.[8] One might call this *post*-metaphysical (to aid the reader's philosophical orientation).

We have, to this point, emphasized the elements in the act of orientation. I would like to deepen our understanding of orientation by drawing our attention to three additional and, somehow, corrective elements. First, we will consider the indexical character of orientation that is due to the standpoint from which an orienting perspective is taken as well as the usage of a local vocabulary to express this very perspective. Second, we will elaborate on the comparative (partly symmetrical, partly hierarchical) relation between a given situation and the means of orientation (a map, rules, policies, etc.). Third, we will examine the idea that orientation occurs not always deliberately, i.e. that we are *already* oriented (or positioned) in a situation before we begin any orientation process – we do not start from 'point zero', rather we find ourselves, at least partly, being oriented by external conditions before we deliberate, choose and make decisions. While suggesting analogies and similarities between very different ways of orienting oneself (or, being already oriented) – spatial, logical, existential – the focus will be on the latter.

2 Orienting oneself: a Kantian theme

Orientation as a philosophical topic is, comparatively, young. Immanuel Kant gave 'orientation' some prominence in responding to a debate between Friedrich Jacobi and

Moses Mendelsohn on the possibility of *pure* reason against the backdrop of the so-called pantheism controversy.[9] In his 1786 essay, *What does it mean to orient oneself in thinking?* Kant tries to characterize the business of reasoning by referring, initially, to the use of the spatial orientations 'right' and 'left'. Kant notes that this vocabulary of 'right', 'left' and other relative terms does refer, but it is not determined by reality; neither perception nor thinking are able to draw the difference between 'right' and 'left' which led Kant to the (provisional) conclusion that this distinction is based on a "feeling". It is interesting to see how Kant – who did not use 'orientation' before this seminal essay or after in any programmatic sense – proceeds from spatial language to mathematical and, then, logical orientation, i.e. from an empirical application to a, one might say, transcendental usage of orientation terminology; what this attribute, 'transcendental', precisely means in this context will become clearer in the course of this chapter.[10] And it is equally interesting to see how Kant – writing the essay between both editions of his *Critique of Pure Reason* (1781/87) – prepares, against his presumable intention, the shift from seeing orientation as a supplement to reason towards the acknowledgement that reason is just one instrument among the manifold means of orienting oneself. Hence, orientation is no longer reason's supporting actor, but conversely, reason serves as an orienting performance.[11]

Let's have a closer look. Kant begins by stating that the

> extended and more precisely determined concept of *orienting oneself* can be helpful to us in presenting distinctly the maxims healthy reason uses in working on its cognitions of supersensible objects.[12]

Before Kant touches on 'supersensible objects' – and he actually does at the end of his essay in talking about faith and/in God – he offers an account of 'right' and 'left'. As noted above, Kant emphasizes the fact that nothing 'outside' settles this binary distinction; however, it is not the business of *a priori* judgements either. Kant, therefore, concludes that a 'feeling' (*Gefühl*) grounds the difference between right and left: 'Thus even with all the objective data of the sky, I orient myself *geographically* only through a *subjective* ground of differentiation [...]' (135). The exclusion of 'objective data' reflects the fact that 'right' and 'left' are not part of the world's furniture, but are rather to be found *in us*.[13]

While 'feeling' is, particularly under Kant's own premises, a fairly unhappy terminological choice,[14] the 'subjective' character articulated by that term is the core element that a philosophy of orientation might take as its starting point. This subjectivity should not be misunderstood as a plea for a merely subjectivistic stance, but it does express the essentially *indexical* character of orientation: it is always an orientation *for* someone who establishes the distinction between 'right' and 'left' in the world by taking up a standpoint.[15] What serves as orientation for x, however, does not have to be one for y; and what is 'right' and 'left' for x, does not have to be 'right' and 'left' for y (for instance, when standing opposite to each other). Moreover, to entertain and apply this distinction is, as Kant holds, a '*need of reason*' (136: '*ein Bedürfnis der Vernunft*'):

> But now there enters *the right* of reason's *need*, as a subjective ground for presupposing and assuming something which reason may not presume to know through objective grounds; and consequently for *orienting* itself in thinking, solely through reason's own need, in that immeasurable space of the supersensible, which for us is filled with dark night.
>
> 137

However, Kant is, of course, not primarily interested in spatial orientation. He moves from mere topology to mathematics, and from there, to logic. In other words, he leaves behind the geometrical space of extension, movement and directions for the 'pure' space of thinking. Here, one might hesitate to accept this metaphorization of space: the contingencies of geographical orientation may not be sufficiently adequate to an abstract notion of space including mathematical and logical necessities.[16] Moreover, space (alongside with time) serves as 'pure form of intuition' in Kant's transcendental aesthetics, while orientation is an act *within* that space; thus, in contrast to geometrical orientation, the orienting distinctions and terms of mathematics and logic not only 'belong' to the relevant space but also are constitutive of it.[17] Nevertheless, Kant seems to think that reason has similar "needs" that could be met by establishing certain distinctions as well as stipulating particular entities (136).[18]

However, in Kant's essay, the (abductive) stipulation (i.e. that reason needs orientation) is not worked out by referring to mathematical or logical deliberations, but rather – and not surprisingly, given the pantheistic context of the debate – within a theological and moral framework. Kant rejects the inference of God's existence from observation or from the course of nature; that would open the gate 'to all enthusiasm, superstition and even to atheism' (143). Divine existence is, thus, not a matter of insight and knowledge, but is rather a particular 'need' of reason. What kind of need is this? Kant sticks to allusions in the essay, but what he has in mind is well known from his moral defence of God's existence in his *Critique of Pure Reason*: God's existence is an implication of the morally necessary postulate of immortality by virtue of which the fulfilment of duties and the prospects of happiness are, eventually, compatible.[19] God – or God as an idea – safeguards morality from an existential void in which following duties achieves no satisfaction.

Without this theological supplement, Kant states, reason would 'feel' its insufficiencies. Without the affirmation of a divine reality there is a breakdown in the relation between being moral and the 'pursuit of happiness'. Rationally believing in God is, hence, not rational by reasonable inferences and empirically secured grounds, but because God is an indispensable '*hypothesis*' for human conduct, both individually and collectively (141). And only this purely 'rational' belief in God can, Kant concludes, serve as a 'signpost or compass' for orienting the 'speculative thinker' in 'the field of supersensible objects', divine as well as moral ones (142).

I will skip the usual critique of Kant's optimism concerning the synchronic unity and diachronic stability of reason – an alleged singular, pure and purified reason yielding orientation for our time, rather than being itself in 'need' of getting oriented in the era of its fragmentation.[20] And I will also skip the rather exegetical, context-bound discussion of the precise relation between orientation as a fruitful topic in its own right and the theological and ethical effort to unify morality and happiness by abduction.[21] What we can learn, however, from Kant's essay is an awareness of the specific traits of the act of orientation: the peculiar status of the orienting vocabulary – with the question of whether its indexicality also applies to non-spatial orientation; the necessarily 'subjective' and, one might add, embodied character of orientation – stressing the relative, but not relativistic involvement of the person being oriented; and the non-'mythological' given of a situation calling for orientation – negotiating anew the relation between actively responding to the need to be oriented and the receptivity of the person needing orientation who is finding herself already within a cluster of orientation(s). We will consider each of these aspects in the argument to come.

3 Orientation's architecture: an extended analysis

To be oriented – in the sense of eliminating disorientation or replacing other ways of being oriented in order to find (a new) orientation for and in a given situation – denotes a *successful* act. Contrary to concepts like 'interpretation' or 'comparison' the term 'orientation' is not externally linked to its 'teleological' fulfilment; orientation entails both the act leading to a goal and the fulfilment of the goal. It is, in this sense, similar to the term 'understanding'. One might interpret a text in a fruitful or a clueless way or one might find insightful comparisons or make a comparison that is not fruitful, but if someone understands an argument or finds orientation in a foreign city, in both cases what has been searched for is actually achieved.[22]

Orientation is never restricted to mere objects or quasi-atomistic entities; rather, it is contextual or even holistic. As noted above, orientation is both particular and unconfined; sometimes more extended 'worlds' do not remain untouched by the act of orientation. The person being oriented is not beyond or outside the given situation, but is part of a concrete arrangement of things whose relevance for the orienting act is not yet fully determined.[23] Hence, what counts as the given situation is bound to the orienting act referring to that situation, whether limiting or widening its scope for creating a 'surveyable representation'[24].

3.1 Defining orientation

The German philosopher Werner Stegmaier presented the notion of orientation as an 'ultimate and basic concept' in philosophy and for human conduct in general.[25] In several texts, he circumscribes orientation as the 'capacity to find one's way around in changing situations and to exploit in them possibilities of acting'.[26] A more analytic account of orientation as an act consisting of several components might look like the following formula *F*:

> *F*: Someone (i: the subject of orientation) locates herself (ii: the self-locating act) in something (iii: the space of orientation) by means of something (iv: points of reference) in relation to something (v: the order or arrangement).[27]

Formula *F* takes us nearer to a real definition because it avoids the circular notion of 'finding one's way around'. In place of this imprecise use of language, orientation is regarded here as a particular form of *performative self-location*. Orientation 'exists' only in and by the act of orienting oneself[28] and, thereby, it constitutes a twofold self-location, namely in the 'subjective' sense of establishing an orienting cluster from the person's point of view as well as in the 'objective' sense of locating oneself within a pre-existing order.[29] This brings us back to the five elements in *F*: Ad (i): orientation presupposes a bearer orienting herself, since orientation as an act is based on a subject performing that act, whether individually or collectively. Thus, one might say that orientation is necessarily agent-centred.[30] Ad (ii): although orientation is bound to a standpoint, it calls, additionally, for a locating act. Having a standpoint does not mean that an agent knows exactly where it is. Hence, the standpoint has to be determined as a particular location. Ad (iii): this self-location implies a surrounding because orientation is contextual, not atomistic. A standpoint is such a point only within an environment, while a self-location is the precise relating of that standpoint to the environment. Ad (iv): this relation, however, presupposes points of reference within the environment, salient markers tentatively defining the space of orientation by qualifying it in highlighting particular things and neglecting others. Ad (v): and all this is done by reference to an order or cluster that might be derived from the situation in which one orients oneself but is not identical with it. A map, for example, might serve as such an order, reflecting that situation in reduced form for the sake of orientation.

The elements (i) through (v) are meant to be an analytic differentiation; in reality they are connected to each other and together constitute the act of orientation. However, they are sufficient for characterizing the orienting act: if all five elements are present, an orientation is not only possible but will follow. It might be debatable whether all five elements are also necessary, particularly regarding the last item. Obviously, there are cases in which (v) is not required or entailed by other elements. For instance, an orientation in the geographical sense is possible without a map. Either the map remains implicit (as a 'mental image') or is redundant due to the triangle of context, standpoint and references.[31]

Now, there are additional and broader characteristics to be considered than merely the five structural ones. A philosophy of orientation has also to take into account the following traits we already touched upon at the beginning of this chapter: first, that orientation is a fundamental mode of existence – 'fundamental' in its significance, but also in the sense of self-reflection and self-correction: a new orientation is always the replacement of a preceding one; second, orientation is, as Stegmaier underlines, 'fluctuant'[32] – it is not stable and cannot be completely stabilized: orientation is always a draft and, as a practice, it vanishes if the subject is eventually oriented; third, the structure of context, standpoint and references does not entirely determine a person's orientation since one has always latitudes of orientation;[33] fourth, orientation is both a capacity (or performance) of the subject/agent by which a situation is addressed and the situation in which the agent finds herself to be (located) in. Most cases have both active and passive elements of orientation.

3.2 Orientation in its element

But do these characteristics of orientation really fit the formula *F*? There are reasons to doubt, and elaborating more on the elements of orientation – or: orientation in its element – will substantiate our doubts about employing *F* and lead to a corrected version. I shall start off by briefly presenting Stegmaier's traditional account of orientation. In the following sections I will attempt to amend that account in three important regards – in keywords: indexicality (3.3), comparability (3.4) and receptivity (3.5).

Trivially, orientation is an act in space and time. It is less trivial that *spatial* orientation – in a literal, hence, geographical sense, and in a metaphorical, for example, moral sense – leads to two concepts of 'world'. On the one hand, there is the abstract notion of world as a meaningless and container-like space in which orientation takes place. On the other hand, orientation concerns an extract of that world that is significant for the agent. Therefore, we are dealing with the duality of a presupposed realm in which all human actions have their place as well as a meaningful and therefore already determined world in which our actual dealings have their home. The first one is not much more, Stegmaier claims, than a 'marginal condition'[34] for our acting; whereas, human beings are actively (and not just 'marginally') involved in the concrete world of conduct. Orientation could be understood as transforming the abstract space into the world as significant context. However, following that path would lead into an impasse since, as we just stated, orientation does not start at a point of nowhere, but replaces – by correcting, amending, rearranging – already existing orientations. Hence, orientation cannot be the transformation of the merely abstract into the concrete world; rather, the abstract world might serve as the realm in which shifts from one orientation to another one (*diachronic*) or the conflict between divergent orientations (*synchronic*) takes place. The abstract world is, then, not to be found beyond the concrete orientation, but is alluded to by the shifts between plural ways of being oriented.[35]

Orientation is always *temporary* in 'temporalizing' the world, as Stegmaier holds.[36] As a performative act orientation 'exists' only in that very performance and dissolves again as soon as the needs of the orienting subject are satisfied. But there is also a structural aspect to orientation's temporality insofar as the act of orientation is both a reaction to a situation calling for orientation while constituting that very situation. Usually, this structure is linked to temporal pressure and, often enough, urgency. Therefore, Stegmaier characterizes orientation as a particular mood (*Stimmung*) of alarm and disquiet. Something is at stake when it comes to orientation, namely, achieving what a certain situation demands from us and calls for. The extent of alarm mirrors, Stegmaier adds, the extent of orientation's relevance; it reflects, rather negatively, the significance of 'finding one's way around' in the face of the possibility of failure. Accordingly, dealing with this persistent uncertainty and the alarming mood that accompanies it requires reacting to with courage and awareness. A situation calls for an orienting reaction and, so it seems, gets intensified by that reaction. This reaction as an immediate response is characterized as mood – in contrast to a feeling, emotion or even knowledge – and leads, as it were, to a second-order-response to that mood with an attitude of courage under uncertain circumstances and increased awareness. Here, orientation as a duality of mood and attitude is already embedded in the psychological setting which comes with the urgency of the situation, the temporalizing orientation and our involvement in that setting somewhere between alarm and coolness.[37]

Orientation is, as we have already noted, the attempt to gain a "surveyable representation" of a given situation. To do this with success (whatever 'success' might mean in detail here) the orienting act must be *reductive* and, therefore, *selective*. Trying to find one's way in a foreign city means denoting particular markers while neglecting the rest. There is no orientation without that kind of reduction.[38] The scope of a "situation" might be widened or limited, broadened or focused according to the orienting needs. Hence, we are dealing here with two forms of latitudes: the selective process of marking optional reference points as well as choosing the adequate scope for approaching the situation.[39] To orient oneself in a situation is thus both structural and practical, structural because it is a necessary reduction of complexity in uncertain conditions and practical because it occurs under the particular pressure of urgency. In Stegmaier's formulation: "orientation is an art of abbreviating the world"[40].

Orientation as an abbreviation of the world is not only structuring the situation but is itself a structure consisting of a standpoint, a horizon and selected reference points. While a standpoint is already given by the subject – the standpoint as, therefore, a 'contingent absolute'[41] – and while a horizon is necessarily linked to that standpoint, the reference points are not simply given, but chosen or adopted according to the requirements within the situation. All these expressions are, obviously, spatial metaphors derived from orientation in a spatial arrangement, but are also meant to be relevant for non-spatial ways of orienting oneself. A crucial question will be whether the 'language-game of orientation'[42] is still in play if used for acts of moral or political orientation (see section 3.4). In any case, the 'sub-metaphors' of orientation – standpoint, horizon and reference points – make it clear that orientation as a philosophical topic raises the question of *perspectivism*, an epistemological doctrine that circumvents the extremes of full-blown realism and a helplessly relativistic position.[43] One might claim that every orientation is taking up a particular perspective (among possible alternatives, since talking of one perspective entails that there are more than just one) while being connected to the contextual concern of 'finding one's way around' (what is, apparently, not the case for every perspective).[44] Speaking is the 'pervasiveness of orientation' does not imply, however, the claim that everything is a question of orientation; and insofar as orientation leads to perspectivism, it would also be beside the point to declare everything as perspectival. There are limits.[45] Nevertheless, orientation remains a highly prominent mode of existence, and thus, taking up a perspective inherits that prominence.

On this account, the orienting act is of a greater specificity than the more general task of taking up a perspective. Think, again, of our example: orientation in a foreign city implies two essential tasks: self-location and determining salient markers in relation to one's own standpoint. One orients oneself by means of something (see (iv) in the formula *F*), i.e., reference points that are selected from alternatives and that serve, by this qualification, as footholds. These footholds are conditionally stable assumptions.[46] Accordingly, a reference point that is also a foothold (or hinge) implements a *paradoxical structure* into the act of orientation: it enables orientation while being itself established by that very act of orientation – a ground that is itself grounded by what it is grounding.[47]

3.3 Orientation, subjectivity and indexicality

As we have seen, without an orienting subject there is no act of orientation, i.e. without someone bringing the elements of orientation – a standpoint, horizon and reference points – 'into the world', this cluster does not exist in the first place. Orientation is thus not 'objective' but an essentially agent-centred act. Just as 'right' and 'left' are not 'out there' but bound to a standpoint for which these indexical demonstratives give precise directions, neither is orientation a part of the objective world. And yet, orientation is objective insofar as its indexical structure provides precise relations for the bearer and the bearer's contingent standpoint. Referring again to the formula, one might say that all further elements given in *F* are dependent on the 'subjective' establishment of a certain indexical structure.

Before turning to the indexical element and the problem of comparing the indexical elements of orientation with a particular environment calling for orientation, let us consider the 'subjective' character of orientation. It is interesting to see the sense in which the paradoxical structure – of a ground that is itself grounded by what it is grounding – is also pertinent for the way in which Kant characterizes the subject orienting itself. It is not only the case that Kant, rather implicitly, inverts the traditional order between reason and orientation by asserting that reason is one orienting tool among others.[48] He also disrupts the assumption of the stable subject of orientation. Accordingly, there is no subject independent of its actions – no subject of orientation without the orienting act – but rather the 'transcendental subject' is itself only 'a form of thinking'.[49] The idea that there is a subject for which, secondarily, things appear is confused, states Kant; rather, a subject is constituted by the fact that things appear for that very subject. Insofar as things are 'given' to that subject, it exists as 'a form', but without that givenness the idea of an underlying subject remains empty.[50]

In other words, the subject posits itself pragmatically through its actions. For Kant, the subject is a 'form of thinking' precisely to the extent that it is *not exhausted in its actions*. Therefore, the transcendental subject is a subject that is *not identical* with its actions (or representations), otherwise it would be a varied and different subject (this danger is apparent in the *Humean* opposing standpoint). However, from this it does *not* follow, that the transcendental subject is fully (or, *de re*) independent of its actions (such as the act of orientation). Take a Kantian parallel case: concepts are different from *Anschauungen*, but without them they, as Kant holds, remain 'empty' (AA IV, 48). Hence, concepts have only content in and by their application and together with *Anschauungen*, i.e. with empirical input. The same applies here: the subject and its actions are distinguishable, but not totally separable. That is to say, there is a *categorical difference, but no detachment*, there is a *distinction without separation*.

Likewise, the subject of orientation is not a substance with additional activities; a 'subject' is a subject only in and by these orienting activities. Or one might stress this inversion by claiming the subject of orientation to be orientation itself, as Stegmaier following Kant (and Heidegger) does.[51]

In this sense there is no substantial, only a formal difference between the self of orientation and the orienting act. The 'subjective' self of orientation takes shape precisely by the act of orientation in which we apply notions such as 'I', 'you' and 'we'.[52] Or in Stegmaier's terminology: 'In talking of orienting oneself the self as self-reference of orientation is already presupposed and not further to be justified within the act of orientation.'[53] Hence, this self-reference as *consciousness* is not to be thought of as substance, but consciousness *is* this act of referring to itself, Stegmaier adds in a Humean fashion. And this self-referential act generates the idea of 'I am thinking', an idea that, as Kant once famously stated, has to accompany all other ideas.[54] This idea of an 'I' is, however, devoid of any specific content and only expresses that a particular idea is *my* idea. By means of the idea and the concept of 'I' Kant understands the objectivity of objects to be grounded on talking about these objects – *objectivity through communication*.[55] The shift from the subjectivity of the 'I' to objectivity among a plurality of 'I's is given, Stegmaier holds, because the pronoun 'I' is individual as well as general: one can only use 'I' in reference to oneself, but everyone is able to say 'I'.[56]

What can we learn from this Kantian intermezzo on subjectivity, self-reference and the 'I' for the act of orientation and its comparative element, i.e., the comparing of a given situation with a means of orientation? First, the self-orienting subject does not only establish the agent-bound elements of a standpoint, horizon and reference points; it exists only in and by this orienting performance; hence, both the act of orientation and its subject are 'fluctuant'. Second, this leads us to the problem of indexicality and comparability: the subject of orientation belongs to the world in which it is situated and in which it locates itself while it is, at the same time, part of the indexical structure that the subject employs on a given situation. Therefore, the subject 'is' only in this double sense of belonging, on the one hand belonging to the 'subjectively' established structure of orientation, on the other hand belonging to a world that is grounded and ordered by that very structure.[57] And insofar as the comparison implied by orientation is the one between a structure for the world and the structured world, and insofar as the subject 'is' only in and by orienting itself in this process, becoming a subject involves an indexical as well as a comparative element.

Let us focus for a moment on the indexical element. The basic observation is simple: an orientation for *x*, as we have seen, does not have to be an orientation for *y*; and what is 'right' and 'left' for *x*, does not have to be 'right' and 'left' for *y*, when they are standing opposite each other, for example. Terms like 'right' and 'left', but also 'I', 'there' and 'tomorrow' are of 'context-sensitive character'.[58] There are several differences, however, among this class of terms. One might, for instance, distinguish between indexicals that are linked to a demonstrative act (*true demonstratives*) and indexicals that do not need such an act (*pure indexicals*).

Our vocabulary for spatial orientation includes terms of both kinds; think of 'up there' or 'over there' for the first group and 'right' or 'left' for the second group (although there is often enough no strict line of demarcation).[59] Now, what both groups, true demonstratives and pure indexicals, semantically capture, is the simple fact that all these terms mean the same for each person – we do not have to interpret what 'left' and 'right' mean here – and yet, all these terms are essentially bound to a standpoint – without which 'left' and 'right' provide no direction.

There are several attempts to give an account of this difference between sense and reference.[60] One way of putting the matter, suggested by David Kaplan, distinguishes between the "character" and the "content" of true demonstratives and pure indexicals. Take, for example, the sentence 'I am a football player'. This sentence has a single character, but different contents with respect to different speakers. There is a stable element in this sentence that is independent of who articulates it, and there is a context-bound element to this sentence in relation to a particular context. If Jules says, 'I am a football player', and Jim does too, they say different things in the same sentence; if Jules says, 'I am a football player', and Jim says (pointing to Jules), 'You are a football player', they say the same thing, Kaplan states.[61]

Obviously, the language of spatial orientation also includes true demonstratives and pure indexicals and thereby the difference between character and content is also at play.[62] As we have seen, the person being oriented has a cluster of reference points based on a particular standpoint. Now, this standpoint, belonging as it does to a particular bearer, entails that these reference points are indexical, since it is always an orientation *for and by someone* without being relativistic or merely 'subjectivistic'. Someone else might apply a similar orienting net of references (hence, of the *same character*), but there is still the difference between the two speakers (hence, of *different contents*). Consequently, orientation is based on the duality between a situation calling for an orienting response on the one side and, on the other, an orienting cluster of reference points that entails several indexicals: the subject of orientation ('I'), the self-locating act ('here') and points of references within a space of orientation ('left', 'right', 'there', etc.).[63] We can conclude, then, that the entire formula F is not only pervaded by indexicals but also the structure it represents is itself of indexical character (and content).

3.4 Orientation as twofold comparison

Our philosophical orientation using the language of spatial orientation looks like this now: orientation as a practice is a reaction to a need to be oriented in a particular situation. In such a scenario, someone is already taking up a certain standpoint such that that context of reality is no longer abstract or distant, since the orienting subject is involved in that situation in 'not knowing her way around'. To illuminate the situation, a cluster of reference points has to be established. The 'subjective' standpoint, along with these salient markers, creates an orienting cluster of elements. In this sense, reality is only given through the lens of this indexical, subject-bound construction. However, this is insufficient for a successful orientation since one needs an idea of the topographical relations between the several orienting references. In other words, one needs a map that objectively represents the scenario in question. Using the terminology of indexicals one might paraphrase this duality, between the 'subjectively' constructed cluster and the 'objective' representation of a situation, by describing the relevant distinction as the one between different contents and one shared character.

And here, the element of comparison is brought to light in two ways. In a consideration of philosophy as orientation we are not directly comparing 'reality' to tools of orientation such as a city map. Reality as such is not plainly given as it is when the subject is oriented. What is, however, relevant for the comparison is the order of reference points entailed by the orienting subject. This order is a construction, not wholly given or forced upon the subject, at least in terms of what counts as the situation in question (what the subject needs orientation to) and in regard to the particular references used in the course of orientation. Both elements, the 'situation' and the reference points, are variable: what counts as the 'situation' could be widened or narrowed, and alternative markers could replace the reference points. Insofar as orientation is a response to a situation in which 'one does not know one's way around' the orienting construction as a tentative attempt to dissolve this frustration has to be chosen and determined in relation to alternative constructions using other reference points. Once this construction is established – despite its uncertain status – it has to be put in relation to the tools of orientation, either an ideal representation of the situation or a city map. This is the other element of comparison in orientation: trying to correlate the information given by the orienting tool, the map, with the real situation while, conversely, correlating that particular situation with what the map shows. We are thus considering three layers and two comparisons in:

$A \leftarrow compare \rightarrow B \leftarrow compare \rightarrow C$

A: Reality in the form of a *situation* calling for orientation;

B: Indexical *constructions* (hence, $B_1, B_2, B_3, \ldots, B_n$) of that reality consisting of the subject's standpoint and reference points;

C: *Tools of orientation* (hence, $C_1, C_2, C_3, \ldots, C_n$) representing ideally (a mental image or picture) or materially (city map) the situational reality in a reductive and selective way.

Spatial orientation implies – that is the crucial point here – the twofold act of comparing both A to B and B to C – without a direct comparison between A and C. First, a situation calls for orientation. One is not oriented to reality itself or as a whole, but in view of a particular setting. 'Reality' is a concrete situation in which the orienting subject finds herself. Second, the situation does not itself determine the salient markers of orientation – again, buildings, street names, background knowledge or assumptions – rather, the subject chooses or adopts these markers as tentative and practical stipulations that reduce and make more manageable the scene by highlighting situational bits. That means that there are different possible clusters of stipulating markers ($B_1, B_2, B_3, \ldots$), which can be internally compared to one another, and then give rise to the question of which cluster meets the need of orientation best (or most efficiently). These various and potential clusters of markers also lead to an *external* comparison between a particular cluster B_n and the situation A concerning whether B_n is a helpful response to A. Third, the internal comparison does not, at least initially, give priority to any particular cluster: $B_1, B_2, B_3, \ldots$ are compared to one another and the comparative question is answered according to which cluster provides the best (or most efficient) orientation. In contrast, the external comparison is temporally hierarchical: a particular orienting cluster ($B_1, B_2, B_3, \ldots$) is adjusted to the situation or one presupposes the cluster B_n and considers the situation accordingly – this is the *hierarchical* element. Usually, we observe an oscillating back and forth between the priority of A and then the priority of B_n and back again – this is the *temporal* aspect.[64] Fourth, this duality of internally and externally comparing is repeated between B_n and an orienting tool C. Once again, the internal comparison is non-hierarchical in the sense that no priority is initially given to any particular cluster: $B_1, B_2, B_3, \ldots$ are compared in relation to C, a map, for instance, by finding out which B_n best fits the topographical reduction. The external comparison between a particular B_n to the map C_n, however, is hierarchical because the map, as an established geographical tool, is authoritative in a way that construction B_n is not. The oscillation here is a kind of probing whether a stipulated cluster B fits what the map shows. That being said, sometimes this hierarchical order between B and C is reversed as when the map does not match the orienting needs by being either too imprecise or too fine-grained.[65]

Fifth, there is, as already stated, no direct comparison between A and C. The reason: there is no orientation without having a stipulated cluster B derived from (but not identical to) the situation calling for an orienting act. This cluster thus stands between the situation (A) and the tools (C) to find orientation in it, sometimes nearer to A, at other times closer to C. Sixth, going from A to B and to C also increases the dependence upon the reductive features of orientation. Orientation is not possible unless there is a reduction of one's situation.[66] And this reduction is performed first by *selecting* reference points and by neglecting others (that are, then, situated outside the stipulated order)[67] (the move *from A to B*); and then by determining how the selected cluster is represented on the map (*from B to C*). Seventh and finally, our philosophical orientation to geographical orientation has an analytic and temporal status: *analytic* insofar as all elements considered here constitute the single act of getting oriented; *temporal* insofar as we are dealing here with a single practice consisting of different steps, or phases, that are neither always simultaneous nor always sequential, but are reductive and selectively sequential depending upon the particular need.

Now, are these considerations also applicable to non-spatial forms of orientation? Instead of responding directly, I shall briefly consider how the double comparison between three layers within the act of orienting oneself takes shape in a moral setting. Think of David Lurie, the protagonist in J.M. Coetzee's 1999 novel *Disgrace*. Lurie lost his university position after being convicted of sexual harassment. He moved in with his adult daughter Lucy who lives on a farm far from Cape Town. Lurie, the urban professor, is now exposed to a rural life dominated by agriculture and animals. Things change considerably after a severe attack by three men in which Lucy is raped, most of the animals are killed, and nearly everything of value is taken from the farm. The catastrophe destroys their form of existence, rendering them victims in need of a new orientation to existence. The novel narrates, among many other things, how Lurie gradually changes his attitude to animals, partly because of being exposed to the farm's dogs that survived the assault. Lucy withdraws herself, becoming much less active, and thus David must take care of the animals, and, eventually, becomes the 'dog-man', as Coetzee expresses this shift.[68]

Obviously, the narrative is built around an existential rupture calling for a new orientation. This call does not remain merely abstract and hazy, but is highly concrete and detailed insofar as Coetzee focuses on particular elements of this search for, and eventual discovery of, a new orientation. One of these elements is Lurie's gradually shifting attitude to dogs – one of Coetzee's major interests, particularly in his later work: the life of animals and our relation to them. Lurie is, thrown into a new situation, trying to find new reference points as he struggles to make sense of his new responsibility for the dogs. In the course of events, his growing and deepening relation to the dogs challenges his complete degradation of animals. His old ethical stance – based on a categorical distinction between humans and animals, between conscious rationality and inferior animal instincts – no longer fits his experience of human crime and the nearness he feels to 'his' dogs.

It is not difficult to identify the situational element A in the story, given the need to reorient oneself after such an attack. It is less easy to find a new ethical framework – in particular with regard to animals – that fits Lurie's behaviour. His initial ethical framework (C_1) remains latent for a long time but is brought to a serious revision (C_2), and even substitution, by what happens to him and his daughter. One might assume that the novel's second part, narrating the events and developments after the catastrophe, is about this transformation from a moral view that leaves animals 'outside ethics' to one that integrates them into our most important moral concerns (from C_1 to C_2).[69] This shift, however, also includes new reference points that take the form of emotional encounters with dogs, a deeper awareness of the human crimes committed against animals, and the growing sense of the animal instincts of humans against the backdrop of South Africa's post-Apartheid society (B – as, also, a shift from B_1 to B_2). In sum: the situation (A) has changed but allows for divergent reactions; the protagonist is almost forced into changing fundamental assumptions (C) that touch on inter-personal relations as well as relations to animals. And this framework of assumptions develops, in detail, through confrontations with new reference points (B) within a particular setting. The situation (A) calls for a new orientation to existence but it does not directly initiate a revised or reformed ethical framework; the framework emerges by virtue of new (or potentially new) reference points within the scenario of disorientation, informing a deepened awareness of one's surrounding, including human and non-human animals.

Admittedly, the example does not serve as a strict argument for the general applicability of the A-B-C structure. The example serves only to allude to that possibility by inviting us to consider non-spatial forms of orientation in a manner that is derived from the language of spatial orientation. We live in the spaces of acting, speaking, feeling and thinking, all of which attest to traces of lost, eroded, regained and newly established orientations. These ways of being oriented are replaceable but the person being oriented, the subject, is not.

3.5 On being already oriented

Orientation is, as noted, an act bound to an individual or collective subject seeking orientation in a particular setting. This phrasing emphasizes the active and, to some extent, sovereign role that the orienting person plays. And this is the standard analysis, presented by Stegmaier, which characterizes orientation as a *basically active practice*.[70]

However, this picture needs some correction through an elaboration of the *passive modes* in which the non-sovereign, and not yet oriented, person finds himself. He might be thrown into a particular situation (*A*) after having lost the confidence of 'knowing his way around' (this is precisely David Lurie's position). The latently valid and, suddenly, challenged routines of being oriented, personally, morally and socially, may get disrupted by external incidents that are not chosen. The loss of a set of convictions and the acquisition of a new set – after an interim of, hopefully, productive disorientation – is not simply a matter of active 'picking and choosing'.[71] Often enough, we resist a new set of orienting background assumptions (*C*) before accepting them as possibilities and, eventually, integrating them into our own self-understanding (Coetzee's novel narrates that ramified process). And, further, this uncertain dynamic is linked to eroding reference points and to finding or being exposed to new salient markers (*B*), derived from and given in a particular situation (recall again, Lurie's experiences of crime and the non-romanticized presence of animals).

All these instances are, often enough, beyond our control. Being disoriented is, by definition, an unsettled stance that is not easily dissolvable by action and decision. However, these are not cases of mere passivity, either. The possibility of relating oneself to one's own disorientation on new grounds might be a first step, despite being involuntarily exposed to a situation in which one does 'not know one's way around'. To capture this space in between – between actively creating a new orientation and being passively thrown into it – one might speak of *receptivity*.

Three observations illustrate this case for receptivity. For one, finding a new orientation is always an act of *reorientation*. Hence, a new orientation comes from an old one. To orient oneself in a new way, one has to be already oriented – somehow. There is no neutral point devoid of every bit of orientation, no complete and all-encompassing disorientation, since we are necessarily (Heideggerians might reserve the term 'existentially') living in a 'world of orientation'[72] by dwelling in this world. The receptive element lies in the fact that there is an orientation precedent that informs the new orientation, which replaces, amends and rearranges that 'world well lost'. There are also deliberately adopted or latently accepted routines, orders and structures by which we orient ourselves. Examples are legion: the orientation by customs, conventions and experiences in our everyday life; the orientation by grammar and style in the way we communicate; the orientation by logic and rationality in thinking and, more rarely, debating; the orientation by law in the legal sphere; moral norms in our sense of duty and the allegiance to certain values; a set of rules in games or for traffic; rituals, confession and prayer as forms of religious orientation[73] – and so on. All of these different and differently authoritative ways of being oriented are commonly shared, but not independently chosen structures. And finally, the orienting routines may be so thoroughly engraved onto our ways of living that the order of action is inverted: it is not we who orient ourselves, but rather, we are being oriented within the dynamics of orientation; the driving force of orientation is – orientation itself.[74]

There can be a sense of relief in having pre-established orientations so that one is not constantly forced to create them or to choose between them. And often enough we react with a *conservative* posture towards alternative orientations, persisting with known options and showing preference for what seems to be trustworthy and reliable. Orientation has its own memory.[75]

4 Coda: the perils and treasures of disorientation

It is time to reconsider the formula F and integrate our findings in this extended analysis of orientation. For this purpose, I will focus on the three essential observations that take us beyond the standard account of orientation: the *indexical character* of orientation that is due to the particular standpoint of the subject who is oriented by a particular cluster of available reference points; the twofold *comparative procedure* of orientation in which a situation is assessed by virtue of a practically justified and indexically structured net of orientation; and the *receptive modes* of orientation, mirroring the 'existential' fact that the subject is already oriented to a situation by established institutions. These three observations alter our formula:

> F^*: Someone (i: the individual or collective subject of orientation) locates herself or is already located (ii: the act or fact of locating the self) in a situation (iii: the qualified space of orientation) by an indexical cluster (iv: the standpoint plus points of reference) that is in a twofold comparative relation to the situation as well as to the means of orientation (v: tools reflecting the situation).

All basic differences between F and F^* are consequences of paying attention to the role that indexicality, comparability and receptivity play in the act of orientation or the fact that one is already oriented. The double comparison of situational need to points of reference and points of reference to an orientation tool, as an essential element of orientation, entails both the indexical cluster of one's own standpoint and reference points in relation to the situation *and* the tools that replicate that very situation. This indexical cluster may be either actively selected or receptively adopted. The comparative element seems to stress, again, the active character, but it may remain implicit or presupposed in those cases in which the receptive element dominates orientation. Therefore, indexicality, comparability and receptivity are not only compatible with, but are essentially connected to each other.

Orientation, however, is an issue only if something significant is at stake. Its relevance is thus derived from situational need, its disoriented counterpart. Further, the relation between orientation and disorientation is not merely complementary. The relations are often complex. Fragments of orientation exist even within disorientation. Multiple and potentially incommensurable offers of orientation may contribute to disorientation. The fact that there is no general orientation available to meet all disorientations may further contribute to our disorientation.

Further sources of disorientation include failures, disturbances or even disruptions within the act of orientation. This leads us to consider again formula F^* since several (not all) of its elements may create a lack of orientation or actual disorientation (which does not have to come to the same thing): the impossibility of locating the self (ii), an insufficient cluster of indexical references for a twofold comparative act (iv) and inadequate tools of orientation (v). Insofar as there is no 'true' or 'false' orientation, there can only be more or less successful acts of orientation.

The predicate of success in orientation then, in contrast to the claims of some authors, is not necessarily a virtue.[76] Should we assume that disorientation is a vice? Even if it is, it might sometimes be a fruitful one that encompasses its own set of 'virtues': an openness to new voices, the stamina to endure periods of uncertainty, the ability to suspend familiar ways of being oriented to reflect on established routines, and even the value of creating disorientation in order to provoke responses in the face of severe irritations. This chapter has provided an orientation to orientation. Consequently, all that has been presented here must be applicable to itself.

5

Comparatively/Descriptively: Wittgenstein and the Search for 'Objects of Comparison'

1 Introduction: after dogmatism

Ludwig Wittgenstein[1] is well known for being a philosopher of description. The fact that he approaches his 'environment' descriptively means that he gives attention to particular cases, an attention that is too often withheld within philosophical inquiry. This means that he guards the particular case against the equalizing usurpation that general and all-encompassing theories are so prone to – in other words, *description as protection*. When it comes to applying such a descriptive philosophy to itself, it is not surprising that we do not receive more general disclosures concerning his 'method' from Wittgenstein, disclosures that would lead beyond description. Here too, he leaves it at 'pure descriptions', or more precisely stated: through his description of relevant and interesting phenomena, we get to know the pertinent information about his descriptive approach; no 'meta-discourse', no 'second-order philosophy', no description 'behind' descriptions (cf. PI 121).[2]

In contrast, Wittgenstein is far less known for being a philosopher of comparison. The fact that he approaches his 'environment' comparatively means that he places the particular cases that are to be compared with one another into a relation that is apparently not (or, no longer) self-evident, as we seem to have lost a stable scale *per se*, i.e. a comparative regard that is equipped with the necessary authority for the cases Wittgenstein is targeting. Often enough, it is precisely this kind of situation that we react to comparatively – *comparison as orientation* (see chapter 4 for a more in depth discussion). When applying a comparatively proceeding philosophy to itself, it is also not surprising that we do not get more general disclosures from Wittgenstein concerning his 'method', disclosures that would lead beyond comparisons. In this context too, he leaves it at 'pure comparisons' – or more exactly: through his comparison of relevant and interesting phenomena, we get to know all the pertinent information about his comparative approach. What could be *said* about the manifold comparisons *shows* itself when Wittgenstein performs these comparisons.[3]

The fact that Wittgenstein is neither a theorist of description, nor a theorist of comparison is because he is not a 'theorist' at all; this is precisely why he is describing and comparing and, at least in his later writings,[4] doing so incessantly. In the course of philosophical considerations on language, we encounter the following passage:

Our clear and simple language-games are not preparatory studies for a future regularization of language – as it were first approximations, ignoring friction and air-resistance. The language-games are rather set up as *objects of comparison* which are meant to throw light on the facts of our language by way not only of similarities, but also of dissimilarities.

PI 130; italics in the original; see also CV, 26

Here, the anti-Cartesian Wittgenstein delineates his favourite term[5] 'language-game' in a similar manner to how Descartes once characterized 'ideas': as clear and distinct (*clair et distinct*).[6] In contrast to Descartes and also to the rationalistic, and later positivistic, programs, Wittgenstein makes it clear and equally distinct that the object in question is not supposed to be informed by an allegedly context-free ideal. On the contrary, language-games are supposed to serve as invocations of a hermeneutic inversion: they should not simply dissolve the apparently unclear 'facts of our language' in favour of an ideal language purified of all ambivalences, but rather, they should elaborate judiciously on 'the language in which we live'.[7] This *ordinary language* is not at all free from friction which stems from our everyday dealings in understanding, not understanding and misunderstanding each other. This language is not aseptic, and therefore, the philosophical work is about comparatively/descriptively creating an order by which the linguistic ramifications come to the fore and become clearer in detecting similarities, dissimilarities and also family resemblances.[8] Language-games function here as '*objects of comparison*' that can be – in changing variations – put into comparative relations with each other and therefore, can enable mindful descriptions of our ordinary and sometimes less-ordinary language.[9]

The passage from the *Investigations* that I just expounded upon is followed by a short methodological commentary from Wittgenstein, along with an equally short reflection on his approach. In PI 131, he writes:

For we can avoid ineptness or emptiness in our assertions only by presenting the model as what it is, as an object of comparison – as, so to speak, a measuring-rod; not as a preconceived idea to which reality *must* correspond. (The dogmatism into which we fall so easily in doing philosophy.)[10]

Here, Wittgenstein is implicitly referring, once again, to the aforementioned ideal language (and all its derivatives). And he takes that idea not only to be an 'empty assertion', but also *moralizes* against the 'dogmatic' adherence to that very idea as a philosophical injustice towards reality.[11] Doing justice to reality is only possible if the variety of phenomena surrounding us is not reduced to 'the hardness of the logical must' (PI 437; see also 374 and 521).[12] Rather – and contrary to the metaphysical line of thinking – we have to 'look and see' (PI 66) what the 'facts of our language' truly are *before* we can construct them theoretically.[13] We will be able to circumvent this philosophical 'immorality' only if we do not solidify the 'objects of comparison' into 'prejudice', but instead manage to apply them as a 'model'. With this approach – by using comparative samples and parallel descriptions – we can contribute to a sensitivity that is located beyond overblown relativisms, as well as excessive ideals. The philosophical interventions that work to directly reform language are then substituted by a descriptively tentative sense – which is very phenomenological – that 'leads back to the issues' ('*zurück zu den Sachen*') and hence, back to language. Therefore, one does not 'interfere' with either the issues at stake or the language in a revisionist manner (cf. PI 124).

Wittgenstein's search for suitable 'objects of comparison' has thus far only been briefly sketched out. Now it is time to elaborate on it more carefully: to begin with, what leads to Wittgenstein's immense appreciation for descriptions and comparisons must be clarified precisely (2); then, the following section is dedicated to the concept of 'language-game' which has already been introduced as the object of comparison (3); finally, we will consider comparisons as a particular mode of description in order to sharpen the relation targeted in this chapter's title, 'Comparatively/Descriptively' (4).

2 The assets of description

Describing is not an end in itself but rather, a reaction to philosophical confusions. These *deep*-seated difficulties, masked often enough by mere *surface* phenomena, are, according to Wittgenstein's conviction, essentially *conceptual* problems.[14] Hence, we are deluded by our language or, more precisely, by a certain way of speaking; like a labyrinth, we are condemned to roaming around a landscape that is difficult to see from above, without – once, having lost our way – finding it again. Thus, the philosophical problem takes on a very simple form: 'I don't know my way about' (PI 123; cf. 664). Accordingly, dissolving the problem would be similar to 'a certain kind of "knowing one's way about"' (PI II 203) – not, however, as a previously achieved answer (as a 'pre-stage' leading to the next theory), but rather as a mode of intellectual discomfort in sketching a 'perspicuous representation' that keeps the adaptation of divergent perspectives in motion (PI 122; cf. RFG, 133).

The object of description is therefore language and its use, which, however, exhibits a highly ambivalent character. This is reflected in Wittgenstein's claim that our ordinary language is 'in order' (PI 98; BlB, 28), while holding at the same time that this language is also responsible for the notorious 'bewitchment of our intelligence' (PI 109). Along these lines, towards the end of the *Blue Book* we can read: 'Our ordinary language, which of all possible notations is the one which pervades all our life, holds our mind rigidly in one position [...]' (BlB, 59). It is also this language that is a 'handicap' (BlB, 52), that exerts a 'fascination' we should fight against (BlB, 27), that is 'pretending' (cf. PI 251), and that inhabits 'the grammar which tries to force itself on us here' (PI 304). Insofar as language not only constitutes the descriptive target, but also provides the tools for every description, it is the *remedy* for the confusions alluded to, as well as their *primary source*.[15]

Precisely because of this unresolved ambivalence between being both the remedy for and the source of confusion, Wittgenstein's emphasis on philosophical descriptions aims at an increased sensitivity to our language, a language that we are *in fact* speaking. This is expressed by the fear that generalizing theories necessarily create a distance between us and the complex usage of language that is entangled in manifold ways with our life. Accordingly, generalizations do not dissolve our philosophical confusions, but an 'ethnological point of view' might dispel them in showing us how our language is embedded in a 'natural surrounding' (CV, 502). Philosophy is, for Wittgenstein, the attempt to regain our language from the *metaphysical* project of searching for its presumable essence and to move our attention away from a particular form allegedly inherent to that language in favour of our *ordinary* usage of that language without these rigid forms (cf. PI 116). This arguably anti-theoretical trait is aptly summarized by the laconic advice 'don't think, but look!' If one happens, in philosophizing and generally, in thinking, to get 'confused' and become 'bewitched' (PI 109; cf. OC, 435), then the actual application and usage of language refers to everything that might contribute to our 'clarity' (CV, 7).

Let me draw on one prominent example: the obstacles in pinning down common features within a set of objects are well known. What is it that is without exception common to all games to justify the application of that term 'game'? Often, however, the way of asking the question in this (Socratic) fashion might already block the way to a (Socratic) answer. Wittgenstein invites us, instead, to pay attention to the practice and the usage of the term 'game' connected to that practice:

> Consider for example the proceedings that we call 'games.' I mean board-games, card-games, ball-games, Olympic games and so on. What is common to them all? – Don't say: 'There *must* be something common or they would not be called 'games' – but *look and see* whether there is anything common to all. – For if you look at them you will not see something that is common to *all*, but similarities, relationships, and a whole series of them at that. To repeat: don't think, but look! – Look for example at board-games, with their multifarious relationships. Now pass to card-games; here you find many correspondences with the first group, but many common features drop out, and others appear. When we pass next to ball-games, much that is common is retained, but much is lost [...].
>
> PI 66

'Anything your reader can do for himself leave to him' (CV, 77), Wittgenstein claims as a kind of stage direction (presumably, to himself as well). Apparently, he does not give his readers much credit, but neither does he to himself: 'How hard I find it to see what is *right in front of my eyes!*' he complains (CV, 39). Therefore, he becomes a 'mirror' in which his reader can recognize him- or herself; the mirrored ways of thinking and being misled become visible as something the reader might already be familiar with as well. Wittgenstein's idea of 'family resemblances' between relative elements (PI 67; see the entire passage 65–7; also BrB, 86–8) is an intriguing example of this procedure of pedagogical training in taking a close(r) look, but also in acknowledging that one must stay with 'what is *right in front of our eyes*' without philosophically escaping too quickly into the merely theoretical realm. Wittgenstein leads his reader – contrary to the usual ideal of taking distance – to linger 'in peace' over the objects in question (PI 133). While on this trajectory, we might find the claim to be unwarranted that there *has* to be something common to all games. It is the gradual illumination by perspective comparisons that enables us to cure ourselves from false pictures – often enough by means of new ones. In this sense, philosophy is 'really more a working on oneself' (CV, 16).

Despite his occasional cautioning against the 'tremendous danger' to want to 'draw subtle distinctions' (see PI II 205), Wittgenstein primarily underlines that it is 'our craving for generality' that makes 'this line of investigation' difficult (BlB, 17; cf. 19). As one looming consequence of this 'craving' he recognizes a 'contemptuous attitude towards the particular case' (BlB, 18) – a danger that a purely descriptive philosophy is supposed to circumvent.

Now, this eschewal can mean at least two very different things, and it is not always totally obvious which reading Wittgenstein truly prefers. What is at issue here will become clearer when addressing the question as to what alternatives to a purely descriptive philosophy there are: the weaker version claims that descriptions fulfil the philosophical purposes outlined above far more 'adequately' than other means; the stricter version, in contrast, claims that there is no alternative to a philosophy characterizing itself as a (very broadly understood) descriptive endeavour and practice.

The alternative that is critically considered by Wittgenstein is a philosophy that is concerned with explanations and, in particular, with justifications – and he comments on this explanatory-foundational project in a highly dismissive fashion: 'Philosophy may not interfere with the actual use of language; it can in the end only describe it. / For it cannot give it any foundation either. / It leaves everything as it is' (PI 124; cf. 98).

It is important to immediately add two qualifications: for one, Wittgenstein is, of course, not advocating that we get rid of all justifications.[16] In the present case, however (in the case of language used not only ideally, but ordinarily) these justifications cannot achieve anything because there are no *philosophical* reasons that would call for remodelling the language by reforming or adjusting it. This means, moreover, that Wittgenstein does not allow for justifying linguistic revisions in the name of philosophy, but in contrast, here we are dealing with practical and purpose-bound considerations that have nothing to do with a genuinely philosophical endeavour (cf. PI 132).[17]

At this point one might object that these qualifications remain faltering at best, considering that Wittgenstein is constantly concerned with language – including ordinary language – so that the descriptive approach focused on clarifications *factually* represents a methodological monopoly that affects all philosophical disciplines. Therefore, Wittgenstein would defend the stricter interpretation according to which a descriptively oriented philosophy does not leave any room for transcendental, analytic, idealistic, deconstructive, etc. accounts.

Now, I assume that Wittgenstein's descriptive philosophy does not stand on exclusively on descriptive grounds. This is why I further simplify things by relying on an even more benign interpretation concerning the status of descriptive philosophy than the weaker version touched upon above. Hence (and in the context of the present argument), I would not even defend the modest claim that a philosophical description deals with its potential subject matter more 'adequately' than the usual approaches; I will just assume that Wittgenstein's style of thinking (*Denkstil*) is philosophically more interesting – and 'interesting' meant in the sense of Richard Rorty, namely, that we can do things with descriptions that are less accessible within an alternative methodological framework.[18] For example, in the language-game of the term 'game', we recognize aspects that are traditionally obscured by game-theories in 'looking' at the various contexts in which we speak of (language) games and how the notion of a game withdraws itself, relative to divergent contexts, from every far-too generalizing harmonization.

In the following section I will elaborate on the concrete shape this philosophical interest might take. In doing so, I will not suppress the oscillation between description as protection and comparison as orientation. The benign character of the very weak reading attributed to a descriptive philosophy might then appear less benign.[19]

3 Language-games as 'objects of comparison'

Up to this point we have brought into focus why Wittgenstein has such an appreciation for descriptions that are specified by comparisons. Based on the concern that theories may block our attention to differences that surround us, Wittgenstein underlines the importance of descriptions that are at least 'interesting', and that are much more 'adequate' for working out the differences *and* similarities among the objects described. This view is no longer directed at the (alleged) *depth* of a metaphysical intuition of essences (the 'nature' of language, the 'substance' of the mind, etc.), but rather at the *variety* of what 'openly lies right in front of our eyes' (cf. BlB, 5; PI 126). In other words, this variety is the (new) depth. Therefore, we are confronted here with a remarkable shift away from the search for an Archimedean external point of reference anchored in 'essential' and invariant structures to the discovery of practical-internal reference points that are – sometimes in an equally stable manner – embedded in ordinary ways of acting and living.

This kind of 'postmetaphysical' philosophy (and not only a philosophy in a postmetaphysical age) regards itself as being an advocate of justice towards the objects of description. 'These objects,' as Hans Blumenberg claims in his arguably idiosyncratic fashion, 'do not allow for sticking with them'; hence, 'to turn sentences about objects into the "object itself"' presents then at least '*one* form of coming back from the objects', given that these objects 'do not acquiesce in remaining with them'. A phenomenology of objects gets intensified by being transformed into a phenomenology of language, and it is this phenomenology which Wittgenstein expects to avoid philosophical 'aspect-blindness'.[20] It is this very context of expectation in which we encounter the aforementioned claim that language-games function as 'objects of comparison'.

By this move, the entire 'operation called comparison'[21] appears on the scene: different *relata* are related to each other according to at least one comparative respect (the so-called *tertium*) within a purpose-bound context (see chapter 1, sections 2.4–2.6).[22] What Wittgenstein presents as 'objects of comparison' corresponds to these *relata*, while he remains rather silent when it comes to making the comparative regard explicit (but this has reasons, as we will see in section 4.3). The 'objects of comparison' are supposed to contribute to clarifying the 'situation of our language' by presenting the (dis)similarities within that language. Wittgenstein contrasts these objects with 'regulating' linguistic structures – with the simple consequence: *either* one compares descriptively *or* one regulates prescriptively. Apparently, one can't have it both ways.

Equating the 'objects of comparison' and comparison's relata might, however, come into conflict with Wittgenstein's refutation of philosophical 'dogmatism'. This dogmatism has to be avoided (see again PI 131) by comparatively applying these objects not as 'prejudices', Wittgenstein claims, but as 'examples' (or as 'scales').[23] This could mean two things: the philosophical dogma might either go back to absolutizing one particular comparative regard that leads to the privilege of one *relatum* over other *relata*; in such a case, the 'object of comparison' is not identical with one comparative *relatum* (contrary to what has just been claimed), but this object as a possible '"prejudice' would be identical with the *tertium comparationes*. Or, identifying the 'objects of comparison' with comparative *relata* is indeed correct, whereas the aforementioned dogmatism is based on a normatively burdened comparison; this includes asymmetrical comparisons (Ver-*gleiche*) – hence, alignments (Ab-*gleiche*) – in which one *relatum* functions as a norm in relation to all others.

I do not think that we necessarily have to decide between both interpretations, since both the absolutizing of a particular regard of a comparison, as well as the standardizing of one of its *relata* are able to feed that dogmatism. We will see that Wittgenstein does not criticize the mere possibility of comparing asymmetrically; he acknowledges that it is possible to use 'objects of comparison' as 'prejudices'. One has only to be aware of applying these 'prejudices' in a transient and tentatively conceited manner that has been chosen relative to a certain purpose. Given other concerns, the asymmetry of comparing items will be transformed as well (see section 4.2).

All these observations, however, hardly contribute to better understanding the operation called comparison; they remain mere comments on Wittgenstein's allusion. A real clarification comes in sight only when we characterize the 'objects of comparison' as language-games (and the other way around). Thus, we should be asking: what is a language-game?[24]

'Language-game' is arguably the best-known concept within Wittgenstein's philosophy. This is the case partly because Wittgenstein managed to introduce a catchy neologism for analogizing deeper meaning, but also because of his pronouncement (that he himself has adhered to all throughout until his very last notes) in the *Blue Book* (1933–4) to prospectively direct attention to what he tries to capture by this term (cf. BlB, 17–18). We are dealing with described, but also with invented, language-games, with language-games as singular terms, as kinds of words and as an entire practice connected to language. We are dealing with language-games as a therapeutic means of elaborating on language's meaning and eventually, with language-games as the undeniable horizon of reasonable justifications (see esp. OC, 559). In a mixture of complaint about the unsurveyable situation of language, as well as diagnosis of why this situation is constantly ignored, Wittgenstein states: 'We remain unconscious of the prodigious diversity of all the everyday language-games because the clothing of our language makes everything alike' (PI II 224). Analogizing[25] language and games already has as its intention to avoid this 'making everything alike'.

There are five central aspects connected to this intention.

(1) *Seeing differences*. We have already emphasized the immense variety of games, making it unnecessary to pin down essential features that every game would share. Speaking a language is something different from participating simultaneously in

several games because, to give just one example, most games have a well-defined goal, which is obviously not the case for a language. Nevertheless, one could consider both kinds of heterogeneity as '*related*' (PI 65). With and through language, we greet people, give monologues, have conversations or make announcements; we can call someone, lie, make jokes, give orders or ask a question. As with games, in speaking a language there are several moves open to us that belong to a particular practice of communicating, weighing pros and cons, giving replies, etc. 'Language-games' are supposed to underline these linguistic differences in contrast to their unifying reduction to merely indicative assertions.

(2) *Context*. The term 'language-game' also stresses the importance of the embeddedness of linguistic actions within certain 'surroundings' (PI 412) and hence, the fact that language is contextually bound. As the movement of a token in Monopoly means something else in chess, similarly, an indicative sentence in the context of a sermon might be used in a different manner to that in a newspaper report. In the light of this close connection between the meaning of language and its relation to practice and context, one could speak of the *transition from a theory of language to a phenomenology of speaking* in Wittgenstein.[26]

(3) *Rules*. The differences relative to divergent contexts can be traced back to at least implicit rules and thus, to different grammars. For instance, as much as a tennis match is constituted by very different rules than, say, orienting oneself, the 'language-game of telling' (PI 363) encompasses a different grammar than, say, the recounting of dreams (cf. PI II 187–8). However, despite all its cogency, this parallel eventually hits a brick wall. One has to acknowledge that, contrary to the rules of games, grammar's reliability in particular word fields or areas of language (in moral or religious language, for example), is not very high. Touching on this aspect Wittgenstein states:

> For remember that in general we don't use language according to strict rules – it hasn't been taught us by means of strict rules, either. *We,* in our discussions on the other hand, constantly compare language with a calculus proceeding according to exact rules.
>
> BlB, 25

(4) *Community*. In the vast majority of cases, speaking constitutes a commonly shared space: we could be debating with someone, answering his questions or talking about a person or an issue. Similarly, games are collectively shared practices as well. Of course, there are monologues or games without any teammates or opponents. However, the pertinent situations when learning a language or a game resemble each other; in some ways, they are interwoven and necessarily entail one another. Just as it is impossible to have and speak a language privately, it is also not possible to learn a game alone and to play it without any connection to a community (cf. PI 202, 243, 248).[27]

(5) *Involvement*. It was not made explicit by Wittgenstein, but it is implied by the language-game analogy that games emphasize the fact that their participants are not necessarily the active part of the game. Rather, the players may be absorbed in this activity to such an extent that there is eventually a decisive inversion: the player is then no longer the master of the game, and his 'playing the game' then turns into 'being

played by the game'. The game befalls the player in desubjectifying him, as Gadamer states.[28] We encounter a similar situation regarding the speaking of a language. Accordingly, Heidegger claims that 'language is not the work of humans: it is language that speaks. Humans only speak (*sprechen*) in corresponding to language (*entsprechen*).'[29] It must be admitted that this inversion is not part of Wittgenstein's focus; however, it is not only compatible with, but it is also a potential result of, what he has to say about one's growing into a language and its world-disclosing character (cf. PI 19, 32b, 241). We follow rules, including those of a language, often 'blindly', in order to be able to understand. As with Heidegger and Gadamer, we are again confronted with the question to what extent – after the breakdown of the rigid subject-object-scheme – we are the (exclusive) subjects of understanding. This question seems to be even more urgent when taking into account our lifeworld-involvement, strongly underlined by Wittgenstein's reference to the notion of a game.

The initial application of 'language-game' takes on a very peculiar form given Wittgenstein's usual mode of articulation; the *Blue Book* almost provides a definition in stating

> [Language-games] are ways of using signs simpler than those in which we use the signs of our highly complicated everyday language. Language games are the forms of language with which a child begins to make use of words. The study of language games is the study of primitive forms of language or primitive languages.
>
> BlB, 17

One has to bear in mind this consciously simplifying character of language-games (cf. OC, 599). However, this is only part of the wide range of possible applications of this label.[30] Wittgenstein himself offers a kind of list, mirroring this heterogeneity: giving orders and acting accordingly, describing and producing an object or thing, telling something and giving a report; but also performing on stage, solving a riddle, making jokes, translating a text, among other things (cf. PI 23; BlB, 67–68). Here, two essential aspects are already alluded to: on the one hand, a language-game as an *object to be described* in focusing on certain linguistic usages and, on the other hand, a language-game as a *mode of description* in relation to particular purposes of philosophical analysis. Therefore, language-games encompass a descriptive, as well as a functional, element, and both together amount to a third aspect: the ultimate *task of a language-game consists of reducing linguistic complexity* for the sake of illuminating the mode(s) of operation of language and its 'environment' (BrB, 157; cf. BlB, 17).[31]

This reduction can take on the following forms: first, Wittgenstein places particular stress on the contexts of *learning a language*. He has different reasons to do so: for one, the linguistic resources are still rather limited and, in this sense, 'primitive' regarding that stage of development (cf. PI 7; BlB, 17). Then, within instances of language-learning, it might become clearer how language is connected to certain practical contexts and the ways in which it is even derived from that context (cf. Z 545). Finally, situations of language-learning highlight the fact that applying (or playing) a language-game presupposes a sovereign mastering of other language-games as well; here, the internal relations among language-games come to the fore and become more transparent (cf. PI II, 224–5).

Secondly, a 'language-game' does not in every case function as a descriptive unit that refers to the *factual* use of language, as Wittgenstein also speaks of language-games that are made up and *fictional*. These latter language-games are mostly modifications of common, yet heuristically reduced, usages of language that help to clarify our ordinary linguistic practices precisely by contrasting them with fictional applications. Moreover, they underline the contingent character of our modes of expression by hinting at obvious or hidden alternatives. For instance, the language-game of denoting colours could be partly, or even entirely, different – a fact that might tell us something about the embeddedness of our factual conventions concerning colours (in comparison with, say, those of Inuits) in the practical environment we live in and through (cf. OC, 525).[32]

Third, and by far most importantly, language-games are *explicit reductions* of communicative situations that intentionally break down linguistic complexity into surveyable units. An almost overused example of such a 'primitive language-game' is the one of the builders in PI 2. The builder's vocabulary is limited to single nouns that function at the same time as commands (see Z 99; BrB, 77–86). One does not have to go much further to see this paragraph as an allegory of modernity losing its formerly rich language.[33] Precisely in view of acknowledging the ramifications of our factual language, this language-game serves as a filter to place stress on the descriptively important aspects.

Accordingly, *language-games do not denote linguistic units that are actually to be found in our language, but they present functional-reductive items of philosophical description whose scope is adjustable relative to certain descriptive purposes*. So much for the language-game of 'language-game(s)', which Wittgenstein uses as an 'object of comparison' in the course of his descriptive philosophy. In the following section, we will turn to the question of how comparative procedures might clarify Wittgenstein's descriptive ambitions.

4 Comparing as a mode of description

We have to ask how comparisons and descriptions can hang together, and how they stand in relation to each other in Wittgenstein's work. To address this question, it is necessary to take a short look at descriptive procedures. Here, we are dealing with a ramified and multi-faceted activity that can be summarized in a very non-Wittgensteinian fashion: *somebody (i) describes something (ii) to someone else (iii) with regard to a specific purpose (iv) by adopting particular means (v)*.

The 'somebody' describing (and comparing) in Wittgenstein's *Investigations* (and his other later writings) is not simply the author himself presenting something that remains at a distance to himself and his readers. We have seen that descriptions are supposed to safeguard us against hasty generalizations, while comparisons are responses to a need for orientation, i.e. a reaction to a philosophical 'not knowing one's way about' (cf. again PI 123). Hence, this 'somebody' is not working on something that is disconnected from himself, but rather, he is always part of the work he is engaged in. Accordingly, Wittgenstein can describe this kind of self-involvement as follows: 'Working in philosophy – like work in architecture in many respects – is really more a working on oneself. On one's own interpretation. On one's way of seeing things. (And what one expects of them)' (CV, 16). This 'working on oneself' is described by example. Hence, the reader's confusions and newly achieved reorientations are mirrored in Wittgenstein's own movements of thought and his resolving of the problems of orientation. In the best case, the *Investigations* would be pursued and updated by another author, who is the reader himself (ad i). (We will soon return to potential objects of description and "objects of comparison" (ii).)

Now, no one can describe something in a void without context but rather, must do so within the framework of shared interests, common (background) knowledge and personal, as well as intellectual, preferences. To a considerable extent, we tailor our descriptions to a particular addressee – with the result that our descriptive endeavours will change as soon as our audience changes (ad iii). Moreover, descriptions can fulfil very different tasks: if I tell my friend enthusiastically about the new novel I have been reading, I might recommend this book to him; if I report the circumstances of an accident, I could try to justify why I am not guilty; if I sketch the relations between, say, religion and sports, I might attempt to hint at similar aspects among both comparative elements. In the first case, the act of describing resembles the search for common appreciation (*description as persuasion*); in the second case, the act of describing is related to providing evidence and assessing it (*description as justification*); in the last case, we are dealing with a comparative contextualization (*description as explanation*). Although there are no clear boundaries between these examples, it is nonetheless important to note the differences among descriptions (ad iv).

And finally, divergent descriptive means determine divergent descriptive results. If human beings are conceived of using a psychoanalytical vocabulary, this might be illuminating in regard to certain aspects, whereas other aspects could be better captured and made more accessible using an alternative terminology.[34] Thus, opting for particular descriptive means does not leave the description itself and its results untouched (ad v).

It is precisely here that comparison, as one means of determining possible descriptive results, comes into play. Accordingly, the formula above has to be amended and adjusted: *someone working on her- or himself (i) compares her- or himself or something (ii) to her- or himself and/or others (iii) in responding to a "not knowing one's way about" (iv) by applying language-games as "objects of comparison" (v).*

Since we have already touched on the first elements, I will now primarily concentrate on (v). Insofar as 'objects of comparison' are supposed to be language-games and if we take seriously what we have compiled so far concerning language-games, a twofold comparison emerges: one may compare (across) different language-games *and* the compared language-games themselves resemble (analogical) comparisons. I will therefore address *external* and *internal* comparisons in regard to language-games (see section 4.1.). However, the question must be posed as to what extent Wittgenstein's comparative description is truly free from particular intentions[35] (which means: in which sense his descriptions are truly presented with the 'purity' referred to above (cf. PI 100 and 108) – instead of descriptions that ultimately serve a certain agenda or point of view). This leads us to the distinction between *pure* and *intentional* comparisons (4.2). Wittgenstein compares by juxtaposing several comparisons of both kinds, often without an explicit comparative regard. Therefore, the comparison would have to find the right balance between self-sublation due to multiple comparisons and the enhancing of our 'knowing one's way about' by taking up different perspectives. This results in a specific *dynamic between the act of comparing and the one who compares* (4.3).

4.1 'Objects of comparison': external and internal comparisons

At the most trivial level, there cannot only be one singular object of comparison, for this object must be compared with other items (in a synchronic or diachronic fashion, or even with itself at an earlier or later juncture). These objects of comparison, along with the *tertium* through which a comparison is performed, constitute an external comparison: 'external' insofar as these objects are compared to something that is 'outside' of them to create transient, dissolvable orders and arrangements that always have alternative possibilities. Because Wittgenstein presents these objects of comparison as language-games and because language-games, as previously noted, can be characterized as analogical comparisons, an additional comparative combination emerges, i.e. a comparison of a second order within objects of comparison. More precisely, the objects of comparison are themselves nothing but comparative objects in that they accommodate a comparison.

Wittgenstein relates different objects of comparison to one another, for example, 'praying' and 'acting' (both are mentioned in PI 23). By doing so, he defines them as language-games. Hence, for this characterization, all intentions are relevant that have initially led to introducing the language-game analogy and that have been sketched in the previous section. 'Praying' and 'acting' teach us to see the differences in using language, to recognize its being as bound to a context – along with its regularity and its communal aspect – and eventually to imagine the person praying or acting as being involved in that very practice. Here we are dealing with an analogical comparison that, therefore, entails its own failure: analogies are not identifications (cf. PI 83), and comparisons are never without alternatives. If we compare 'praying' and 'acting' (and praying and acting), both could be compared with other items or with one another via a different regard. All of this is also relevant for language-games (as internal comparisons): if we compare 'language' with 'game' (and language with games), both could be compared with other items or with one another via a different regard. And this is what Wittgenstein himself is doing – not necessarily systematically, but on occasion. Besides the language-game analogy, he uses other analogies that might be more adequate for other purposes; these are taken to be alternatives to analogizing language and games or they can serve as a refinement of that analogy:

- language – tool (cf. PI 11)
- language – calculus (cf. BlB, 17; PI 31)
- language – set of regulations (cf. PI 81)
- language – playing chess (cf. PI 30–31 & 136) – etc.

In our context here, we do not need to be concerned with the problem of how adequate these analogies really are in relation to certain descriptive and comparative purposes. What is important is their status *as* analogical comparisons since it would be too premature to object that language is not a game, a tool, a calculus, etc. This underlined difference between language and its analogical counterparts is already conceded in the figure of analogical comparisons that excludes strict identification. The analogy's relevance depends rather on how the analogy might illuminate pertinent aspects of language.[36]

Therefore, when comparing the objects of comparison 'praying' and 'acting' *externally*, both are – as language-games and as activities – themselves part of an *internal* comparison. And now, it won't come as a surprise to claim that the comparative ambitions within internal comparisons may influence the emphasis when comparing externally (and vice versa). When considering 'praying' as a tool for achieving certain goals, as opposed to thematizing 'acting' under the regard of its regularity, then the external comparison between both language-games might likely bring other aspects to the fore instead of treating 'praying' and 'acting' as moves in a chess game. The potential results always remain dependent upon the comparative regard that has been previously stipulated.

4.2 Pure and intentional comparisons

It has already been noted in passing that one may distinguish between comparisons whose objects are symmetrically and equitably related to one another and comparisons in which one object is normatively loaded in such a way that the other 'object of comparison' must be measured according to the first object. This is the distinction between comparing (*ver-gleichen*) and aligning (*ab-gleichen*). With the latter, Wittgenstein appears to view an act of holding to one's prejudices (cf. PI 131; CV, 29) as amounting to an instrumentalization of comparison and, more generally, of description for purposes that had already been determined outside of the context. A similar charge obtains for certain comparative regards that may lead to privileging one of the *relata* while devaluing the other ones (one prominent, while unfortunate, example is the process of recruiting staff in which the employment description is already formulated in view of a specific candidate; under the disguise of transparent fairness, the comparison then turns into a recursive legitimization of (in Wittgenstein's sense) a 'dogmatic' background decision; cf., again, PI 131).

However, the intentional bias for a comparative item can fulfil descriptive tasks as well, of course. Preferences do not have to be problematic *per se*; they only turn into blind spots when they are absolutized. There is nothing necessarily objectionable about transient privileges relative to particular purposes, and this option is also presented in Wittgenstein's work. Hence, he is aware that we do not use language according to strict rules, but rather, he emphasizes that it is *us*, as comparing subjects, who establish this counterfactual presupposition of language's strict rules in order to compare language with same clarity as a calculus (see BlB, 17).

Another difference is linked to the one sketched above. One has to distinguish further between comparisons that are open in terms of their potential results, i.e. void of (or liberated from) particular interests (descriptive, or even normative, ones) and comparisons that are really bound to particular intentions. In the first case, we can speak of purely descriptive comparisons that proceed from describing something and end up with an *initially open result,* whereas in the second case, we are dealing with functional structures assuming the form of comparative descriptions that, conversely, are constructed *on the basis of a result having already been intended.* Therefore, comparisons work either by really surveying 'what lies in front of us' (see again PI 126–7), or they serve as examples for something hidden and lurking 'behind' the comparative act. *Pure comparisons are, in this sense, never exemplary (they do not stand for something else other than themselves); intentional comparisons, however, always represent something else (they are replaceable by other tools and means).*[37]

When referring to Wittgenstein's approach to the concept of a game, we can find *both* of these interpretations of comparison (pure and intentional). It is either Wittgenstein's aim to simply juxtapose divergent types of games to then criticize the claim that they all 'must' share a common structure, or this critical ambition may serve as a starting point by relying on the game example to eventually contribute to the old, as well as famous, debate on nominalism as critique of stipulated, yet unnecessary, essences. Due to *hermeneutical* considerations, we do not have to go for one of both readings; rather, one might concede the essential circularity between both options. In any case, it may have now become clearer as to why the supposedly benign character of a philosophy proceeding comparatively/descriptively does not have to have the final word – insofar as it is shown what one is able to do by and with and through comparisons.[38]

4.3 Incompleteness: on the dynamics of comparing

It is precisely this combination of internal and external – as well as pure and intentional – comparisons that constitutes a dynamic that amounts to an incompleteness or openness. Wittgenstein does not present *one* – as it were, *the* – definitive comparison, but rather, he offers several comparisons as 'activities' dependent on certain patterns of objects and their construction (which is visible in his mode of invitation: 'Let us assume that . . .', 'You might see it like this . . .', or 'Seen from here, it might look like . . .'). This training, to accurately see and recognize, is apparently at odds with taking the distance to present definitive theses prescribing what has to be seen and recognized. This caution turns Wittgenstein's *Investigations* (*Untersuchungen*) into a real search (*Suche*), possibly a search for certain traces (*vestigia*). However, this is an ambivalent feature: this training, where the reader has to assist and to collaborate, is not easy since she does not remain a mere reader – and she ought not remain what she is – but rather, must work on herself. *Wittgenstein's hope is, therefore to prevent ourselves from having an understanding without it having any effect on us; the philosopher is supposed to leave everything as it is, and precisely by doing this, she might allow herself to be changed.*[39] Here, the focus turns away from the objects of comparison to those who engage in comparison.

Let us recall Wittgenstein's description of the diversity laden within the concept of the game (see again PI 66). Here we also encounter an invitation to the reader:

'Consider for example the proceedings that we call "games". This is then followed by the anticipated confusion and the attempt to circumvent false expectations: 'Don't say: "There *must* be something common [to all these games], or they would not be called games" – but *look and see* whether there is anything common to all.' Here, Wittgenstein does not exclude the fact all games have something in common, but neither does he plainly presuppose that there is such a nucleus of essential features. In contrast, he 'looks and sees' descriptively and by dint of this, comparatively, at how things really stand. A sketch of this kind of looking and seeing however remains incomplete because the reader's hoped-for transformation – a transformation of a voice initially relying upon metaphysical necessities – is not simply brought about through presenting new arrangements that have been comparatively/descriptively created. Rather, the reader must be enabled to find these 'similarities', 'multifarious relationships', yet also 'common features [that] drop out' between 'board-games, card-games, ball-games, Olympic games and so on'. As with musicians, from whom one learns most when seeing them play their instruments, there is something *personal* about philosophizing as soon as this transformative and self-involving act of looking and seeing is trained and responsibly acknowledged.

As claimed at the outset, describing takes on this protective function: 'Don't say that ..., but *look* whether ...'. It has been stated that these comparisons accomplish an orienting task which enable 'a certain kind of "knowing one's way about"' (PI II, 203). However, what becomes of orientation given the fact that Wittgenstein created no definite orders, arrangements, stable overview or survey, and given that he seems generally to distance himself from sustainable results?

These concerns can be amplified: if we look at how Wittgenstein treats different games, his (de)emphasizing of similarities, dissimilarities and the 'familiar relationships' between them (cf. PI 67), one might get the impression that the comparisons he offers actually neutralize each other. The plurality of comparisons would amount to nothing but untenable relativisms, while it remains unclear, or at least implicit, which regard it is that these different games are related to. The situation becomes even trickier when one considers that Wittgenstein often integrates counterfactual elements into his descriptions and comparisons in a manner that is twofold: on the one hand, as purposeful *reductions* (this is exactly the aforementioned task of language-games: simplifying language in a way that risks oversimplifying it), and on the other, as *imaginations* (the potential of language-games extends beyond the real to also encompass the conceivable).

Both aspects – reduction as well as imagination – are by no means concealed by Wittgenstein: language-games are procedures that simplify the actual usage of everyday language – that is the reductive element (cf. BlB, 16–17). And conversely, Wittgenstein is nevertheless interested in inventing new parables and comparisons – that is the imaginative element (see CV, 19 and 20; also PI 400). Hence, a determination or stipulation of 'a particular way of looking at the matter' (PI 308) is challenged by both aspects. Nevertheless, there are also some restrictions in Wittgenstein's approach:

Methodologically. In juxtaposing different games against one another merely through a latent (or silent) comparative regard, Wittgenstein neither intends to enact any semantic shifts reforming meaning, nor any constructivism detached from a real linguistic practice. Rather, the conceptual difficulties sketched above are met by getting released from oversimplifications through tentatively established arrangements as well as by structures that are made visible perspectively. As a result, we will be more inclined to be – without any disappointment – content with acknowledging the variety within the irreducible range of using language and therefore, content with 'enduring comparisons' as they illuminate this diversity.[40] Otherwise, Wittgenstein states, the 'most obvious may become the hardest of all to understand. What has to be overcome is a difficulty having to do with the will, rather than with the intellect' (CV, 17).

Structurally. Wittgenstein not only helps to liberate us from our confused longings for definitively foundational structures, but also from an unnecessary relativism that emerges as an allegedly inevitable result after saying goodbye to essentialism (and all its derivatives). Such a choice between relativism and essentialism is a more than unhappy one. This is demonstrated by the fact that there is a *via media* between the either/or of the abstractly general on the one hand, and the mode of merely remaining with particular cases on the other. Across different games are indeed *clusters,* which sometimes pervade the web of several games more extensively and, at other times however, abruptly come to an end. Nevertheless, here we have moved beyond the purely general and the purely particular by paying heed to both aspects and, in so doing, have elaborated on the relationships between games. Therefore, the relativism that is so often feared does not emerge here, and neither does the arbitrariness of constructivism allegedly promoted by testing out different 'objects of comparison'. Dismissing the 'contemptuous attitude towards the particular case' (BlB, 18) does not leave us with a vacuum; rather, it is replaced by a newly achieved attentiveness concerned with the complicated relations among particular cases. And it is these cases which force us to learn again and again to 'look and see'.

5 Comparatively/descriptively: a concluding note

Initially, I anticipated to encounter *descriptions as refined by comparison.* It might have become obvious that, throughout this discussion, I have provided exactly the opposite. I have, in keeping with the distinction presented above, described comparisons not in a pure manner, but intentionally (i.e. in view of certain purposes) in order to capture the significance and weight that comparative procedures take on in Wittgenstein's later writings. Thematizing comparisons in the framework of his descriptive philosophy ultimately amounts to presenting *comparisons refined by descriptions*:

- firstly, as *elements of critique*, as objections against a philosophy that understands itself as explanatory, foundational and dedicated to concrete contexts only in so far as the particular represents a sample for the general;
- secondly, as *regaining* the particular case, which aims philosophically to turn the noncomparative and nondescriptive necessities upside down and transform them into the (nonlogical) necessities of the comparative-descriptive mode of philosophizing;

- thirdly, as procedures with 'objects of comparison' that are illuminated by features characteristic of language-games, such as: communality, reference to practice, regularity despite the limitations of rules, etc.;
- fourthly, as concerns which turn out to be not at all benign, given the differences between language-games as internal comparisons, given the external comparisons between different language-games, as well as their mutual influences, and given the differences between pure and, hence, open (as well as purpose-bound) comparisons, including their circularity;
- finally, as dynamic processes whose movements involve the person who is comparing within the attempt to fulfil what is for Wittgenstein the decisively moral task of preventing philosophical results from turning into the injustices of everyday 'dogmatism'.

However, dangers will remain because, in contrast to deductive inferences, comparisons do not guarantee their validity; they are precarious and fragile. And hence, only those comparativists might appreciate the case for comparisons that do not regret the 'decomposing of comparisons' (cf. PI 308), but rather, are willing to re-enact that decomposition playfully.

6

Comparative Ironism: Richard Rorty on Plural Vocabularies and the Comparisons Between Them

> *That is to say, while it is because of a big gap in philosophy that we can give no general account of the concept of virtue or of the concept of justice, but have to proceed, using the concepts, only by giving examples; still there is an area where it is not because of any gap, but is in principle the case, that there is no account except by way of examples: and that is where the canon is 'what's reasonable': which of course is* not *a canon.*
>
> G.E.M. Anscombe[1]

1 Introduction: theories or examples?

Richard Rorty is as popular among his 'analytic colleagues' as Kierkegaard had once been with the Christian bourgeoisie. This is how Alasdair MacIntyre phrased it,[2] and this analogy does indeed have some merit. Both renegade ironists attracted the rage of the opposite side by criticizing it from within. Hence, it is not external critique that is in the foreground but, rather, the dangers of misunderstanding the subject matter itself. Apparently, God and the world are equally affected by this problem.

What Rorty articulates is the distinctive reservation against the claims of theoretical generalizations. The reason for this refutation does not solely lie in the assumption that we can no longer afford to use these generalizations – concerning truth, knowledge, morals, the 'nature' or 'essence' of the human – but also in the belief that we do not have any use for them. The limitations of theories are here accompanied by their practical redundancy. However, the difficulty of this claim is fairly obvious as soon as one applies this claim to itself: repudiating generalizations in the form of a theory seems itself to be somewhat general, as well as in danger of neglecting the particular case – possibly in the name of theoretical premises. As we will see later, Rorty anticipates this countermove not by pretending to disprove the opposite side, but by trying to make it 'look bad'.[3]

Let's focus for a moment on the methodological, and thus metaphilosophical, problem of the accessibility and scope of theories. This difficulty plays an eminent role in Rorty's criticism of the Western philosophical tradition; generally, it can be found among writers influenced by Wittgenstein. Put more concretely, we are dealing with the question of whether theories in moral philosophy are possible in contrast to richer and more comprehensive descriptions of morally significant conflicts. Onora O'Neill transforms the opposition that concerns us here into the simplified choice between norms and examples, as well as between the strict orientation by principles for solving specific problems on the one hand, and, on the other, an exemplary mode of thinking that is interested in understanding the particular case.[4] It does not come as a surprise which preferences the Kantian O'Neill has, and therefore, the Wittgensteinian refutation of theoretically-stable principles has to appear to her as a farewell to philosophical thinking in general. The stumbling blocks are statements such as the following by Peter Winch: 'All we can do, I am arguing, is to look at particular examples and see what we *do* want to say about them: there are no general rules which can determine in advance what we *must* say about them.'[5] This statement might not only appear to Kantians as far too weak. And yet, O'Neill appreciates the reflexivity and sensitivity entailed by ethically-motivated descriptions in order to eventually find fault with the concentration on issues of individual ethics without sufficient awareness of social and political challenges. For these challenges, O'Neill thinks, it is required to have a 'moral theory' that enables judgements beyond 'particular examples', while referring to examples merely for illustrative purposes.

What we are dealing with here is the domestication of examples by reducing them to merely illustrative ornaments of theories formulated independently from the examples chosen. And it is precisely this reduction that is feared by Winch and Rorty. The conflict that becomes apparent at this point is particularly visible in cases where literature is included philosophically: are the references to narratives and novels in the work of Winch and Rorty just exemplifications of the general, or does something more essential lie in the narrative concreteness of literature than merely illustrating more abstract claims? It is obviously the latter for Winch and Rorty (and many others), but this is itself a matter of interpretation.[6] By contrast, most of the numerous opposing voices may agree with O'Neill – namely, that it is difficult to reach morally-relevant decisions from literary, and hence hypothetical, examples without relying on principles and theories to which these examples correspond.[7]

But the question emerges as to which status the chosen examples enjoy or what exactly these examples stand for. Critical commentaries on O'Neill often stress the fact that she just presupposes that these examples are lying in wait for an ethical evaluation. Contrary to that view, Winch's reading of *Billy Budd* by Herman Melville or Rorty's interpretations of Orwell and Nabukov function as examples for the ways in which people reach moral judgements in the first place. And in the course of these readings, it becomes clearer how different the ways of achieving moral judgements really are.[8] Thus, examples do not wait for their generalization to become significant; rather, they already entail everything that is ethically relevant if we are dealing with 'good' examples – and that 'goodness', one might hope, is implied by the 'thick descriptions' represented in and provided by novels. Therefore, criticism of theories is not put forward in order to submit a new one, but for making a case for a new approach in philosophy. Exactly such a plea is to be found in the work of Richard Rorty.[9]

The background just explained comes to the fore within two contexts in Rorty's work. On the one hand, Rorty stresses the plurality of descriptions concerning ourselves and our environment – not only through the mode of acknowledging this plurality, but also through an imaginative gesture of inventing additional descriptions.

However, the chances of achieving adequate theories decrease in a parallel fashion to the amplified heterogeneity within already-existing or invented descriptions. On the other hand, Rorty trusts in the power of literature to prevent the readers from activating their self-referentiality, which helps to transform them into more sensitive beings.[10] It is especially the novel that serves as supplier of examples for alternative modes of self-understanding that cannot be captured by theoretical generalizations, Rorty states.

The following reflections are dedicated to both interrelated contexts by recalling, first, the relevant argumentative background assumptions, as shown in the double reservation against theory, and then, secondly, by clarifying the exemplary character of new descriptions and literary examples. This is done to finally address the so-far marginalized topic of how to evaluate and weigh up descriptions and ideas from a novel as appropriate, helpful, eye-opening, and also interesting versions of ourselves and our surroundings. For this, Rorty calls for comparisons *between* new descriptions and *within* the plurality of literary sources.

2 Irony and the plurality of our vocabularies

The first context in which comparative procedures become essential for Rorty is an epistemic one. It is well known that Rorty is among those authors who refute the correspondence theory of truth, and that refutation leads to the question of how to deal with the competing descriptions of reality, as soon as they no longer match reality in a substantial sense. The *vertical match* is now substituted by a *horizontal comparison*; the relation of our vocabularies to their 'real' references does not lie at the core of truth, but rather, the relation between these vocabularies is what Rorty is interested in. And these interrelations bring comparisons between vocabularies into play. This is also relevant to the second context that will concern us here. This context is a methodological one, addressing the status of philosophical work in general. Rorty claims that philosophy is no longer about picturing reality, but about educating people in a possibly interesting manner. Philosophy is then transformed into literary criticism insofar as theorems appear as narrative offerings that have to be carefully considered, deepened or eliminated. Here too, comparative procedures are necessary, procedures through which it becomes clearer why philosophy and comparative literary studies are increasingly converging.

2.1 A farewell to truth?

One of the most disputed segments in Rorty's neo-pragmatist approach is his critique of the classical account of truth. This account is built on the idea according to which truth consists in the correspondence between language and world – more precisely, between assertoric speech and those units of reality referred to by that very speech. Rorty vehemently repudiates this theory of truth, without entering into the complicated debate about different versions or details of that theory. He instead attacks the kernel of that account which runs through all of its variations. This attack, Rorty says, represents the heart of pragmatism,[11] and it is essentially based on two critical considerations.

One cannot, on the one hand, give credence to the idea of correspondence in general. Proponents of the correspondence theory claimed that reality functions as truth- (or falsehood-) maker in relation to sentences and assertions. It is presupposed here that units of speech would 'match' units of reality in the case of truth, whereas this match is absent when something false is asserted. Apart from thereby limiting truth exclusively to assertoric language (while truth in ethics, aesthetics, religion and also with regard to taste or preference remains precarious), this theory brings together two ontologically distinct areas. Linguistic units are supposed to correspond to fragments of reality. Rorty, however, refutes that this 'nasty broad gap' (G.E. Lessing) can be overcome by a kind of correspondence, and more to the point, he claims that this supposition is senseless and philosophically futile.[12]

On the other hand – and connected to the first aspect – Rorty presents the following argument: truth does not exist 'out there' but constitutes a feature of sentences. Sentences, however, are elements of human, i.e. human-created, language. It is not the world that tells us which way we should describe and categorize that world, but rather, this description and categorization is part of our contingent forms of life. If language and its highly-divergent modes of articulation are contingent, then truth is as well – without our being able to determine which of the various vocabularies fits reality better than others, reality remains indifferent towards our modes of describing it. Hence, sentences refer only to other sentences, but never to a language-independent reality.[13] Therefore, Rorty programmatically eliminates epistemological representationalism because language would be misunderstood as medium or interface between mind and world. Rather, language is part of our behaviour and of our practice; it resembles a tool rather than being a mode of representation.[14]

Given our purposes here, it is impossible, but also not necessary, to enter the ramified debate about Rorty's criticisms and their background assumptions. There is not only critique, but even indignation concerning, for instance, Rorty's claim that Galileo Galilei's paradigm just worked 'better' than the Aristotelian one,[15] without it being substantially and significantly 'closer' to the physical reality described by that paradigm.[16]

The way in which Rorty describes the superiority of modern physics[17] over its ancient ancestor is simply inadequate, some critics claim.[18] And especially in an age that suffers from relativistic positions which threaten to dissolve the difference between truth and falsehood, one would have to rely again on more robust forms of epistemic realism.[19]

Insofar as Rorty still cherishes the idea of truth, he does so in a conventionalist, as well as coherentist, manner – truth as a relatively-stable convention within a community of speakers and their fairly-consistent background assumptions and convictions.[20]

I do agree with the discontent concerning Rorty's elimination of a substantial and, thus, theoretically considered correspondence-concept of truth. And yet, I think that his reflections on the plurality of vocabularies and, connected to this, his allusions to comparing these vocabularies remain highly relevant. I will leave it an open question as to what degree this relevance can be claimed, also in relation to the realm of the natural sciences, by restricting myself to areas within which the notion of a more-or-less evident correspondence of our sentences to external facts has traditionally met with difficulties. Our moral vocabulary and the ways of describing ourselves may serve as an example here. In these 'softer' domains, Rorty's conventionalism and coherentism seem to be far less spectacular, and his considerations regarding the status of these life-orienting and identity-forming vocabularies appear to be more helpful and appropriate.[21]

2.2 Irony and the plurality of descriptions

In his 1989 book *Contingency, Irony and Solidarity*, Rorty summarizes his concern as follows:

> The fundamental premise of the book is that a belief can still regulate action, can still be thought worth dying for, among people who are quite aware that this belief is caused by nothing deeper than contingent historical circumstance.[22]

Passages like this one try to find the right balance between the contingency of even our deepest convictions, i.e. their evolution and changeability on the one hand, and, on the other, the certainty that remains possible regarding the validity of these convictions and the necessity to act according to them. It is again a Wittgensteinian insight that prevents Rorty from succumbing to the abyss of relativism, namely the insistence on the fact that certain convictions are embedded in our lives in such a way that negating them is not at all an option and is thus meaningless.[23] This element is marginalized, as Rorty himself is in fact guilty of at times, when historical contingencies are emphasized and when ironists are characterized as those who just celebrate doubt concerning 'final vocabularies' – considering that everything could always be different. However, irony does not solely consist of refuting final vocabularies and the readiness to constantly check out new descriptions, but it equally consists – even despite this double openness – of adhering to potentially variable convictions as an expression of one's own identity.[24]

This irony is only attainable within the private sphere, Rorty claims; he does not speak of a public irony. Now, this dualism between privacy and the public realm is an unhappy one (one might here think of a merely private religion[25]) and, often enough, a failing remnant of the old Cartesianism between the inner and the outer. Irony can indeed be made public, given the fact that descriptions and constantly new vocabularies do not remain within a private sphere, but affect our ways of being together.

There are further consequences of Rorty's account, based on his critique of the correspondence theory of truth and his refutation of the realistic ambition of that theory. First, he repudiates the idea that there can be a final and ultimate vocabulary. By a final way of speaking, Rorty means a language – be it in religion, be it in the natural sciences – that ultimately fits reality. If the idea of correspondence is gone, so is the finality of vocabularies insofar as a standard of correctness cannot be determined. Neither reality, nor its allegedly hidden structure, nor the ordinary use of language, nor a grammar to be detected are able to establish this standard.[26] And this leads to Rorty's project of leaving the 'mirror of nature' behind and of embracing the plurality of articulations without any mirror.[27]

Secondly, Rorty sticks to the idea of language's causal relation to the world,[28] but underlines the fact that there is still linguistic contingency. Therefore, language cannot determine which way of speaking is the 'correct' one; language is not simply there to be found, but evolves permanently. Hence, truth – as codified by language – is not to be discovered, but also made up and created.[29] One could compare, as Wittgenstein did,[30] language with tools, as long as one does not neglect the differences within that analogy. While the purposes of using an instrument are clearly defined, this is different with regard to language and remains a matter of openness and discursive negotiation.[31]

Thirdly, Rorty advocates the metaphorization of language. Following Donald Davidson, he negates the attempt to distinguish between ordinary and figurative ways of speaking, as this attempt would imply the characterization of metaphors as having their own genuine, yet 'improper', meaning. However, Rorty replaces this duality of ordinary and figurative meaning with the intentionally vague distinction between familiar and surprising (or even alien) ways of expression. Then, metaphors would not have their own meaning, but represent nothing other than a so-far unfamiliar area of speech.[32] Insofar as one deals with constantly finding new modes of (self)description, there is the 'expansion of the combat zone' (Michel Houellebecq) by way of metaphorics.

Given this backdrop and his own premises, Rorty is not in a position to prescribe which way of speaking we should prefer; he is not even able to justify his claim according to which we are called to multiply our modes of expression – our 'vocabularies' or our 'descriptions' that are often inspired by literature.

It is not an imperative that governs here but, rather, an invitational gesture to eventually make that invitation look suggestive and exciting. The dubious hope that one single vocabulary could be sufficient for describing everything has to be abandoned when facing the variety of contexts, along with the richness of expressions, metaphors, and theories for one specific context.[33] To do this, fantasy is required, and fantasy is, according to Rorty, no longer a faculty that produces representational images, but he characterizes it 'as the ability to change social practices by proposing advantageous new uses of marks and noises'.[34]

In later texts, Rorty leaves this invitational gesture behind when presenting the possibility of constantly redescribing oneself as a task to be undertaken; this would be necessary if privileging education over knowledge is to be taken seriously.[35] On the other hand, he characterizes the plurality of (and pluralizing) languages as a 'cultural politics' that is a debate about which concepts should be used in which way. However, in doing this, new purposes and new norms are established.[36]

There are in fact normative intentions behind this oscillation between invitation and the imperative to engage in redescriptions. Concerning the link between literature and morals, and between reading and self-extension, Rorty adds: 'The hope is that if one understands enough poems, enough religions, enough societies, enough philosophies, one will have made oneself into something worth one's own understanding.'[37] There is an additional aspect motivating the celebration of redescribing oneself – a therapeutic one.[38] However, the focus lies on the hope, maybe even the late-humanistic expectation, that our language has educative force, that the plurality of languages makes us richer by new and alien experiences and that this richness won't cause the distancing of the other, but will rather strengthen the sensitive insight into the variety of ways of living, as well as into the limits of one's own way. It is this understanding and acknowledgement which, in Rorty's terminology, makes us 'liberal' – as a beneficial mixture of sensitivity to other things, as well as curiosity for the new. For liberals – here, Rorty follows Judith Shklar's definition – the worst that people can do is to behave cruelly towards other sentient creatures.[39] The plurality of (and pluralizing) languages has one single and, in the end, genuinely moral sense: to become humble and to never be cruel again.[40]

This idea of linguistic and narrative identity invites criticism, or at least a bit of reservation: hasn't Rorty's educational humanism already been disproven for a long time? Isn't his fight against cruelty merely negative and, hence, reductive? And how could Rorty justify the implicit, and also latent, norm of 'cultural politics' under his self-imposed premises? But one might recall: Rorty does not pretend to be able to justify a 'theory' or an 'account'; he only claims to make his approach look more attractive than the alternatives.

There is also an additional concern that entails an internal criticism. Rorty does not pay sufficient heed to the biographical limitations to adopting constantly-new – religious, political, social, psychoanalytical, etc. – descriptions. There are some descriptions which are a better fit, and then there are others with which we are connected in such a way that the search for alternatives is tantamount to suspending our already-developed identity. Not all options are 'vivid options' for someone or for everyone.[41] The limits of linguistic and narrative self-extension, or the self-metaphorization of the human are neglected by Rorty. However, this prescribed nonconformism suppresses the fact that excessive self-extension might lead to the dangerous loss of oneself. With all due sympathy for Rorty's metaphorical humanism, the endless search for additional forms of articulation rather undermines a strong self, instead of making it sustainably immune to antiliberal cruelty.[42] Self-affirmation resembles in Rorty – and contrary to Nietzsche's account – the permanent pressure of expansion; it does not represent a form of sovereign self-acceptance.[43]

One might try to constructively combine these limitations with attempts to constantly redescribe and understand oneself differently in the framework of Rorty's postmetaphysical hermeneutics. In doing this, one has to study the scientifically and literarily acquired vocabularies and their relation to one another. And then, the comparisons between them become as illuminating as they are unavoidable.

2.3 Between vocabularies, or philosophy as comparativism

As we have seen, Rorty makes a great case for transforming the *vertical alignments* between representation and that which is represented to *horizontal comparisons* between different vocabularies that no longer have a representative role. As we have also seen, the attempt to relate two ontologically different elements to one another is given up here; hence, we are now dealing with two different modes of articulation that ontologically belong to the same category.[44] This alternative can also be expressed using a comparative vocabulary: accordingly, in the first case we are dealing with two elements that represent different categories where the possibility of comparing them becomes precarious; in the other case, this problem is no longer there because the elements belong to the same class and their comparability is secured.[45]

Rorty himself puts comparison at the centre of philosophical activity – and this move is completely consistent with the line of thinking expressed by refuting the correspondence between language and world. As soon as the alignment of linguistic units with reality is no longer possible, we are left with comparing different ways of expressing and understanding ourselves. As Rorty says, 'all (that) philosophy should do is compare and contrast cultural traditions', to which he adds: 'So (philosophy) is a study of the comparative advantages and disadvantages of the various ways of talking which our race has invented.'[46] Rorty also introduces alternative labels for the comparative tasks of philosophy. For instance, he considers Hegel's 'dialectical method' not primarily as a mode of argumentation but, rather, an expression of literary craft which plays off vocabularies against others – without a higher synthesis. Instead of dialectics, Rorty states, one could also speak of literary criticism.[47]

What could be meant by 'literary criticism' becomes clearer when one accepts Rorty's broader concept of 'literature'. It is not an artistic genre that is primarily meant here; rather, Rorty invites us to treat other modes of existential and theoretical articulation in the same way as literature by suggesting that the difference between theories, models, literary writings, religious texts, etc. should be disclaimed by virtue of their closeness or distance to an allegedly external truth. 'Literature' functions, then, synonymously with what Rorty calls descriptions, redescriptions or vocabularies. He is not so much interested in clarifying these concepts as he is in the idea, expressed by these identifications, of giving up a robust criterion for the 'right description' in the sense of having a neutral reference in relation to something non-linguistic. In this sense, the world is in fact 'well lost'.[48]

What is left are comparisons between vocabularies, i.e. inter-literary connections that refer to the general structure of comparisons and the concrete practice of comparing:

F: *a subject of comparison (1) compares different comparative items (2) in view of a comparative regard (3) within a particular context (4) and with a comparative purpose (5).*[49]

This (slightly simplified) formula F could be applied to two scenarios that are dealt with as supposedly belonging together with Rorty but that should rather be distinguished. The call for understanding oneself through constantly new descriptions, for trying out new vocabularies, could be interpreted in two ways: either as a *conditional acknowledgement of already-existing articulations* or as *a mode of creating new 'literature'*. And this heuristic alternative between reception and creativity has consequences for the form that comparisons might adopt.

The first case concerns comparing different, already-existing vocabularies. This is the specialty of Rorty's ironist who does not have better access to the 'facts', but who has simply seen more, experienced more, read more. Rorty hopes that this plurality counterbalances the temptation to be caught in one single vocabulary.[50] It is this plurality that drives comparisons to relate different literatures to one another, which amounts to divergent procedures of comparing. We can distinguish between three versions.

(i) *The standard comparison.* By referring to the formula F above, one can describe the standard comparison as follows: a person (1) compares, for instance, a democratic system with a meritocratic one (2) in regard to the question as to which one will be more beneficial for mutual coexistence (3), while this choice has to be made in the framework of a liberal order (4) and for the purpose that as many people as possible can participate in it (5). (1) represents the often-implicit individualism in Rorty; collectives, as comparative agents or subjects of self-understanding, are not the focus here. This is even true when political alternatives as incompatible forms of governance are at stake (2); the criterion of adequacy of these forms is open to interpretation and different ways of making sense of it (3) – however, this criterion is closely connected to the context of comparison, which is, in Rorty's case, always the context of liberalism as avoidance of cruelty (4). In this qualification of purpose in supporting an inclusive political participation lie the remnants of consequentialism that Rorty does not consider to be a 'moral theory' (5). The reason for this is the aforementioned reservation against any theory; moreover, it is based on the fact that the elements (3: comparative regard) and (5: purpose of comparison) call for justification whereas justifications, as Wittgenstein once said, 'come to an end at some point' and underline the contingency of our social environment.

(ii) *Circularity.* Scenario (i) remains slightly innocent because it is based on the mostly unfulfilled condition that those comparative elements are stable or at least sufficiently invariant. In a playful setting of trying out different ways of understanding and self-understanding, this condition is not fulfilled; hence, the comparative elements are in a dynamic, often-circular relation to one another. Two examples: imagine a person trying to understand herself by relying on religious language-games from the Christian tradition and exploring, as an alternative or supplement, the vocabulary of psychoanalysis. The question of whether this comparison is really that active or is, rather, performed in this sovereign way can remain an open one. What is relevant here is the simple fact that the comparing subject (1) does not remain unaffected by the choice of comparative objects (2) and by the purpose of the comparative procedure (5). The comparing subject changes herself by preferring a particular vocabulary or by subsequently adopting it. Put in a stronger way: people are nothing but webs of narrative (self)descriptions – a notion which is itself just another narrative option, not a thesis on how things are 'in reality'.[51] Rorty's repeated claim that one should create an 'interesting' self is already an assertion that concerns the qualification of the subject. Thus, there is a dynamic and comparative relation between (1), (3) and (5). The practice of comparing does not always rely, however, on stable comparative elements; there are also arrangements – depending on the context – in which the choice of a *tertium* or *relata* may transform the subject of comparison.

Here is a second example that does not illustrate the dynamics but, rather, comparative circularity: Rorty links the idea of liberalism to the avoidance of cruelty. He thinks that authors like Orwell and Nabukov have done the most for that liberal sensitivity. A rather static reading of that claim might say that a novel like *1984* is preferable to other critical future scenarios; one might also emphasize the circularity between novels, comparative regards and comparative purposes by putting the stress on the possibility that vocabularies such as the one in *1984* have brought about our sense of what cruelty means in the first place and how it shows itself. Therefore, the comparative setting is inverted: the comparative items (2) establish the *tertium comparationis* (3) in relation to concrete contexts (4) and the purposes of comparative descriptions (5) that are already determined by the comparative regard.

(iii) *Revisions.* Another case considers the diachronic element of comparing and, hence, the historical effect on comparative items. A paradigmatic example is the confrontation between religion and natural sciences – a constellation that gains prominence in Rorty's later work.[52] The rivalry between confessionally-fragmented religion and modern science leads to religion's defeat through the (self)diversification of the sciences – but, after that defeat, it also became a kind of self-transforming religion. In other words, the question as to which vocabulary could more successfully take on the explanatory tasks regarding the genesis and development of the universe brought the victory to physics and, much later, to evolutionary biology. However, the consequence drawn from this defeat can also be expressed in a comparative manner: namely, that the inferior item of the comparison has to be understood differently, by acknowledging that this item begins to redescribe itself: no longer in an explanatory way (*why-questions* regarding the world), but in an existential-orientational manner (*how-questions* regarding ways of living). Hence, a completely new comparison is required after having – in a quasi-revolutionary fashion – replaced the relevant *tertium*. The traditional comparison between science and religion presupposed that both items had the same task: adopting explanatory and justifying aims. Insofar as this is taken to be correct, we already have an evident result. But it is precisely this result that caused a different understanding as to what religion is all about: not about explanations and justifications, but about a way of leading one's life.

Let us now turn to the second half of the heuristic opposition above. After considering comparisons *between* already-existing vocabularies, we now have to deal with comparisons in the creation of *new* vocabularies. It must be acknowledged that the limits between both versions are not firm, and yet, this distinction might nevertheless be helpful. Rorty describes the creation of new ways of articulation using a rather activist vocabulary. Following Nietzsche and the literary critic Harold Bloom, Rorty speaks repeatedly of "strong poets."[53] These poets not only 'poeticize' their way of life through interesting modes of expression and metaphors, but also expand, or even create, these linguistic and imaginary tools. They achieve this by discovering or inventing alternatives and, in some cases, better-functioning descriptions in relation to particular purposes. Here, the structure of comparisons seems to remain rather stable: the *tertium comparationis* (3), in relation to which established or new ways of talking are compared to one another, is stable – and hence the context (4) and purpose (5) of the comparative arrangement are as well. Therefore, a new comparative item has to be found that is able to assert itself against the ones that are already there. This new item might fulfil the goal of finding 'interesting' expressions in a more satisfactory way. However, it still must be asked: *fulfilling better – better for whom? In front of which audience?* One could speak of an explorative comparison that takes on different forms, three essential versions of which must be distinguished.

(iv) *Self-extension*. Here too, this kind of comparison might be described by way of an example used by Rorty himself (although in a slightly different context): Freud's psychoanalysis. According to Rorty, Freud is the first who presented – relying on similar accounts in Schopenhauer – a comprehensive and, to a large extent, consistent description of human beings. Rorty stresses the fact that psychoanalysis is an example for a new vocabulary and that its central notion of the 'unconscious' is not a 'lower' register, but just another additional way of thinking about ourselves. It is one mode among many that has to be sufficiently consistent to be distinguishable from other kinds of self-description.[54] Rorty, following Donald Davidson, states that, within the framework of a holistic approach to personal identity, a person *is* identical with 'a coherent and plausible set of beliefs and desires' (147). Rorty does not clarify how far that consistency goes – i.e. in the face of biographical discontinuities and the *intra*-personal diversity of self-understanding. Instead, Rorty highlights the essential idea that consciousness, passions, the unconscious, as well as the doctrine of instances (including its triad of I, Thou and Super-Ego) do not stand for things as-of-yet undiscovered, but rather they represent 'alternative extrapolations from a common experience' (151).

At the same time, Rorty limits the range of relevance of the vocabulary of psychoanalysis to relate it exclusively to projects for private improvement and intimate self-expansion, but not to social or public purposes. For these, we would need a totally different set of tools. Freud, Rorty thinks, did not contribute to a social theory, but he has been of invaluable significance for the development of an aesthetic life with interesting descriptions – with the intention of turning us into more sensitive human beings. Rorty adds:

> The availability of a richer vocabulary of moral deliberation is what one chiefly has in mind when one says that we are, morally speaking, more sensitive and sophisticated than our ancestors or than our younger selves.
>
> 155

Obviously, Rorty himself mixes up this precarious dualism between the private and public domains, considering that becoming 'more sensitive and sophisticated' is in fact a socially significant feature of a liberal society whose first and foremost aim is to avoid cruelty. This fight is not restricted to the private sphere. However, for our purposes it is more important that Rorty calls for an orienting comparison between different vocabularies of 'moral reflection' (154) with the conclusion that Freud had opened up new ways of leading an aesthetic life – through irony, playfulness and new choices for self-description. Hence, one should prefer psychoanalysis over alternative kinds of identity-forming narratives (cf. 155).

We can leave it open as to whether this claim is justified – an answer would depend on additional factors belonging to a sufficiently-exact description of comparisons: the comparing subject and its audience, the relevant contexts and comparative purposes. What is important, however, is the presupposed stability of those comparative acts. For stabilizing comparisons, one has to fix the available descriptions (older narratives, psychological or religious vocabularies), as well as the comparative regards (for instance, the degree of 'interestingness' with its own subcriteria). This fixation is necessary to bring about a new comparative item that might win the ironic-comparative competition. The success of psychoanalysis is, for Rorty, identical with winning that battle.[55]

(v) *Transforming the comparative regard.* New comparative items (*relata*) could sustainably transform the character of the comparative regard (*tertium*) and, especially, its concrete (sub)features. This is true for psychoanalysis as well. Rorty's late-romantic criterion of 'interestingness' as *tertium* could be understood in a new way within a psychoanalytic frame. Now the fascination with 'unconscious' aspects of ourselves and the acknowledgment of the non-transparency of our own selves becomes revitalized. This extension does not leave the initial comparison untouched. The meaning of the comparative regard has shifted in a crucial and effective way. The Enlightenment ideal of self-transparency and self-control is not only substituted by the acceptance of the impossible completion of that very ideal; rather, the *tertium* is even turned into its complete opposite.

This transformation is hard to understand and to appreciate without the historical context of a rational 'disenchantment" of our world.[56] Only then, the acknowledgment that one is not "the master in one's own house' is by no means a sign of a shortcoming but, rather, an expression of one's own inscrutability. Through therapy and dream interpretation one tries to get access to one's own personality; hence, the promise of a secret is no longer 'out there' or to be found in nature but lies instead somewhere 'inside'. Rorty, however, weakens this extension of a criterion for what it means to be an 'interesting' self by refuting the idea of a true or false insight concerning that self. Integrating 'hidden' facets of one's own character represents just another narrative, not a hidden truth. This narrative, Rorty adds, might fulfil the aim of helpful self-descriptions 'better' than other pro-romantic descriptions.

(vi) *Plural narratives.* We have, so far, distinguished between two cases of dealing creatively with vocabularies: introducing an original vocabulary (iv), as well as transforming the *tertium comparationis*, including different comparative results (v). For Rorty, the significant role, however, is played by a third case, namely a certain dealing with literature and here especially with novels. This case too oscillates between the reception of already-existing vocabularies and the introduction of new ones. In adopting existing ways of articulation, the creative element consists of bringing plural narratives into a more-or-less coherent relation to one another in order to expand oneself as self (similar to (iv)). Rorty's appreciation for literary authors does not come as a surprise because these writers sometimes suggest completely new ways of considering people, contexts and values. And they bring these plural ways in tension with one another.

As already mentioned, 'literature' is, for Rorty, not a term for a genre of artistic expression; rather, it signifies a function of texts that provides interesting means to think in new ways. Thus, every text could potentially turn into literature, although Rorty usually speaks of literature in the sense of narratives and stories or of novels. Paying attention to literature is, for Rorty, linked to ambitious expectations. These expectations even include a history of successive substitutions ranging from religion via philosophy, to privileging literature over theory.[57] If one characterizes Rorty's appreciation of literature – i.e. reading as many texts as possible or even creating these texts, as 'strong poets' do – in terms of moral philosophy, an affinity to virtue-ethical accounts is hard to overlook. Then, intentions or consequences of actions are no longer the central interest but, rather, persons whose education informs their actions become the focus.[58]

Appreciating literature – and nowadays also film[59] – on behalf of moral philosophy is already an established part of today's ethical discourse. Here, an important role is played by the questions of whether literature, as mentioned at the outset, just has the character of an example for general, independently formulated theories or whether there is a concreteness in literature that is not captured by the generality of theories. Put in more technical terms: does literature have a cognitive content which goes beyond merely illustrating theories or is literature an exclusively noncognitive form, from which one could extract more general claims? Rorty, however, does not seem to embrace this opposition that is itself theoretical in nature. His reservation against moral theories leads him to see an intrinsic value in narratives. Following John Dewey, Rorty states that the most important instrument for the good is not abstraction but imagination.[60] Literature as example thus entails everything necessary for a morally relevant 'self-transformation'.[61]

Novels, Rorty says, specifically contribute to emphasizing the contingency of our forms of life. Therefore, we may circumvent our 'self-referentiality' insofar as literary alternatives clarify to which extent our standpoints are variant, but also how divergent and potentially alienating life can be.[62] Novels confront the reader with this variety; they expand our self-understanding, as well as the readiness to tolerate alterity and otherness or even to appreciate them. Purification through the 'true' story is not within reach here. It is rather about extending one's own horizon, which has consequences for one's own self-image and ideas of mutual coexistence.

At this point, comparisons become relevant again because it is not sufficient to merely juxtapose plural narratives. Two forms of comparative-creative irony should be distinguished here. And for this distinction, we can refer to Rorty's own literary examples: as shown above in (ii), Rorty's main liberal concern is to strengthen our sensitivity to cruelty. For doing this, Rorty relies on novels by Orwell and Nabukov that have informed not only our sensitivity, but also our awareness of what can be considered to be cruel in the first place. If one takes these novels to be moral instruments for cultivating and extending this sensitivity, a specific regard emerges in relation to which literary sources may be compared to one another to eventually recognize which ones best fulfil that purpose. Extending the spectrum and the sources – as in (v) – might cause a shift in the meaning of the comparative regard. Then, the criterion according to which one compares transforms itself through additional comparative items. This dynamic may also be relevant to the second case in which the focus is not on a comparison in regard to an already established *tertium*. Rather, it is about extending the self by adopting more and more narratives and exposing oneself to them.

This becomes clearer when turning to Rorty's reading of classical novels with female protagonists from nineteenth century literature.[63] Here, the question is not so much about whether Ibsen's *Nora* or Flaubert's *Madame Bovary* fulfil certain purposes more effectively. Rather, comparing aspects and traits of these characters can contribute to expanding our sense of what is possible and deepen our understanding of the different forms that life can take on. In this broader sense, comparative regards, contexts and purposes are not predefined, but emerge latently to be replaced again by new comparative constellations – for example, seeing Fontane's *Effi Briest* performed on stage may broaden the 'wide field' of possibilities once again. Both forms are creative because they are based on the active acquisition, as well as on new combinations, of narrative possibilities. In the first case, one refers to novels within a particular frame and setting to compare different narratives in view of an established *tertium*. In the second case, one integrates more and more comparative items into the comparing act only to find out recursively which regard one could – or even should – use to compare these items.

3 Nearing the end: irony, comparatively

Rorty's comparative ironism of constantly finding new descriptions might suffer from numerous internal difficulties: for instance, the largely neglected fact that we do not always choose vocabularies, but are rather thrown into them; the existential limitations of these ironic choices; the somehow-artificial compulsion towards nonconformism that is in serious tension with the desire (and even the necessity) to develop a sufficiently-stable self. Despite this need for correction, there is a decisive relevance in Rorty's comparativism. In the case of dealing with already-existing vocabularies, there are dynamic structures that allow for ordinary comparisons (in which all comparative elements are fixed; (i)), as well as for circular and revisionary versions (that try out certain comparative elements to replace them with other elements or to transform one comparative item in the course of comparing; (ii) and (iii)).

Things are slightly different in cases where new descriptions prevail against traditional articulations in fulfilling the comparative regard 'better' (iv). How one should assess the potential results depends on several background assumptions: for instance, whether the new is appreciated; to what extent the privilege is given to or taken away from the conservative; what is concretely meant by the comparative regard (for example, interestingness); and in which way this regard is qualified on its sublevel (for example, interestingness ... *as* relevance, surprise, creativity, nonconformity, etc.) (v). According to Rorty, it is especially literature that is capable of extending our vocabularies and to intentional ambivalences between juxtaposed vocabularies or newly created ones. In the one case, the value itself lies in the spectrum of possibilities and their expansion; in the other case, it is about a narrative that promises to better fulfil particular purposes (vi).

Rorty advocates for the replacement of problem-solving philosophy with a form of comparative literary criticism. Therefore, he bids farewell to metaphysical hopes for 'final' vocabularies in the name of an irony that constantly tries out new kinds of exemplary articulations in bringing them into a comparison – while doing this, as Anscombe says in the motto at the outset of this chapter, in 'an area where it is not because of any gap, but is in principle the case, that there is no account except by way of examples'. Despite this narrative which calls for substituting philosophy with literature, Rorty distances himself from so-called 'meta-stories'.[64] However, his plea for a playful engagement with manifold examples and plural narratives is itself based on a new, exciting – yet also strained – re-narration, i.e. a 'meta-story'.

Part III

On Relocating Incomparability

Comparisons are obviously an important part of our everyday discourse, as well as integral elements of scientific procedures. And the same goes for the notion that something is incomparable with something (or even anything) else. To speak of incomparability in ordinary contexts usually means that x is not only incomparable to y, but that it is beyond comparison in general. Withdrawing x from the possibility of being comparable *tout court* is an attempt to highlight x's specific status as something singular or unique. To compare x to y would then undermine x's status – which also means that comparability would exclude singularity and uniqueness. However, the question remains whether this inference is correct and valid; it depends on the precise grammar of the concepts involved, and it oscillates between two different cases subsumed under the label of 'incomparability': namely, cases in which particular comparisons meet difficulties and cases in which a concrete comparison is impossible. It is important to distinguish between these two scenarios, and some of the confusion from which the debate about incomparability suffers stems from neglecting this distinction.

These difficulties of confounding cases are also relevant within more technical and scientific discourses. In aesthetics, speaking of the 'sublime' often suggests incomparability and, conversely, the danger of losing this element of sublimity through comparison. In ethics, dealing with a plurality of values leads often enough to the idea that these values (or some of them) entertain a relation of incomparability to one another. In science and the philosophy of science, the notion of incommensurability between rival theories has already become a classic and is sometimes combined with the claim that being incommensurable (or incompatible) entails incomparability as well. However, the idea that x's sublimity would be subverted by the comparability of x (to what?) is, in this form, either unclear or contradictory as long as sublimity might itself be the result of a particular comparison. The plurality of values is a culturally pressing problem, and valuing particular traditions can bring the conflict with other traditions to the fore, but this does not *per se* imply incomparable scenarios. Finally, incommensurable theories may, and often do, confront us with the problem of deciding which theoretical offer is preferable. These uncertainties could be caused by other difficulties, such as the fuzzy relation between empirical facts (data) and general claims (theory), or the notion of incommensurability is itself based on the comparison of theories.

Therefore, it is essential to differentiate between the following alternatives:

- difficulties in comparing x and y (for instance, lacking a form of measurement or scale) versus a strict incomparability of x;
- an incomparability of x to y versus an incomparability of x to everything else;
- comparability including clear results (such as 'better than . . .') versus a fuzzy constellation that is itself a comparative result (and not an instance of incomparability);
- incomparability as the technical impossibility of comparing x and y versus incomparability as the impossibility *for someone* to compare x to y (or anything else).

This final part of the book attempts to pay specific attention to these complex difficulties, and it amounts – as the title suggests – to 'relocating incomparability'. At the centre of this section lies the distinction between what might be called *structural versus normative incomparability*. This opposition reflects what was just presented as incomparability on technical grounds versus incomparability as someone's unwillingness or personal incapacity to compare in the first place. Chapter 7 is dedicated to this first case by analytically entering the ramified debate about the potential limits of comparing x and y to eventually repudiate the idea that there is something like structural incomparability. Chapter 8 deals with a particular kind of incomparability that combines structural, as well as normative (meaning evaluative or moral), considerations. The specific element of this combination is an *indexical aspect* integrating the standpoint of the comparing person into an account of comparisons and their limits. The last chapter strengthens the indexical element by focusing on *incomparability on normative grounds*: one could compare, technically speaking, but one is not able to do so due to evaluative or moral reasons. What this precisely means might be more easily grasped by referring to an example from literature and its 'thick description'. J.M. Coetzee's novel *Elizabeth Costello* not only circles around a highly provocative comparison and its refutation in the name of morality; it also underlines, once again, the embeddedness of comparing as a practice (in relation to other practices; see chapter 6 on comparative irony). Then, we will be in a position to better understand the 'curious case of normative incomparability' and its challenges for its heterogenous audience to which we, as readers, also belong.

7

Against Structural Incomparability

1 Introduction: incomparability as a marginalized classic

While 'the incomparable' denotes something extraordinary, the use of that term, however, is not. The fact that a person, an event or an experience appears to be incomparable for someone is a common feature of our ordinary language. Incomparability is, some would hold, based on a certain structure and its limits or even breakdown; but more to the point, the incomparable as a language-game played by certain speakers expresses their perceiving a particular and peculiar constellation or their being confronted with someone truly special, respectively. It indicates something absolutely spectacular or totally horrendous combined with an enigmatic appearance of being beyond every scale and measurement or belonging to the elite class of pure uniqueness and singularity.

In this sense, a lover might say that her loved one is unique; remember Sinéad O'Connor singing the 1990 Prince cover *Nothing Compares to You*. Or recall again the constant warning not to relativize the Holocaust by comparing it to other instances of mass murder and mass destruction. Or take the cinematic masterpiece *Citizen Kane*, for which Orson Welles – himself an 'incomparably' charismatic figure – was especially praised in terms of the cinematography, musical dramaturgy, the experiments with lighting and use of shadows, and the narrative anachronisms and flashbacks in that movie, which have been regarded as truly innovative in redefining cinema. Accordingly, there is a telling tension between the widespread application of the incomparable as an evaluative notion on the one hand, and on the other, the extraordinary character of the content deeply appreciated or intensely feared by someone for whom the incomparable is exactly that – incomparable.

There are only two more concrete issues in which comparative moves and their limits do play a significant role in contemporary philosophy, namely the incommensurability of different scientific theories and the plurality of divergent moral, political or private values. In this chapter, I will concentrate primarily on this second dimension because I take the classical debate about incommensurable theories to be wrong-headed. The debate overemphasizes theoretical differences, neglecting the diachronic and synchronic resemblances between theories, even to the point of compartmentalizing them and thus, also, their underlying conceptual schemes or even world-views.[1] Hence, in overviewing the current debate on incomparability we are left with comparing values – but comparing in a very broad sense, as the examples usually referred to for illustrating the pertinent theoretical points show: valuing friendship more than money, weighing up divergent goods such as security over freedom, or as lingering over the different career paths of being a lawyer or a musician.[2]

Now, claiming that incomparability represents a prominent issue in current philosophical thinking would be an exaggeration. Where one actually deals with this problem, the approaches in question suffer from several methodological limitations. The contextual embeddedness and indexical character of 'the incomparable' (here just used to embrace all instances of incomparability) have often been neglected. But this is not the only problematic restriction within the philosophical discourse, insofar as all its considerations are, to a large extent, focused on two aspects: number one, the relation between comparison and choice linked to a particular idea of rationality; number two, and more importantly, incomparability as a structural impossibility of comparing items. And both aspects are debatable.

As we will see in greater detail, it has often been stated that rational choice is based on the possibility of comparing options at hand.[3] The rationality of decisions, then, is bound to the act of comparing, whereas incomparability seems to threaten that justification in eventually leading to irrationality in theory and in our practical life. But this, as we shall see too, is based on an impoverished notion of making choices and decisions; it relies on an unnecessarily narrow idea of rationality, disregarding the actual depth of being confronted with conflicting values as well as the ways we are in fact dealing with these tensions – not irrationally, but not comparatively either. So much, for now, on the first problematic aspect. The second concerns characterizing incomparability as a structural breakdown, i.e. the impossible application of positive value relations (such as 'better than . . .') to two or more items to be compared. Almost the entire debate on incomparability is concentrated on pinning down the precise reasons for that breakdown by finding it, mostly, in divergent instances of indeterminacy and vagueness, either ontically or semantically.[4] Here again, we meet problematic and partly confused moves based on an overexertion of comparisons and too high expectations towards comparative procedures.

A side debate that in fact claims some prominence within the discussion about incomparability is the 'possibility of parity'.[5] It is a critique of the standard view according to which two items are comparable as long as A is better than B, or the other way around, or both are equally good. The standard view, then, implies this 'trichotomy thesis' and is challenged by arguing for a fourth relation between A and B labelled as 'being on a par'.[6] In parity cases, none of the three traditional value relations hold between A and B – and yet, they are nevertheless comparable and, for that reason, a justified choice in favour of A or B is still possible. This brings us back to the narrow notion of (practical) rationality and a too hasty defence of comparability. Parity extends, it is assumed, the scope of comparability and justified choice. However, this somehow mysterious fourth relation is hard to describe on logical grounds as a 'properly basic'[7] and irreducibly additional value relation. Moreover, it unfortunately remains an open question of what exactly to do in practice if two items are on a par.

Up to this point, I have done no more than introduce the kind of approach that dominates the debate about incomparability: its narrowing focus on comparison and justified choice; its decontextualizing focus on structural limits of comparisons as the source for incomparable cases; and its critical focus on parity to expand the realm of comparability. The next four sections of this chapter will be dedicated to this kind of account including its threefold focus – to then create conceptual space for a fresh start in thinking about incomparability. I will be, first, defending a necessarily imprecise fourth relation between two items to be compared called *fuzzy equality*. Second, I will be critical of structurally based cases of incomparability by attempting to present a 'therapeutic' explanation for confusions on which these alleged cases rely, and in casting doubts that structural incomparability is intelligible in the first place. I will, thirdly, elaborate on what has been called "constitutive incomparability"[8] amounting to a new interpretation of that equally vague, but intriguing concept. This enables us to integrate the person for whom something counts as incomparable and to do tentative justice to incomparability as a language-game by which we articulate the evaluative uniqueness of a person, an event, or an experience. In this course, a rather technical account of incomparability has to be deepened by a sensitivity for those people using 'incomparability' to express their appreciation for something taken out of comparative exchangeability. An underlying interest lies in the attempt to redescribe potentially hard choices by asking which resources we actually refer to in making decisions – beyond pure and mere comparisons.

2 Choices and comparisons

Why should we philosophically care about incomparability at all? Many don't, but for those who do, incomparability is part of a much larger debate concerning practical reasoning and deliberation. This is particularly relevant for 'hard cases' defined as instances in which there is no overall preference for *A* or for *B*, but in which, nevertheless, a decision has to be made.[9] These 'hard cases' are linked to (in)comparability in a certain way. Ruth Chang describes this connection as follows:

> Indeed, if, as many philosophers believe, the comparability of the alternatives is necessary for justified choice between them, hard cases are very plausibly at the root of moral dilemmas and the most intractable sorts of practical conflict generally.[10]

As mentioned at the outset, the possibility of comparing *A* and *B* is here considered to be a necessary (and sufficient?) condition for rational choice; or put the other way around: without the comparability of alternatives a rational choice between them is deemed to be impossible. What is called 'rational' here might be translated as 'justified by reason and weighing up preferences'. Hence, the act of comparing is or belongs, for authors like Chang, to the arsenal of practical justification that is, in 'hard cases', undermined as soon as comparisons are not available. This pairing of rationality of choices with the comparing of its options explains, first, why rational choice scholars take problems concerning incomparability to be philosophically more urgent than those more prominent ones running under the heading of the incommensurability of (scientific) theories. And it explains, second, why many authors invest in either denying the existence of incomparability by explaining merely alleged cases away (*epistemicists*); or tracing the limits of comparisons back to other grounds, such as indeterminacy and vagueness (*indeterminists*), or by extending the realm of comparability by extending its scope through an additional value relation (*comparabilitists*). Hence, the defence of comparability is tantamount to securing practical rationality that is, again, threatened by repudiating all three exit strategies, partly by having a different idea of rationality in relation to comparing alternatives (*incomparabilitists*).[11]

Accordingly, the anti-incomparability-fraction commits itself to a standpoint introduced as 'comparativism' and circumscribed, again by Chang, as 'the view that a comparison of the alternatives with respect to an appropriate covering value "determines" a choice as justified, where this relation of determination is to be filled out in due course'.[12] Additionally, it is claimed that these comparative procedures are *always* possible and that *every* plausible theory of practical reason must be 'comparativist' in holding that a comparative (value) relation between the options in respect to what is relevant in a particular choice determines a justified outcome. Hence, the idea that there is no justified decision between alternatives without comparing them turns here into the far stronger claim that this justification is always achievable because of comparisons being ubiquitous.[13]

There are far-reaching metaphysical assumptions in order to implement comparisons as being ubiquitous and to eventually substantialize comparativism. I will quickly refer to two versions of that move based on establishing one single and all-embracing aspect ultimately relevant for every comparison of values and evaluative options. The one option is utilitarianism and its claim that the bottom line of all acting and deciding is, or should be, maximizing utility (leaving here all problems of defining 'maximizing' and 'utility' aside).[14] The other option is based on the Good in a Moorean sense that is, it is said, the formal while unanalysable object of all wanting, whereas this wanting creates the background of our deeds and decisions.[15] The first version appears to be *procedural* in not saying what is right or wrong, but in delivering a procedure to determine right and wrong on the basis of utility as the covering value; the second version appears to be *substantial* in introducing the Good in reference to which comparing acts and justified decisions are possible. In both cases, one single comparative regard is metaphysically assumed by claiming that one ultimate and overall value structures our forms of life.

To summarize, we are dealing here with the three following claims:

(i) A rational and therefore *justified choice* between A and B is constituted by comparing A and B;
(ii) *Comparativism* is true, which means that weighing up A and B comparatively is always possible and, hence, a justified choice is at hand;
(iii) It is possible to establish comparativism *metaphysically* by defending an all-embracing value by which comparative acts are enabled.

The claims (i), (ii) and (iii) are logically independent of each other though factually related in the debate about incomparability. I will leave (iii) aside since this claim is burdened by strong assumptions that I take to be wrong because of convincing objections to utilitarianism and because of doubts that a Moorean Good (even if it 'exists') would help in comparative scenarios.[16] I am also critical of (ii) because comparativism is either plainly false – there *are* cases of incomparability – or it is based on conceptual stipulation labelling cases of comparative limits in such a way that in fact there remains space for incomparability, but not for 'incomparability', hence for the phenomenon in question without labelling it as 'incomparable' (see section 6.1). The crucial claim for the relevance of incomparability as a philosophical topic is (i) which also suffers from shortcomings. It is just wrong that a rational choice between *A* and *B* always implies comparing *A* and *B*. Take a passionate football player having been confronted with all sorts of professional career alternatives. Did he necessarily choose that life option due to his preference for it compared to other paths open to him? No, he might have felt the duty to pursue his talent without comparatively weighing up alternatives. Or imagine someone confronted with a very important life choice, for instance having to decide what to study, medicine or fine arts. Maybe every comparison fails in this case, and this student 'jumps into' one option and makes it right for herself by being committed to it, not for antecedent reasons, but through realizing and adopting that option existentially. There is no comparison at work, but there is no irrationality or lack of rationality either. Far richer and 'thicker' descriptions of cases like these are required than the ones presented by rational choice defenders.[17] Only then will we really appreciate the ramified usage of comparisons and their limits. These limits, however, do not undermine, but rather clarify the philosophical importance of comparisons and the debate about incomparability. To not always compare does not mean not to compare at all.

3 Incomparability: a first sketch

There are different ways to think of incomparability as being *structurally* impossible, i.e. dealing with a notion of incomparability that is not based on existential, moral or political convictions ruling out certain, potentially possible comparative acts, but on formal difficulties within the comparative structure. Leaving contextual considerations aside for a moment, the structural breakdown of a comparison has to be retraced, then, either to the comparative items (*relata*) or to the comparative regard (*tertium*). Both versions will play a role; a preliminary sketch might be concentrated on the regard of comparing items.

A first and common attempt to think of incomparability might state that the absence of a shared scale or measurement for *A* and *B* causes the impossibility of comparing *A* and *B*. While it is simple to hold that Christiano Ronaldo scored more often than Toni Kroos did in the last season (just for the record, both are football players for Juventus Turin and Real Madrid, respectively), it is not that simple to hold that Christiano Ronaldo scored fewer than LeBron James did in that period (playing basketball for the LA Lakers). In the first case we have scalable items and a common scale; in the second case we have, again, scalable items, but different kinds of sports that may call for different scales. A comparison might be considered to be possible but seems to be rather ill-suited. This last problem is more evident in cases in which we lack scalable items as well as a common scale: who was more creative in and more influential on rock music, David Bowie or Roxie Music with Bryan Ferry? Most would go with Bowie, but I am not that sure, and what kind of disagreement is looming here?

While delaying meeting this important question we could draw three lessons from this first and too simple account: one, as long as we have a scale and items belonging to the category to which the scale is applicable, incomparability does not arise. Two, this first lesson begs, obviously, the difficult question of how to implement the idea that different items belong to the 'same' (Ronaldo – Kroos) or to the 'relevant' category (Ronaldo – James?) (we will come back to this in section 6.2). Three, the claim according to which the absence of a shared scale for *A* and *B* causes the impossibility of comparing *A* and *B* is – in this generalized fashion – wrong. As already stated, for the majority, I suppose, David Bowie is more important than Bryan Ferry in regard to creativity and artistic influence. That I might disagree here does not render their comparison impossible although there is no clear measurement like scoring charts. Hence, comparability does not presuppose scalability; and incomparability is not coextensive with lacking a scale; often enough we *do* compare *A* and *B* without having a measurement at hand.

A second and a bit more sophisticated account of incomparability is focused less on the comparative regard, but more on the possible relations between the items. Starting off with comparability, it means (or, according to the standard view, is defined as) the relating of *A* to *B* by either being 'better than', 'worse than' or 'equally good' in terms of a particular regard.[18] This view is expressed by the so-called trichotomy thesis claiming that one of these three relations must hold between *A* and *B* to be comparable and that all three relations together exhaust the logical space in comparing *A* and *B*. This second claim is under pressure since authors like Ruth Chang are refuting the trichotomy thesis by defending a fourth comparative relation called parity (see section 5).[19]

Apart from this ramified debate one has to clarify what counts as a 'relation' between *A* and *B*. There are two limitations: (i) what we are talking about in this context are *logically irreducible* and therefore basic relations; the trichotomy thesis, thus, entails the claim that 'better than', 'worse than' or 'equally good' are of that kind, whereas, the parity thesis adds a fourth element enjoying, it is assumed, the same status. This does not exclude, however, that there are several other relations available – 'not worse than', 'at least as good as', etc. – but they are derivative in being definable by those basic relations.[20] (ii) For comparability to be possible, it is held, one needs a *positive value relation* stating what is actually the case between *A* and *B* (e.g. *A* is better than *B*) and not only saying what is not (e.g. *A* is not worse than *B*).

Given the fact that there are no comparisons between *A* and *B simpliciter*, but only in regard to a certain respect, a *tertium comparationis*, it follows that incomparability – like comparability (at least) a three-figure-relation – presupposes also a comparative respect while lacking a positive value relation (not necessarily a negative one). Or in definitive terms: 'two items are incomparable with respect to a covering value if, for every positive value relation relativized to that covering value, it is not true that it holds between them.'[21] Taking (i) and (ii) together, if 'better than', 'worse than' or 'equally good' (and 'being on a par') all fail in a comparative setting between *A* and *B*, both items are in fact incomparable.

The first account to define incomparability by reference to scalability was, in its generalized form, incorrect, but nevertheless instructive in giving us some lessons to learn; the second strikes me as showing opposite features by meeting well our intuitions about comparisons while remaining silent about the real reasons for incomparable cases. Incomparability between *A* and *B* is here based on lacking a positive value relation between them, which directs the attention to the real reasons of why that lack might have occurred (coming back to this point in section 6).

Before following that path, it is necessary to measure the conceptual neighbourhood of '(in)comparability'. To begin with, there are some specific features that comparability possesses. Among them are *categoriality, complementarity, reflexibility, transitivity*: meaning if *A* is comparable (with *B*) this is either true or false and not a matter of degree or grades; *A* is either comparable to *B* or not, no third option open;[22] while *A* might be comparable to something else, it is not comparable to itself (it is not better or worse than itself, but it is not equally good either, or on a par); and finally, if *A* is comparable with *B*, and *B* is with *C*, *A* is also with *C*. Now, when we refer to *in*comparability nothing changes in terms of categoriality, complementarity and reflexibility. Slightly different is the case of transitivity: it does, one might argue, *not* follow that if *A* is incomparable with *B*, and *B* is with *C*, that *A* is also incomparable with *C*. Take again an example: if you cannot decide what to prefer, an orange or an apple, and if you cannot decide between an apple and a banana, it does not follow that you do not know what to do when confronted with the admittedly trivial choice between an orange and a banana.[23]

One of the biggest sources for conceptual confusion is incomparability being often confounded with incommensurability as a covering term for relative, but different (moral) concepts.[24] However, it is helpful to preserve these differences that are only hidden by unqualified talk of incommensurable options.[25] One might denote options as *incompatible* (and not incomparable) if the choice in favour of the one option is only possible at the cost of the alternative – you can't have it both ways.[26] Different items, values for instance, are incommensurable, according to another account, if they cannot be reduced to one superior value (think of the comparativist claim in John Stuart Mill and Jeremy Bentham that 'happiness' could do that job); this is the problem of *plurality* or *diversity*. Then, there is a phenomenon called – unintentionally, but actually very ironic – *trumping*, i.e. a case in which the duty not to perform *x* outweighs the benefitting from *x*; so, for example, one's obligation not to lie 'trumps' the utility to do so in a given situation. Again, another case is what is called *non-substitutability*, meaning that the loss in one value cannot be compensated by the gain of (or in) another one; this applies particularly to values that are taken to be 'sacred' and by definition not replaceable, such as human dignity.[27] Finally, there is *incommensurability in a narrower sense* meaning that items are incommensurable if there is no cardinal scale according to which both could be measured. This version has, again, two other subversions: either it is meant that there are scales for measurement, but only for certain and limited regards (*weak incommensurability*) or there is no scale available, not on the sub-level, and not for an overall comparison either, so that we have to accept the items to be 'unrankable'[28] (*strong incommensurability*).[29]

Obviously, the ordinary and technical vocabulary for relating items comparatively is ramified, while 'incomparability' and 'incommensurability' entertain overlapping elements despite being far from identical. However, 'incommensurability' is semantically so widespread in covering cases in which comparisons turn out to be problematic (for instance, in lacking a scale) as well as in serving as a tool to describe certain conflicts between incompatible values. As we shall see, 'incomparability' occupies a much more restricted conceptual area.

4 A traditional and a less traditional view: Raz and Broome

To gain a deeper understanding of (what) incomparability (is not), one might refer to two approaches, the ones by Joseph Raz and John Broome, that sustainably informed the pertinent discussion. Raz himself summarizes the difference between these two accounts by presenting, first, the view that to be incomparable for A and B means not being related by 'better than', 'worse than' or 'equally good'; or put in a propositional form: it is *wrong* that one of these predicates hold between A and B. This is Raz's own position.[30] John Broome, however, is taken by Raz to defend a different view that sticks to the trichotomy thesis since it is *neither right nor wrong* that one of the three predicates is applicable to the relation between A and B.[31] Raz is prepared to speak of incomparability in these cases, whereas Broome prefers to talk of indeterminacy and vagueness. It is obvious that both accounts are incompatible, since it cannot be true that the trichotomy is wrong and neither right nor wrong.[32]

Let us first take a look at Raz's defence of incomparability that really set up the way in which the debate has been structured and approached. To begin with, Raz does not distinguish sharply between 'incomparability' and 'incommensurability' using both concepts, often enough, interchangeably. Moreover, Raz does not only follow, but initially suggested to investigate incomparability within the bigger context of rational choice and decision-making. For that purpose, he regards the rationalist to be holding that acting is determined by reason alone, while the counterpart labelled as 'classical' holds that our will is not solely determined, but limited by reason.[33] The rationalist, Raz states, has no use for the idea of the incomparable, while the classic position allows for the incommensurability of different kinds of reasons, including wants, wishes, desires and ends (120). However, all these kinds of reasons[34] do not determine what we do – partly because of their conflict.[35] Rather these reasons could limit the frame in which we are acting and have options in the first place (126–7).

Even without entering the ramified debate about reasons and actions, it seems that Raz traces the source for incomparability back to conflicting values informing our reasons – a situation that cannot occur in an entirely rationalist world, Raz suggests. These incomparably conflicting values, such as freedom versus security,[36] do not allow for being related by 'better than', 'worse than' or 'equally good'.

Now, what Raz gives us, relying on cases like these conflicts, are two major lessons. The first one is a more precise characterization of the relation between A and B said to be incomparable. Here, Raz distinguishes incomparability from equality insofar as in the former, a judgement about the relative value of A or B is impossible, while equality is exactly such a judgement (324). More important is the second lesson, namely a 'test' for incomparability consisting of the following consideration: two items A and B are incomparable if neither is better than the other while there being another item *C* that is better than one, but not better than the other (324–5). An alternative way to put this is the so called 'small improvement argument'[37] saying: given that neither is better than the other, if improving one of them 'just a bit' does not turn it better than the other; or if there is another option *C* which is better than one of them but not better than the other, then *A* and *B* are incomparable.[38] For Raz, this test is based on the *lack of transitivity* of a comparative predicate between *A*, *B* and *C* being better than *A* but not than *B*. Equality would, however, show that very transitivity. Raz underlines that this mark of intransitivity serves just as a test, not as a definition for incomparability, not even as a necessary feature thereof (326).

Raz defends this account against the possible objection according to which what he presents as being incomparable is, in the end, nothing else than what has been called 'rough equality' by James Griffin and Derek Parfit.[39] In contrast to that, Raz locates two essential differences between incomparability and rough equality. The first one leads back to the small improvement scenario: as we have seen, for Raz, if a small improvement of *B* does not turn *B*+ better than *A* they are incomparable if *C* is better than *A*, but not than *B*. This is different in cases of rough equality that just mean that the gap between *A* and *B* is not big but is in fact so small that all items *C* being better (or worse) than *A* are also better (or worse) than *B* (330). Hence, rough equality does not pass the intransitivity test. Now, Raz, and in a different respect Chang, are correct in insisting on several differences between plain equality (that has to be measurable) and a certain kind of vagueness between two similar items. Raz's test is an attempt to substantiate this difference, and we will have a chance to come back to his first argument in favour of it, the small improvement argument (see section 5). However, I do not think that he really established a resilient difference between incomparability and rough equality in referring to the above improvement scenarios, since, in the course of it, Raz just implicitly approximates rough to plain equality. Saying that the gap between *A* and *B* is actually 'so small' that all items *C* being better (or worse) than *A* are also better (or worse) than *B* tends to erase that difference in question between plain scalability and, let's say, the vague character of roughness. Hence, it seems, Raz only repeats the existing difference between incomparability and plain equality when turning to the relation between incomparability and rough equality, neglecting the once stated different features of plain and rough equality, respectively.

The second difference lies in divergent practical implications entailed by incomparability and rough equality: in the latter case, Raz holds, one is entitled to remain *indifferent* concerning the choice between *A* and *B*. This is not so in the case of incomparability between *A* and *B*; take them to stand for different careers, which turns that choice between *A* and *B* into a highly significant one not allowing for remaining indifferent when taking oneself seriously (332).[40] This supporting idea referring to indifference as being possible in the case of plain equality while being inadequate in the case of rough equality strikes me as, more or less, correct. Plain equality, as we have seen, entails scalability, and if two items are truly equal in this sense, one might make an arbitrary choice like throwing a coin. All situations, however, that do not allow for such an indifference – and decisions of personal, social or political impact belong to this type – are never scalable, Raz seems to imply. If one accepts that hidden premise, it follows that in these non-scalable cases we have always to do with rough equality that calls for decisive resources other than just arbitrary decision-making. Raz sums up:

> Incomparability does not ensure equality of merit and demerit. It does not mean indifference. It marks the inability of reason to guide our action, not the insignificance of our choice. [...] Incommensurability speaks not of what does escape reason, but of what must elude it.
>
> see above 334

As we have seen, Raz is a proponent of what serves as the standard view on incomparability: the trichotomy of 'better than', 'worse than' and 'equally good' is, then, not applicable to the relation between A and B or, in the amended form, no positive value relation holds between A and B.[41] Moreover, he tries to distinguish between incomparability and rough equality. Both claims are challenged by John Broome. I will turn to his account in a manner that skips some of the most extensively discussed issues raised by Broome and will instead concentrate on three aspects Broome has introduced into the debate that I take to be relevant for the argument here.

Raz already distinguished between two versions of thinking about incomparability (or incommensurability):

> His own standard position: it is *not true* that 'better than', 'worse than' and 'equally good' hold between A and B;

and

> the indeterminacy position: it is *neither true nor false* that 'better than', 'worse than' and 'equally good' hold between A and B.[42]

John Broome, however, presents also a slightly different version than the last one in holding:

> the indeterminacy position*: it is *true as well as false* that 'better than', 'worse than' and 'equally good' hold between A and B.[43]

Broome adds that as long as it is indeterminate whether A or B is better, both are, in a sense, comparable and not comparable. Is this characterization – if not taken to be helplessly counter-intuitive – of any help here? Let us, again, take the example of two career paths, to be a lawyer or a musician: does the standard view or one of the indeterminacy positions better reflect that binary scenario? According to the standard view, being a lawyer is not better or worse than or equally as good as being a musician. That seems to be correct since a *negative* value relation saying what is *not* the case between A and B is compatible with cases of, according to Raz, incomparability between A and B. A positive value relation concerning anything that articulates what is actually the case between A and B is, however, just not available here. Moreover, we have seen, that for both, comparability and incomparability, complementarity holds;

hence, we have to deal here with a strict either-or. I think, the phenomenology of pertinent examples creates instead a reservation against adopting Broome's proposal.

But only in one regard, namely in the sense of using truth values. In a different sense, I think, it is indeed helpful to characterise incommensurate cases as suffering from indeterminacy. For this purpose, Broome describes the 'zone of indeterminacy' – and it has to be a zone, not only a single point (71–2) – as the range that allows for small improvements (or degradations) without turning the indeterminate situation between A and B into a determinate one (69, 88). There are two further important observations that Broome puts to the fore: one is the difference between indeterminacy and vagueness. If I understand Broome's position correctly, he means to say that indeterminacy is a feature concerning attributes while vagueness concerns the question whether indeterminacy holds in a particular case. Hence, it could be clear and obvious that the value relation between A and B is indeterminate; it might, however, be the case that it is not clear whether A and B stand in a determinate or indeterminate relation. That is why Broome discusses the possibility that vagueness might prevail at the borders of the indeterminate zone – which leads to the additional difference between hard and soft indeterminacy, i.e. an indeterminacy either without or accompanied by vagueness to, eventually, deny the possibility of hard indeterminacy (73, 84). The second addition lies in pinning down the root of indeterminacy to find it, again, in two areas: on the one hand in the indeterminacy of predicates (such as 'bald') and their comparatives (such as 'balder than'); on the other hand in the fact that some predicates (such as virtuous, but not, for instance, 'red') consist of underlying predicates (such as prudent, honest, just for 'virtuous') that may create difficulties in comparative settings. It might not be clear whether A or B is more virtuous because of struggling with determining who is more prudent, honest, just – and how to combine these comparisons on the sub-level in view of the overall predicate 'virtuous' they constitute (67).

In sum, I argued for sticking to Raz's standard view in leaving it with the negative assertion that in cases of incomparability the trichotomy does not hold; however, Broome helps us immensely to better understand the source of potential incomparability by referring to instances of indeterminacy to be distinguished from cases of vagueness. I will draw on this lesson when discussing the question of whether incomparability might just *factually* not exist or whether incomparability is indeed *unintelligible* (see section 6.4).[44]

5 Ruth Chang on being on a par

It is not self-evident to stick to the trichotomy thesis when fully taking into consideration what Broome and others put the stress on: cases of indeterminacy and vagueness between items to be compared. Obviously, the possibility of stating that A is better or worse than B or that equality holds between them presupposes (some sort of) determinacy. Hence, we need a conception that allows for capturing these cases of *relational fuzziness*. It is Ruth Chang who suggested such a fourth relation beyond 'better than', 'worse than' and 'equally good', in repudiating, therefore, the trichotomy thesis defended by Raz and to which Broome still remained allegiant. This fourth relation is called 'parity' or 'being on a par' extending the scope of comparability: if *A* and *B* are on a par neither is better or worse and they are not equal either – and, yet, they are comparable, making a decision between *A* and *B* rationally justifiable. Extending the scope of comparability could imply two very different claims: the weaker reading sticks to extending comparability by parity without fully substituting it; even the trichotomy plus parity leaves space, then, for incomparable cases; the stronger reading does, on the contrary, not leave that room in introducing the fourth relation to entirely replace incomparability as a threat for rational choices (see, again, section 2). Chang presupposes this latter version in subscribing to a comparativist position,[45] without having explicitly met the ambivalence between the weak and strong interpretation.

Chang is, however, very aware of the difficulties of really grasping the idea of 'parity'. Therefore, she argues not directly for the existence of that fourth relation, but for its *possibility*. In making this rather modest move more plausible, Chang analogizes the situation for a defender of a fourth relation with the one a trichotomist had to face when confronted with a dichotomist knowing only 'better than' and 'worse than'. Chang suggests that 'paritists' are dealing here with exactly the same sort of reduction by an undiscerning trichotomist (662–3). However, this analogical consideration does not show much, since it could always be repeated in favour of an allegedly additional relation. And here, the analogy begins to turn into a slippery slope.

In attempting to undermine incomparability Chang attacks, she thinks, the best argument for incomparable cases, namely the small improvement argument that has already been used by Joseph Raz. According to Chang, it has the following form:

> if (1) A is neither better nor worse than B (with respect to V [as the covering regard or the *tertium*]), (2) A+ is better than A (with respect to V), and (3) A+ is not better than B (with respect to V), then (4) A and B are not related by any of the standard trichotomy of relations (relativized to V). Assuming the Trichotomy Thesis is true, A and B are therefore incomparable.
>
> 667–8

Chang does not criticize this argument along epistemicist lines assuming that the trichotomy factually holds and that to claim something different is just an error based on a lack of information (671). Accordingly, her intellectual counterparts are rather indeterminists like Broome and all defenders of rough equality. The task, then, consists of acquiring a deeper understanding of parity and its logical features to eventually be able to demarcate it from all sorts of equality, plain and, especially, rough equality. My claim, here, will be twofold: first and critically, Chang does not succeed in distinguishing parity from rough equality; second and constructively, this is not bad news since what Chang has to say about being on a par could well be used for characterizing equality in its rough version.

Chang elaborates, once again, on the small improvement argument in reconstructing it into what she calls the 'unidimentional chaining argument' based on the idea of improving an item in only one particular regard, hence unidimentionally (673). Here, Mozart and Michelangelo are starring in being supported by a very bad sculptor named

Talentlessi. In using these three figures, the main consideration circles around the idea that where comparability has been, incomparability cannot emerge (674). The concrete argument takes the form of a *reductio* in presenting the following scenario: suppose the trichotomy holds and both Ms are incomparable, i.e. neither is better than the other and they are not equal either. Now, imagine, there is this poor Talentlessi, a very, very bad colleague of Michelangelo. Obviously, he is also far worse than Mozart in terms of creativity. Now, imagine that we successively improve Talentlessi to T+, T++, ..., and so on – and in the end, we will end up, again, with Michelangelo as T_n. However, the standard view and its 'small improvement argument' entail also the decisive claim according to which a tinily improved element in *A* – given that *A* and *B* are taken to be incomparable – does not turn *A*+ better than *B* (although *A*+ is trivially better than *A*).[46] Hence, if Talentlessi is worse than Michelangelo (and, hence, comparable with him), and if the small improvements (T+, T++, ...) cannot make a crucial difference, that is, one not able to trigger incomparability, T++++++++... *equals* Michelangelo, who was said to be not comparable with Mozart. In other words, insofar as Mozart is comparable with Talentlessi, he is comparable with Talentlessi+, since the difference between T and T+ is just a small one, and such a difference cannot cause incomparability between different items when we had comparability before. If Mozart is comparable with T+, then applying the principle anew, it follows that he is comparable with T++, and so on. Therefore, comparability with Mozart is secured throughout the reapplication of small differences, and hence we are led to the conclusion that Mozart is, finally, comparable with Michelangelo. However, Mozart is, by hypothesis, not more or less creative than Michelangelo nor are both equally creative (675). Yet it seems that they are nevertheless comparable. Thus, there is a fourth relation between them.[47]

I think that Chang brings us to the correct conclusion by using a problematic tool. As indicated at the beginning of this section, I agree with Chang in holding that we in fact need a fourth relation beyond the trichotomy of 'better than', 'worse than' and 'equally good' in order to really cover all cases in relating *A* and *B* comparatively. The traditional restriction to trichotomy does not encompass evaluatively similar *relata* that are not plainly equal. Raz and others take them to be incomparable, but, obviously, we do and we can compare here even under these fuzzy circumstances. However, Chang's way of arguing for this view suffers from a simple difficulty: the 'unidimentional chaining argument' entails the sorites problem. In consequence, one is not allowed to unlimitedly repeat the small-improvement-move. Imagine that if one were, then a completely bald man would easily turn into one abundant with hairs, since adding one does not make a difference – and so on. That there is no clear cut here does not mean that there is not a cut at all.

Now, it would be unfair to ignore that Chang had been aware of that very problem. All that she adds, however, to meet this problem consists in holding that not every scenario seeming to be or to resemble a sorites-argument is actually one.[48] But this is not a sufficient reply since one would have to show that the examples such as the one used against the incomparabilitists is a non-sorites-argument. That has not been shown, and there is, I think, no good reason to maintain that poor Talentlessi has a decisively different relation to T+++ ... than the bald man has to the one visiting his barber on regular basis.[49]

In defending her view on comparable cases being on a par, Chang adds the idea of a conceptual 'neighborhood.' She states:

> I suggest that qualitatively very different items are on a par if they are also 'in the same neighborhood' of value overall. Mozart and Michelangelo are both 'in the same neighborhood' of creativity – they are both creative geniuses – and yet qualitatively very different in creativity. I suggest that parity holds when two items are (i) qualitatively very different with respect to the covering value, and yet (ii) in the same neighborhood overall with respect to the covering value.[50]

Both concepts here in play – 'being qualitatively different' as well as 'being in the same neighbourhood' – are vague since what really counts as 'different' in the one case and 'same' in the other is a matter of convention or even stipulation. By "qualitatively different" Chang seems to refer to comparing two artistic branches, music and sculpting, but we do not need that difference to make the relevant point of non-scalability and, hence, a certain kind vagueness because of being confronted with the same difficulty already in comparing Mozart and Beethoven (or Bowie and Ferry). Whether both items to be compared are located within the 'same neighbourhood' in respect to a particular *tertium comparationis* is not a given fact, but a highly *constructive* undertaking – a point that is neglected by Chang. The fixation of a covering value, one could say, turns two items to be comparable not by uncovering, but by creating the neighbourhood comparatively required. In other words, there is no neighbourhood *per se* between both artists (Mozart and Michelangelo) and not even between two musicians (Mozart and Beethoven), but there are potentially multiple neighbourhoods as soon as we assign different comparative regards. However, this assignment does have limits leading us to the problem of categoriality (to which we turn in section 6.2).

The intention behind speaking of conceptual neighbourhoods is, I take it, to secure comparability by defending a fourth relation as being logically distinct from trichotomy relations. And we should follow that intention. First, being obviously different from 'better than' and 'worse' than, what is called parity shows also differences to equality. To the logical properties of parity, Chang holds, belong *inter alia* irreflexibility (nothing is on a par with itself) and nontransitivity (if A is on a par with B, and B is on a par with C, it doesn't follow that A is on a par with C).[51] Equality, in contrast, does possess reflexibility (everything is equal to itself) and transitivity (if A is equal to B, and B is to C, it does follow that A is equal to C). Furthermore, Chang characterizes the relation between A and B as being on a par if there is a nonzero while unbiased difference between them. Insofar as parity is an imprecise cardinal relation there is some sort of magnitude between A and B (since $A+$ is better than A, but not than B), but there is no preference in favour of either of them.[52] Chang, I think, manages here to distinguish between parity and equality, but only in relation to its plain (and reflexive as well as transitive) form. Everything, however, she brings to the fore to establish a fourth relation is an applicable to rough equality too.[53]

Parity is characterized as being a fourth, unbiased, nonzero, logically independent relation of comparability. There are no cases of being on a par as long as we refer only to items that have a clear measurement or scale. If we have, the trichotomy thesis holds;

if not, parity is a possibility for the relation between *A* and *B*.⁵⁴ Not having a clear measurement or scale confronts us with a particular fuzziness between cases such as comparing Mozart and Michelangelo in regard to creativity. At times, Chang herself stresses the importance of giving an account of the phenomenology of comparative acts under these circumstances⁵⁵ – without sticking to her own advice. Now, comparing Mozart and Michelangelo might be surrounded by a hesitancy and uncertainty, but I take that reaction rather to be an expression of seeing them on the roughly same level than as an instance of being incomparable. In these cases we do compare, and the potential repudiation of saying who is better articulates a sense of equality in also acknowledging the comparative vagueness due to a lack of scale.

In conclusion, I agree, first, with Chang in the defence of a fourth comparable relation; the relevant cases cannot be adequately described by the traditional trichotomy.⁵⁶ Second, we have to restrict this additional relation to non-scalable cases; we need that relation to capture equality that is not plain. Third, since we are dealing here with instances of equality, I prefer using the term *fuzzy equality* instead of 'being on a par'. Contrary to what Chang thinks, however, comparability despite fuzziness does not facilitate decisions and choices: both alleged incomparability and fuzzy equality entail that either choice of *A* or *B* is rationally permissible and neither choice is rationally required, whereas the choice is not 'rationally indifferent' either. In both cases reason under-determines the choice. Hence, connecting 'rational' choices to comparisons does not lead to stronger justifications, but rather to a deeper understanding of the difficulties of finding a preference called for.⁵⁷

6 On explaining structural incomparability away

It is interesting to see that there are several terms circulating within the debate about (in)comparability used to denote cases of factual or intrinsic vagueness and indeterminacy. We already encountered Parfit's notion of 'rough equality' that is connected to the concept of 'imprecise comparability' (alongside 'imprecisely better than' and 'imprecisely worse than').⁵⁸ The roughness of the kind of equality in question does not, Parfit holds, exclude these roughly equal items as still being comparable. However, it is, as we have also seen, important to underline the difference between being 'imprecisely better (or worse) than' to 'imprecisely equal': the first is still of the same kind as the 'traditionally better (or worse) than', whereas imprecise equality is not just another species of equality.⁵⁹

Why is this so? In cases of plain equality, a small improvement (or degradation) does in fact mark a difference in triggering a bias and turning equality between two items into one being better (or worse) than the other. Imprecise equality, in contrast, allows for – small – improvements (or degradations) while maintaining the status of being equal. The question is, of course, what 'small' really means here;⁶⁰ but one could put the case also upside down in stating that the zone of imprecise equality holds as long as no bias is triggered by any small improvement (or degradation). Moreover, as we have also seen above, the imprecision of equality entails its intransitivity while plain equality is transitive (if *A* is equal to *B*, and *B* is equal to *C*, it does follow that *A* is equal to C). The reason for this asymmetry brings us back to the problem of scalability, and hence commensurability, in reference to comparing items. Two cases have to be distinguished: different items are *precisely comparable* when they are cardinally comparable and their (evaluative) differences can be measured by a unit of the pertinent regard, in short: if they are commensurable. If this precise comparability is not available, we are left with imprecise comparability: two items are *imprecisely comparable* when they are cardinally comparable but their (evaluative) differences cannot be measured by a scale. In other words: precise comparability is based on having a scale, imprecise comparability implies a non-countable magnitude between the items to be compared.[61]

Incomparability cannot occur in cases of scalability, and thus in cases of commensurability, and hence precision. If it existed, incomparability as the structural impossibility of comparing A and B would represent a consequence of an imprecision between A and B. However, we do not have to draw that very consequence. My claim will be simply that *there is no such thing as structural incomparability*. To show this we should, first, fully appreciate the difference between in- and noncomparability to trace alleged cases of the former back to real instances of the latter; we may, second, scrutinize one major source of 'incomparability', namely semantic vagueness of predicates and their comparatives to see how we actually do compare even under these circumstances; we may, third, also pay heed to another source of 'incomparability', namely the multidimensionality of different comparative regards to see on which level we actually can compare and what that might mean for an overall comparison hoped for; and finally, we shall linger over the intelligibility of structural incomparability – to, eventually, suggest that this is an empty concept.

6.1 Three forms of non-comparability

Let us start off by distinguishing between incomparability and noncomparability. The first was circumscribed (or, some would say, is defined) as the case where the traditional trichotomy fails or, as one could also say, where no positive value relation – better than, worse than, equally good – holds between A and B (see section 2). In contrast, two items are noncomparable if the formal conditions required for there to be a claim of comparability or incomparability are not fully met. The question of whether A and B are (in)comparable has significance only if noncomparability can be excluded in the first place. While incomparability could be called a substantial failure – a comparison is unavailable although all conditions for its possibility are fulfilled – noncomparability is a matter of a formally conditioned breakdown or limit of comparing A and B – a comparison is unavailable because of unfulfilled conditions for its possibility.[62]

Two forms of noncomparability must again be distinguished. Either there is no covering value to put A and B into a comparable setting; a comparative regard, a *tertium*, is necessary for every comparison to be possible, since there is no comparison *simpliciter*; this is, admittingly, a fairly trivial case. Or one has a covering value but it does not apply to the comparative items A and B; this is a far less trivial case.[63] And it confronts us with the so far rather marginalized problem of categoriality. Take the following examples we partly used already before:

(i)   Christiano Ronaldo scored more often than Toni Kroos did in the season 2016/17;
(ii) Christiano Ronaldo scored less often than LeBron James did in the season 2016/17;
(iii) Christiano Ronaldo scored more often than Kant's categorical imperative in the season 2016/17;
(iv) Christiano Ronaldo is a better football player than the categorical imperative is;
(v)   Christiano Ronaldo is a better football player than Toni Kroos;
(vi) Christiano Ronaldo is more creative than Mozart and Michelangelo together.

(i) is a simple (and correct) comparison based on a scale; this is a case of precise comparability. (iii) is a simple case of noncomparability because the *relata A* and *B* do not belong to the category that the covering value presupposes; the categorical imperative does not score; the comparison is, hence, nonsense. (ii) is a more interesting case located between (i) and (iii), i.e. between precise comparability and noncomparability: on the one hand, one could argue that Ronaldo and James are comparable, even precisely, due to the covering value 'scores in sports'; on the other hand, one might hold that a comparison is near its limits or even beyond, since football and basketball do not have 'scores' as a shared covering value. (ii) shows a potential borderline case for only potentially fulfilling the condition of categoriality in testifying to the difficulty that finding a category is not only a question of grammar, but also of convention and, in some cases, of stipulation.[64]

The cases (iv) to (vi) refer to incommensurable scenarios and, if comparisons are possible, to imprecise comparability. In case (iv) this is, again, combined with the problem (or the lack) of categoriality and, hence, noncomparability. In case (v), one might miss a covering value leading to the task of either introducing one or of explicating the only latent one; the 'better than' might mean here something like 'all things considered' that begs the question to the vagueness of what 'all' means in regard to the quality of football players. The last case (vi) amplifies these problems while creating another version of the categoriality problem: in (vi) we do have a covering value (creativity) and we do have comparative items falling under this category (players and artists are candidates of creativity) – and yet, comparability is not secured since the way in which players and artists potentially fulfil that criterion are 'too different'. Accordingly, the condition of comparability has to be restricted: we need, *formally*, a covering value; the covering value has, *categorically or conceptually*, to be applicable to the comparative items; and these items have, *contextually*, to instantiate the comparative regard in a sufficiently similar manner. Again, and as with categoriality, this last phrasing allows intentionally for borderline cases and vagueness – or in reference to case (iv): whether Christiano Ronaldo is in fact more creative than Mozart and Michelangelo together is either open for a telling comparison or, due to the difference between their 'areas of competence', to be taken as another case of noncomparability, but *not* of incomparability.

Therefore, we have to extend the concept of noncomparability now to three forms: the lack of a *tertium comparationis*, the non-applicability of the regard to the comparative items, and the (too) divergent ways in which comparative items realise the regard in question. As we can now see, many instances traditionally taken to be incomparable rather belong to the realm of the noncomparable.

6.2 Vagueness: predicates and comparatives

Usually, drawing comparisons is not a difficult thing to do – often enough, it is, in fact, too easy. Here, however, I am interested in the other side of the spectrum in holding that the comparative problems are rooted in or expressed by the vagueness of predicates.[65] My point is, that these problems are not limits for comparing items, since we can still make comparisons, even under vague conditions. The vagueness of predicates is, obviously, a highly ramified philosophical debate, and it is neither possible nor required here to give more than a sketch of the relevant issues in favour of factual comparability and in explaining alleged incomparability away. Take the following predicates:

(i)   Max is 6 feet tall;
(ii) Max is tall;
(iii) Max is a bachelor;
(iv) Max's eyes are blue;
(v)   Max is bald;
(vi) Max is a virtuous person.

Now, (i) is a sharp while scalable predicate not allowing for any vagueness.[66] There are also non-gradable, but nevertheless crisp predicates also excluding vagueness in not admitting of degrees and gradation. One might say that (iii) and (iv) belong to this category: 'bachelor' is well defined and, hence, either applicable to a person or not without leaving much room for debate (however, is an unmarried young man who is already a widower still a bachelor?);[67] a similar case we have with colour predicates that are usually sharp enough allowing only for rare borderline cases (is this colouring still blue or rather 'deep purple'?). The two last cases, however, point to a different direction confronting us with genuine vagueness. There are people who have lost all or much of their hair, and if Max were one of them, (v) did not suffer from any vagueness. Usually, things are not that clear, and the zone of vagueness is more extended when it comes to pinning down whether a person is bald or not. A similar result with a slightly different background we have in case (vi). What we mean by being 'virtuous' is a topic of dispute, not in everyday scenarios, but in ethical debates: what counts as a virtue and how to combine these 'ingredients' for being truly virtuous?

In the cases (ii), (v) and (vi) (perhaps also in (iv)) we meet the traditional features of potential borderline cases, namely tolerance, indefiniteness and sorites-susceptibility. These three aspects all go back to a move one can make without undermining the applicability of the predicate, and this move is similar to the small improvement (degradation) argument: change Max just a bit (taller, his eyes more blue, with less hair, showing more justice), yet it does not change the predicate in relation to its bearer or in comparative settings. This last consideration brings us already to the next step, the step from predicates to their comparative forms. Consider, again, our list above, now with a comparative twist:

(i*)   Max is 6 feet taller;
(ii*) Max is taller;
(iii*) — ;
(iv*) Max's eyes are more blue;
(v*)   Max is balder;
(vi*) Max is a more virtuous person.

Now, there is no comparative for being a bachelor; hence (iii) drops out. This goes also, in a slightly different way, for (i), since (i*) adopted a new meaning because 'taller' refers to different circumstances in both sentences: in the first case it is a proposition about Max, in the second about the difference in height between Max and someone else. In neither case is vagueness involved.

This is, again, different in the rest of the proposed cases. And among them there is an interesting difference. Take, first, sentences (ii) and (ii*); 'tall' is a vague predicate, but turning it into its comparative form does not preserve that vagueness since 'taller than' is perfectly commensurable. In the cases (iv) to (vi), by contrast, the vague predicates have comparatives, but they too resist precise measurement and quantification. Here, again, one might detect a difference among them, namely the one usually referred to as the duality between genuine and derivative vagueness.[68] Genuine vagueness is meant to denote the case in which the specification (for instance, by stipulation) on the level of the predicates does not lead to the exclusion of the potential vagueness of its comparative form, while this is precisely the case in derivative cases. If one clarifies the notion of being virtuous and its sub-elements in (vi*), i.e. the underlying virtues, one might claim that a comparison in terms of virtuousness is not a vague matter either. And one might claim the opposite in regard to cases such as (iv*) and (v*) because clarifying the predicate does not lead to clear and distinct comparatives.[69]

6.3 Multidimensionality

The cases (v*) and (vi*) lead, again, to another source of vagueness. Apparently, it is not always easy to determine whether Max is balder or more virtuous than someone else. However, both predicates supervene on sub-features together constituting the predicate in question:

(v*)   baldness: supervenes on, say, the number of hairs, their thickness, and their distribution, etc.;
(vi*) virtuousness: supervenes on, say, a list of virtues, such as the classical cardinal virtues like justice, prudence, courage, etc.

Both cases entail two different versions of vagueness that inform, eventually, the vagueness of the relevant predicates as well as their comparative forms. In (v*) all supervened sub-features allow for a rather exact measurement and quantification, and yet, the supervening covering item of baldness does not share that feature of quantifiability. In contrast, in (vi*) all supervened virtues are incommensurable and that very feature is preserved by the supervening trait of being a virtuous person overall.

Both cases are examples of multidimensionality. And it confronts us with another root of vagueness, namely the problem of how to combine the supervened features in regard to an overall comparative. As we have seen, this problem arises in cases in which the predicates on the sub-level represent commensurable features (v*) as well as in cases in which they represent incommensurable features (vi*). In both cases, the vagueness is, again, derived from two independent sources. The first is a *semantic* one, meaning that it is not clear which features are constituting the supervening comparative. Is baldness sufficiently determined by the number of hairs, their thickness and their distribution? This is an open question and it is easy to extend this list. This is even more evident in the moral case. Is the list of virtues complete in encompassing all cardinal virtues? Again, that is an ethically controversial debate, since some may argue that there are further virtues or that there is another, non-moral kind, for instance, epistemic or dianoetic virtues.[70] Hence, how to analyse 'bald' (and 'balder') and 'virtuous' (and 'more virtuous') is not intrinsically determinate. The second issue in play is a *combinational* one, meaning that it is not clear how the values of the features on the sub-level bear on the overall value of the supervening predicate or comparative; as we have seen, this goes for commensurable as well as incommensurable sub-features. The reason is that there is no unit that all features share to constitute an overall value for the supervening feature. How to weigh the number of hairs, their thickness, etc. in regard to baldness, or how to weigh a person's justice, prudence, etc. in regard to her virtuousness is not determinate.[71]

In sum, what brings us to the difficulty in comparing A and B is . . .

- the vagueness of the *predicates* A and B;
- the potential vagueness of their *comparative* forms;
- the *multidimentionality* (which dimensions?; and how to weigh them up?) of the predicates and their comparative forms, if A and B are analysable features consisting of distinguishable sub-features.

Traditionally, these cases are candidates potentially taken to be incomparable. The trichotomy of 'better than', 'worse than' or 'equally good' does not hold; a positive value relation is not in sight (see section 3).[72] But if comparative statements such as 'Max is balder than . . .' or 'Max is a more virtuous person than . . .' do not lead to a clear result, this lack of clarity is based on a comparison. While it is true that the claim that both comparative items are equal is not correct either, it is, phenomenologically, not adequate to say that we do not compare or that we cannot compare at all in cases like (v*) and (vi*). Instead, it is more appropriate, I conclude, to hold that A and B are *fuzzily* equal – and, hence, comparable.[73]

6.4 Choices, comparisons and beyond

Being fuzzily equal means that A and B are in the same 'neighbourhood' without being equal on a scale (because there is none), while allowing for a nonbiased, nonzero magnitude (see section 5). To expect a higher degree of clarity under such circumstances—eventually replacing fuzzy equality by plain equality – is not even desirable, since that very expectation is confused. As long as we deal with incommensurable items the potential comparative result of them being equal is necessarily surrounded by that fuzziness. Therefore, to claim that this is a breakdown of a comparative act seems to be wrong-headed, simply because stating this kind of equality – all things considered – while not allowing for a comparatively justified preference is itself nothing but a legitimate result of comparing A and B.

This does not exclude strategies to establish a preference in favour of A or B. These attempts refer, again, to the roots of vagueness, either the one of the predicates and comparatives or the one based on multidimensionality. In cases of the first sort, one might stipulate criteria to conditionally clarify what, for instance, counts as being bald and balder. This, sometimes, does dissolve comparative difficulties, but not always. In cases of the second sort, one might presuppose an evident list of pertinent items constituting the supervening feature (restricting the list to, for example, justice, prudence, courage) or one might, given a particular context, put the stress on only one element of the list (valuing prudence most, compared to the remaining virtues). And here too, this could dissolve comparative difficulties, but it does not always. Where it, eventually, does not, A and B remain connected in fuzzy equality. However, all of these possible outcomes testify to the comparability between A and B.

Accordingly, we might change the way in which we approach situations of genuine indifference based on comparative results not justifying one option over an alternative. Leaving the abstract talk of vagueness, incommensurability, and divergent versions of equality behind, we might, as Charles Taylor suggested, ask instead what we actually *do* in situations of abeyance while being confronted with the practical urgency to decide.[74] Let us, for these more severe cases, replace the level of predicates and comparatives for more ramified and ponderous life choices: being a lawyer or rather a musician? Now, the epistemicist will maintain that there is something to 'find out' by answering this question truthfully and thoroughly which life one really wants. However, this introspection does not necessarily lead to more existential clarity; it might even undermine it.

If the comparison between A and B, between being a lawyer or a musician, is not sufficiently precise, one could enrich the comparative act or one could go beyond it in leaving the comparative setting altogether. The first way resembles the strategies sketched above in stipulating possible meanings of involved items or, more importantly, in pinning down the elements really constituting one option. What does it mean to be a musician, what is it that seems to be so attractive to linger over this option? In meeting these questions, one might be able to establish an emphasis on particular aspects over others within a multidimensional spectrum, or one extends or reduces this spectrum in coming to see what really counts. This process does not have to lead back to the logic of 'finding out' a hidden truth; it might rather be an innovative act that really creates the possibility of comparing both career paths.[75]

At some point comparisons come to an end and their clarifying potentials are finally exhausted. However, contrary to rational choice thinking a decision in favour of being a lawyer or a musician does not have to be based on comparisons. Often enough it is not – without losing its rational character (see section 2). The scope of rational choices is not coextensive with the range of comparative justification; rather, choices that are justified (or justifiable) often enough transgress our comparative capacities. And here we are taking leave of comparisons and have to go beyond them. But where, exactly?

I close this section with two suggestions for *post-comparative decision-making* under fuzzy conditions. If one prefers to be a musician rather than to be a lawyer, this does not necessarily imply that one has compared both options before: wanting or desiring x does not entail having compared x with samples of non-x. One might have had indeed a range of 'living options' instead of the one chosen, and yet the choice was a matter of duty to one's talent, not of a comparatively achieved preference. This, again, could be an insight leading back to a merely latent or even explicit comparison, but it does not have to. 'Living options' – a notion taken from William James's seminal paper 'The Will to Believe' – alludes already to another way of creatively dealing with post-comparative decision-making. Referring to the phenomenon of interpersonal trust, James holds that existentially adopting one particular life option does not have to reflect a precedent preference but rather creates the integrity and rightness of a choice precisely by committing oneself to it: the trust once given might cause receiving trust in return. This choice could have been arbitrary in favouring *A* over *B*, but choosing *A* is a conscious 'jumping' into a reality that is not *per se* the right one, but becomes so in making it real, vivid, vital.[76]

The often-feared threat of regretting the choice once irreversibly made is lingering here everywhere: to have realized a possibility at the cost of another one.[77] The joy of what is gained might go hand in hand with the melancholy, even the regret in thinking of what has been lost at the same time. But in all these cases and in all our divergent dealings with them, sometimes in blindness, sometimes thoughtfully, incomparability is not in sight.

What does all this amount to? It means that we shall say farewell to the idea of *structural* incomparability. We can explain all alleged instances of a structurally caused breakdown of comparisons away by either tracing them back to forms of *noncomparability* or by describing them as presenting *fuzzy equality* in cases where expecting more precise results is a confusion, given divergent forms of vagueness at play. Moreover, the urgency against incomparability is not only out of place here because of ubiquitous comparisons but also due to the ways in which we deal post-comparatively with decisions and choices. The concession above was intentionally stated in a cautious manner: *if* structural incomparability really 'exists,' it has the form roughly described by Raz and in the standard view enriched by Broome's help. However, the antecedent in that conditional is not fulfilled. And this does not come as a surprise since in all these cases we can and do compare, whereas imagining that we could not is as impossible as holding we could not decide when confronted with alternatives. Therefore, I take structural incomparability not only to be accidentally excluded, but to be *unintelligible*.[78] Everything outside the realm of *non*comparability *is*, in fact, comparable.

8

On Indexical Incomparability

Up to this point, we have concentrated on several candidates for *structural* breakdowns of a comparing act. This breakdown could take different forms, but, as we just have seen, none of them is able to establish incomparability.[1] In explaining this version away – by referring to alternative, more convincing accounts – I am, therefore, refuting that something like structural incomparability really 'exists'.

Now, I shall consider another kind of incomparability that is called 'constitutive'. According to Joseph Raz, this is a distinct form of a comparative breakdown.[2] The 'constitutive' element, however, is not based on the impossibility of relating items to be compared with one another in regard to a *tertium comparationis*, but rather is rooted in the character or status of an item put into a comparative setting. Friendship versus money serves here as the representative example entailing the (normative) privilege of the former over the value of the latter. Friendship as a particular institution, one might say with Raz, has to be given the priority over monetary considerations. The core element of constitutive incomparability of an item is, then, an *institutional* one.[3] In generally sympathizing with Raz's claim, I shall offer a slightly different background for this 'institution' in regaining the specific context in which a constellation is considered to be incomparable – *for someone*. Here again, the structural element disappears, and an *indexical* dimension emerges.

The idea of constitutive incomparability is, in its most general interpretation, a severe repudiation of the claim that literally everything lies within the realm of universal exchangeability. Insofar as crude forms of consequentialism and utilitarian approaches subscribe to this claim, defending constitutive incomparability is, latently or explicitly (as in Raz)[4], a critique of all-embracing trade-offs informing particular forms of moral theory. Steven Lukes circumscribes the very idea of constitutive incomparability (or 'incommensurability', as he says) by, interestingly, relying on our potential reactions to its denial. He writes:

> It is the claim that someone who makes certain comparisons with respect to the worth of valued alternatives thereby exhibits, at the very least, misunderstanding – misunderstanding that may in turn merit condemnation.[5]

In which cases is such a 'condemnation' understandable or even called for? We may think of, at least, two scenarios. The highly controversial case of harming people might serve as a first example. Here, a potential or actual trade-off between benefit and harm is taken to be acceptable or even necessary, but within certain boundaries beyond which this trade-off turns to be objectionable or morally untenable. Accordingly, one can harm people in cases of punishment, while the kind of punishment has restrictions in terms of duration, extent and kind. This is why one has to deal with a noncomparative conception of harm.[6] Take another example from Derek Parfit's *Reasons and Persons*: in comparing different future outcomes regarding potential populations and their well-being for the whole or only parts of it, Parfit invites us to consider different cases in which we have a small number of people enjoying a very high standard of living – while, then, increasing the population significantly and letting the standard of living decline in alternative scenarios while these populations still have a life worth living.[7] Here again, we encounter a trade-off between the quantity of people and the quality of their lives up the point where this sort of bargaining comes finally to an end as soon as human beings have to live beneath a certain standard of existence.

This case already touches upon the second example of constitutive incomparability. Think of human rights and human dignity secured by these rights. The language we use to express the suspension of every trade-off in these cases is telling: human dignity is 'untouchable' (precisely because it, in fact, has been touched so many times); human rights are 'sacred' (as a, somehow, post-religious concept inheriting a theological dimension even for a 'secular age'); or, more Kantian, human beings have to be regarded as 'ends in themselves' (and never as 'mere means' for achieving something else). Here, again, a clear demarcation is not easily at hand, while our 'reactive attitudes' (Peter Strawson) towards questioning, threatening, even attacking this 'untouchable sphere of sacredness' are important symptoms for constitutive incomparability – in the moment of its denial: 'attitudes of discomfort, embarrassment, shock, outrage, or horror that is displayed when such calculation of commensuration is engaged in by others', as Lukes aptly states.[8]

Accordingly, Raz tries to establish a stronger relation between cases beyond trade-offs and our existential or moral attitudes to them, an *internal* relation, one might say. In illustrating this internalism Raz refers repeatedly to choices between money and friendship or money and parenthood. Raz claims that a couple really desiring to become a parent does not only not compare both options – money *versus* parenthood – but would firmly repudiate this comparison:

> For many, having children does not have a money price because exchanging them for money, whether buying or selling, is inconsistent with a proper appreciation of the value of parenthood.
>
> 348

Raz speaks of a kind of incomparability that is not based on the breakdown of the three traditional predicates 'better than', 'worse than' and 'equally good', but rather on the refusal to compare in the first place. In that course, he invites us, as I read him, first, to question the intuitively understandable assumption that 'incomparability' refers necessarily to a structure and its potential breakdown and, second, to contemplate alternative possibilities in view of the precise *grammar* of that notion.

The refusal to compare is itself to be regarded as an expression of the deep appreciation for the value in question. What puts this severe case at the threshold between structural and normative incomparability is the ambivalent status of that refusal. Structurally, a comparison is, obviously, possible; normatively, one might ask, whether the refusal of weighing up parenthood comparatively is, by any means, more substantial than an emotive or evaluative attitude turning this kind of incomparability into a mere 'noncognitive' expression.

Raz wants to exclude this metaethical reduction in characterising this refusal as of 'symbolic significance' for their parenthood (349). And this symbolic refusal, Raz adds, is an integral element of the symbolized value itself. Thus, there is no essential distinction between the judgment of incomparability and the case of incomparability. Raz states:

> My claim regarding incommensurability is that belief in incommensurability is itself a qualification for having certain relations. [...] Certain judgments about the non-comparability of certain options and certain attitudes to the exchangeability of options are constitutive of relations with friends, spouses, parents, etc.
>
> see above. 351 and 352

Moreover, the constitutive character of this incomparability implies, for Raz, that only those refusing to compare parenthood, friendship and the like with money are able to be good parents or to have real friends.[9] Someone insisting that money is more valuable than friendship is, then, neither confused nor claiming something wrong, but is just incapable of true friendship (352–3). Raz concedes not to have shown that life is impossible without the institution of constitutive incomparatives, but one is very near to that insight when really appreciating the depth and morality as well as the practical significance of this kind of incomparability (357).[10]

Raz's characterization of constitutive incomparability has met several critical responses. First, how is it possible to give friendship the privilege over money when both are said to be in an incomparable setting? Is this not exactly what has been denied, a comparison? And second, how could the denial of comparing x with something else be constitutive for x? Is this not, also, a question of the concrete context? Imagine someone has already more than 'enough' friends but is struggling financially. Would that person be incapable of friendship, preferring money over an additional friendship under the particular conditions of having a vivid social life and, yet, an empty wallet?[11]

Ruth Chang, in critically responding to Raz's account, proposes to speak of 'emphatical comparability' in cases previously running under the heading of constitutive incomparability.[12] It is possible to compare friendship with money precisely because one wants to underline the significance of a particular good. Put in an abstract manner: A is emphatically better than B if all improvements of B are not able to make B better than A. Applied to our example: there is no amount of money that would make that sum better than a friendship to someone.

Now, I do not want to claim that Chang's critical reaction is just wrong, but rather raise doubts about whether it really captures the existential and, sometimes also, the moral depth and significance regarding the asymmetry between friendship and money Raz tries to express. While Chang describes the cases in question in a distant, technical way, Raz changes the perspective in paying attention to the language used by those being involved in situations just sketched. One might assume that this involvement is (part of) a language-game to which it, first, entails that particular moves are suspended – namely, not to even consider putting the valued good into a sort of ranking with other goods; and not as a *normatively* laden dealing with that value, but as an expression of what that value *means* for that person; and hence, second, to express that refutation explicitly if necessary, as an essential element of a person's deep valuation of the good in question. The 'will *not* to compare' – to, once again, adopt William (not: LeBron) James' phrasing – comes to the fore if one is confronted with the structurally possible, but personally misplaced comparison (*first person perspective*), as well as if others express their alienation from someone actually drawing these comparisons (*third person perspective*).

Speaking of a language-game here might sharpen our awareness in two different regards: it underlines that 'incomparability' is part of our ordinary language and, for some, an integral element of the grammar constituting particular values. Here – and in contrast to normative incomparability – the relation between that value and our talk of its incomparable character is not one of moral deliberation, but is based on a way and a form of life, to which it belongs that comparisons are, in certain arrangements, suspended – not out of duty, but as an entailment of how we live and how we express ourselves. Speaking of a language-game might, furthermore, highlight that one is involved in a – serious – game with others, a game whose rules are not completely settled without being arbitrary. Seen from the first person perspective it might be the attempt to reach out to others in tentatively extending one's own rules to others while finding out whether there is agreement with others, whether the 'I' could speak for a 'we' and what this 'we' might do to the 'I', as Stanley Cavell suggests.[13] Seen from the third person perspective it might be, conversely, the expression of a deep reservation against someone not playing one's own game or playing it while breaking the rules consciously; here, the 'we' already realizes a gap to the 'I' and gives that very difference an expression by refuting comparison. Does someone who does not welcome that refutation still share the same form of life with me, we might ask taking Raz's argument further and following Cavell's line of thought.

Therefore, I suggest we reconsider the idea of constitutive incomparability as a result of changing the way we approach cases of deep valuation. Instead of asking whether a comparison is structurally possible or whether it merely hints at an attitude leading to the resistance to compare items, one might linger over the ways in which people articulate their existential and moral valuations challenged by other values and considerations; the ways we as sentient as well as responsible human beings find expressions that do not remain in the linguistic realm, but that do mark a difference in life; and how we actually play the language-game of incomparability in finding out whether a situation is only incomparable *for me*, or whether I share this conviction *with others* (from the 'I' to the 'we'), or – if not – what this lacking common ground might mean for my own stance (from the 'we' back to the 'I'). Incomparability serves, then, as a language-game in which I, as an individual voice, have to find out who is playing that game with me too—a voices among voices. Incomparability is, therefore, an essentially *indexical* statement expressing that something is incomparable *for someone*—while, eventually, finding out how extended the 'we' really is to which the individual voice always belongs.

9

The Case of Normative Incomparability: Comparisons, Animals, and the Quest for Adequacy

For that which befalleth the sons of men befalleth beasts;
even one thing befalleth them:
as the one dieth, so dieth the other;
yea, they have all one breath;
so that a man hath no preeminence above a beast:
for all is vanity.

Ecclesiastes 3:19

1 Introduction: 'for all *is* vanity'

There can be nothing genuinely unique. Insofar as uniqueness entails the claim that something is either the only element within a particular class or kind, or that it does not belong to any class or kind whatsoever, the idea of uniqueness itself remains an empty set. To be the singular element within a class is self-contradictory because it is constitutive for a class to include more than just one single item; the very idea of being a class is bound to the plurality of its members or units. And the notion of being beyond every class is an equally confused conception since it is always possible to create a class to which the presumably unique item could belong. Classes and kinds are not 'out there', but are made up and created for heuristic arrangements.

Incomparability seems to share the same fate as uniqueness because of its impossibility – not because the one presupposes the other, but rather because the arrangements allowing for a comparison are always available. It is always possible to find a particular avenue to compare A and B. This is at odds with the exclusive idea of incomparability, which means not only that A and B cannot be compared from the point of view of a T, but that there is no T at all by which A and B could possibly be brought into a comparative setting. But again, this idea leads nowhere or, at best, to an impasse.

Nevertheless, uniqueness and incomparability have their place in our ordinary and less-ordinary speech: the incomparable character of a person's performance, or the horrendous evil of a unique historical event. The incomparability of these extreme instances is an expression of deep appreciation, admiration and love; or of horror, disgust and indignation; but always a superlative in its best or worst sense. Given the tension between its structural impossibility and the fact of its everyday application, the language game of incomparability is not played on a literal, but rather (for lack of a better term) on an 'expressive' level. It does not refer to a structural breakdown of potential comparisons, but signifies the withdrawal of an item from comparative arrangements.

Therefore, speaking of incomparable instances is *normatively loaded* (or sometimes even *burdened*), since the reason for declaring an item to be incomparable is either rooted in an *evaluative judgement* or goes back to a *moral reason*. In all these cases, structurally speaking, a comparison is not excluded or impossible, but the comparative act itself has been put into question. It is not the technical possibility of a particular comparison that is denied here; rather – precisely when facing this possibility – the comparative performance and its implementation is taken to be normatively (i.e., evaluatively or morally) problematic, dubious, or even forbidden. This *normative* form of incomparability is based on the conviction, or sometimes even the moral duty, *not* to compare. It is a reaction to the predicament that a comparison is structurally possible, and yet for many evaluatively counterintuitive or morally untenable. Put technically: normative incomparability presupposes structural comparability.

However, the range and concrete instances of normative incomparability are not self-evident or beyond dispute. On the contrary, a person might be deemed incomparable by one person, but not by others, because of the existence of totally different relationships to that same person. Instances of war, destruction and injustice could be characterized as incomparable by some or taken to be in line with similarly mundane events by others. Consequently, the claim that A is incomparable with B (in relation to T or any other regard) is not a judgement restricted to the item A, but represents an expression of a person's relation to that A, an evaluation of A by someone according to taste, preference, or affection; or a determination of A's moral status with reference to our obligation, concern and care, or commitment to A. Contrary to instances of structural incomparability, their normative counterparts are essentially based on a personal and hence, an indexical, as well as contextual, element. Without a normative assessment of A, the incomparability of A would not be reachable. Normative incomparability is, thus, bound to an individual or collective judgment that is either latent or explicit.

This obviously has far-reaching entailments for a methodological approach to this kind of incomparability. Characterizing A as incomparable is not a reflection of an 'objective' setting or of matters of fact, but it is itself a highly normative claim. Questioning A's incomparable character in response bears witness to a deep disagreement – a gap between divergent, opposite, and most importantly, incompatible convictions regarding A's status, as well as our different relations to A. Comparing A with other items stands then for an equally normative claim refuting the normatively incomparable character of A, but not necessarily its normative significance. In any case, what comes to the fore here is the *moral dimension of the act of comparing* item A as a claim about A's status, as well as, more generally, the institution of drawing *comparisons as a theme of ethical reflection*.

Leaving the merely structural difficulties of comparisons for the contextual embeddedness of normatively disputed comparative acts now forces us to confront the quest for comparative adequacy and the dangers of missing it. Again, whether one does (or does not) and what counts as 'adequate' here is itself part of the discourse in which comparisons are either part of that semantic problem or an ingredient in (dis)solving it. To be able to give a philosophically satisfying account of normative incomparability, along with the debate about the precarious status of comparisons, calls, I think, for concreteness as opposed to hasty generalizations. This means doing justice to different takes on a particular case, instead of reducing ramifications within a complicated constellation, calling for 'think descriptions' instead of a merely technical vocabulary.

In October 1997, John Maxwell Coetzee, future recipient of the Nobel Prize for literature, was invited to give the prestigious Tanner Lectures on Human Values at Princeton University. The South African writer did talk about 'human values', but in an unexpected manner. He did not, as usual, present a philosophical talk with more-or-less abstract considerations on a topic of common and recently urgent concern, but instead gave two lectures that playfully mirrored the same occasion at Princeton that he had been invited to. Coetzee performed a reading of a literary text about an older and fairly successful writer, named Elizabeth Costello, who was invited to give two guest lectures at a prestigious college somewhere in the US – clearly a *mise en abyme*. Both lectures by Coetzee were published, together with commentaries by Peter Singer and others, as *The Lives of Animals*, which is a fitting title for what Costello had presented – or rather, confronted – the audience with at the fictional Appleton College. Costello is deeply concerned with our relation to and our treatment of animals, and she eagerly criticizes both the immoral lack of mindfulness towards these fellow creatures on a private, as well as political, social, and economic level; and, in her view, the wrong-headed (yet philosophically prominent) accounts that already critically address that untenable situation for animals. In Coetzee's lectures, there is a constant oscillation between literary fiction and philosophical allusion, including arguments, examples, counter-voices and even some footnotes, an oscillation that later becomes more pronounced by integrating these two lectures into a longer piece (to avoid the term 'novel') simply called *Elizabeth Costello*, published in 2003. This book consists of eight 'lessons' in which Coetzee's Princeton lectures are republished as the third and fourth lessons (excluding the notes) and to which the author adds different scenes where Costello, as well as her concern for animals, plays a major role.

We will return to Elizabeth Costello again later for a more lengthy discussion, but by way of introduction, I shall focus here on one element that is particularly relevant to our theme. Early on in her first lecture and then from time to time again, Elizabeth Costello draws a precarious, yet not completely new, comparison: our treatment of animals, she claims, is like the treatment of Jews in Nazi concentration camps, in this case turning the Holocaust into a daily business. With what exactly are we, as readers and as potential addressees of Costello's critique, confronted here? A fair, responsible, mindful comparison? An act of genuine moral concern tied to an adequate manner of expressing this concern? Or an exaggeration based on obliterating the categorical difference between human beings and animals by hinting at their potentially common features – 'for all *is* vanity'? Or a comparative act to be met with indignation and protest to safeguard the incomparable character of what has been done to the Jewish people?

Coetzee – himself both an author and a voice who has a highly peculiar relation to Elizabeth within the complex narrative structure – not only presents Costello's moral insurrection, but also divergent and conflicting reactions to her eagerness to defend the lives of animals in her lectures, as well as during her stay at Appleton in general. On various levels, her account not only elicits reservations and objections, but also causes irritation and many misunderstandings. It is the delicate comparison and its context within Coetzee's lectures and 'lessons' in particular that gives rise to a ramified and intriguing debate which eventually combines three major issues: animal ethics as a general matter, literature that 'hosts' this philosophical issue as a mode of approaching it, and the theme's amplification by a severe comparative provocation that sets the framework for a quest for adequacy. And this quest leads to a plain conflict: comparing something with something else or securing its status by declaring it as incomparable. The following chapter will draw on Coetzee's Costello 'lessons' *not* to answer the problem of normative incomparability (I do not even know what that could possibly mean), but rather to give a careful account of the difficulties, conflicts and tensions in trying to find the adequacy of comparative acts and of meeting their limits, while ultimately touching upon the evaluative or moral impossibility of comparison in the first place, as well as the notion of what it means to belong to the realm of incomparability.

2 Meeting Elizabeth Costello

Elizabeth Costello is invited to give an honorary lecture on a topic of her choice at Appleton College. She is an Australian writer, best known for a James Joyce adaptation called *The House on Eccles Street*, and is now, late in her career, probably expected to reflect on her work and development as an artist at this honourable occasion created on her behalf. However, not only the theme chosen, but also the way in which she approaches the topic is surprising, if not irritating, to the audience. Under the heading *The Lives of Animals* she gives a two-part lecture, narrated by Coetzee with the title 'The Philosophers and the Animals' and then, for the following day, 'The Poets and the Animals'.

Nothing in her work prepares her readers and listeners for this ramified issue, while Costello herself is also described as slightly unprepared both thematically and emotionally. It becomes increasingly obvious that Costello is deeply concerned, even frustrated and outraged, about the treatment of animals, not only about the industry built around meat production – which includes the imprisoning, fattening and finally, slaughtering of animals – but even more so, about the ordinary devaluation of animals as our fellow beings, as sensitive and often suffering creatures. And this engagement with the topic ultimately amounts to a presentation that is not distanced, balanced, fluent or well argued, but it does testify to her real involvement und true concern about 'the lives of animals', even though she appears unsure about how to approach the issue. In her lectures, and even more so in the following discussions and encounters at Appleton, Costello is characterized as vulnerable and sensitive. In her responses to critical, but mostly benevolent questions, she appears almost rude, uncertain in a manner that exhibits impoliteness, latent aggression, and finally, a lack of 'self-insight', as her son John says.[1]

John plays a major role within the architecture of both 'lessons'. He is a professor of physics at Appleton College; however, his mother's invitation has nothing to do with his position there. From the beginning of the narrative, it is quite clear that Elizabeth's relationship tp her son, and to his wife Norma, is tense, distanced, burdened by missed chances in the past, and may even be characterized by a lack of genuine love – or a love that had been eventually substituted by a superficial sense of duty that one might suppose to be part of familial commitment. This is not to say that there are no scenes of tenderness and care – Coetzee demonstrates a concern that John feels for his mother in a few instances, yet leaves it unclear as to how Elizabeth really feels about her son – but the gulf between the two characters dominates their relationship. Here, Coetzee creates a telling contrast between her awareness of animals and their lives, and her latent, and sometimes explicit, ignorance towards her human fellow beings. At times, one gets the impression that Elizabeth simply forgets, or is even ignorant of the fact, that the young man accompanying her is her son.

In particular, John (but also Norma and some of the other figures who appear in the course of the events at Appleton) serves as a counter-voice to Costello's claim that our relation to animals and their ethical status, as well as our moral duties towards them is in tension with our factual behaviour towards nonhuman animals of all sorts. Hence, objections, hesitations and reservations, as well as alternative accounts of Costello's activism, are put into the mouths of John, Norma and others. Often enough, they represent well-known and prominent positions that have actually been defended by philosophers and animal activists, past and present, including Peter Singer, Tom Regan, Mary Midgley and, in a different respect, Thomas Nagel. Here again, the demarcation between fiction and the realities of an ongoing debate becomes blurred in interesting ways.

So, does Elizabeth Costello have a general message? To ask this straightforward question invites the danger of neglecting the setting which Coetzee has prepared for his central character and his readers. As much as Coetzee himself has refused to give a standard talk at Princeton, Elizabeth Costello also does not give us a detailed argument, a well worked out treatise, a message to be easily taken home. Rather, Coetzee seems to have created a resonance chamber constituted by Costello's attempts to express her deep concerns and by the divergent reactions to those concerns. Both her lectures and the various responses to them are literary offerings to which we, as readers, might respond without necessarily adopting one single stance. Coetzee, as well as Costello, both remain writers, authors in the fictional genre, not theorists under the consistent pressure to have intellectual clarity. The clarity that literature in fact provides is the capacity to reflect on the irreducible difficulty of taking sides in these debates, as well as on the conflict between divergent and (potentially) equally appalling or appealing standpoints – which may eventually involve the reader in this struggle to the point that it becomes his or her own, if it is not already.

Despite this polyphonic constellation, one can still pin down several aspects within Costello's ramified and somewhat meandering speech and responses to questions –

aspects that seem to be essential for appreciating her concern, and for understanding her impatience and dedication. The major thread running through Costello's remarks on animals is the cruelty against them; she alludes to the abattoirs and the industrialized animal farms that she had to pass on her way to Appleton College. However, Costello is even more concerned with the reasons behind our constant neglect of the reality of ongoing violence against animals, as well as their functionalization. It is this context in which Costello repeatedly comes up with the comparison of our treatment of animals with Nazi concentration camps like Treblinka (63) – combined with the desperate and exasperated question of how it had been possible to be blind to the disappearance of Jewish people, to have allegedly not known about the camps these people were transported to, to not have smelled their burning bodies. Costello states that these ignorant people, mostly Germans, 'lost their humanity' (64), and then adds: 'The crime of the Third Reich, says the voice of accusation, was to treat people like animals', while the thrust of her comparison is based on turning this 'accusation' upside down by seeing animals as subject to the same treatment as prisoners in concentration camps (65).

Without a doubt, Costello's comparison – and we will return to it in greater detail in due course – is the peak of her talk and, at the same time, its main source of irritation, anger, and even resentment. However, Costello's comparative performance belongs to a longer tradition (along with severe critiques of it) in which the reference to the Nazi past and the horrendous evil perpetrated against Jewish people has been placed in the context of our dealings with animals. The term *holocaust* is itself connected to the significance of animal sacrifices given to God, a historical and semantic background that might even help to elicit this comparison and its terminology.[2] Moreover, there are several prominent predecessors to Costello who have used this specific comparison to underline, in their view, the unacceptable industrial, but also experimental, treatment of animals. This group includes the Jewish writer and Nobel Prize laureate Isaac Bashevis Singer, as well as Jacques Derrida who reflects on the 'pathetic' self-evidence of this comparison, along with the pictures and images it provokes.[3] There are also voices without a Jewish background that rely on that comparison and the reference to genocidal mass murder. In the words of the philosopher and animal rights activist Tom Regan: 'Do we dare to speak of a Holocaust for the animals? May we depict the horror they must endure, using this fearful image of wanton inhumanity, without desecrating the memory of those innocents who died in the death camps?'[4] Regan replies to this rhetorical question in the affirmative, as many others do.[5] Nevertheless, this comparison remains, for some, objectionable, whereas it seems for others to be 'potentially useful and illuminating, and may help to underline the gravity of our oppression of nonhuman animals', as the philosopher and descendent of Holocaust survivors David Sztybel aptly states.[6] In this context, it is not without relevance *who* it is that is drawing this comparison.

Besides Costello's controversial comparison, there are further salient critiques in her lectures and replies. To begin with, Costello is highly critical of the idea that justifying our concern for animals lies in specific features common to human and nonhuman animals. Among the prominent candidates are reason, sensitivity, self-consciousness – all of which Costello is ready to refute by stating:

> The question to ask should not be: Do we have something in common [...] with other animals? (With the corollary that, if we do not, then we are entitled to treat them as we like, imprisoning them, killing them, dishonoring their corpses.) I return to the death camps. The particular horror of the camps, the horror that convinces us that what went on there was a crime against humanity, is not that despite a humanity shared with their victims, the killers treated them like lice. That is too abstract. The horror is that the killers refused to think themselves into the place of their victims [...].
>
> see above. 79

Critically, Costello distances herself from the logic of shared features for the obvious and often repeated reason that this line of thinking necessarily excludes every being not possessing the feature in question. Human beings – children, mentally-challenged people, people suffering from dementia – could easily drop out of moral concern.[7]

The second part of that passage leads to an additional aspect in Costello's account: '... the killers refused to think themselves into the place of their victims', she says. This is at the core of her diagnosis, as well as her demand on us which is derived from this diagnosis: to think oneself into the place of someone else. It is a kind of relocation of oneself 'into the place of' someone else. It is an intentional act of cognition ('to think'), but apparently also of acknowledging, discerning, understanding, feeling.[8] The 'crime against humanity' consists here in a refusal to perform that capacity for sympathy and empathy. It is Costello's conviction that this capacity for empathy is far less limited than usually assumed. In an almost deprecatory response to Thomas Nagel's seminal paper 'What it is like to be a bat?'[9] Costello explains that it is her task as a writer to think herself into characters that have never existed in order to infer from this imagining 'what it is like to be (...)' and that it is also open to our imagination to think oneself into an animal. Thus, she states: 'If I can think my way into the existence of a being who has never existed, then I can think my way into the existence of a bat or a chimpanzee or an oyster, any being with whom I share the substrate of life' (80).

Here, Costello is in danger of reactivating what was previously criticized, namely that the fact of sharing something with an entity that one tries to think oneself into is also the condition of doing so successfully. And it remains unclear and vague what this 'substrate of life' – allegedly shared by bats, apes, marine animals and human beings alike – really is. However, what becomes clear is Costello's interest in a completely different approach to the 'lives of animals' that is not dictated by the Western rationalism connected to the names of Thomas Aquinas, Descartes, and Kant (all of whom have their appearance in Costello's talk and are targets of her critique, esp. 67). This approach hints at the possibility of what she calls 'sympathetic imagination', which has more to do with the abilities of the 'heart' than with the capacities of our reasoning (80).

All these hints are really no more than hints. These three aspects of Costello's concern – the comparison between the treatment of animals and the Holocaust, the refutation of the notion of shared features as a justification for our moral duties towards others (including animals), and the attempt to change our thinking about animals through regarding this kind of 'thinking' as a matter of 'heart', and not primarily of reason – will accompany us in the sections to come.

3 A delicate comparison and its aftermath

First, it is disputed whether Costello's references to the Holocaust, concentration camps and the Nazi past really constitute an actual comparison, not just another trope. A few commentators suggest that, instead, we are dealing with a *metaphor of persuasion* in passages like the following in which Costello claims: 'We are surrounded by an enterprise of degradation, cruelty, and killing which rivals anything that the Third Reich was capable of, indeed dwarfs it, in that ours is an enterprise without end, self-regenerating, bringing rabbits, rats, poultry, livestock ceaselessly into the world for the purpose of killing them' (65). The South African philosopher Ward Jones comments on this:

> Elizabeth Costello is here redescribing the animal industry by way of a metaphor: the animal industry, she says, is a Holocaust. A metaphor works by claiming that a target object is susceptible to the properties of a new, introduced object. In saying that the animal industry is a holocaust, Elizabeth Costello is inviting us to take the moral attitude appropriate to the Holocaust – that of moral horror – and to apply it to the animal industry that surrounds us.[10]

There are different possible reactions to this characterization. One could insist on Costello's claim that we are in fact dealing with a comparison here without denying the metaphorical element within it, insofar as – such as in the Aristotelian tradition – every metaphor entails, or is based on, a comparative act.[11] In this case, one should be ready to explain which exact sense this metaphorical element, that presumably goes beyond the comparative act, consists in. Alternatively, if one does not want to commit oneself to this explanation, one could, generally, refute Jones's interpretation. Then, however, one must accept another commitment, namely to at least circumscribe the way in which a metaphor works and to take a stance within the wide field of theories on metaphors and metaphorical meaning in order to pin down why the above passage is not metaphorical. For the sake of the argument, there is a less difficult way out of this bind: by *not* refuting Jones's take and in regarding, heuristically, Costello's claim as a comparison – a modest approach that will be justified in the course of subsequent interpretation and by the aspects and details it brings to the fore.[12]

A similar move might prove useful for the alternative claim that Costello does not present a comparison or a metaphor, but an *analogy*.[13] One could, in response, deny that Costello's reference to the Holocaust entails an analogical element, but then we confront a problem similar to the one encountered in the case of metaphors: due to the close relation between comparisons and analogies, one would be committed to elaborating on the structural differences between both tropes – an obligation that again serves to separate us from the initial issue under discussion. Hence, I will stick to the comparative claim as heuristically fruitful without necessarily repudiating an analogical dimension. And there is another, simple reason for this focus on Costello's comparison between our treatment of animals and mass murder: it is she who presents this as a comparative act while being aware of its ambivalent status (62 and 65–6).

3.1 Costello, Kafka's Red Peter and the Holocaust

Now, what does Elizabeth Costello's comparison look like? First, there are *two* crucial comparisons at play. Right at the beginning of Costello's first lecture we find Elizabeth comparing herself to Red Peter in Kafka's 'Report for an Academy', an ape named Peter who conveys his life story before the members of a learned society. Peter adopts the behaviour of a human in the attempt to gain his freedom from conditions of confinement, eventually claiming that he is no longer capable of feeling like an ape (a fact which indicates that his transformation had been, in a way, successful, since Peter seems to be content with his achievement).[14] Elizabeth, also standing in front of a learned audience, alludes to this 'Report' by stating that she feels like Red Peter. However, it remains vague what she means to express by that surprising opening. Is she referring to Peter's transformation and the loss of his animal existence and experience? Then, Peter's development might be mirroring the ontogenesis of every single human being – something which may be considered 'successful' if an animal has become human and is no longer able to feel the animalistic existence anymore, or return to it.

Or is Costello's introductory remark a critique of the suppression of our existence to rules, customs and standards that are alien to us, and hence, by effect, alienating? A passage that indicates Costello's pervasive criticism of rationalism and reason might be taken to confirm this reading. She quotes Kafka's Peter: 'Do I have a choice? If I do not subject my discourse to reason, whatever that is, what is left for me but to gibber and emote and knock over my water glass and generally make a monkey of myself?' (68). Costello describes Red Peter as a 'branded, marked, wounded animal' – exactly how she sees herself while speaking to her audience. From the start, her lecture is enigmatic not only because she leaves it to her audience to discover the comparison's payoff, but also because of the status of her comparison. She comments on this status as follows: 'I did not intend it [the remark that I feel like Red Peter] ironically. It means what it says. I say what I mean. I am an old woman. I do not have the time any longer to say things I do not mean' (62).

She means what she says – she feels like the ape in front of an academy. Elizabeth is the 'branded, marked, wounded animal' whose existence thus far had been a kind of preparation for playing a human being not only in its mode of constant pretence, but also for playing a human being to the point where no return to animal life is possible. Her 'second nature'?

However, apart from both standing in front of an academy, the comparison between Peter and Elizabeth begins to dissolve, and differences emerge that Costello just ignores or suspends. Peter's journey is an attempt to gain the freedom to eventually experience freedom's ambivalences,[15] while Costello stands at Appleton because of an invitation she has freely accepted. After all, Peter leads a human life that he reports in some detail to be fairly happy and not at all similar to that of a 'wounded animal'. He intentionally underlines, at the end, that he just 'reports' to the academy. This is the final sign that the mere report cannot be just that (a report), since underlining the name of the genre is not part of the genre of a report, but functions on a different level. Costello seems to miss the absurd irony in Kafka's short story that either narrates an impossible gathering between a monkey and the silent members of an academy, or that *all* participants in that scene are animals struggling to become human, surrounded by other animals, nonhumans, or no-longer-nonhumans. In any case, contrary to Costello, Red Peter cannot only mean what he says; there is much more to it, and not giving space to this surplus shows Costello to be lacking the humour required to appreciate the joke in all its seriousness.

The question is now whether (or to what extent) this one-sided first comparison touches on the more prominent and dangerous second one. Some of the passages in which Costello presents the comparison between our treatment of animals and the Holocaust have already been quoted. This comparison appears repeatedly. Here is another passage taken from a later chapter of the book called 'The Problem of Evil': 'The massacre of the defenseless is being repeated all around us, day after day [...] a slaughter no different in scale or horror of moral import from what we call *the* Holocaust; yet we choose not to see it' (156). It is obvious that Costello is referring primarily to industrialized animal farms that function as slaughterhouses for effective killing. She intentionally only hints at this industry with which everyone is at least vaguely familiar to make the impression even stronger by calling on everyone's imagination (63). She also uses the comparison to react critically to objections against this comparative act. She states:

> And to split hairs, to claim that there is no comparison, that Treblinka was so to speak a metaphysical enterprise dedicated to nothing but death and annihilation while the meat industry is ultimately devoted to life (once its victims are dead, after all, it does not burn them to ash or bury them but on the contrary cuts them up and refrigerates and packs them so that they can be consumed in the comfort of our homes) is as little consolation to those victims as it would have been – pardon the tastelessness of the following – to ask the dead of Treblinka to excuse their killers because their body fat was needed to make soap and their hair to stuff mattresses with.
>
> see above. 66

Costello shows here that she is very aware that she is entering into a precarious zone by admitting the 'tastelessness' of what her comparison has to offer. Immediately after this passage she reflects on this polemical move and its 'cheap point-scoring'; although, the coolness of philosophical expression, 'the language of Aristotle and Porphyry, of Augustine and Aquinas, of Descartes and Bentham, of, in our day, Mary Midgley and Tom Regan' is 'available' to her (66). After all, she speaks not as a member of philosophers, but as a writer. And a twist in the comparative act belongs to the heated polemic of that intellectual guild by not only relating a concentration camp to an 'animal farm', but also by using the difference between them precisely to amplify the initial comparison: accordingly, the fact that the killing of animals is part of our food production is, Costello implies, by no means the justification for this institution of industrial killing. If this means-ends logic were truly valid, the use of dead bodies killed at places like Treblinka would at least soften the horror of mass murder and destruction.[16] The 'tastelessness' of this suggestion is supposed to strengthen the adequacy of comparing Treblinka with these farms – with a blunt, but consistent conclusion: 'Each day a fresh Holocaust' (80).

In sum, Costello wants first to bring awareness to this killing industry by comparing it to a past that elicits moral horror, anger, shame and disgust – in order to generate the same reaction in the case of animals, regarding their lives and deaths. Secondly, Costello admits to trying to consciously and intentionally chastise people, not for primarily failing to engage their thoughts and reasoning, but rather their 'hearts' (79; see also section 4). The 'wounded' animal is not part of a deductive argumentation, but the embodied result of a perverse system, while these oppressed and maltreated corpses bear an evidence that eventually leads to similar reactions and 'reactive attitudes' as it does in the case of Nazi concentration camps. It is a transfer of moral evidence. Thirdly, this hope is nothing more than a hope, and not a reality yet. Comparing the treatment of animals with mass killing also entails its comparative inversion: our blindness and ignorance regarding the lives and suffering of animals reminds Costello of the blindness and ignorance of the people living in close proximity to these camps and, allegedly, not knowing – or being unable to 'afford to know' – what was really going on there (64). Not knowing is then a way of being guilty too. 'Only those in the camps were innocent,' Costello concludes (ibid.). This is a fourth aspect, namely that the expectation that this wrong-doing will be punished by being 'inwardly marked by the after-effects of that special form of ignorance' remains unfulfilled, as it does when it comes to our wrong-headed practice of treating animals – although, 'we cannot accept that people with crimes on their conscience can be healthy and happy' (65; cf. also 80).

Stirring up, changing and reforming our attitude and moral stance concerning animals and our relation to them cannot leave our real actions untouched. Here, the truthfulness of a belief and conviction lies in its consistency with the deeds derived from it.[17] Accordingly, Costello not only points to a perverse system and our neglect of it, but also alludes to the effects of giving up our ignorance: having an awareness of, wanting and 'affording' to know about, the treatment of animals; and by implication, feeling guilt in terms of our wrongdoing in the past while not being able to live 'healthy and happy' without that change of 'heart'. There are also more practical effects that are important to Costello: obviously, the protest against the inhumane practices of factory farming in all its forms; moreover, vegetarianism as a consequence of refusing to 'put in your mouth the corpse of a dead animal'; and to really find it 'nasty to chew hacked flesh and swallow the juices of death wounds' (83). In a conversation after her lecture, Costello uses this response taken from Plutarch's moral essays to underline the awkward differences we are ready to implicitly draw in regard to our dealings with fellow humans and animals, dead and alive.[18] This is, for Costello, an inconsistent way of acting, whereas her way of presenting this inconsistency is, for her son John, who is standing next to her and listening to her already well-known 'Plutarch response', an unnecessarily harsh way of putting the matter. 'Plutarch is a real conversation-stopper. [...] He wishes his mother had not come' (83).

Red Peter and the Holocaust – is there any relation between both comparisons presented in her lectures? It is fair to say, I think, that there is some tension here. While Kafka's 'Report for an Academy' reflects ironically on the development of a particular being towards his second and, more-or-less, human nature as a gradual loss of his animalistic pre-existence, these potential transitions are not among Costello's most critical issues. Rather, our irresponsibility towards animals, given our dominance and power, is the target of her severe admonition. She might feel displaced, standing there in front of her academic audience at Appleton; Red Peter, however, does not appear as the 'wounded animal' that Costello considers him to be, despite his long, dangerous journey from the 'Gold Coast' to a music hall in Hamburg. Hence, if one wants to defend Costello's comparative reference to the Holocaust, one must disconnect it from the fact that she misinterprets Red Peter's story, as well as from – as we shall see later – other problematic aspects within Costello's speech and personality.

Costello, as we have already seen, is not unaware of the precariousness of her comparisons, especially between animal industries and the Holocaust. She is also aware of addressing her audience as irresponsible, since those sitting there in front of her are the ones who are in danger of becoming like all the ignorant people who neglected the reality of mass killing during the Nazi era and wilfully deceived themselves in remaining passive.[19] Costello's comparison does not only concern past atrocities, but contemporary ones too; her audience resembles those living around Treblinka. Stephen Mulhall comments on Elizabeth's comparative suggestion as follows: 'But what wounds her most deeply is not the likelihood that her comparison and charge will be thought morally incompetent and intellectually disreputable to the point of insanity; it is the fact that the position into which she places herself by making both is one that makes *her* seriously contemplate the possibility that she is going mad [...].'[20] In following Mulhall and by evaluating Costello's comparisons, one should pay attention to two different dimensions at play here (that are, of course, not completely separable from each other), namely the *factual adequacy* of Costello's advocacy for the 'lives of animals' and the *personal involvement* of herself, as well as her audience, who turn out to be some of the comparison's addressees. The first dimension dominates the comments on and reviews of Coetzee's novel (although it has often been denied that *Elizabeth Costello* belongs to this genre of novel)[21], and I shall begin with this 'factual' layer as well.

3.2 Three objections

The comparison between our treatment of animals and the killing of Jews in concentration camps has encountered three basic objections that touch on the general legitimacy of that comparative act: for one, there is a serious danger, some argue, of *playing off* one sort of 'difficulty of life' against another.[22] Comparing A and B is then tantamount to a certain kind of 'play-off' totally inadequate to the status of both *relata* A and B. It is not the comparison as play-off that is the problem, but the character of the items to be compared with one another seems to prohibit that comparison. The concern consists, in this case, in the impression that Costello is already committed to this play-off by simply relating A and B comparatively. However, that charge is based on far-reaching assumptions concerning the comparative intention and turns out itself to be inadequate because it does not leave any space for the possibility of underlining aspects in A – precisely on behalf of B. What Costello is really doing then, is not mutually playing A off B, but reciprocally amplifying aspects of both items.

The second objection underlines crucial differences between animals and victims of inhumane treatment, differences that are in danger of being neglected in the act of *comparing as equalizing*. At Appleton Professor O'Hearne is the one who expresses this reservation. According to him: 'Animals live, and they die: that is all. Thus, to equate a butcher who slaughters a chicken with an executioner who kills a human being is a grave mistake. The events are not comparable. They are not on the same scale' (109). The point here is not so much the technical question of whether comparability really presupposes scalability (in fact, it does not) or what it exactly means to say that both events are truly 'on the same scale'. The point here lies rather in our different reactions to the butcher and executioner. I do think that these 'reactive attitudes' are telling and important for an open debate about this issue. However, it is questionable that these differences justify the inference from the gap between *A* and *B*, to the incomparability of *A* with *B*, as O'Hearne seems to suggest. Comparisons are, after all, not identifications.

The most prominent concern is the charge of undermining the *unique and singular character* of the Holocaust – a character that removes this event from every comparative setting and declares it to be incomparable. The claim is not that the Holocaust could not be technically compared to other items or *relata*; in this sense, singularity is compatible with comparability (since singularity might even be considered to be a result of a comparison). The claim is rather that no comparison can do justice to that particular event and to those involved in it. It would, as Abraham Stern, another character in Coetzee's 'novel' and also a professor at Appleton, states in his response to Costello's lecture, 'insult the memory of the dead' (94). Stern is invited to join the dinner after Costello's talk. Instead of doing so, he writes a letter to her stating that she 'misunderstand[s] the nature of likeness' by inverting the initial comparison: the fact that Jews had been treated like animals does not, Stern holds, allow for claiming that animals are now treated like those imprisoned in concentration camps. Assuming that *A* is like *B* does not automatically allow for assuming that *B* is like *A*. This again presupposes a certain attitude to the Holocaust and its horror, as well as its victims. The inversion does not necessarily imply 'blasphemy', as Stern puts it; rather, it might underline and highlight the horrendous character of the Holocaust, and in presupposing this character, she turns her attention to another instance of moral collapse. It is quite the opposite of denying or belittling anything; on the basis of the gravity of the Holocaust, something else – that entertains particular similarities with that event – becomes the focus of our attention. Costello does not react to Stern's letter. The critique remains unanswered – and maybe unanswerable (cf. 117).[23]

Critically, the historical integration of the Holocaust into a chain of events might, then, already be regarded as an expression of relativizing it.[24] This is, of course, a real danger, but by no means a historiographic necessity. Constructively, to dissolve the triad of integration, comparison, and potential relativization, one might argue for a specific, 'ontologically' extraordinary status of the Holocaust, either to justify its incomparability, or to severely restrict the items to which the Holocaust could possibly be compared. This second version can be found in what Robert Nozick has to say about the Holocaust. This event, he claims, is 'so momentous' that it is almost impossible to grasp its 'full significance'.[25] Hence, the uncertainties when it comes to the question of how to react to it today – remembering, forgiving, forgetting? Nozick adds: 'I believe the Holocaust is an event like the Fall in the way traditional Christianity conceived it'.[26] As a consequence, 'the Holocaust has shut the door that Christ opened',[27] and it changed the situation of mankind altogether. Christ might have died for all our sins – but not for *this* one, not for what happened in Auschwitz, Treblinka and all those places the names of which are engraved into a history that has 'ruined the reputation of the human family'.[28] Nozick, a layman in theology, draws two major conclusions from this: one, what Christ has done for us, is something that humans now have to do for themselves; two, the death of a particular person can still be a true tragedy, but after the Holocaust there is no further tragedy and additional loss to be found in the death of humankind.[29]

What Nozick is presenting here is not necessarily the claim of full-blown incomparability regarding the Holocaust. Rather, he seems to refer to a very limited range of items that have the status to be comparable to the Holocaust: the mythological fall and the reconciliation by Christ. This is itself a comparison insofar as Nozick is not intentionally giving a doctrinal statement, but is rather comparing the status of the Holocaust with the status that both events have for Christianity and its dogmatic company. However, Nozick leaves room for two readings: either he merely sticks to a comparative mode by stating that the Holocaust has a similar weight in a secular age as the Fall and the work of Christ have had for the Christian tradition – which is in fact a claim *for* the singularity of the Holocaust (insofar as the Fall and Christ's work are of no existential significance outside of Christianity); or Nozick maintains that the Fall and the work of Christ both had an exclusive status – and the Holocaust is the third event 'enjoying' that 'ontologically' transformative privilege (which is indeed a theological statement). Thus, either he claims the Holocaust to be truly incomparable (precisely by using comparison), or he severely limits the comparative range and restricts the incomparable status to this range.

Both readings are, indirectly, challenged by Costello's comparison. Obviously, she does not restrict incomparability to certain quasi-theological items, nor does she think that the Holocaust is incomparable, hence the question of whether the comparison she presents is factually defensible. There are several possibilities for potentially fruitful comparisons between the Holocaust and our treatment of animals that are based on different suggestions for comparative regards: for instance, '"degradation and destruction' (vivisection, skinning, displacement from homes), a particular 'apparatus' (secrecy, namelessness, bureaucratization), 'forms of agency' (ordinary perpetrators, disowning of responsibility, conditioned indifference), etc.[30] Elizabeth Costello herself is not explicit when it comes to these possibilities, at least not in this structured way of scrolling through the *tertia comparationis*, but it is in line with her intention, and some of the listed comparative regards do play a role in her lecture.

Is this list of any help in assessing the Holocaust's incomparability? Those presenting these suggestions think, of course, that it is helpful in maintaining (referring to Costello) that, for her and in certain significant respects, comparisons between the Holocaust and what one might refer to as the oppression of animals can be delivered. This, one could add, is for Costello not a means of lowering the Jews, but rather of raising the animals to their level, as one commentator has it.[31] But again, this repeats the initial problem, rather than dissolving normative concerns. Professor Stern might still be convinced that – whether by lowering or raising them – bringing the Jewish victims and the maltreated animals to a shared level is insulting to (the memory of) these dead humans. We can at least specify the incomparability claim to mean not only that a comparison between *A* and *B* is (technically possible, but) normatively prohibited, but, more precisely, that (despite the partial adequacy of certain comparative regards) by bringing certain similarities to the fore, the overall comparison is, nevertheless, not justified. This can be expressed in the following manner:

(i) there are some comparative regards that are inadequate for *A* or *B*; and in sum, the entire comparison between *A* and *B* then turns out to be inadequate;
(ii) even if all comparative regards for *A* and *B* were normatively unproblematic, an overall comparison between *A* and *B* is still not allowed.

(i) stands for a *logic of addition*, meaning that if one or more (how many?) comparative regards are inadequate for *A* or *B*, then the overall comparison itself becomes inadequate. (ii) represents, in contrast, the *logic of emergence*, meaning that the overall comparison is, in any case, inadequate, independent of the (in)adequacy of particular comparative regards. While in (i), cases of adequate comparison are possible, this is excluded in (ii). The claim that the Holocaust is incomparable follows the logic of emergence.

3.3 Costello's (un)belief

At the end of section 3.1, I distinguished between the *factual adequacy* of Costello's advocacy for the 'lives of animals' and the *personal involvement* of herself as the one who compares. It is this second aspect that will occupy us in the following section. This brings us to the relation between the person as subject of the comparative act and its potential impact on the comparison's adequacy. Here, we encounter two telling, almost disturbing, elements in Coetzee's narration, namely Elizabeth Costello's character as shown in her relationships to her family members and to her colleagues at Appleton, and her far-reaching critique of reason and a 'Western' notion of rationality.

If one generally categorizes ethical approaches into those focused on a person's actions and the effects of those deeds, on the one hand (*action-centred*), and on the other hand, those concentrated on the personality of a particular moral agent (*agent-centred*), then it is not difficult to guess which program Costello would prefer. The latter account is often enough identified with virtue ethics, being concerned not with acting and its consequences, but rather with its precondition, the person and his or her character. This has enormous consequences not only for what ethics engages with and might be reacting to, but rather, and more fundamentally, for what ethics itself really *is*. Obviously, Costello is not interested in these methodological labels, but what she has to say about our treatment of animals and our particular kind of moral failure refers to one of the most central issues in virtue ethics, namely character formation. 'Ethical knowledge' is then not primarily about the righteousness of a particular act, but about the 'possession of a good character'. It is not about acting correctly, but about becoming a virtuous person. Hence, the moral flipside of this approach lies in the more fundamental criticism that falling short of attaining goodness is not just a mistake among others, but a vice informing (or even infecting) the entire personality.[32]

Elizabeth Costello is not merely addressing our deeds and misdeeds in her talks, but also our personal lack of awareness for the 'lives of animals'. She points to our moral blindness to their being, our ignorance that is, to her, comparable (and similar) to its counterpart in Germany during the 1940s. Although Costello is aware of her own inconsistency in her dealings with animals, she lacks an equally acute sensitivity when it comes to her immediate surroundings, her family, and work life. She criticizes herself for her own inconsistency in advocating vegetarianism while accepting the 'obscenity' of using products made of animal skin (89); in contrast, her behaviour towards other people shows traces of misanthropy, bordering on contempt and disdain.[33] Given the importance she attaches to 'sympathetic imagination', it is remarkably infrequent that we see it at work in her interactions with others.

It is not an exaggeration to say that Coetzee portrays his main character as an unlikable person in almost every scene in which the reader encounters her. She regards her own childhood as a rather sad period (4–5), and her relationship with her sister (a whole chapter is dedicated to indirectly exploring that theme) is highly distanced and reserved (117). Costello's Appleton stay is plagued by latent, and sometimes explicit, tensions, along with arguments with her son John and her daughter-in-law, Norma (59–60), and Costello seems unaffected by the fact that her grandchildren have to eat at a separate table since they get meat for dinner (60). Moreover, there is almost no attempt on her part to stop this cascade of self-isolation. On the contrary, the disputes, especially with John, lead to impasses or a burdened silence, preventing any true closeness with her son, which is particularly visible during the scene in which they meet again after two years' absence, and in the instance where she claims that her sister Blanche is 'merely a sister in blood. The others are truer sisters, sisters in spirit' (126).

Coetzee, however, does not merely portray Costello's isolation as plain distance; he also creates scenes of open impoliteness and irreconcilability in which others are hurt. In her discussion following the talks at Appleton, her colleagues try to reach out. This might be part of the usual academic small talk, but it is also an attempt to better understand her position. Costello, however, reacts almost rudely by refusing all overtures from the other side to explain her position and by answering their questions with even less clarity. The dean asks her if her advocacy for animals is based on moral grounds. She refutes this laconically, adding that she wants to save her soul (89). In her reference to Red Peter, Costello states that if he 'had any sense, he would not have any children' (75). Apart from the difficulty of combining this statement with her general account of the status of animals, this claim must be more than irritating for her son, given her initial identification with Red Peter.[34]

Costello's actions are not always well-considered. Seeing Norma and her kids, Costello says to herself: 'Everyone comes to terms with [life], why can't you? *Why can't you?*' (115) and comes to the point where she considers the thought that she herself might be truly mad. And it is an intriguing move by Coetzee to present some of Elizabeth's reactions to others as indications of a deep tension in herself, which show the inconsistency between her actions and judgments, and, eventually, even provide the reader with more pleasant glimpses into her character. In a letter to her sister who espoused a form of religious conservatism in a talk that Elizabeth also attended, Costello wrote something that might just as easily apply (if not more so) to her own advocacy for animals: 'Blanche, Blanche, Blanche, who would have thought you would end up such a hardliner?' (133).

Costello has become a hardliner herself. She not only criticizes our treatment of animals, but also the dominant mode of thinking about them. First, she repudiates the prominent tradition of philosophical rationalism in the wake of Descartes and Kant (112). Then, she extends this critique by attacking reason in general, and declares: 'Both reason and seven decades of life experience tell me that reason is neither the being of the universe nor the being of God. On the contrary, reason looks to me suspiciously like the being of human thought; worse than that, like the being of one tendency in human thought. Reason is the being of a certain spectrum of human thinking' (67). While her audience does not react to this sweeping blow, it is Norma who hints at this contradictory gesture: 'There is no position outside of reason where you can stand and lecture about reason and pass judgement on reason' (93). The criticism of reason and rational thinking presupposes what is refuted by that very critique.

Costello does not end with reservations against reason and rationality, but even goes on to express doubts about thinking and believing, a criticism that remains obscure and vague. 'I don't know what I think, says Elizabeth Costello, I often wonder what thinking is, what understanding is. Do we really understand the universe better than animals do?' (90). This last stage of refusal is the main theme in the Kafkaesque final chapter of *Elizabeth Costello*. In a dream-like setting adapted from Kafka's parable 'Before the Law', Costello is asked to write down what she believes in. In several attempts, she radicalizes her doubts concerning belief. Either the refutation of reason also applies to beliefs: 'she no longer believes very strongly in belief' (39); or she distinguishes between having a belief and the belief in believing: 'I have beliefs but I do not believe in them,' she concludes (200). Her unbelief might also be nothing other than a belief, but in the end, she wants to get rid of that propositional state by giving space to our feelings and 'heart' (39 and 203).[35] She not only lacks certain required beliefs, but she seems to be incapable of belief itself; she wants beliefs without belief, and aims at persuading others without reasoning. This is the unresolved conflict of Elizabeth Costello, her tragedy, if you like.[36]

What is the point of both aspects – Costello's isolation and her anti-rational 'hard line' – for the quest for comparative adequacy? Is her engagement on behalf of animals challenged or even undermined by her latent, and sometimes, explicit disengagement from her fellow humans? Is it authentic to deny a crucial, or even categorical, difference between animals and human beings while continuing to treat both creatures differently (here turned upside down in her calling for awareness for animals and yet being insensitive towards her son, her sister, her colleagues)? Is it not hypocritical to call for sensitivity despite one's own vast personal insufficiencies? And how should we deal with Costello's bizarre confession of disbelief, her all-encompassing scepticism concerning reasoning, rationality and understanding? Is this just a reminder of all the shortcomings of Western rationalism in favour of the 'heart' as an alternative site for our moral sense, or rather, a self-contradictory announcement only justifiable by exactly that institution that has been attacked before, reasoning? And, in the end, is not Costello's comparison of our treatment of animals harmed and damaged by her twofold unbelief?

Comparing is an activity and a practice performed by someone, and the comparison's adequacy does not – at least, within Coetzee's setup – seem to be totally independent of and disconnected from the person standing behind that comparative performance. The delicate comparison referring to the Holocaust gives an example of this link: it does not come as mere accident that the major objection levelled against Costello's comparison is presented by Abraham Stern, a Jew. If this Jewish background does give his critique additional weight, then Costello's lack of awareness and empathy for her surroundings, as well as her whimsical (or at least, whimsically presented) disbelief in belief and reasoning, must equally be given critical attention. Accordingly, it is interesting to see how difficult it becomes now – given the constellation created by the author – to appreciate Costello's comparative reference to the Holocaust. If one, nevertheless, sticks to the initial comparative arrangement, the hurdle to be overcome for defending the delicate comparison is essentially raised, and so is its significance and pertinence. In this sense, Stern's objection and Costello's personal withdrawal and (anti)intellectual scepticism do not exclude the comparison's adequacy; rather, they allude to its embeddedness in a highly ramified and truly complicated context that has to be fully taken into account in order to appreciate the real weight of comparing our treatment of animals with what happened in German concentration camps. Simple and simplistic responses are no longer in sight here – and Coetzee tells us why this is so.

4 On extending our sense of possibilities

Is there a connection between a claim X and the person P representing and eventually defending X? Coetzee does not answer this directly, but he uses a narrative detour for his affirmative reply by making the main objection against Costello's comparison come from Stern's mouth. This connection might seem less plausible in the framework of an *action-centred* ethics that tends to uncouple X from P, while an *agent-centred* account relies on a P-bound X-claim in mirroring the contextual ramifications in which claims like X and non-X – including the assumption that a comparison is possible, as well as the opposite claim that an item is incomparable with others – have their sense and weight. In consequence, individuals involved in the relevant debate come into focus, particularly Elizabeth Costello herself who claims to feel like the ape Peter. From here, it is not far away to suggest, as Robert Pippin does, that her stories, parables, and comparisons are indeed about the 'lives of animals', while we, the humans, are the animals at issue, given what we do to other animals and what these deeds and misdeeds do, conversely, *to us*.[37]

There are, of course, further aspects to the relation between human beings and animals that inform and complicate that very relation: diachronically, the historicity of our attitudes towards animals;[38] synchronically, the divergent responses to animals that are far from any universal consensus, as Norma underlines (87–8); moreover, the mostly implicit differentiations we make between different groups of animals; and also, the impact of religious (or other) convictions on our treatment of animals, reaching from sacralization to contempt and disdain, as John maintains (104), while animal sacrifices can represent both extremes.[39]

It is a common move within animal ethics to justify the peculiar moral status of animals by referring to certain features shared by animals and human beings.[40] The catalogue of these features is long and includes reason, shared sensory modalities, self-consciousness or the ability to suffer[41] (a derivative position based on this idea of shared properties is used by the animal rights movement).[42] However, it belongs to the logic of 'sharedness' that animals fall short of the sufficient criteria and rights as soon as they do not possess or lose the feature(s) in question.[43] The same goes for human beings, especially in the case of disabled people and babies (cf. 90).

Elizabeth Costello also refers to this topic by indicating that most animals do not seem to have any sense of history, or that their being-in-the-world (to use Heidegger's notion; 95)[44] is a completely different mode of existence than ours, or that (to apply Derrida's example)[45] animals cannot be nude and know what nudity is. Costello asks rhetorically what one should conclude from animals lacking a particular feature. She says:

> No consciousness that we could recognize as consciousness. No awareness, as far as we can make out, of a self with a history. What I mind is what tends to come next. They have no consciousness *therefore*. Therefore what? Therefore we are free to use them for our own ends? Therefore we are free to kill them? Why? What is so special about the form of consciousness we recognize that makes killing a bearer of it a crime while killing an animal goes unpunished?
>
> 90

Costello refuses this logic of shared features. Instead, she puts the stress on overcoming one's personal ignorance by stating:

> they [the 'killers' in concentrations camps and those of animals] closed their hearts. The heart is the seat of a faculty, *sympathy*, that allows us to share at times the being of another. Sympathy has everything to do with the subject and little to do with the object, the 'another'.
>
> 79

This is not a 'self-contradictory plea for an archaic animal ethics',[46] as some commentators would have it, and it is not about humanizing animals either.[47] It is also not about a stable structure, securing an equally stable status – features to be uncovered, or rights to be formulated. Rather, it is about creating, eliciting, and invigorating a 'faculty' of the subject. And this sympathy does not belong to the realm of deductive arguments and 'reason', but to the 'heart' as an ability to emotionally respond to a being and to be affected and touched by it. Hence, Costello envisages a kind of moral sense, based not primarily on ethical deliberation, but on emotional responsiveness.[48]

In another, thematically related novel, *Disgrace* from 1999, Coetzee describes the development of such a responsiveness to animals through following the main character David Lurie. He experiences a sort of spiritual transformation from being an arrogant humanist, as well as a sexual predator, to a decent human and, yes, a human animal that has lost almost everything that was once meaningful to him. Regarding his relation to animals, especially to dogs, he goes through different stages, from a severe lack of care and a deep ignorance, to a growing love and real compassion. Eventually, Lurie is able to see himself and his disgraced condition reflected in these dogs. It is a growth of understanding by gradually beginning to recognize – while the reader is invited to grasp that understanding along with David – that he himself has an animal vulnerability as well. If this is a return to the logic of shared features – here, the attribute of being vulnerable – then it is not a feature that is just 'out there', as something that has 'to do with the object', but rather something that has to be endowed or even created by being exposed, in reality or in the reality of literature, to the 'lives of animals'.[49]

Literature – i.e. being involved in and captured by the act of reading, as well as being exposed to a peculiar, sometimes even alien, constellation and its characters – can enable such a growth in understanding by extending what we take to be possible, meaningful and relevant for ourselves and others. To examine our example again, David Lurie is rather unwillingly exposed to animals, their lives, and deaths, and for him it is this evidence of an undeniable experience that triggers a latent process of changing his attitude towards these creatures. There is no necessity for this silent, unlikely upheaval to occur. Coetzee's narration is precisely about the manifold obstacles to such a personal change, embedded in highly peculiar – biographical, social, historical – circumstances.

In contrast to generalizations by ethical theories, literature pays attention to particular cases. In this sense, the mode of argumentation and deductive reasoning is either replaced, or at least accompanied and hopefully enriched, by showing other possibilities for responding to, acting in, and mindfully discerning a particular situation. Literature, then, does not prescribe or provide advice about what one should do – it is not about alleged necessities; it unveils another way of doing things – and hence, it is about possibilities that may be uninteresting, irritating or exciting.[50] Literature is able to potentially touch and change the reader by participating in the nature of an experience by narratively circling around that very experience and eventually, by creating another, namely literary, experience with its own evidence.

This is exactly what happens when reading *Disgrace* and *Elizabeth Costello*. Far from being cowardly by hiding himself behind 'mere' literature and its façades, or lacking the guts to bring to the fore what is philosophically at stake,[51] Coetzee presents a tableau of divergent points of view that all are embedded in a concrete context that is either alluded to or made explicit. Costello's claims and concerns can only be appreciated within that ramified setting, and that applies equally to the objections expressed by John, Norma and Professor Stern. It is accurate to state that this is a precarious endeavour, since it 'has everything to do with the subject', and these subjects are obviously very different. Here, the reader has an important job to do as well, insofar as literature offers possibilities, but no ready-made conclusions.[52] 'Do you really believe, Mother,' John asks, 'that poetry classes are going to close down slaughterhouses?' (103). It is not sufficient to answer in the negative, but it is still required to hint at the dangerous potential that literature possesses. Thus, Costello is right in stating at the end: 'We can put ourselves in peril by what we write; or so I believe. For if what we write has the power to make us better people then surely it has the power to make us worse' (171).[53]

As already noted, Costello wants to move beyond the point of sympathy. Additionally, she calls for thinking oneself into the existence of a foreign and alien being in order to fully overcome our ignorance and carelessness. It is a theme which runs through almost all her 'lessons' that Costello has this imaginative capacity to think herself into very different beings, and that as a writer, she must do so. She claims that if she is able to think her way into the existence of a being that has never existed, then she must be able to think her way into the existence of 'any being with whom I share the substrate of life'. Moreover, there are no boundaries to this kind of 'sympathetic imagination' (80; cf. 22, 98).

By exploring this ambitious claim, Costello attacks 'realistic' positions as being at odds with this unbounded imagination and defends a distinctive realm beyond our epistemic, as well as linguistic, grasp. Hence, Thomas Nagel's depiction of the limits of sympathetically imagining 'what it is like to be a bat' is then a major target of Costello's critique.[54] Not that she has an actual argument against Nagel's position beyond referring to her own imagination in 'sharing the substrate of life' (whatever that might mean); rather, she turns the argument upside down by claiming that neglecting this imaginative capacity for thinking (or, rather feeling?) oneself into someone else, has been and still is the root of ignorance regarding the weak and downtrodden, may they be in concentration camps or in animal farms. In both types of scenarios, we meet a dangerous, almost immoral refusal to exert this faculty, Costello suggests.

5 Finally: the curious case of normative incomparability

Thus far, the line of argument has run from the delicate comparison between our treatment of animals and the Holocaust (as well as several objections to this comparative act), to the interrogation of different background assumptions concerning the status of human beings in relation to nonhuman animals, over to the debate about shared features and the relevant moral duties we have towards animals, to finally a debate about literature's impact on the reader in creating a 'sympathetic imagination'.

It might now be clear that I did not try to finalize, end or close the debate concerning our relationship to animals; or, put more precisely, that I did not aim at answering the question of whether Costello was 'right' in referencing the Holocaust (or, for that matter, in which sense Professor Stern was justified in protesting against that move). Instead, I attempted to gradually make explicit what constitutes the concrete context – as well as the emotional, biographical and intellectual surroundings – of the voices involved in this ramified conversation. Accordingly, I performed 'close' and, sometimes, rather 'distant' readings of relevant passages from *Elizabeth Costello* and *Disgrace* that exhibit the manifold connections between claims about comparative potential or their refutation in the name of incomparability, on the one hand, and the person presenting these constructive or critical claims, on the other. Insofar as there is such a link, Coetzee's readers encounter several obstacles to appreciating Costello's comparison and its adequacy, as well as David Lurie's conversion and its authenticity.

The major concern in this chapter has been to give a mindful account of what I have labelled as *normative* incomparability in contrast to its *structural* counterpart and its *constitutive* and *indexical* siblings. The first form of incomparability is a structural breakdown of a comparison that goes back to the relation between the comparative *relata* and their *tertium comparationis*. The relation between relevant items is such that a comparison is structurally impossible. I cannot give an example of this because there are no cases of this sort of incomparability that have been traditionally promoted and defended. Constitutive incomparability, however, goes back to a particular item that is to be compared with another one. Its incomparable character is due to the constitution of that item. For example, friendship is supposed to be constitutively incomparable with money because friendship is undermined at the moment of being integrated into a comparative setting, or because 'friendship' as a concept is *grammatically* misunderstood when compared with money (or anything else, for that matter). The indexical element to it lies in the fact that most (if not all) constitutive instances entail a personal element, meaning that, for example, friendship is incomparable with money *for someone* confronted with this comparison. Hence, there is a tension between the 'objective' aspect of incomparability, based on an institution or grammar that is independent of somebody's stance, and the necessarily person-bound perspective implying the claim that something is beyond comparison for someone, but not necessarily for others. This leads already to the normative version. Here, structurally speaking, a comparison is in fact possible, but nevertheless, there is another form of impossibility at work that literally forbids comparison. Either there are *evaluative* reasons (preferences, tastes) based on which a person refuses to actualize the comparative potential (for instance, comparing a loved one with someone else), or there are *moral* grounds that stand in way of performing a comparison (Stern's protest against Costello belongs to this version).

Normative (hence, evaluative or moral) incomparability is not located in the comparative setting (the structure and relation between the *relata* and the *tertium*), or in the relevant object (its constitution) or in the object's concept (its grammar). Rather, the normativity here is about the subject (not) performing this comparison. Accordingly, structural and constitutive incomparability is 'objective', i.e. it can be discovered and is a matter of fact and givenness. Normative incomparability is, in contrast, 'subjective', i.e. it is an assertion and a matter of concern and commitment.[55] Constitutive-indexical incomparability stands, as it were, between the structural and normative version by participating in aspects of both: it shares the 'objective' element with structural incomparability, since the limits to compare are not primarily based on person-bound considerations, but on the comparative setting and the item itself; and it shares the 'subjective' element with the normative counterpart, insofar as a comparison is not logically excluded – which is why the incomparable character of the relevant item has to be acknowledged by someone. Here, constitution and indexicality go hand in hand. To sum up:

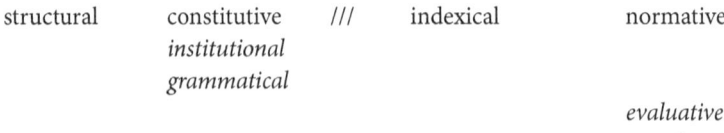

structural	constitutive	///	indexical	normative
	institutional			
	grammatical			
				evaluative
				moral

Obviously, Costello vs. Stern is a case of normative incomparability. Stern might be happy to call his protest 'moral', insofar as he regards the comparison between Jews and animals to be an 'insult', with an obligation or duty to avoid it. Costello, however, is not content with characterizing her stance on comparability as based on moral grounds (cf. 88–9), but it is not just an evaluative claim – in the sense of preferences and tastes – either. I assume that we might stick to calling it a genuinely moral stance, considering her reservation towards and uneasiness with generalized labels that belong to a philosophical tradition (a tradition already shown to be problematic in Costello's view).

The personal and, hence, indexical element in the claim that something enjoys the status of incomparability (or the refutation thereof) explains why cases of (alleged) incomparability are often highly disputed. This is the reason for referring to literature as a 'dense description' of such a severe dispute. This literary reference, I hope, provides an opportunity to do justice to conflicting – even incompatible – standpoints, as well as to show which contexts and divergent backgrounds inform these voices, counter-voices, and their normative weight.

I tried not to succumb to the temptation of playing the judge to determine who is right or wrong, justifying Costello's still delicate comparison against the deep concerns expressed by Stern, the Jew, with his particular experiences, expectations, and fears. And this hesitation might be applied to the philosophical business in general: is our primary task to decide between normatively loaded concerns in their peculiar tension, friction, and incompatibility; or is the task, rather, to give a thoughtful survey and 'perspicuous representation' (Wittgenstein) of the irreducible choir of divergent, and possibly even convergent, voices? Asking that question is to entertain sympathies with the latter option (see chapter 5).

In the end, we are not only dealing with different *standpoints*; we are also dealing with *ways of expressing* them. If there is an ethical element to comparisons, it is not merely about the (lack of a) justification of comparatively relating items with one another; it is also about comparisons as tropes and prominent parts of our language. The question of whether Elizabeth Costello was 'correct' in presenting her Holocaust reference to trigger our awareness of animals and their endangered existence then turns into the more subtle question of whether the language of comparisons was an appropriate choice for capturing the vulnerability of humans and animals. Here too, philosophy's task is not to play the role of a referee, but rather, it is about illuminating – or even suggesting – different, useful, surprising, exciting, irritating, even alien ways of articulating oneself. This affinity to contemplating alternatives – instead of advocating just one of them – might itself be a *moral* demand on the philosopher.

Epilogue: Living in an 'Age of Comparison'? An Interpretation with Diagnostic Intent

1 In the 'age of comparison'

In was in 1878 that Friedrich Nietzsche, then thirty-four years old, published 'a book for free spirits'. *Human, All Too Human* is also a volume 'for free associations', since this book touches rather abruptly on, among many other themes, the 'age of comparison' in § 23. It is the twilight of the nineteenth century in which Nietzsche presents his ambivalent consideration: the 'age' of industrialization, commercialization, quantification, professionalization. If deliberately approximate classifications are to be allowed, then the previous century could be regarded as one of trying out modern taxonomies: class, order, species, kind. And the natural scientist Carl von Linné, born in 1707, was the great initiator of that genre of thought during that time.[1]

About one hundred years later, such thinking in terms of 'orders' became increasingly accompanied by thinking in terms of 'assessments' (along with comparisons), and consequently with explicit or latent evaluations and assimilations. It is also the age in which cultural comparisons in the face of increasing experiences of otherness and alienation – think, for example, of the then-emerging travel literature – became more prominent, yet at the same time more precarious.

Comparisons do not only accompany a particular 'thought style', in which similarities and differences are stated, but they are themselves also a symptom of complicated historical transformations. These shifts are associated with catchwords such as 'disenchantment' and 'rationalization', as well as, in a critically-negative sense with the loss of transcendence or of even sublimity. What prevails – after the romantic era which provided the ultimate attempt to fight against these obituaries for bygone notions – are horizontal clusters and relations. The exceptional, the sublime gets substituted – here again, if approximations may be allowed – by flat hierarchies. And for this, comparisons are perfect for presupposing, or even creating, a certain degree of equality in kind and category.

It is still difficult, yet possible, to engage in a more comprehensive diagnosis of modernity as the era of the similar, of assimilation, of making things equal by standardization. Modernity could even be characterized as an epoch that became aware of and called for a norm-creating equality: 'Opinions all provided / The future pre-decided / Detached and subdivided / In the mass production zone.' This is what the

Canadian rock band Rush was singing about in 'Subdivisions' at the beginning of the 1980s, while the accompanying music video shows architectonic wastelands of indistinguishable suburbs in the late-Fordist era. However, the mass production zone is by no means just a North American phenomenon, when one takes into account that the lower-middle-class society of the GDR generated similar scenarios.

Nietzsche and Rush stand at the beginning and the end, respectively, of that long 'age of comparison', and, as we shall see, there is a new beginning of that age again today. The following reflections resolve the chapter title's genitive in order to sketch in which way the texture of the present age might affect practices of comparing and, more importantly, which role comparative procedures could assume when facing the structure of our late-modern 'age'.

2 On Nietzsche's assumption

To meet this twofold concern, we might take a look at Nietzsche's relevant assumption that is expressed as follows:

> The less men are bound by tradition, the greater is the fermentation of motivations with them, and the greater in consequence their outward restlessness, their mingling together with one another, the polyphony of their endeavours. Who is there who now still feels a strong compulsion to attach himself and his posterity to a particular place? [...] Such an age acquires its significance through the fact that in it the various different philosophies of life, customs, cultures can be compared and experienced side by side; [...] There is likewise now taking place a selecting out among the forms and customs of higher morality whose objective can only be the elimination of the lower moralities. This is the age of comparison! It is the source of its pride. [...] And then posterity will bless us for it – a posterity that will know itself to be as much beyond the self-enclosed original national cultures as it is beyond the culture of comparison, but will look back upon both species of culture as upon venerable antiquities.[2]

Nietzsche's statement entails a diagnostic as well as an instigating dimension. In contrast to his previous work, the *Untimely Meditations* (especially its second part), Nietzsche does not refute tendencies toward levelling down, or even toward equivalence among all values as a "historical malady"[3] here. Rather, he sticks to a more benevolent reading of the situation that is characterized by the dissolution of old attachments. Local cultural connections and affinities are coming increasingly under pressure and are being replaced by a 'polyphony of [...] endeavours' that are playfully exposed to different voices, influences, and 'customs'. And here, comparisons come to the fore so that the theoretical and practical approaches to the world are not just abstractly juxtaposed with one another. Comparing these approaches turns out to be performative, in the sense that the reader is invited to explore these alternatives.

Nietzsche derives his mission from this invitation: the playful trying-out of alternatives in fact implies serious ambitions in the name of a "higher morality." He leaves no doubt that the pertinent cultural comparison is normatively upgraded in a double sense. On the one hand, the 'age of comparison', that is also the age of relativism-friendly historicism and of the 'end of metaphysics', allows not only for lining up 'forms and customs', but also for choosing the best of their options. What we can see here is the highly topical 'dialectics' of comparatively levelling down – the juxtaposition of options by a *tertium comparationis* – combined with 'strong evaluations' precisely by means of comparisons that uncover or even create new differences.

On the other hand, Nietzsche applies that cultural comparison between 'various different philosophies of life, customs, cultures' to itself. With this move the synchronic comparison turns into a diachronic one between cultural epochs: that comparative age justifies, Nietzsche says, 'pride', because it contributes to the 'elimination' of inferior approaches to the world. One not only leaves behind the provinciality of a culture of local identities, but Nietzsche also lingers with the possibility that the 'age of comparison' itself could soon belong to the past. This would be the case if that age turned out to be a specimen of 'lower moralities'. In this view, there are subtle elements of a cultural history of progress that does not look back with resentment – or that even calls for a purifying forgetfulness – but that rather remains thankful with veneration for what made the comparison possible. Not untypical for Nietzsche, as he already anticipates the potential retrospective view here.

3 The dangers of levelling down

So far, we have talked about a comparatively facilitated 'dialectics' between levelling down and separation, between an all-encompassing identification and, at the same time, a singularity amplifying potentially everything. This mechanism that nowadays unfolds its full dynamics is already to be found in Nietzsche: comparative procedures level down the unequal to be able to compare in the first place – either in the mode of *reducing the variety* of one phenomenon to a comparatively-relevant aspect, or by pushing the not-simply scalable into an *alleged scalability*. However, within the comparison this levelling down turns into its opposite by exchanging assimilations for evaluations. Only what has been made equal by comparison allows for new differences, with the result that surprising evaluations and unexpected downgrades might occur. This age that finally wants to escape the 'mass production zone' as metaphor for an entire 'philosophy of life' and that celebrates the special, outstanding, singular and the dialectical balance between comparative levelling down and furnishing differences tends to favour, or even dissolve into, this second alternative. First, let's look at the option of levelling down.

In a short, overly-tendentious text entitled 'Theatre and Film. The Misery of Comparing', Peter Handke lambasts this figure of thinking and speech.[4] The writer appears as a patron of the particular, and he recognizes the dangers of that particularity in comparing as symptom of even-bigger difficulties. Three motives may be distinguished. First, Handke refutes the strange attempt to constantly compare oneself to the infinite (cf. 65). Such an attempt leads to the theologically well-proven idea that all are equal before God, i.e. that *coram Deo* all differences vanish. But, for Handke, it is not God as transcendent equalizer that is the problem but, rather, the impulse – and the 'misery' of wanting – to compare everywhere and even *in extremis* (66–7). Secondly, Handke alludes to the interventional element within comparative practices: comparisons do not leave their elements 'as they are', but adjust them for the purpose of comparing in the binary manner through reduction and scalability sketched above. Thirdly, Handke psychologizes comparing as an 'obsession' that does not stay with particularities, but that burdens the particular with evaluations. For Handke, evaluating something is tantamount to devaluing it (cf. 71).

Handke's critique of comparisons itself belongs to the subject matter of that very critique because his comparison between theatre and film vehemently advocates cinema. Nevertheless, the mechanics of levelling down become clearer. On the one hand, the presupposition of equality that is essential for comparisons gives licence to privilege the categorically equal over the different. The methodological paradox of cultural comparisons consists precisely in the ambivalence that what has been excluded by identification is integrated into its opposite;[5] put differently, even in cases where one thinks that something escapes from the order, one refers to that very order through comparison. Therefore: may the difference be big, the equality shall be bigger.

On the other hand, the often-porous comparability of the *relata* threatens the comparison between them. As long as the comparative items are scalable, comparative procedures are almost trivial. Hence, it appears to be a simple solution to reduce the not-yet scaled, and hence not-yet quantifiable, to something that is measurable. Comparability would then be fabricated using a reductive method. This move has to remain precarious when one thinks of ideal entities such as values, ideas, preferences. The problem is visible even in Handke's contradictory critique of comparisons when theatre and film or cinema are exposed to the 'misery of comparing', just to make that misery a bit bigger. Where the 'success' of theatre and film are measurable – by the number of viewers – the artistic element is no longer in focus, and where one tries to regain that focus, meaningful comparisons seem to be misplaced.

And yet, some mechanisms are clearer now due to this 'miserable' excursus: comparisons entail a somehow-intrinsic inclination to give preference to the equal. This tendency is combined with the constructive element of comparisons that do not simply find their *relata*, but that rather create their conditions by reductively adjusting the comparative items and their presupposed scalability. A mindful critique of comparisons would have to contemplate the unavoidability of that comparative intervention, as well as the limitations of comparisons. And such a critique is necessary as soon as one takes Handke's concerns seriously according to which a 'comparative addiction' is pervasive (cf. 65). This addiction, one could add today, might be increased and animated by the new potentials of all-encompassing and, yet, preference-driven search engines. Comparisons are becoming globalized by digitalization. And so does the levelling down that nevertheless turns into its equally global opposite.

4 And today: a 'society of singularities'?

This brings us now to the antipode of the aforementioned dialectics. And that counterpoint might be sketched best by looking at the thesis and theory claiming that we are living in a (self)singularizing society. Nietzsche's assumption that we would leave behind 'the self-enclosed original national cultures' and thereby loosen local ties can be read as an aphoristic precursor to that theory. A similar concern is expressed by the German sociologist Andreas Reckwitz who does not refer to Nietzsche. He says:

> In late modern times there is a structural transformation in society that consists in a social logic of the general losing its predominance to the *social logic of the particular*. This particular, the unique, i.e. what seems to be irreplaceable and incomparable, I would like to describe by the concept of singularity.[6]

Turning to the semantic milieu of his main concept, Reckwitz adds:

> If the general-particular denotes the variation of the same and if idiosyncrasy stands for the pre-social oddity, then singularity is socio-culturally fabricated uniqueness. These uniquenesses could be qualified, first, negatively: as *non-generalizability, non-interchangeability* and *non-comparability*.
>
> 51

Conceptually speaking, Reckwitz follows Kant's mereological qualifications in his *Critique of Judgment*. There, Kant introduces concepts as the general abstraction of the particular from perception. This qualification sticks to the domain of the 'general-particular', since the single element is here nothing but an example of general clusters.[7] But the idiosyncratic is also not meant either, because it is located beyond the social order and convention. Singularities, however, acquire the inheritance of what Kant has called the 'sublime': they do not reproduce general orders, but neither are they mere oddities outside known and acknowledged arrangements. Rather, singularities emerge within socio-cultural processes and are produced there. They represent a possible alternative to the 'mass production zone'; here, the 'dreamer or the misfit', as Rush has it, is not alone, but is rather the most 'popular guy'. Reckwitz investigates different areas and numerous social practices to elaborate on what he coins '*doing singularity*': no standard vacations anymore, but the documentation of remote travel paths; not the clothing size of what everyone's wearing, but stylistic conspicuousness and fashionable combination; not labour as merely providing earnings, but as an essential part of one's authentic self-expression. All the modes of self-presentation, individually and through organizations (especially politics), are also alluded to: leaving the standard behind and turning towards the unmistakable that is produced and presented, but that has also to be, as such, acknowledged and evaluatively and affectively accepted (cf. esp. 246 and 265).

Reckwitz combines his singularity thesis, first, with a diagnostic explanation for the genesis of today's 'sublimities' and, secondly, with a revitalization of the concept of class. He claims that three elements have become unified since the 1970s, which together catalyzed an '*authenticity revolution*' (19). We are its inheritors today: one, the development of a middle class with a transformed lifestyle; two, the transformation of the economy in a post-industrial age; and three, the digitalization of society (cf. 103).[8] A new class – this is the second element – has been created that has established itself along the lines of the old model with the emergence of a standard-oriented group, along with a poorer subclass left behind. Within this new class, evaluating success is no longer bound to money and material goods, but to the particularity of one's life-plan. The predesigned value-cluster that had been mandatory for the old middle class is no longer relevant, but the celebration of the different and particular, including the devaluing old orientations, has become central. One third of society, Reckwitz states, is successful in this, whereas the rest is marginalized and treated accordingly.

The 'comparison as social practice' (54) takes up, Reckwitz says, essential functions in terms of producing singularities, although he only alludes to this aspect *en passant*. The age of singularities is dominated by self-presenting and self-creating selves who have a particular 'profile' (246). Making the allegedly singular visible is based on comparing the supposedly incomparable. To dissolve this contradiction, one could refer to the techniques of reduction and scalability described above. Put in Reckwitz's own terminology: the status of singularity is suspended for the sake of comparability and in order to transform the singular into something 'general-particular' (see 175–6). Hence, according to the sociological class model, comparisons had to belong to the lower class or the old middle class. Consequently, the act of comparing would represent a sort of leftover that latently goes up against the 'logic of the singular' (54) and that repudiates the incomparability that was hoped for.

5 A hybrid ending: on the future of comparison(s)/comparing

Thinking about the prospects of comparison as structure and comparing as practice is in fact a hybrid endeavour. To mitigate this problem, a theoretical framework is required in which comparative procedures can be classified and in which their development can be portrayed or meaningfully anticipated. Such a theoretical frame is provided by Reckwitz's theorem of singularity.

However, this grand narrative of an all-encompassing singularization beginning around 1970 calls for corrections. Such singularizing inclinations have always been around, not just in late-modern times. One might think of such opposed projects as the Enlightenment and the romantic period, or epicentres like Paris, Berlin and California as localized promises of singularization. Hence, Reckwitz's assumptions concerning the genesis of these new societies are not without alternatives, and they do not necessarily require the developments after 1968 or a post-industrial economy. One might ask whether, during this development, new classes have been created or whether one should rather speak of a constant transformation of divergent modes of social affiliation. 'Singularization' is understood as fabricated particularity (in terms of its *mode*), as one's intended speciality (in terms of its *reflexivity*), and as evaluative-affective acknowledgement of a *unicum* (in terms of the *medium and its audience*). However, the modal-reflexive element has always been at home in singularization-friendly contexts. What, in contrast, has truly been new are the modes of presentation and reception, with the consequence that one has to postdate the emergence of the 'society of singularities', as it is not imaginable without digitalization. Thus, here we are dealing with a telling tension between singularity as latently existing subtext *and* as dynamics of singularity that has become prominent no earlier than during the last decade.

With these adjustments in mind, it is hard to overlook the fact that comparisons enjoy an eminent significance and that their practical relevance will be increased in an age with affinities for singularization. What might this development look like? Three figures of comparative ambivalence might be suggested:

(i) *Levelling down – singularization*. It is not quite right when Reckwitz connects singularization with incomparability in order to qualify comparability as methodical de-singularization (see the quotations above). Comparisons emerge only if a comparative regard is defined; 'before' that determination, one is not dealing with incomparability but, rather, with no comparison at all. 'Incomparability' does not denote anything, but functions – again, following Kant – as a limiting concept: as an idea without content and which does not refer to something concrete. As soon as a comparison is established, comparability is either presupposed or created. As mentioned before, this is simple in cases with quantifiable items in comparisons; hence, the challenge only awaits in cases of non-scaled *relata*. Absolute differences are not only dissolved by comparative relations; rather, a quantification is made possible by digital means of evaluation and, hence, alongside the transformation of intrinsic values into external evaluations, i.e. transforming properties into attributions, aka '*likes*'. Now, even ideal entities are comparable, and the markets of attraction are in fact calling for such a comparability by means of the massive potential within global search engines.

Up to this point, Handke is quite right to be afraid of comparative miseries: absolute differences are 'comparatively' levelled down. However, the initially equal and pure quantities disappear, because of what Reckwitz calls a *"winner take all/most"* logic (159). This logic amplifies small advantages into huge differences. The one who can accumulate attention – which is the new currency – has better chances of increasing his/her reputation. Hence, the purely quantitative generates new and quasi-absolute differences (cf. 179). This is an economic dynamic that is also pervasive in social contexts, that is comparatively amplified, but that cannot be easily arrested.

(ii) *The particular of the general – generalizing the particular*. The wider the range of addressees of the call to 'get singularized!' becomes, and the more intensely this invitation is accepted, the more contradictory this invitation appears to be. Singularizations create new elites that have a postmaterialistic self-image. Elites, however, are incompatible with an equal status for all, and they dissolve as such as soon as everyone is enjoying that status. Extravagance, niche-existence, subculture – all these 'institutions' rely on idiosyncrasies that are acknowledged as singular. If these idiosyncrasies become highly popular, an excessive acknowledgement ensues. Formerly marginal values, locally limited styles, and cultural peculiarities then become objects within a potentially global comparison. Urban design looks similar in San Francisco to how it does in Berlin-Neukölln; the much-maligned hipsters are indistinguishable in Brooklyn and Belgrade; and a blog, an Instagram account, or vacations in Georgia have already lost their flavour of particularity. An all-encompassing comparison has to amount to an equally all-encompassing thrust-reversal, if one sticks to the regulative idea of becoming singularized. What is left are phenomena of withdrawal; they might make us rethink our design; they could lead to what has been called 'detox', i.e. temporally abstaining from social media; or they may let us find new forms of traveling and tourism, etc. If one does not succeed in finding a more sovereign way of dealing with the not-so individual – which is rather more of a collectively-structured *Lebenswelt* than a permanent comparison in the name of the new – then the dance between the particular and the general will go on *ad infinitum*.

(iii) *Comparison's ubiquity – the anticomparative*. Scenarios (i) and (ii) are still based on the readiness to latently, or even explicitly, compare via rankings, lists, and scales of popularity. Therefore, in a globalized and digital world, attachments via descent, origin or biographical affiliation are increasingly coming under pressure, as Nietzsche already suggested. 'Natural' differences are replaced by extending the comparative matrix by means of *de-regionalization* (right up to cosmopolitanism), by *multiplying* comparative regards (including the possibility of processing them through algorithms), by *de-contextualization* of comparative procedures through eliminating more specific parameters or by aligning them comparatively, and by *de-subjectivization* of comparative agents through nonpersonal procedures of comparison. It is true: 'an age acquires its significance through the fact that in it the various different philosophies of life, customs, cultures can be compared and experienced side by side'. Comparisons also have an interventionist element that could lead to preferring regional extracts, to carving out certain regards, to only allowing for certain procedures in specific contexts, and to revitalizing anonymous comparisons through the use of search engines. And in fact, we experience these modes of limiting potentially all-encompassing comparisons everywhere: often enough the members of the new middle class, and hence the protagonists of singularization, only exist within reflexive, yet isolated, echo chambers of self-affirmation; the same goes for those trying to get rid of the comparative game by reactivating 'self-enclosed original national cultures'. Therefore, one has also to speak of the self-limitations, or even negativities, of singularizing societies. Here, the ultimately impossible ubiquity of comparisons is, understandably, limited. Or one cannot resist those comparative gestures to eventually defend the old affinities and attachments.

Scenario (i) reflects the quasi-capitalist element in comparisons, along with the destructive tendency towards monopoly; (ii) mirrors the impossibility of letting the particular become egalitarian, which makes new comparisons necessary; (iii) stands for a reaction critical of comparisons in order to suspend them or at least to regionalize, or even nationalize, them. All three ambivalences may become amplified in the future, given the fact that comparisons already enjoy the status of unavoidability. There is much evidence that we are in fact – and again – living in an 'age of comparison' whose final episode thus far is a society of self-singularizing ways of living.

The limits of comparisons, however, can only be circumvented by comparisons, and this calls for trying out additional *tertia* within a comparative arrangement. The one-sidedness of a particular comparative act might then be dissolved by considering alternative comparative regards. This explorative game of carefully handling divergent perspectives has to be practised anew time and again. If we expose ourselves to this kind of comparative training, we should not continue to speak of the 'misery' of comparing; rather, comparisons now testify to a methodological thoughtfulness. Therefore, it is all about adequate ways of dealing with comparisons and not at all about their abandonment. It is not necessary to broadcast thankfulness and veneration towards those who will eventually look back to the 'national cultures' and 'the culture of comparison'. Because the foundation of the 'age of comparison' already entails the endlessness of that very age, a 'posterity' to this epoch is, and may remain, beyond reach.

Notes

Introduction: Comparisons – A Marginalized Classic

1. For a similar observation, see Joachim Matthes, 'The Operation Called "Vergleichen"', in idem (ed.), *Zwischen den Kulturen? Die Sozialwissenschaften vor dem Problem des Kulturvergleichs* (Göttingen: Schwartz, 1992), 75–99, 75; Mathias Gutmann, 'Der Vergleich als Konstruktion – Systematische Bemerkungen zur Bestimmung entwicklungstheoretischer Ansätze in der Biologie', in Michael Weingarten and Wolfgang Friedrich Gutmann (eds.), *Geschichte und Theorie des Vergleichs in den Biowissenschaften* (Frankfurt a.M.: Kramer, 1993), 45–60, 47; Johannes Grave, 'Vergleichen als Praxis. Vorüberlegungen zu einer praxistheoretisch orientierten Untersuchung von Vergleichen', in Angelika Epple and Walter Erhart (eds.), *Die Welt beobachten. Praktiken des Vergleichens* (Frankfurt a.M./New York: Campus, 2015), 134–59, 134–5; Guy G. Stroumsa, 'In Search of a New Paradigm', in idem (ed.), *Comparative Studies in the Humanities* (Jerusalem: Israel Academy of Sciences and Humanities Press, 2018), 7–13, 9.
2. See Ruth Chang on 'comparativism': it 'is the view that a comparison of the alternatives with respect to an appropriate covering value "determines" a choice as justified, where this relation of determination is to be filled out in due course'; see Ruth Chang, *Making Comparisons Count* (London/New York: Routledge, 2002), 43; see also Donald Regan, 'Value, Comparability, and Choice', in Ruth Chang (ed.), *Incommensurability, Incomparability, and Practical Reason* (Cambridge, MA/London: Routledge, 1997), 129–50.
3. On Kuhn and Feyerabend, see Eric Oberheim and Paul Hoyningen-Huene, 'The Incommensurability of Scientific Theories', in Edward N. Zalta (ed.), *The Stanford Encyclopedia of Philosophy* (2016), https://plato.stanford.edu/archives/win2016/entries/incommensurability/
4. Else Oyen, 'The Imperfection of Comparisons', in idem (ed.), *Comparative Methodology. Theory and Practice in International Social Research* (London: Sage, 1990), 1–18, 8.
5. A helpful overview is to be found here: Anna Kosmützky and Romy Wöhlert, 'International vergleichende Forschung. Eine interdisziplinäre. Metaanalyse disziplinärer Zugänge', *SWS-Rundschau* 55: 4 (2015), 279–307.
6. For instance, Hartmut Kaelble, *Der historische Vergleich. Eine Einführung zum 19. und 20. Jahrhundert* (Frankfurt a.M./New York: Campus, 1999).
7. Cf. Charles C. Ragin, *The Comparative Method. Moving Beyond Qualitative and Quantitative Strategies* (Berkeley/Los Angeles/London: University of California Press, 1987), esp. chapters 4 and 9.
8. See *The Methodology of Comparative Research*, eds. Robert T. Holt and John E. Turner (New York: The Free Press, 1970).
9. Cf. Hartmut Kaelble and Jürgen Schriewer (eds.), *Diskurse und Entwicklungspfade. Der Gesellschaftsvergleich in den Geschichts- und Sozialwissenschaften* (Frankfurt a.M./

New York: Campus, 1999); here particularly the papers by both editors; idem (eds.), *Vergleich und Transfer. Komparatistik in den Sozial-, Geschichts- und Kulturwissenschaften* (Frankfurt a.M.: Campus, 2003); cf. esp. the papers by Will Arts and Loek Halman, Lars Mjoset, Michel Espagne and Jürgen Osterhammel.
10 See: https://www.uni-bielefeld.de/(en)/sfb1288/
11 As one (former) 'spokesman' of that project has it: Johannes Grave, 'Vergleichen als Praxis. Vorüberlegungen zu einer praxistheoretisch orientierten Untersuchung von Vergleichen', 139.
12 Cf. Rolf Elberfeld, 'Überlegungen zur Grundlegung "komparativer Philosophie"', *Allgemeine Zeitschrift für Philosophie* 24 (1999), 125–54; Ralph Weber, '"How to Compare?" – On the Methodological State of Comparative Philosophy', *Philosophy Compass* 8:7 (2013), 593–603.
13 See Ann L. Stoler, *Carnal Knowledge and Imperial Power: Race and the Intimate in Colonial Rule* (Berkeley: University of California Press, 2002).
14 Cf., for instance, Ruth Chang, *Making Comparisons Count* (London/New York: Routledge, 2002); idem, 'The Possibility of Parity', *Ethics* 112:4 (2002), 659–88; idem, 'Are Hard Choices Cases of Incomparability?' *Philosophical Issues* 22: 'Action Theory' (2012), 106–26.
15 On this topic see esp. Jürgen Schriewer, 'Problemdimensionen sozialwissenschaftlicher Komparatistik', in Hartmut Kaelble und Jürgen Schriewer (eds.), *Vergleich und Transfer. Komparatistik in den Sozial-, Geschichts- und Kulturwissenschaften* (Frankfurt a.M.: Campus, 2003), 9–52; Michael Eggers, *Zur Wissenschaftsgeschichte und Epistemologie des Vergleichs und zur Genealogie der Komparatistik* (Heidelberg: Winter, 2016); Guy G. Stroumsa (ed.), *Comparative Studies in the Humanities* (Jerusalem: Israel Academy of Sciences and Humanities Press, 2018); *Regimes of Comparatism. Frameworks of Comparison in History, Religion and Anthropology* (Jerusalem Studies in Religion and Culture, Vol. 24), eds. Renaud Gagné, Simon Goldhill and Geoffrey Lloyd (Leiden: Brill, 2018).
16 Cf. Michel Foucault, *The Order of Things. An Archaeology of the Human Sciences* (London/New York: Routledge, 1989), chapter 3: 'Representing'.
17 Hans Blumenberg, 'Light as a Metaphor for Truth: At the Preliminary Stage of Philosophical Concept Formation', in David Michael Levin (eds.), *Modernity and the Hegemony of Vision* (Los Angeles/Berkeley: University of California Press, 1993), 30–86, 56 and 77.
18 See Christian Strub, '"Das hinreißendste Wort, über das wir verfügen, ist das Wort WIE, ganz gleichgültig, ob es ausgesprochen wird oder ungesagt bleibt." Eine These zur Geschichte der Ähnlichkeit', in Andreas Mauz and Hartmut von Sass (eds.), *Hermeneutik des Vergleichs. Strukturen, Anwendungen und Grenzen komparativer Verfahren* (Würzburg: Königshausen & Neumann, 2011), 243–66, 249.
19 On this ambivalence and with special regard to Herder, see Eggers, *Zur Wissenschaftsgeschichte und Epistemologie des Vergleichs und zur Genealogie der Komparatistik*, ch. 6.
20 See Claudia Brodsky Lacour, 'Grounds of Comparison', *World Literature Today* 69:2: 'Comparative Literature: States of the Art' (1995), 271–4, esp. 271.
21 Cf. Arend Lijphart, 'Comparative Politics and the Comparative Method', *The American Political Science Review* 65:3 (1971), 682–93, esp. 682–83.
22 The entire passage reads: 'Comparison essentially presupposes that the knowing subjectivity has the freedom to have both members of the comparison at its disposal. It openly makes both things contemporary. Hence we must doubt whether the method

of comparison really satisfies the idea of historical knowledge. Is it not the case that this procedure – adopted in some areas of the natural sciences and very successful in many fields of the human sciences, e.g., linguistics, law, aesthetics – is being promoted from a subordinate tool to central importance for defining historical knowledge (...).' (Hans-Georg Gadamer, *Truth and Method*. Second and revised edition, trans. Joel Weinsheimer and Donald G. Marshall (London/New York: Continuum, 2004), 227).
23 Cf. Dirk Baecker, *Wozu Kultur?* (2000), 3rd ed. (Berlin: Kadmos, 2003), 47 and 67; Willibald Steinmetz, '"Vergleich" – eine begriffsgeschichtliche Skizze', in Epple and Erhart (eds.), *Die Welt beobachten. Praktiken des Vergleichens*, 85–134, 97.
24 See Jonathan Culler, 'Comparability', *World Literature Today* 69:2: 'Comparative Literature: States of the Art' (1995), 268–70, 270.
25 Cf. Carlos Spoerhase, 'Rankings: A Pre-History', *New Left Review* 114:6 (2018), 99–112.
26 James Sully, 'Comparison', *Mind* 10:40 (1885), 489–511, 490.
27 See Melvin Richter, 'David Hume on Comparison. From Philosophy to Political Theory and History', in Lothar R. Waas (eds.), *Politik, Moral und Religion – Gegensätze und Ergänzungen. Festschrift Karl Graf Ballestrem* (Berlin: De Gruyter, 2004), 343–58, 343–4; cf. also Benson Saler, 'Comparison: Some Suggestions for Improving the Inevitable', *Numen* 48:3 (2001), 267–75, 268.
28 For a slightly different view, see Jürgen Raab, 'Wissenssoziologisches Vergleichen', in Mauz and von Sass (eds.), *Hermeneutik des Vergleichs*, 91–113, esp. 98.
29 Cf. Peter Janich, 'Der Vergleich als Methode in den Naturwissenschaften', in Michael Weingarten and Wolfgang Friedrich Gutmann (eds.), *Geschichte und Theorie des Vergleichs in den Biowissenschaften* (Frankfurt a.M.: Kramer, 1993), 13–28, 20; Bettina Heintz, 'Numerische Differenz. Überlegungen zu einer Soziologie des (quantitativen) Vergleichs', *Zeitschrift für Soziologie* 39:3 (2010), 162–81, 169.
30 See Susan Stanford Friedman, 'Warum nicht vergleichen?' in Epple and Erhart (eds.), *Die Welt beobachten*, 63–83, 67; Chris Lorenz, 'Comparative Historiography: Problems and Perspectives', *History and Theory* 38:1 (1999), 25–39, 39.

1 Comparisons. A General Account

1 Edmund Husserl, *Erfahrung und Urteil. Untersuchungen zur Genealogie der Logik* (Hamburg: Meiner, 1954), 224; cf. also 230; translation mine.
2 On this influential distinction (with all references), see Paul Hoyningen-Huene, 'Context of Discovery and Context of Justification', *Studies in History and Philosophy of Science* 18 (1987), 501–15.
3 Cf. Arend Lijphart, 'Comparative Politics and the Comparative Method', *The American Political Science Review* 65:3 (1971), 682–93, esp. 682.
4 See Ian Hacking, 'Styles of Scientific Thinking or Reasoning: A New Analytical Tool for Historians and Philosophers of the Sciences', in Kostas Gavroglu (ed.), *Trends in the Historiography of Science* (Dortrecht: Kluwer Academic Publishers, 1994), 31–48, 33–4; idem, 'Language, Truth, and Reason', in idem, *Historical Ontology* (Cambridge, MA/London: Harvard University Press, 2002), 159–77, 161–2 – alluding to Ludwik Fleck's notion of 'thought styles' (*Denkstile*); see Fleck's 1935 central work *Genesis and Development of a Scientific Fact* (Chicago/London: The University of Chicago Press, 1979), 39.

5 Cf. Bettina Heintz, 'Numerische Differenz. Überlegungen zu einer Soziologie des (quantitativen) Vergleichs', *Zeitschrift für Soziologie* 39:3 (2010), 162–81, esp. 162–3; see James Sully, 'Comparison', *Mind* 10:40 (1885), 489–511, 490.

6 See Keith J. Holyoak, Dedre Gentner and Boicho N. Kokinov, 'Introduction', in idem (eds.), *The Analogical Mind. Perspectives from Cognitive Science* (Cambridge, MA/London: MIT Press, 2001), 1–19, 1; on the role of imagination in Descartes see Peter Galison, 'Descartes's Comparisons: From the Invisible to the Visible', *Isis* 75:2 (1984), 311–26, esp. 323 and 326.

7 See Melvin Richter, 'David Hume on Comparison. From Philosophy to Political Theory and History', in Lothar R. Waas (ed.), *Politik, Moral and Religion – Gegensätze und Ergänzungen. FS Karl Graf Ballestrem*, (Berlin: De Gruyter, 2004), 343–58, 343.

8 Cf. ibid., 347 and 357.

9 Cf. Michael Eggers, *Zur Wissenschaftsgeschichte und Epistemologie des Vergleichs und zur Genealogie der Komparatistik* (Heidelberg: Winter, 2016), chapter 8; with references to Kant's primary sources.

10 Referring to literary studies, see Francesco Loriggio, 'Comparative Literature and the Genres of Interdisciplinarity', *World Literature Today* 69:2 (1995): 'Comparative Literature: States of the Art', 256–62; and more recently Carlos Spoerhase and Steffen Martus, 'Die Quellen der Praxis. Probleme einer historischen Praxeologie der Philologie. Einleitung', *Zeitschrift für Germanistik* 23:2 (2013), 221–5; Steffen Martus, 'Wandernde Praktiken "after theory"? Praxeologische Perspektiven auf "Literatur/Wissenschaft"', *Internationales Archiv für Sozialgeschichte der deutschen Literatur* 40 (2015), 177–95, esp. 181.

11 Cf. Andreas Reckwitz, 'Grundelemente einer Theorie sozialer Praktiken. Eine sozialtheoretische Perspektive', *Zeitschrift für Soziologie* 32:4 (2003), 282–301, 288–9 and 292.

12 This transition from comparisons to comparing lies at the methodological heart of the interdisciplinary research project at the university of Bielefeld, Germany, called 'practices of comparing' (SFB 1288; see https://www.uni-bielefeld.de/(en)/sfb1288/profil.html). It very much relies on leaving comparison as structure behind and on giving the practice(s) of concretely comparing its due. And therefore, it subscribes to the praxeological claim that comparing – as all practices – is an embodied, situated, context-bound, materialized activity; see, for instance, Johannes Grave, 'Vergleichen als Praxis. Vorüberlegungen zu einer praxistheoretisch orientierten Untersuchung von Vergleichen', in Angelika Epple and Walter Erhart (eds.), *Die Welt beobachten. Praktiken des Vergleichens* (Frankfurt a.M./New York: Campus, 2015), 134–59, 139–40; Angelika Epple, '*Doing Comparisons* – Ein praxeologischer Zugang zur Geschichte der Globalisierung/en', in ibid., 161–99, 173.

13 Charles Tilly, *Big Structures. Large Processes. Huge Comparisons* (New York: Sage Foundation, 1985), 447; this notion goes back to Alfred N. Whitehead's *Science and the Modern World. Lowell Lectures, 1925* (New York: Pelican Mentor Books, 1948).

14 Kerstin Stüssel, 'Das "Zeitalter der Vergleichung" – Philologie, Ethnographie, Literatur und Medien', in Epple and Erhart (eds.), *Die Welt beobachten. Praktiken des Vergleichens*, 265–83, 278.

15 Cf. Husserl, *Erfahrung und Urteil*, § 46.

16 See Peter Janich, 'Der Vergleich als Methode in den Naturwissenschaften', in Michael Weingarten and Wolfgang Friedrich Gutmann (eds.), *Geschichte und Theorie des Vergleichs in den Biowissenschaften* (Frankfurt a.M.: Kramer, 1993), 13–28, 24; Ralph

Weber, 'Comparative Philosophy and the Tertium: Comparing What with What, and in What Respect?' *Dao* 13 (2014), 151–71, 152.
17 Cf. esp. Ruth Chang, 'The Possibility of Parity', *Ethics* 112:4 (2002), 659–88.
18 See Wolfgang Kaschuba, 'Anmerkungen zum Gesellschaftsvergleich aus ethnologischer Perspektive', in Hartmut Kaelble and Jürgen Schriewer (eds.), *Vergleich und Transfer. Komparatistik in den Sozial-, Geschichts- und Kulturwissenschaften* (Frankfurt a.M.: Campus, 2003), 341–50, 347.
19 Cf. Michael Werner and Bénédicte Zimmermann, 'Beyond Comparison: Histoire Croisée and the Challenge of Reflexivity', *History and Theory* 45:1 (2006), 30–50, 33.
20 Cf. Joachim Matthes, 'The Operation Called "Vergleichen"', in idem (ed.), *Zwischen den Kulturen? Die Sozialwissenschaften vor dem Problem des Kulturvergleichs* (Göttingen: Otto Schartz, 1992), 75–99, 90.
21 See Ralph Weber, '"How to Compare?" – On the Methodological State of Comparative Philosophy', *Philosophy Compass* 8:7 (2013), 593–603, 596.
22 The indication 'structurally speaking' is important because there are cases of incomparability that are not based on structural or formal limitations but, rather, on normative, i.e. moral or evaluative considerations; see chapter 9 on normative incomparability.
23 Cf. Robert A. Segal, 'In Defense of the Comparative Method', *Numen* 48:3 (2001), 339–73, 344.
24 See, in particular, Hartmut Kaelble, *Der historische Vergleich. Eine Einführung zum 19. und 20. Jahrhundert* (Frankfurt a.M./New York: Campus, 1999), 103; Michael Werner and Bénédicte Zimmermann, 'Vergleich, Transfer, Verflechtung. Der Ansatz der Histoire croisée und die Herausforderung des Transnationalen', *Geschichte und Gesellschaft* 28:4 (2002), 607–36, 609.
25 See Alberto Abadie, Alexis Diamond and Jens Hainmueller, 'Comparative Politics and the Synthetic Control Method', *American Journal of Political Science* 59:2 (2015), 495–510, 496.
26 The so-called *transfer research* in historiography serves as a prominent example for this *independence problem*: China and 'the West' may be compared in terms of cultural activity while investigating, at the same time, the relationships, interactions and circulations between both regions – which, again, informs the initial comparison; see Jürgen Schriewer, 'Vergleich und Erklärung zwischen Kausalität und Komplexität', in Hartmut Kaelble and Jürgen Schriewer (eds.), *Diskurse und Entwicklungspfade. Der Gesellschaftsvergleich in den Geschichts- und Sozialwissenschaften* (Frankfurt a.M./New York: Campus, 1999), 53–102, esp. 70–81.

The problem of independent *relata* is especially prominent in what has been coined 'Galton's Problem', named after the English scientist Sir Francis Galton. The key concern is that similarities between *A* and *B* (in Galton's case, societies or ethnicities) go back to a hidden influence of *A* on *B* (or conversely). Galton put great emphasis on this widespread problem of concealed interactions; it is a methodological difficulty particularly within historical, sociological and ethnological studies and crucially, it is amplified under globalized circumstances – accompanied by attempts to solve this challenge statistically; see Raoul Naroll, 'Galton's Problem: The Logic of Cross-Cultural Analysis', *Social Research* 32:4 (1965), 428–51; Marc Howard Ross and Elizabeth Homer, 'Galton's Problem in Cross-National Research', *World Politics* 29:1 (1976), 1–28, esp. 2; Paul Warwick, 'Galton's Problem In Comparative Political Research', *Political Methodology* 5:3 (1978), 327–46; Jürgen Osterhammel,

'Transferanalyse und Vergleich im Fernverhältnis', in Kaelble and Schriewer (eds.), *Vergleich und Transfer*, 439–66, esp. 465.
27 See Charles C. Ragin, *The Comparative Method. Moving Beyond Qualitative and Quantitative Strategies* (Berkeley/Los Angeles/London: University of California Press, 1987), 5; Mathias Gutmann and Benjamin Rathgeber, 'Vergleichen und Vergleich in den Wissenschaften. Exemplarische Rekonstruktionen zu einer grundlegenden Handlungsform', in Andreas Mauz and Hartmut von Sass (eds.), *Hermeneutik des Vergleichs. Strukturen, Anwendungen und Grenzen komparativer Verfahren* (Würzburg: Königshausen und Neumann, 2011), 49–73, 58.
28 Dirk Berg-Schlosser, 'Vergleichende Politikwissenschaft im Vergleich – multidimensionale Verortung und mögliche Anwendungen', in Kaelble and Schriewer (eds.), *Vergleich und Transfer*, 117–40, 119.
29 Peter V. Zima, 'Vergleich als Konstruktion. Genetische und typologische Aspekte des Vergleichs und die soziale Bedingtheit der Theorie', in idem (ed.), *Vergleichende Wissenschaften. Interdisziplinarität und Interkulturalität in den Komparatistiken* (Tübingen: Francke, 2000), 15–28, 18, see also Mathias Gutmann, 'Der Vergleich als Konstruktion – Systematische Bemerkungen zur Bestimmung entwicklungstheoretischer Ansätze in der Biologie', in Michael Weingarten and Wolfgang Friedrich Gutmann (eds.), *Geschichte und Theorie des Vergleichs in den Biowissenschaften*, 45–60, 47–8 and 52; William H. Sewell, Jr., 'Marc Bloch and the Logic of Comparative History', *History and Theory* 6:2 (1967), 208–18, esp. 213.
30 Cf. Josef Kopperschmidt, 'Vergleich und Vergleichen aus rhetorischer Sicht', in Mauz and von Sass (eds.), *Hermeneutik des Vergleichs*, 223–42, 226.
31 See Philipp Stoellger, 'Unvergleichlich? Vergleich als Umgang mit dem Inkommensurablen. Ein Beitrag zur Hermeneutik der Differenz', in ibid., 321–45, esp. 330.
32 See Bettina Heintz, 'Numerische Differenz. Überlegungen zu einer Soziologie des (quantitativen) Vergleichs', 169; idem, '"Wir leben im Zeitalter der Vergleichung." Perspektiven einer Soziologie des Vergleichs', *Zeitschrift für Soziologie* 45:5 (2016), 305–23, 308 and 319.
33 Cf. Ralph Weber, 'Comparative Philosophy and the Tertium', 154.
34 See Rodolphe Gasché, 'Das Vergnügen an Vergleichen. Über Kants Ausarbeitung der Kritik der praktischen Vernunft', in Michael Eggers (ed.), *Von Ähnlichkeiten und Unterschieden. Vergleich, Analogie und Klassifikation in Wissenschaft und Literatur (18./19. Jahrhundert)* (Heidelberg: Winter, 2011), 167–82, 181.
35 Martin Heidegger, *Being and Time*, trans. John Macquarrie and Edward Robinson (Oxford: Basil Blackwell, 1962), esp. §§ 15–16.
36 Heidegger, as is well known, uses the hammer as an example: we are acquainted with hammers by being involved in practical engagement with tools; however, if the hammer breaks, the routine stops – and the transition from the hammer's status as present-at-hand to its readiness is possible; see ibid., § 15.
37 See Husserl, *Erfahrung und Urteil*, esp. 28.
38 Cf. Robert B. Brandom, *Tales of the Mighty Dead. Historical Essays in the Metaphysics of Intentionality* (Cambridge, MA/London: Harvard University Press, 2002), 76, 309, 326.
39 See Mark Okrent, *Heidegger's Pragmatism. Understanding, Being, and the Critique of Metaphysics* (Ithaca, NY/London: Cornell University Press, 1988), chapter 5: 'The Argument for the Primacy of Purposive Action'.
40 More sophisticated examples, taken from historical and religious contexts, are given by Hartmut Kaelble, *Der historische Vergleich*, 112, and by Volkhard Krech, 'Wie lassen

sich religiöse Sachverhalte miteinander vergleichen? Ein religionssoziologischer Vorschlag', in Mauz and von Sass (eds.), *Hermeneutik des Vergleichs*, 149–76, 151–2.

41 Hence, one has to have an awareness of the 'politics of comparing', as well as a sensitivity to an 'ethics of comparisons'; see Susan Stanford Friedman, 'Warum nicht vergleichen?', in Epple and Erhart (eds.), *Die Welt beobachten. Praktiken des Vergleichens*, 63–83, 67 and 75.

42 See Robert Segal who underlines the fact that the crucial distinction relevant for comparisons is not whether they are true or false, but whether they are useful or useless; cf. his 'In Defense of the Comparative Method', 350; a slightly different emphasis entails the term comparatively 'illegitimate'; cf. Helga Lutz, Jan-Friedrich Missfelder and Tilo Renz, 'Einleitung: Illegitimes Vergleichen in den Kulturwissenschaften', in idem (eds.), *Äpfel und Birnen. Illegitimes Vergleichen in den Kulturwissenschaften* (Bielefeld: transcript, 2006), 7–20, esp. 10 and 13.

43 See also Ralph Weber, 'Comparative Philosophy and the Tertium', 152.

44 See Bettina Heintz, 'Numerische Differenz. Überlegungen zu einer Soziologie des (quantitativen) Vergleichs', 164; cf. also James Sully, 'Comparison', 495.

45 Michel Foucault, *The Order of Things. An Archaeology of the Human Sciences* (London/New York: Routledge, 1989), 64; see chapter 3: 'Representing' (51–85).

46 For a critique of Foucault, see Christian Strub, '"Das hinreißendste Wort, über das wir verfügen, ist das Wort WIE, ganz gleichgültig, ob es ausgesprochen wird oder ungesagt bleibt". Eine These zur Geschichte der Ähnlichkeit', in Mauz and von Sass (eds.), *Hermeneutik des Vergleichs*, 243–66, esp. 246 and 253; and Eggers, *Zur Wissenschaftsgeschichte und Epistemologie des Vergleichs*, 46.

47 See Anil Bhatti and Dorothee Kimmich, 'Einleitung', in idem (eds.), *Ähnlichkeit. Ein kulturtheoretisches Paradigma* (Konstanz: Konstanz University Press, 2015), 7–31, 13, 17, 26.

48 Albrecht Koschorke, 'Ähnlichkeit. Valenzen eines post-kolonialen Konzepts', in ibid., 35–45, 36–7.

49 This is also true for Wittgenstein's idea of *family resemblances* exemplified by the term 'game' and the diversity among different games; see his *Philosophical Investigations. Part I*, 3rd edition, eds. G.E.M. Anscombe and Rush Rhees, trans. G.E.M. Anscombe (Englewood Cliffs, NJ: Prentice Hall, 1973), 1–172, § 66. It is worth noting, as Stanley Cavell did, that Wittgenstein does not deny the possibility of necessary features shared by all items belonging to one class; what he is contemplating are cases in which a term seems to lack such a core element while giving a different account of (partly) shared features; see Stanley Cavell, *The Claim of Reason. Wittgenstein, Skepticism, Morality, and Tragedy* (Oxford/New York: Oxford University Press, 1979), chapter 7.

50 Cf. Husserl, *Erfahrung und Urteil*, §§ 44–5; see also Stoellger, 'Unvergleichlich? Vergleich als Umgang mit dem Inkommensurablen. Ein Beitrag zur Hermeneutik der Differenz', 335.

51 See Nelson Goodman, *Problems and Projects* (Indianapolis: Bobbs-Merrill, 1972), esp. 445; cf. also David Decosimo, 'Comparison and the Ubiquity of Resemblance', *Journal of the American Academy of Religion* 78:1 (2010), 226–58, 227 and 231; Lieven Decock and Igor Douven, 'Similarity After Goodman', *Review of Philosophy and Psychology* 2:1 (2011) 61–75, 68.

52 Cf. Eberhard Jüngel, *God as the Mystery of the World. On the Foundation of the Theology of the Crucified One in the Dispute Between Theism and Atheism* (Grand Rapids, MI/Cambridge: William B. Eerdmans Publishing, 1983), § 17: 'The Problem of Analogical Talk about God'.

53 See Thomas M. Olshewsky, 'Demea's Dilemmas', *British Journal for the History of Philosophy* 11:3 (2003), 473–92, 475; Timothy M. Costelloe, 'In every civilized community: Hume on belief and the demise of religion', *International Journal for Philosophy of Religion* 55:2 (2004), 171–85, 171–2.
54 David Hume, *Dialogues Concerning Natural Religion* (1779), ed. Dorothy Coleman (Cambridge: Cambridge University Press, 2007), 19; page numbers in brackets refer to this text.
55 See Paul Bartha, 'Analogy and Analogical Reasoning', in Edward N. Zalta (ed.), *The Stanford Encyclopedia of Philosophy* (2016), https://plato.stanford.edu/entries/reasoning-analogy/
56 On these dynamics, see Andrea Albrecht, 'Analogieschlüsse und metaphorische Extensionen in der interdisziplinären literaturwissenschaftlichen Praxis', in Andrea Albrecht, Lutz Danneberg, Olav Krämer, Carlos Spoerhase (eds.), *Theorien, Methoden und Praktiken des Interpretierens* (linguae & litterae 49) (Berlin/Boston: De Gruyter, 2015), 271–99, esp. 275; cf. also Guy G. Stroumsa, 'In Search of a New Paradigm', in idem (ed.), *Comparative Studies in the Humanities* (Jerusalem: Israel Academy of Sciences and Humanities Press, 2018), 7–13, 9.
57 Cf. Karen Gloy, 'Versuch einer Logik des Analogiedenkens', in idem and Manuel Bachmann (eds.), *Das Analogiedenken. Vorstöße in ein neues Gebiet der Rationalitätstheorie* (Freiburg i.Br.: Alber, 2000), 298–323.
58 On the (very good) reasons for which Demea rejects Cleanthes' analogical thinking see Hartmut von Sass, 'Beyond Hume: Demea. A Rehabilitation with Systematic Intent', *International Journal for Philosophy of Religion* 86:1 (2019), 61–84.
59 For instance, see Aristotle, *Rhetorics*, Book III, 1406b; cf. also Christian Strub, '"Das hinreißendste Wort, über das wir verfügen, ist das Wort WIE, ganz gleichgültig, ob es ausgesprochen wird oder ungesagt bleibt." Eine These zur Geschichte der Ähnlichkeit', 243–4.
60 See Janet M. Soskice, *Metaphor and Religious Language* (Oxford: Oxford University Press, 1985), 25.
61 Max Black, 'How Metaphors Work: A Reply to Donald Davidson', *Critical Inquiry* 6:1 (1979), 131–43, 143.
62 See Ivor A. Richards, 'Metaphor', in idem, Lecture V of *The Philosophy of Rhetoric* (Oxford: Oxford University Press, 1936), 89–138; Max Black, 'Metaphor', *Proceedings of the Aristotelian Society*, New Series 55 (1954/1955), 273–94, esp. 276; sometimes, Black speaks, instead of 'frame' and 'focus', of principal subject' and a 'subsidiary subject'; see Max Black, 'More about metaphor', *Dialectica* 31:3/4 (1977), 431–57, esp. 441 and 451.
63 Cf. Monroe C. Beardsley, 'Metaphor', in Paul Edwards (ed.), *Encyclopedia of Philosophy* (New York: Macmillan, 1967), Vol. 5, 284–9.
64 See ibid., 439–41.
65 Cf. John Searle, 'Introduction' to his *Expression and Meaning. Studies in the Theory of Speech Acts* (Cambridge: Cambridge University Press, 1979), x.
66 Donald Davidson, 'What Metaphors Mean', *Critical Inquiry* 5:1, Special Issue on Metaphor (1978), 31–47, 32.
67 Cf. Richard Rorty, 'Unfamiliar noises I: Hesse and Davidson on metaphor', *Proceedings of the Aristotelian society*. Supp. vol. 61 (1987), 283–96.
68 Hans Blumenberg, 'Ausblick auf eine Theorie der Unbegrifflichkeit', in Anselm Haverkamp (ed.), *Theorie der Metapher*, 2nd edition (Darmstadt: WBG, 1996), 438–54, 438 and 450.

69 The German original reads: '[D]ie Metaphorologie sucht an die Substruktur des Denkens heranzukommen, an den Urgrund, die Nährlösung der systematischen Kristallisationen, aber sie will auch faßbar machen, mit welchem 'Mut' sich der Geist in seinen Bildern selbst voraus ist und wie sich im Mut zur Vermutung seine Geschichte entwirft' (Hans Blumenberg, 'Paradigmen zu einer Metaphorologie', in ibid., 285–315, 290).
70 Ibid.
71 See Hans Blumenberg, 'Beobachtungen an Metaphern', *Archiv für Begriffsgeschichte* 25: 2 (1971), 161–214, 164–5.
72 Ibid., 170.
73 Cf. Benson Saler, 'Comparison: Some Suggestions for Improving the Inevitable', *Numen* 48:3 (2001), 267–75, 268.
74 See Henrik Birus, 'Das Vergleichen als Grundoperation der Hermeneutik', in Henk de Berg and Matthias Prangel (eds.), *Interpretation 2000: Positionen und Kontroversen. FS Horst Steinmetz* (Heidelberg: Winter, 1999), 95–117, 97, for a similar statement cf. Niklas Luhmann, *Soziale Systeme. Grundriß einer allgemeinen Theorie* (Frankfurt a.M.: Suhrkamp, 1987), 83–4.
75 Cf. also Peter V. Zima, *Komparatistische Perspektiven. Zur Theorie der Vergleichenden Literaturwissenschaften* (Tübingen: Francke, 2011), 20–2.
76 Cf. Willibald Steinmetz, '"Vergleich" - eine begriffsgeschichtliche Skizze', in Epple and Erhart (eds.), *Die Welt beobachten. Praktiken des Vergleichens*, 85–134, 101 and 103.
77 Josef Kopperschmidt, 'Vergleich und Vergleichen aus rhetorischer Sicht', in Mauz and von Sass (eds.), *Hermeneutik des Vergleichs*, 223–42, 232.
78 Lawrence D. Walker, 'A Note on Historical Linguistics and Marc Bloch's Comparative Method', *History and Theory* 19:2 (1980), 154–64, 159.
79 See Schriewer, 'Vergleich und Erklärung zwischen Kausalität und Komplexität', 68–9.
80 See José Casanova, *Public Religions in the Modern World* (Chicago and London: University of Chicago Press, 1994), chapter 1: 'Secularization, Enlightenment, and Modern Religion'; see also William H. Sewell, Jr, 'Marc Bloch and the Logic of Comparative History', *History and Theory* 6:2 (1967), 208–18, who says: 'The comparative method is a method, a set of rules which can be methodically and systematically applied in gathering and using evidence to test explanatory hypotheses. It does not supply us with explanations to be subjected to test: this is a task for the historical imagination' (217).
81 Cf. Peter V. Zima, *Komparatistik. Einführung in die Vergleichende Literaturwissenschaft* (Tübingen: Francke, 1992), 74.
82 See Stanley Cavell, *Cities of Words* (Cambridge, MA/London: Harvard University Press, 2004).
83 See especially Michael Eggers, '"Vergleichung ist ein gefährlicher Feind des Genusses." Zur Epistemologie des Vergleichs in der deutschen Ästhetik um 1800', in Ulrich Johannes Schneider (ed.), *Kulturen des Wissens im 18. Jahrhundert* (Berlin/New York: De Gruyter, 2008), 627–35, 628.
84 Alexander G. Baumgarten, quoted in Günter Schenk and Andrej Krause, Art. 'Vergleich', in *Historisches Wörterbuch der Philosophie*, vol. 11 (Basel: Schwabe, 2001), 679; the German original reads: 'In manchen Fällen geschieht daher die Vergleichung bloß in ästhetischer Hinsicht, zur Belehrung der Einbildungskraft und zur Belustigung des Gemüths.'
85 Cf. Andreas Dorschel, 'Einwände gegen das Vergleichen. Ein Versuch, sie zu beantworten', *Philosophisches Jahrbuch* 113:1 (2006), 177–85.

86 Cf. Francesco Loriggio, 'Comparative Literature and the Genres of Interdisciplinarity', *World Literature Today* 69:2 'Comparative Literature: States of the Art' (1995), 256–62, 259.
87 See Luhmann, *Soziale Systeme*, 91; see also Robert A. Segal, 'In Defense of the Comparative Method', *Numen* 48:3 (2001), 339–73, 350–1.
88 Cf. Stroumsa, 'In Search of a New Paradigm', 9.
89 For a similar reservation, see Dorschel, 'Einwände gegen das Vergleichen', 181–2.
90 See John L. Gittleman and Hang-Kwang Luh, 'On Comparing Comparative Methods', *Annual Review of Ecology and Systematics* 23 (1992), 383–404, 384.
91 Cf. also Dorschel, 'Einwände gegen das Vergleichen', 181.
92 See Sewell, Jr, 'Marc Bloch and the Logic of Comparative History', 217.
93 Matthes, 'The Operation Called "Vergleichen"', 92.

2 Comparisons. A Typology

1 One might also contemplate the possibility of pairing particular practices with certain relational constellations between comparative items. See Johannes Grave, 'Vergleichen als Praxis. Vorüberlegungen zu einer praxistheoretisch orientierten Untersuchung von Vergleichen', in Angelika Epple and Walter Erhart (eds.), *Die Welt beobachten. Praktiken des Vergleichens* (Frankfurt a.M./New York: Campus, 2015), 134–59, esp. 144–5.
2 Obviously, the converse case, namely that we have nonquantifiability on the sublevel, but quantifiability on the overall level, does not exist.
3 See Neil Cooper, 'Paradox lost: understanding vague predicates', *International Journal of Philosophical Studies* 3 (1995), 244–69.
4 Here, one can repeat the same move again in describing 'originality' by referring to additional features on a sub-sublevel, and so on.
5 The restriction 'mostly (but not always)' is necessary because, in some cases, it might be possible to measure the impact that subcomparisons (according to T_n, T_{n+1}, and T_{n+2} ...) have on the overall result. For example: who is the best student in the class? That leads to the question as to who is best in maths, biology, history, sports, etc. Since all students get grades, the results in each subject translate into an overall result. The grading, as it were, equalizes all subjects by introducing a common scale while latently presupposing that an A-grade in maths is equivalent to an A-grade in sports.
6 Attempts to reduce nonquantifiable regards to quantifiable ones for the sake of comparability (or for making it less difficult) are understandable, but – given the problems sketched above – doom to fail. An example for this kind of reduction is to be found in Derek Parfit's 'population ethics', comparing different future scenarios using several parameters (such as life expectancy, quality of life for different groups both on an individual and collective level, etc.). There is no overall scale allowing for a straightforward answer to decide which scenario is (morally) preferable in most cases; see his *Reasons and Persons* (Oxford: Oxford University Press, 1984), chapter 16. However, utilitarian and consequentialist ethicists traditionally have the tendency to present measurements for life expectancy, quality of life, etc. to address the nonquantifiability problem.
7 These terms are used by Johannes Grave; see his 'Vergleichen als Praxis', 144.
8 Cf. John L. Gittleman and Hang-Kwang Luh, 'On Comparing Comparative Methods', *Annual Review of Ecology and Systematics* 23 (1992), 383–404, esp. 392–3.

9   A different example can be found in Ludwig Wittgenstein's work (in *Philosophical Investigations* § 18), comparing language (*A*) with an old city, its streets and crossings (*B*), whereas the concrete regard between *A* and *B* is unclear and has to be found, tried out, (re)defined; see, for an illuminating interpretation, Geert-Lueke Lueken, 'On Showing in Argumentation', *Philosophical Investigations* 20:3 (1997), 205–23, esp. 219.
10 This example is meant to be merely illustrative; hence, I do not claim that parables are nothing but comparisons or that they belong to that category. Concerning the difficulties of exegetically relating these different tropes to one another, see Ruben Zimmermann, 'Die Form bzw. Gattung der Gleichnisse', in idem et al. (eds.), *Kompendium der Gleichnisse Jesu* (Gütersloh: Gütersloher Verlagshaus, 2007), 17–28.
11 There have been attempts to consider this kind of a reader's involvement as essential part of religious discourse in general; cf. Dallas M. High, *Language, Persons, and Belief. Studies in Wittgenstein's Philosophical Investigations and Religious Uses of Language* (New York: Macmillan, 1967), esp. 20, 125, 165–9.
12 Regarding this comparative productivity, see also Angelika Epple, 'Doing Comparisons – Ein praxeologischer Zugang zur Geschichte der Globalisierung/en', in Epple and Erhart (eds.), *Die Welt beobachten. Praktiken des Vergleichens*, 161–99, 164 and 193.
13 On the distinction between individualized and generalized (inclusive) comparisons, see Hartmut Kaelble, *Der historische Vergleich. Eine Einführung zum 19. und 20. Jahrhundert* (Frankfurt a.M./New York: Campus), 1999, 26–7; see also Charles Tilly, *Big Structures. Large Processes. Huge Comparisons* (New York: Sage Foundation, 1985), 81 and 480–1.
14 Cf. Willibald Steinmetz, '"Vergleich" – eine begriffsgeschichtliche Skizze', in Epple and Erhart (eds.), *Die Welt beobachten. Praktiken des Vergleichens*, 85–134, 88–9.
15 See Peter V. Zima, 'Vergleich als Konstruktion. Genetische und typologische Aspekte des Vergleichs und die soziale Bedingtheit der Theorie', in idem (ed.), *Vergleichende Wissenschaften. Interdisziplinarität und Interkulturalität in den Komparatistiken* (Tübingen: Francke, 2000), 15–28, 21.
16 See Charles J. Halperin, Robert J. Loewenberg, George Yaney, Peter Kolchin, Rowland Berthoff, David Moltke-Hansen, Forrest McDonald, Grady McWhinehy, Joan Leopold, Alette Olin Hill and Boyd H. Hill Jr, 'Comparative History in Theory and Practice: A Discussion', *The American Historical Review* 87:1 (1982), 123–43; see, for sociological contexts, Charles C. Ragin, *The Comparative Method. Moving Beyond Qualitative and Quantitative Strategies* (Berkeley/Los Angeles/London: University of California Press, 1987), esp. 168.
17 See Jürgen Osterhammel, 'Transferanalyse und Vergleich im Fernverhältnis', in Hartmut Kaelble and Jürgen Schriewer (eds.), *Vergleich und Transfer. Komparatistik in den Sozial-, Geschichts- und Kulturwissenschaften* (Frankfurt a.M.: Campus, 2003), 439–66, esp. 455–9 (on China and the 'West').
18 This methodological problem is known as 'Galton's problem'; see chapter 1, section 2.4. Cf. esp. Raoul Naroll, 'Galton's Problem: The Logic of Cross-Cultural Analysis', *Social Research* 32:4 (1965), 428–51; Michael Werner and Bénédicte Zimmermann, 'Beyond Comparison: Histoire Croisée and the Challenge of Reflexivity', *History and Theory* 45:1 (2006), 30–50.
19 For this example see Jürgen Schriewer, 'Vergleich und Erklärung zwischen Kausalität und Komplexität', in Hartmut Kaelble and Jürgen Schriewer (eds.), *Diskurse und Entwicklungspfade. Der Gesellschaftsvergleich in den Geschichts- und Sozialwissenschaften* (Frankfurt a.M./New York: Campus, 1999), 53–102, 95.

20 One might alternatively use the distinction between *neutrality in comparing A and B* versus *comparative engagement* for *A* at *B*'s expense; see Philipp Stoellger, 'Unvergleichlich? Vergleich als Umgang mit dem Inkommensurablen. Ein Beitrag zur Hermeneutik der Differenz', in Andreas Mauz and Hartmut von Sass (eds.), *Hermeneutik des Vergleichs. Strukturen, Anwendungen und Grenzen komparativer Verfahren* (Würzburg: Königshausen & Neumann, 2011), 321–45, 324.

21 See Joachim Matthes, 'The Operation Called "Vergleichen"', in idem (ed.), *Zwischen den Kulturen? Die Sozialwissenschaften vor dem Problem des Kulturvergleichs* (Göttingen: Otto Schartz, 1992), 75–99, 90; cf. also Friedrich H. Tenbruck, 'Was war der Kulturvergleich, ehe es den Kulturvergleich gab?' in ibid., 13–35, esp. 22–31.

22 One of the classical references is Aristotle, *Nicomachean Ethics*, ed. and trans. by Robert C. Bartlett and Susan D. Collins (Chicago: University of Chicago Press, 2011), book 2, section 6, 1106b–1107a; see also Robert Audi, 'Acting From Virtue', *Mind* 104:415 (1995), 449–71.

23 See https://www.businessinsider.de/pope-francis-says-abortion-hitman-unlawful-as-state-laws-pass-2019-5?r=US&IR=T (25 May 2019).

24 Cf. https://www.theguardian.com/politics/2017/nov/26/anna-soubry-interview-brexit-history-will-condemn-this-period (26 November 2017).

25 See https://www.businessinsider.com/pope-francis-authorizes-pro-life-choice-catholic-priests-forgive-abortion-2016-11?_ga=2.178592996.1176723989.1568021766-1263474600.1568021766&IR=T (21 November 2016).

26 See *DER SPIEGEL*: https://www.spiegel.de/plus/brexit-ex-tory-politikerin-anna-soubry-ueber-boris-johnson-und-ihre-fruehere-partei-a-00000000-0002-0001-0000-000165813276 (6 September 2019).

27 'Focus' is used here with the intention of hinting at the similarity between pointed comparisons and metaphors; as noted above, 'focus' is itself a metaphorical term to characterize the structure of metaphors; see chapter 1, section 4.2.

28 On normative incomparability, see chapter 9; one might make the case that not allowing for comparisons (as in the case above) is *always* a normative (and not a structural) matter.

29 There are two versions of 'wild comparisons'. Number one, wild comparisons are synonymous with what has been called *experimental* or *explorative comparisons* (in contrast to *result-oriented comparisons*), i.e. the constant trying-out of different elements within a particular comparative setting; see section 2.2. Number two, wild comparisons are those that relate items in a surprising, irritating and even bold and risky manner, as pointed comparisons do; see, on this latter version (including the link between collecting and 'wildly' comparing), Michael Cahn, 'Das Schwanken zwischen Abfall und Wert. Zur kulturellen Hermeneutik des Sammlers', *Merkur* 509 (1991), online: https://www.merkur-zeitschrift.de/michael-cahn-das-schwanken-zwischen-abfall-und-wert/

3 On Comparative Injustice

1 See Hans-Jörg Rheinberger, *Toward a History of Epistemic Things* (Palo Alto, CA: Stanford University Press, 1997); Mary Tiles, 'Is Historical Epistemology Part of the "Modernist Settlement"?' *Erkenntnis* 75:3 (2011), 525–43.

2 This program of 'genealogical' and 'archeological' analysis is, of course, best known from the work of Michel Foucault; see, *inter alia*, his *The Archaeology of Knowledge*:

and the Discourse on Language, trans. Alan Sheridan (New York: Vintage Books, 1982); this book also contains a passage on 'comparative facts' discussing the danger of reducing comparisons to merely unifying things, instead of enabling awareness of the manifold functions that comparisons might adopt; ibid., section IV.4.

3 Cf. Ian Hacking, *Historical Ontology* (Cambridge, MA/London: Harvard University Press, 2002), esp. chapter 4 ('The Archaeology of Michel Foucault', 73–86) and 5 ('Michel Foucault's Immature Science', 87–98).

4 'Comparative injustice' is formulated in parallel to Miranda Fricker's term 'epistemic injustice', referring to instances of refuting epistemically relevant testimonials by someone for *non-epistemic* reasons to intentionally undermine the authority of that person or group. Accordingly, one deals here with instances of epistemic suppression due to race, colour, or gender; see Miranda Fricker, *Epistemic Injustice: Power and the Ethics of Knowing* (Oxford: Oxford University Press, 2007), esp. chapter 1: 'Testimonial Injustice'. For an extension of Fricker's account see Gaile Pohlhaus, Jr, 'Relational Knowing and Epistemic Injustice: Toward a Theory of Willful Hermeneutical Ignorance', *Hypatia* 27:4 (2012), 715–35.

5 To name but a few titles from a voluminous body of literature: Bill Ashcroft, Gareth Griffiths, Helen Tiffin, *The Empire Writes Back. Theory and Practice in Post-Colonial Literatures*, 2nd edition (London/New York: Routledge, 2002); Ann Stoler, *Carnal Knowledge and Imperial Power: Race and the Intimate in Colonial Rule* (Los Angeles/Berkeley/London: University of California Press, 2002); Lutz H. Eckensberger and Ingrid Plath, 'Möglichkeiten und Grenzen des "variablenorientiereten" Kulturvergleichs: Von der kulturvergleichenden Psychologie zur Kulturpsychologie', in Hartmut Kaelble and Jürgen Schriewer (eds.), *Vergleich und Transfer. Komparatistik in den Sozial-, Geschichts- und Kulturwissenschaften* (Frankfurt a.M.: Campus, 2003), 55–98.

6 This 'silencing' within multidimensional comparisons may take two forms: a *radical* one that completely ignores other *tertia*, or a *hidden* one that weighs up different *tertia* in an inappropriate way. 'Inappropriate' could mean, drawing again on the example above, to refer to criteria that have little or nothing to do with qualifying for the job in question, such as privileging a certain sex within the application process, etc.

7 See Colin Crouch, *Post-democracy* (Cambridge: Polity Press, 2004), esp. chapter 1, in which Crouch describes the usage of democratic structures while undermining them – again in the mode of simulation.

8 See, on the problem in general (and not restricted to one country) esp. Richard Forgette and John W. Winkle, 'Partisan Gerrymandering and the Voting Rights Act', *Social Science Quarterly* 87:1 (2006), 155–73; Kenneth C. Martis, 'The Original Gerrymander', *Political Geography* 27:4 (2008), 833–9.

9 One could also distinguish between (a) through (d) in terms of *precomparative* and *intracomparative injustice*, meaning that all of these instances could take place *before* a comparison is conducted or, given the experimental setting, *during* a comparison while trying out different possible constellations.

10 See Guy G. Stroumsa, 'In Search of a New Paradigm', in idem (ed.), *Comparative Studies in the Humanities* (Jerusalem: Israel Academy of Sciences and Humanities Press, 2018), 7–13, esp. 8.

11 These adventurous encounters – for which Alexander von Humboldt might provide the best example – has also led to a new genre, travel literature; see Natalie Melas, 'Versions of Incommensurability', *World Literature Today* 69:2 'Comparative Literature: States of the Art' (1995), 275–80; cf. also, drawing on Adelbert von Chamisso, Walter Erhart, '"Beobachtung und Erfahrung, Sammeln und Vergleichen" – Adelbert von Chamisso und

die Poetik der Weltreise im 18. und 19. Jahrhundert', in Angelika Epple and Walter Erhart (eds.), *Die Welt beobachten. Praktiken des Vergleichens* (Frankfurt a.M./New York: Campus, 2015), 203–33, esp. 209 and 213; Kerstin Stüssel, 'Das "Zeitalter der Vergleichung" – Philologie, Ethnographie, Literatur und Medien', in ibid., 265–83, 268–9.

12 See Dirk Baecker, *Wozu Kultur?* (Berlin: Kadmos (2000) ³2003), 66.
13 Ibid., 68; my trans.; see also 9, 47 and 66.
14 Rajagopalan Radhakrishnan, 'Warum vergleichen?' in Epple and Erhart (eds.), *Die Welt beobachten. Praktiken des Vergleichens*, 35–61, 46.
15 See Albrecht Koschorke, 'Ähnlichkeit. Valenzen eines post-kolonialen Konzepts', Anil Bhatti and Dorothee Kimmich (eds.), *Ähnlichkeit. Ein kulturtheoretisches Paradigma* (Konstanz: Konstanz University Press, 2015), 35–45, esp. 35 and 39.
16 Cf. Edmund Husserl, *The Crisis of European Sciences and Transcendental Philosophy* [1936/54], trans. David Carr (Evanston: Northwestern University Press, 1970).
17 See Martin Heidegger, *Pathmarks*, ed. and trans. William McNeil (Cambridge: Cambridge University Press, [1967] 2014), 123–4.
18 Cf. Michael Eggers, *Zur Wissenschaftsgeschichte und Epistemologie des Vergleichs und zur Genealogie der Komparatistik* (Heidelberg: Winter, 2016), chapter 6.
19 See Rolf Elberfeld, 'Überlegungen zur Grundlegung "komparativer Philosophie"', *Allgemeine Zeitschrift für Philosophie* 24 (1999), 125–54, esp. 140; the same issue also includes a research bibliography by the same author; cf. ibid., 211–20.
20 Cf. Ludwig Wittgenstein, *Philosophical Investigations. Part I*, 3rd edition, eds. G.E.M. Anscombe and Rush Rhees, trans. G.E.M. Anscombe (Englewood Cliffs, NJ: Prentice Hall, 1973), 1–172, § 244.
21 See Peter Winch, 'On Understanding a Primitive Society', in idem, *Ethics and Action (Studies in Ethics and the Philosophy of Religion)*, (London: Routledge & Kegan Paul, 1972), 8–49, 8–9; page numbers in brackets refer to this article.
22 Winch only alludes to a constructive reading of Azande culture beyond a causal framework when speaking of a 'symbolic' interpretation. It is beyond the scope of this chapter to elaborate on Winch's proposal; see John Cottingham, 'What Difference Does It Make? The Nature and Significance of Theistic Belief', *Ratio* 29:4 (2006), 401–20.
23 In one of his later papers, Winch comes back to the basic idea in 'On Understanding a Primitive Society' to engage in the precarious attempt to understand and eventually compare not only cross-culturally and diachronically, but in regard to one's own culture, as well as synchronically; see Peter Winch, 'Can We Understand Ourselves?' *Philosophical Investigations* 20:3 (1997), 193–204, esp. 199.
24 On these epistemological questions in Winch's paper, see Hartmut von Sass, *Sprachspiele des Glaubens. Eine Studie zur kontemplativen Religionsphilosophie von Dewi Z. Phillips mit ständiger Rücksicht auf Ludwig Wittgenstein (Religion in Philosophy and Theology 47)*, (Tübingen: Mohr Siebeck, 2010), 256–62.
25 Applying 'other comparative regards' could mean relying on *tertia* derived from the Azande culture, but that is, one has to admit, very hard to deliver for someone who is alien to the culture in question. Here one can see an unavoidable asymmetry and, hence, an impure comparison at work.

4 Orientation, Indexicality and Comparisons: A Theme from Kant

1 For all cinephiles, think of *Pulp Fiction*'s sixth chapter, the so-called 'Bonnie Situation'.

2   Cf. Hans Blumenberg, *Paradigms for a Metaphorology* [1960], trans. Robert Savage (Ithaca, NY/London: Cornell University Press, 2010), esp. 46 and 123.
3   See Günter Abel, 'Quellen der Orientierung', in Andrea Bertino, Ekaterina Poljakova, Andreas Rupschus, Benjamin Alberts (eds.), *Zur Philosophie der Orientierung* (Berlin/New York: De Gruyter, 2016), 147–69, 150; Ingolf U. Dalferth, 'Verstehen als Orientierungspraxis, Eine hermeneutische Skizze', in ibid., 171–84, 179.
4   Just one interesting example: Palle Yourgrau, *Death and Nonexistence* (Oxford: Oxford University Press, 2019), esp. chapter III and IX.
5   Martin Heidegger, *Being and Time*, trans. John Macquarrie and Edward Robinson (Oxford: Basil Blackwell, 1962), §§ 25 and 41; see Hubert L. Dreyfus, *Being-in-the-world: A Commentary in Heidegger's* Being and Time, Division I (Cambridge, MA: MIT Press, 1991), section 3, esp. 46 and 58.
6   Cf. Werner Stegmaier, 'Zur Philosophie der Orientierung. Fragen und Antworten', in Andrea Bertino et al. (eds.), *Zur Philosophie der Orientierung*, 375–408, 380.
7   This triarchy serves, at least, for Werner Stegmaier as the most important influence; see (among other texts) his '"Was heißt: Sich im Denken orientieren": Zur Möglichkeit philosophischer Weltorientierung nach Kant', *Allgemeine Zeitschrift für Philosophie* 17:1 (1992), 1–16; see also 'Die Wirklichkeit der Orientierung. Perspektivität und Realität nach Nietzsche und Luhmann', *Nietzscheforschung* 22:1 (2015), 93–112.
8   See, in particular, Werner Stegmaier, *Philosophie der Orientierung* (Berlin/New York: De Gruyter, 2008), chapter 18, esp. 647 and 652; hereafter *PO*, there is also an English, but essentially shortened version of this book; hence, I will refer to the German original one.
9   On this background cf. Werner Stegmaier, '"Was heißt: Sich im Denken orientieren". Zur Möglichkeit philosophischer Weltorientierung nach Kant', 1–3.
10 Cf. Francesco Totaro, 'Orientierung, Perspektive, Wahrheit. Versuch einer Verbindung', in Andrea Bertino et al. (eds.), *Zur Philosophie der Orientierung*, 197–213, 199.
11 See Stegmaier, *PO*, xix. Kant's call for enlightenment as a mode of self-thinking also belongs to this context. In other words, the emphasis on orientation with reason as one of its tools is connected to the imperative to use one's own thinking to take leave 'from his self-imposed nonage' (Immanuel Kant, 'Answering the Question: What is Enlightenment?' [1784], trans. Mary C. Smith, available from Columbia University Press at: http://www.columbia.edu/acis/ets/CCREAD/etscc/kant.html#note1).
12 Immanuel Kant, *What does it mean to orient oneself in thinking?* [1786], ed. and trans. Allen W. Wood and George di Giovanni (Cambridge: Cambridge University Press, 2012), 1–18; 8:134.
13 Cf. Ingolf U. Dalferth, *Die Wirklichkeit des Möglichen. Hermeneutische Religionsphilosophie* (Tübingen: Mohr Siebeck, 2003), 41.
14 Kant repudiated forcefully the philosophical usage of 'feeling' in his *Groundwork for the Metaphysics of Morals* [1785]. *A German-English Edition*, ed. and trans. Mary Gregor and Jens Timmermann (Cambridge: Cambridge University Press, 2011), 133–5; see also Werner Stegmaier, 'Orientierung. Einleitung', in idem (ed.), *Orientierung. Philosophische Perspektiven* (Frankfurt a.M.: Suhrkamp, 2005), 14–50, 21, note 14.
15 See, on the 'subjective' character of drawing a distinction from a particular stance, Thomas Nagel: 'And if there is such a thing as the correct view, it is certainly not going to be the unedited view from wherever one happens to be in the world. It must be a

view that includes oneself [...].' ('Subjective and Objective', in idem, *Mortal Questions* (Cambridge: Cambridge University Press, 1979), 196–213, 209.

16 Cf. Dalferth, *Die Wirklichkeit des Möglichen*, 42.
17 See Stegmaier, 'Orientierung. Einleitung', 23.
18 This motive is not restricted to spatial orientation: this orientation, in Kant, is just one prominent example for a typical entanglement of 'subjective' and 'objective' elements – also to be found in the 'respect for the moral law'. This respect ('*Achtung*') is also a 'feeling' that is required to have a reason to act according to the general law. Moral orientation, in Kant, is then the combination between an 'objective' structure (consisting of a moral and coherent law) as well as the 'subjective' feeling of respect; thanks to Michael Hampe for this observation; see also Rae Langton, 'Objective and Unconditioned Value', *The Philosophical Review* 116:2 (2007), 157–85, esp. 165–9.
19 See Immanuel Kant, *Critique of Pure Reason* [1781/87], eds. Paul Guyer and Allen Wood (Cambridge: Cambridge University Press, 1998), A 812/B 840; see also Andrew Chignell, 'Rational Hope, Moral Order, and the Revolution of the Will', in Eric Watkins (ed.), *Divine Order, Human Order, and the Order of Nature: Historical Perspectives* (Oxford: Oxford University Press, 2013), 197–218, esp. 212–3.
20 See Ian Hacking, *Historical Ontology* (Cambridge, MA/London: Harvard University Press, 2002), chapter 1 and 3.
21 Cf. Sven Bernecker, 'Kant on Spatial Orientation', *European Journal of Philosophy* 24:4 (2012), 519–33, 524–7; for a phenomenological interpretation see Peter Woelert, 'Kant's hands, spatial orientation, and the Copernican turn', *Continental Philosophical Review* 40:1 (2007), 139–50, esp. 143–5.
22 However, I don't want to overstretch this case since there are, obviously, several grades of understanding and different levels of orientation, nevertheless, the difference to 'interpretation' and 'comparison' holds, if only heuristically.
23 See Hans-Georg Gadamer, *Truth and Method*. Second and revised edition, trans. Joel Weinsheimer and Donald G. Marshall (London/New York: Continuum, 2004), 283.
24 Ludwig Wittgenstein, *Philosophical Investigations. Part I*, 3rd edition, eds. G.E.M. Anscombe and Rush Rhees, trans. G.E.M. Anscombe (Englewood Cliffs, NJ: Prentice Hall, 1973), 1–172, § 122; see on the idea and term 'surveyable representation' Beth Savickey, 'Wittgenstein and Hacker: Übersichtliche Darstellung', *Nordic Wittgenstein Review* 3:2 (2014), 99–123.
25 Stegmaier, *PO*, xv.
26 Stegmaier, 'Orientierung. Einleitung', 16; the German original reads: 'Orientierung als die *Leistung* zu verstehen, *sich in wechselnden Situationen zurechtzufinden und in ihnen Handlungsmöglichkeiten zu erschließen*'; see also *PO*, 1–2.
27 Here, I am following Stefan Berg's (*Spielwerk. Orientierungshermeneutische Studien zum Verhältnis von Musik und Religion (RPT 60)* (Tübingen: Mohr Siebeck, 2011), 38) and Andreas Luckner's (*Klugheit* (Grundthemen Philosophie) (Berlin/New York: De Gruyter, 2012), 9–23) accounts; Luckner distinguishes between six elements of orientation and pairs them with reverse sources for disorientation; see section 4.
28 Claiming that orientation 'exists' only in the act of orienting *oneself* does not exclude that one could also orient others – that, then, are oriented by someone else. It does say, however, that not every orientation is self-orientation.
29 In a very insightful paper on Stegmaier's philosophy of orientation, Konrad Ott contemplates an analysis of orientation's 'presuppositions', to, eventually, refute the sense of such an endeavour by stating that orientation as basic concept is supposed to be independent from antecedent conditions; see his 'Zum Selbst der Orientierung', in

Andrea Bertino et. al. (eds.), *Zur Philosophie der Orientierung*, 115–26, 119–20. This critique, I think, confuses Stegmaier's actual interest in characterizing orientation as *practically* basic form of acting without denying, by the former characterization, the possibility of orientation to have logical, conceptual, or even factual presuppositions.

30 Speaking here of a 'bearer' of the orienting act or that orientation is 'necessarily agent-centred' is, by no means, a return to activate the formerly criticized subjectivism, i.e. the depiction of the orienting bearer as sovereign and detached actor. Hence, this phrasing here is compatible with the *receptive* element of orientation; see also section 3.5.

31 See also Günter Abel's account integrating this structure into his philosophy of signs and interpretation while turning orientation itself into a hermeneutic act based on the usage of signs and symbols; Abel, 'Quellen der Orientierung', 147–8.

32 Werner Stegmaier, 'Weltabkürzungskunst. Orientierung durch Zeichen', in Josef Simon (ed.), *Zeichen und Interpretation* (Frankfurt a.M.: Suhrkamp, 1994), 119–41, 137–8.

33 Cf. Werner Stegmaier, 'Spielräume der Moral in Orientierungssituationen', in Stefan Berg and Hartmut von Sass (eds.), *Spielzüge. Zur Dialektik des Spiels und seinem metaphorischen Mehrwert* (Freiburg im Br./München: Karl Alber, 2014), 264–77.

34 Stegmaier, 'Weltabkürzungskunst', 128.

35 This diagnosis resembles Heidegger's distinction between 'presence-at-hand' (*Vorhandenheit*) and 'readiness-to-hand' (*Zuhandenheit*); see Heidegger, *Being and Time*, §§ 15, 16 and 18; cf. also Denis McManus, *Heidegger and the Measure of Truth* (Oxford: Oxford University Press, 2012), chapters 3 and 7.

36 Stegmaier, 'Weltabkürzungskunst', 131.

37 Cf. Stegmaier, *PO*, 162–4 and 174.

38 See Dalferth, *Die Wirklichkeit des Möglichen*, 35.

39 Cf. Stegmaier, *PO*, 155; idem, 'Spielräume der Moral in Orientierungssituationen', 271.

40 Stegmaier, *PO*, chapter 8, esp. 282; idem, '"Was heißt: Sich im Denken orientieren"', 13.

41 Stegmaier, *PO*, 200 and 203.

42 Ibid., 194.

43 See Grace A. de Laguna: 'This is admittedly a relativism, but inasmuch as perspectivity is itself objective, and since a character ascribable to an object in a given perspective really belongs to it in that perspective, the relativism is held to be objective.' ('Appearance and Orientation', *The Journal of Philosophy* 31:3 (1934), 72–7, 73).

44 On an account of perspectivism in an epistemological, hermeneutical and ethical sense cf. Hartmut von Sass (ed.), *Perspektivismus. Neue Beiträge aus der Erkenntnistheorie, Hermeneutik und Ethik* (Hamburg: Meiner, 2019); see also idem, 'Perspektiven auf die Perspektive. Eine Einleitung', in ibid., 9–33.

45 One might think of the examples discussed by G.E. Moore as 'common sense' and, following him, by Ludwig Wittgenstein as 'certainties', such as 'this is my hand' (pointing to one's hand), 'my name is …' (first person; self-reflective), etc. Here, taking up a perspective (and not another one) is, obviously, not the issue.

46 Stegmaier characterizes the project of 'classical metaphysics' by regarding it as an attempt to get rid of the merely provisional status and only conditional stability of reference points. This is not meant to be repudiating metaphysics *tout court*, but rather correcting its ambitions by stating that metaphysics is not in contrast to orientation but one possibility of (the philosophy of) orientation itself; see *PO*, 647.

47 See, in reference to Søren Kierkegaard's notion of paradox, Stegmaier, 'Orientierung. Einleitung', 30.

48 Kant's heading 'To Orient Oneself in Thinking?' has often been taken to propose that orientation is given by the act of thinking. It is rather meant to be claiming the opposite, namely that we are dealing here with thinking in need of being structured by orientation; see Ott, 'Zum Selbst der Orientierung', 125.
49 Kant, *Critique of Pure Reason*, B 411.
50 See Jörg Volbers, *Die Vernunft der Erfahrung. Eine pragmatistische Kritik der Rationalität* (Hamburg: Meiner, 2018), 186–205.
51 See Stegmaier, *PO*, 302; the German original reads: '*Das Selbst der Orientierung ist die Orientierung selbst*'; cf. Martin Heidegger on the notion of 'Dasein' in *Being and Time*, esp. § 25: 'An approach to the existential question of the "who" of Dasein'; also Ott, 'Zum Selbst der Orientierung', 124.
52 Cf. Stegmaier, *PO*, 303; see also Ian Hacking, 'The Archaeology of Michel Foucault', in idem, *Historical Ontology*, 73–86, esp. 82.
53 Stegmaier, *PO*, 302; the German original reads: 'In der Rede vom Sich-Orientieren ist das Selbst als Selbstbezüglichkeit der Orientierung schon vorausgesetzt und in der Orientierung darum nicht weiter zu begründen.' However, passages like this one seem to downplay Kant's distinction between the transcendental and the empirical subject; see also Werner Stegmaier, 'Nach der Subjektivität. Selbstbezüglichkeit der Orientierung', in Ingolf U. Dalferth and Philipp Stoellger (eds.), *Krisen der Subjektivität. Problemfelder eines strittigen Paradigmas* (Tübingen: Mohr Siebeck, 2005), 79–101, esp.82.
54 See Kant, *Critique of Pure Reason*, B 132.
55 Cf. Stegmaier, *PO*, 296.
56 See ibid.; cf. also Tyler Burge, 'Demonstrative Constructions, Reference, and Truth', *The Journal of Philosophy* 71:7 (1974), 205–23, 209; Howard Wettstein, 'Referent and Fixing Reference', in *Prospects for Meaning. Current Issues in Theoretical Philosophy*. Vol. 3 (Berlin/New York: De Gruyter, 2012).
57 For a different account re-establishing the subject as object (*Gegenstand*) see Tobias Rosefeldt, 'Kants Ich als Gegenstand', *Deutsche Zeitschrift für Philosophie* 54:2 (2006), 277–93, esp. 279–81.
58 David Kaplan, 'Demonstratives. An Essay on Semantics, Logic, Metaphysics, and Epistemology of Demonstratrives and other Indexicals', in Joseph Almog, John Perry and Howard Wettstein (eds.), *Themes from Kaplan* (Oxford: Oxford University Press, 1989), 481–563, 506 and 531.
59 On this distinction cf. ibid., 490–1. I won't enter the debate about essential indexicals, i.e. indexicals that are not translatable into non-indexical (or non-demonstrative) descriptions; see John Perry, 'The Problem of the Essential Indexical', *Noûs* 13:1 (1979), 3–21; for a critique of essential indexicals (that are, for Perry, supposed to entail only 'I' and 'now') see Ruth Millikan, 'The Myth of the Essential Indexical', *Noûs* 24:5 (1990), 723–34, 724 and 727.
60 This is a difference that mirrors Gottlob Frege's classical distinction between 'sense' and 'reference' (*Sinn* and *Bedeutung*); see his seminal paper 'On Sinn and Bedeutung', in Michael Bearney (ed.), *The Frege Reader* (Oxford: Blackwell, 1997).
61 See Kaplan, 'Demonstratives', 505–6; cf. also Robert Stalnaker who expresses the difference in question as follows: 'The content of a sentence will of course be a function of what is expressed or denoted by the constituents of the sentence, and of its structure, but concepts, objects, senses and semantic structure are part of the means by which content is determined, and not components of the content itself' ('Indexical Belief', *Synthese* 49:1 (1981), 129–51, 134).

62 Cf. Bernecker, 'Kant on Spatial Orientation', 525 and 527.
63 Sometimes a distinction is drawn between indexicals (like 'here' and 'there') and terms anchored to or being dependent on indexicals, as one reviewer of this journal suggested. And 'left/right' may belong only to that second group. I am not sure whether this distinction is apt or helpful, but will only state that even in the case of accepting the sketched difference, one does not have to modify anything said concerning the indexical element of 'left/right'.
64 This oscillation could also be described as feedback, known from early cybernetics: take two systems; P is coupled to R so that P's changes affect, or determine, what R's changes would be, und P's changes depend on what state R is at; a similar mutual coupling we have here too; see W. Ross Ashby, *Introduction into Cybernetics* (London: Chapman & Hall Ltd., 1957), 51–4 and 81.
65 Stegmaier holds that there is no hierarchical relation between the orienting act and the situation; the passage above is meant to correct this claim; see his 'Orientierung. Einleitung', 16; 'Weltabkürzungskunst', 134; *PO*, 42.
66 On the necessarily reductive element of orienting tools see Stegmaier, *PO*, 652.
67 Cf. Berg, *Spielwerk*, 45.
68 John Maxwell Coetzee, *Disgrace* (New York: Penguin Books, 1999), 64, 88, 146; see also the slightly controversial, but illuminating paper by Adriaan van Heerden, 'Disgrace, Desire, and the Dark Side of the New South Africa', in Anton Leist and Peter Singer (eds.), *Coetzee and Philosophy. Philosophical Perspectives on Literature* (New York: Columbia University Press, 2010), 43–63, esp. 54–9.
69 See, for the phrase 'inside/outside' ethics, Alice Crary, *Inside Ethics. On the Demands of Moral Thought* (Cambridge, MA/London: Harvard University Press, 2016), esp. 11–12 and passim.
70 This is also critically addressed by Stefan Berg in his *Spielwerk*, 38–9.
71 See Edna Ullmann-Margalit and Sidney Morgenbesser, 'Picking and Choosing', *Social Research* 44:4 (1977), 757–85.
72 Stegmaier, *PO*, 312: 'Orientierungswelten'.
73 Cf. Max Black, 'Rules and Routines', in idem, *Margins of Precision. Essay in Logic and Language* (Ithaca, NY/London: Cornell University Press, 1970), 41–56; Ingolf U. Dalferth, 'Leben angesichts des Unverfügbaren. Die duale Struktur religiöser Lebensorientierung', in Werner Stegmaier (ed.), *Orientierung. Philosophische Perspektiven* (Frankfurt a.M.: Suhrkamp, 2005), 245–66, 249 and 252.
74 See Ott, 'Zum Selbst der Orientierung', 125. One might also think of what Hans-Georg Gadamer claims for the routines of language, namely that, sometimes, it is not us speaking a language, but rather, we are spoken by it; see *Truth and Method*, 483.
75 Cf. Stegmaier, *PO*, 304–8.
76 Cf. Paul van Tongeren, 'Der "Pflock des Augenblicks". Über die Situation und die Tugenden der Orientierung', in Andrea Bertino et al. (eds.), *Zur Philosophie der Orientierung*, 233–45, 243–4.

5 Comparatively/Descriptively: Wittgenstein and the Search for 'Objects of Comparison'

1 The following abbreviations are used for Wittgenstein's writings:

BlB – *The Blue Book*, in *The Blue and the Brown Book*, ed. Rush Rhees (New York: Harper & Brothers, 1958), 1–74.
BrB – *The Brown Book*, in *The Blue and the Brown Book*, ed. Rush Rhees (New York: Harper & Brothers, 1958), 75–185.
CV – *Culture and Value*, ed. G.H. von Wright in collaboration with Heikki Nyman, trans. Peter Winch (Chicago: The Chicago University Press, 1984).
NL – 'Notes on Logic' [1913], in *Notebooks 1914–1916*, ed. G.H. von Wright and G.E.M. Anscombe, with an English translation by G.E.M. Anscombe (Oxford: Basil Blackwell, 1961), 93–106.
OC – *On Certainty*, eds. G.E.M. Anscombe and G.H. von Wright, with an English translation by Denis Paul and G.E.M. Anscombe (New York/San Francisco/London: Harper & Row, 1972).
PI – *Philosophical Investigations. Part I*, 3rd edition, eds. G.E.M. Anscombe and Rush Rhees, trans. G.E.M. Anscombe (Englewood Cliffs, NJ: Prentice Hall, 1973), 1–172.
PI II – *Philosophical Investigations. Part II*, 3rd edition, eds. G.E.M. Anscombe and Rush Rhees, trans. G.E.M. Anscombe (Englewood Cliffs, NJ: Prentice Hall, 1973), 173–232.
PR – *Philosophical Remarks*, ed. from his posthumous writings by Rush Rhees and translated by Raymond Hargreaves and Roger White (Oxford: Basil Blackwell, 1975).
RFG – 'Remarks on Frazer's *Golden Bough*', in *Philosophical Occasions*, ed. James C. Klagge and Alfred Nordmann (Indianapolis/Cambridge: Hackett, 1993), 119–55.
T – *Tractatus Logico-Philosophicus*, ed. and trans. David Pears and Brian McGuinness (London: Routledge, 2001).
Z – *Zettel*, eds. G.E.M. Anscombe and G.H. von Wright, trans. G.E.M. Anscombe (Berkeley/Los Angeles: University of California Press, 1967).

2. See, however, what Wittgenstein says regarding descriptively philosophizing in his *Philosophical Investigations* (cf. esp. PI 89–133). Here, one might get the impression that he is doing what he, on other occasions, repudiates, namely presenting 'a second-order philosophy' (PI 121). The claim according to which philosophy must be conducted descriptively is to be found in several passages of Wittgenstein's work. This claim had already been formulated in 1913, despite very different theoretical background assumptions (cf. NL, 106). It is also evident in his 'Remarks on Frazer's *Golden Bough*' (cf. RFG, 121), as well as in some of his interim writings during the 1930s, for instance in the *Blue* and the *Brown Book* (cf. BlB, 18: 'purely descriptive', and BrB, 127–8). Also, *Zettel* from twelve years prior contains references to descriptive philosophy (cf. Z 311 and 314).
3. On the distinction between *saying* and *showing*, see T 6.41–6.522. Also, on this topic, see Dieter Mersch, 'Die Sprache der Materialität: Etwas zeigen und Sich-Zeigen bei Goodman und Wittgenstein', in Olaf Scholz and Jörg Steinbrenner (eds.), *Symbole, Systeme, Welten. Überlegungen zur Philosophie Nelson Goodmans* (Heidelberg: Winter, 2004), 141–61.
4. And it is these later writings I will focus on in the following chapter. Despite all continuities between Wittgenstein's earlier and later work, it is safe to state that his take on the possibility of an explanatory, foundational and, so far, *not* 'purely descriptive' philosophy has been shifting considerably. Thus, his appreciation for an essentially comparative mode of thinking comes to the fore only in his later work. The *Tractatus* is obviously not a specimen of a comparatively oriented philosophy.

5 Klaus von Stosch, *Glaubensverantwortung in doppelter Kontingenz. Untersuchungen zur Verortung fundamentaler Theologie nach Wittgenstein* (Regensburg: Pustet, 2001), 16, note 3.
6 René Descartes, *Meditations on First Philosophy*, trans. by John Cottingham (Cambridge: Cambridge University Press, 1996), 93.
7 Hans-Georg Gadamer, *Truth and Method*. Second and revised edition, translated by Joel Weinsheimer and Donald G. Marshall (London/New York: Continuum, 2004), xxiv.
8 See esp. PI 66 on the notion of 'family resemblances'. One has to be aware of the danger of falsely ascribing the complementary theory to Wittgenstein, according to which there are no essential properties anymore. This has been rightly underlined by Stanley Cavell; see his *The Claim of Reason. Wittgenstein, Skepticism, Morality, and Tragedy* (Oxford/New York: Oxford University Press, 1979), 187. The idea of having a 'complicated network of similarities' (PI 66) is primarily linked to a therapeutic function; cf. also von Stosch, *Glaubensverantwortung in doppelter Kontingenz*, 40.
9 This account might show a possibility for how to react to the (often critically intended) observation that comparisons play at best a marginal role in contemporary philosophy; see on this point Rolf Elberfeld, 'Überlegungen zur Grundlegung "komparativer Philosophie"', *Allgemeine Zeitschrift für Philosophie* 24:2 (1999), 125–54, 126.
10 Wittgenstein articulates this point in a similar fashion in CV, 37.
11 See also Peter Winch's phrasing of a 'moral demand' on the philosopher to do justice – a notion that is transferred into philosophy of religion by Dewi Z. Phillips; cf. his *Religion and Friendly Fire. Examining Assumptions in Contemporary Philosophy of Religion* (Aldershot/Burlington, VT: Ashgate, 2004), 88–9. Under considerably different assumptions, Gadamer determines the opting for a method to be a problem of '*moral relevance*'; see *Truth and Method*, 311.
12 However, one might dissolve this tension between doing justice to reality and its variety of phenomena, as well as 'the hardness of the logical must' and its reductive dangers, by pointing to practice: the logical hardness could be the hardness of being forced to accept certain judgements. Wittgenstein does not deny that there is this hardness, but he underlines the fact that this hardness has no reason or underpinnings outside of a certain practice.
13 It is nevertheless not excluded (but not *per se* problematic either) that, even under the conditions just described, a descriptive bias is possible; cf. Hans Blumenberg, 'Ausblick auf eine Theorie der Unbegrifflichkeit', in Anselm Haverkamp (ed.), *Theorie der Metapher*, 2nd ed. (Darmstadt: WBG, 1996), 438–54, 449.
14 This does not preclude that the deep-seated difficulties could – directly or symptomatically – show themselves on the *surface*.
15 See Paul Feyerabend, 'Ludwig Wittgenstein', in *Beiheft 1 zu Wittgensteins Schriften* (Frankfurt a.M.: Suhrkamp, 1960), 30–47, esp. 45; cf. also Joachim Schulte, *Chor und Gesetz. Wittgenstein im Kontext* (Frankfurt a.M.: Suhrkamp, 1990), 138.
16 This is the case simply because of descriptions potentially entertaining the status of justifications; see below.
17 Cf. Schulte, *Chor und Gesetz*, 140.
18 For this claim and its phrasing, see Richard Rorty, *Contingency, Irony, and Solidarity* (Cambridge: Cambridge University Press, 1989), 37. However, it is important to emphasize that this weak version is only a reaction to the potential contradiction between a descriptive philosophy and its non-descriptive grounds. I do think that

Wittgenstein wants more than just to present 'interesting' things in the sense of Rorty. Wittgenstein, for instance, finds it very problematic to think about language in a wrong way; and this wrongness is deeper than being merely 'uninteresting'. Thanks to Jörg Volbers for this point.

19 What is presented here as an 'even weaker' interpretation is not necessarily *my* opinion. It is a manner of circumventing some of the problems that are doubtlessly looming in this context. I have opted for this rather defensive approach because the present chapter is not primarily concerned with giving and defending a consistent reading and formulation of a purely descriptive philosophy in the wake of Wittgenstein. In any case, I have doubts that this is possible and I also have reservations against the interest in such an endeavour. However, it has to be clear that a descriptive philosophy reacts to a genuinely 'modern' situation, according to which Reality – capitalized – as guaranteeing truth has gone astray. This might also explain Wittgenstein's reluctance towards reductive theories. On this point, see Hartmut von Sass, 'Broken Mirrors – Contemplative Nowheres. Rorty and Phillips on Description, Imagination, and Literature', in Ingolf U. Dalferth and Hartmut von Sass (eds.), *The Contemplative Spirit. Dewi Z. Phillips on Religion and the Limits of Philosophy* (Tübingen: Mohr Siebeck, 2010), 55–95, esp. 57–65.
20 It might have become clearer that pure descriptions cannot *per se* guarantee the philosophical justice sought after here; it is possible to be descriptively unjust too – an objection that has also been raised against Wittgenstein himself; cf. Hans Blumenberg, *Zu den Sachen und zurück*, ed. Manfred Sommer (Frankfurt a.M.: Suhrkamp, 2007), 346; for the quotations above see ibid., 342, translations mine.
21 See Joachim Matthes, 'The Operation Called "Vergleichen"', in idem (ed.), *Zwischen den Kulturen? Die Sozialwissenschaften vor dem Problem des Kulturvergleichs* (Göttingen: Otto Schartz, 1992), 75–99; the title refers to Theodor Abel's 1948 paper 'The Operation Called Verstehen'.
22 On the details of comparative structures, see part I, esp. chapter 1.
23 It should be mentioned just in passing, that there are other, more favourable takes on the notion of 'prejudice' than Wittgenstein's; one might compare it to Gadamer's rehabilitation of prejudices as being necessary for every act of understanding; this appreciation belongs into the context of Gadamer's hermeneutic elaboration of heritage and tradition that is itself not without problems; see *Truth and Method*, 277–306.
24 On this question, see also Hartmut von Sass, *Sprachspiele des Glaubens. Eine Studie zur kontemplativen Religionsphilosophie von Dewi Z. Phillips mit ständiger Rücksicht auf Ludwig Wittgenstein* (Tübingen: Mohr Siebeck, 2010), part II, section I.1.
25 I presuppose here that Wittgenstein's term 'language-game' actually works to *analogize* language with games – and is not merely a metaphor to describe such a process. For this characterization, I refer to PI, 83 & 494 and PI II, 231. If 'language-game' is an analogy, then one not only compares other things with it, but it is itself (or it entails) a comparison, insofar as an *analogia proportionalitatis* is a comparison of relations. It is characteristic for analogies to be more modest than identifications. This means that analogizing things implies the concession that the analogy might clarify some aspects, while not being helpful in other aspects. Hence, the language-game analogy often fails, a fact that has been highlighted, especially, by Rush Rhees. What Rhees misses in Wittgenstein's later writings is an account of the *unity of language*; see his *Wittgenstein and the Possibility of Discourse*, ed. Dewi Z. Phillips (Cambridge: Cambridge University Press, 1998), 108, 114–15, 170, 204–5.

26 Cf. Peter Winch, 'Judgement: Proposition and Practices', *Philosophical Investigations* 21:3 (1998), 189–201, esp. 190.
27 Wittgenstein's emphasis on the communal character of language has been, rightly I think, criticized by Ian Hacking for neglecting the *political dimension* of how language is shared by speakers. Hacking states: 'One paradoxical effect of his [Wittgenstein's] work has been to depoliticize the idea of language as essentially public. Language becomes regarded as an abstract phenomenon.' ('How, Why, When, and Where Did Language Go Public', in idem, *Historical Ontology* (Cambridge, MA/London: Harvard University Press, 2002), 121–39, 136).
28 This idea of an inversion between player and game is best known from the game-chapter in Gadamer's *Truth and Method*; see esp. 102–10.
29 Martin Heidegger, 'Phenomenology and Theology' [1927], in idem, *Pathmarks*, ed. William McNeill (Cambridge: Cambridge University Press, 1998), 39–62, 58; translation is my own.
30 Here, I will neglect two problems connected to the concept of language-game, namely the questions of how wide or extended a language-game is (linked to Wittgenstein's speaking of the 'completeness' of a language-game; cf. BrB, 79–80), and how we are able to discriminate different language-games from one another (the problem of internalism). Regarding these aspects, see Hans Julius Schneider, 'Offene Grenzen, zerfaserte Ränder: Über Arten von Beziehungen zwischen Sprachspielen', in Wilhelm Lütterfelds and Andreas Roser (eds.), *Der Konflikt der Lebensformen in Wittgensteins Philosophie der Sprache* (Frankfurt a.M.: Peter Lang Verlag, 1999), 138–55.
31 On this aspect, see Gunter Gebauer, *Wittgensteins Anthropologisches Denken* (München: C.H. Beck, 2009), 39, 83, 113. The descriptive reduction by language-games must be distinguished from the reduction by theories criticized as being inadequate: in the first case, the reduction is taken to be explicitly heuristic; in the second case, this pragmatic concession is given up in favour of theoretical truth claims.
32 Hence, it is claimed that the language-game of denoting colours, firstly, (partly) follows other rules in our case than in the case of Inuits, and, secondly, that this difference is due to divergent contexts of life-practice.
33 See Stephen Mulhall, *Philosophical Myths of the Fall* (Princeton: Princeton University Press, 2005), 111.
34 Cf. Richard Rorty, 'Freud and moral reflection', in idem, *Essays on Heidegger and Others*. Philosophical papers. Volume II (Cambridge: Cambridge University Press, 1991), 143–63. Rorty claims: 'The availability of a richer vocabulary of moral deliberation is what one chiefly has in mind when one says that we are, morally speaking, more sensitive and sophisticated than our ancestors or than our younger selves' (155).
35 The comparative purposelessness has, however, to be specified insofar as *all* descriptions, according to Wittgenstein, are bound to a purpose, namely to dissolve a philosophical problem. This mode of 'being bound to a purpose' turns out to be 'contaminated' as soon as *substantial* interests start to accompany the comparison's *formal* ambition. This, for Wittgenstein, would have to be criticized in the name of 'purity'.
36 This is also critically noted in view of Rush Rhees's critique of analogizing language and games; see Rhees, *Possibility of Discourse*, chapters 5 and 9; on Rhees's criticism, see also David Cockburn's illuminating paper 'Critical Notice: Rush Rhees, Wittgenstein and the possibility of discourse', *Philosophical Investigations* 25:1 (2002), 79–93, esp. 90.

37 One might criticize and eventually repudiate the mere possibility of descriptive and comparative 'purity' in holding that every description and comparison is loaded with preferences and unavoidably, a certain bias. This is one way of understanding the term 'thick descriptions', as seen in the work of Gilbert Ryle and Clifford Geertz; if one subscribes to this reservation, one could still hold that pure descriptions are a regulative idea (not necessarily an ideal); see Clifford Geertz, 'Thick Description: Toward an Interpretive Theory of Culture', in idem, *The Interpretation of Cultures: Selected Essays* (New York: Basic Books, 1973), 3–30.
38 The critique of a compulsory 'must' is aptly circumscribed by Cora Diamond as the reservation against 'the *laying down of philosophical requirements*'; see her 'Introduction II: Wittgenstein and Metaphysics', in idem, *The Realistic Spirit. Wittgenstein, Philosophy, and the Mind* (Cambridge, MA/London: MIT Press, 1991), 13–38, 20.
39 See Stanley Cavell, 'The Availability of Wittgenstein's Later Philosophy', in idem, *Must we mean what we say? A Book of Essays*, 9th ed. (Cambridge, MA: Harvard University Press, 2000), 44–72, 72.
40 For this phrasing, 'enduring comparisons', see Herta Müller, 'Wenn wir schweigen, werden wir unangenehm – wenn wir reden, werden wir lächerlich', in idem, *Der König verneigt sich und tötet* (München: C.H. Beck, 2003), 87; translation mine.

6 Comparative Ironism: Richard Rorty on Plural Vocabularies and the Comparisons Between Them

1 'Modern Moral Philosophy', *Philosophy* 33:1 (1958), 1–19; reprint in: *The Collected Philosophical Papers of G.E.M. Anscombe*. Vol. Three: 'Ethics, Religion and Politics' (Minneapolis: University of Minnesota Press, 1981), 26–42, 39.
2 See Alasdair MacIntyre, 'Philosophy, the "Other" Disciplines, and their Histories: A Rejoinder to Richard Rorty', *Soundings: An Interdisciplinary Journal* 65:2 (1982), 127–45, 143–4.
3 Cf. Richard Rorty, *Contingency, Irony and Solidarity* (Cambridge: Cambridge University Press, 1989), 44.
4 Cf. Onora O'Neill, 'The Power of Example', *Philosophy* 61:1 (1986), 5–29, esp. 5–6; on a philosophy of examples Mirjam Schaub, *Das Singuläre und das Exemplarische: Zu Logik und Praxis der Beispiele in Philosophie und Ästhetik* (Zürich/Berlin: Diaphanes, 2010), ch. VI.
5 Peter Winch, 'Moral Integrity', in idem, *Ethics and Action* (London: Routledge & Kegan Paul, 1972), 182.
6 On this aspect see Cora Diamond, *The Realistic Spirit. Wittgenstein, Philosophy, and the Mind* (Cambridge, MA/London: MIT Press, 1991), 306.
7 See O'Neill, 'The Power of Example', 18.
8 Cf. Dewi Z. Phillips, 'The Presumption of Theory', in idem, *Interventions in Ethics* (Albany: SUNY Press, 1992), 61–85, 70 and 79.
9 See ibid., 68.
10 See Richard Rorty, 'Der Roman als Mittel zur Erlösung aus der Selbstbezogenheit', in Joachim Küpper and Christoph Menke (eds.), *Dimensionen ästhetischer Erfahrung* (Frankfurt a.M.: Suhrkamp, 2003), 49–66, esp. 59; originally published in German.

11 Cf. Richard Rorty, 'Pragmatism and romanticism', in idem, *Philosophy as Cultural Politics*. Philosophical Papers, Vol. 4 (Cambridge: Cambridge University Press, 2007), 105–19, 105.
12 Richard Rorty, 'Introduction: Pragmatism and Philosophy', in idem, *Consequences of Pragmatism (Essays: 1972–1980)* (Minneapolis: University of Minnesota Press, 1982), xiii–xlvii, esp. xvii.
13 This argument is presented by Rorty in different passages; the most concrete is the first chapter of his book on irony; cf. *Contingency, Irony and Solidarity*, 5–6, 8, 15–6; see also *Philosophy and the Mirror of Nature*. With a new introduction by Michael Williams (Princeton and Oxford: Princeton University Press, (1979) 2009), 345.
14 Cf. Richard Rorty, 'Introduction: Pragmatism and Philosophy', in idem, *Consequences of Pragmatism*, xix.
15 Cf. Jaegwon Kim, 'Rorty on the Possibility of Philosophy', *The Journal of Philosophy* 77:10 (1980), 588–97, 596.
16 See Rorty, 'Pragmatism and romanticism', 109; critically commented on by Charles Taylor, 'Rorty and Philosophy', in Charles Guignon and David R. Hiley (eds.), *Richard Rorty (Contemporary Philosophy in Focus)* (Cambridge/New York: Cambridge University Press, 2003), 158–80, 172–3.
17 See Richard Rorty, 'Texts and Lumps', *New Literary History* 39:1 (2008), 53–68, 55.
18 Cf. Ruth Anna Putnam, 'Poets, Scientists, and Critics', *New Literary History* 17:1, 'Philosophy of Science and Literary Theory' (1985), 17–21, 21.
19 Surely, that is one of the reasons why the program of a 'new realism', defended by authors like Maurizio Ferrari or Markus Gabriel, is getting so much credit in advance.
20 See Richard Rorty, *Philosophy and Social Hope* (London: Penguin Books, 1999), 149.
21 There are passages suggesting that Rorty sometimes sticks to the extremely vague difference between robust and soft areas of our *Lebenswelt*. This becomes apparent when he relates the natural sciences to the practice of solving problems, whereas humanities are restricted to narrating stories and our transformation by them; see Richard Rorty, *Philosophie & die Zukunft. Essays* (Frankfurt a.M.: Fischer, 2001), 68 and 71; slightly different idem, 'A pragmatist view of contemporary analytic philosophy', in idem, *Philosophy as Cultural Politics*, 133–46, esp. 134–5 and 137.
22 Rorty, *Contingency, Irony and Solidarity*, 189.
23 Cf. Ludwig Wittgenstein, *On Certainty*, eds. G.E.M. Anscombe and G.H. von Wright, trans. Denis Paul and G.E.M. Anscombe (New York/San Francisco/London: Harper & Row, 1972), §§ 125, 235, 414.
24 See Rorty, *Contingency, Irony and Solidarity*, ch. 4, esp. 73 and 113.
25 Cf. Hartmut von Sass, 'Religion in a Private Igloo? A Critical Dialogue with Richard Rorty', *International Journal for Philosophy of Religion* 70:3 (2011), 203–16.
26 See Rorty, *Philosophie & die Zukunft*, 49; also Niklas Forsberg, 'Philosophy, Literature, and the Burden of Theory. Review of Toril Moi's *Revolution of the Ordinary: Literary Studies after Wittgenstein, Austin, and Cavell*', *Graduate Faculty Philosophy Journal* 39:2 (2019), 1–15, 6 and 12.
27 There are further reasons why final vocabularies may appear to be dubious and inadequate. If one criticizes traditional epistemologies for presupposing a factually-invariant reality, and if one attempts to philosophically capture the constant transformation and unforeseeable evolution of reality, then there can be no final and closed vocabularies for that very 'realistic' reason; see already John Dewey, 'The Practical Character of Reality' (1907), in idem, *Philosophy and Civilisation* (New York and London: G.P. Putnam's Sons, 1931), 36–55, 37–8.

28 See Rorty, *Contingency, Irony and Solidarity*, 5–6.
29 See ibid., 7.
30 See Ludwig Wittgenstein, *Philosophical Investigations. Part I*, 3rd edition, eds. G.E.M. Anscombe and Rush Rhees, trans. G.E.M. Anscombe (Englewood Cliffs, NJ: Prentice Hall, 1973), 1–172, §§ 11 and 589.
31 See Richard Rorty, 'Is Derrida a transcendental philosopher?' in idem, *Essays on Heidegger and others*. Philosophical papers. Volume II (Cambridge: Cambridge University Press, 1991), 119–28, 126.
32 Rorty offers two interpretations for the semantics of metaphors: either metaphors have a different usage compared to the usual one; or, he refutes the idea that metaphors have a meaning whatsoever – precisely because we haven't yet found a usage for them, insofar as having meaning implies possessing a place within our language-games; on this point *Philosophy and the Mirror of Nature*, 12; *Essays on Heidegger and others*, 13 and 87; *Contingency, Irony and Solidarity*, 17.
33 See Rorty, *Philosophy and Social Hope*, 6 and 12–13.
34 Rorty, 'Pragmatism and romanticism', 107.
35 Cf. Rorty, *Philosophy and the Mirror of Nature*, 359.
36 Cf. Rorty, 'Cultural politics and the question of the existence of God', in *Philosophy as Cultural Politics*, 3–26, 3.
37 Rorty, 'Professionalized Philosophy and Transcendentalist Culture', in *Consequences of Pragmatism*, 60–71, 66.
38 Rorty expects from new descriptions not only to solve problems directly but, rather, to dissolve them by transformed linguistic configurations; see *Philosophie & die Zukunft*, 72–3.
39 Rorty, *Contingency, Irony and Solidarity*, xv.
40 Cf. ibid., 173.
41 This is the way in which William James expresses this point within the context of religion and facing the plurality of religious orientations; see 'The Will to Believe' (1897), in *Pragmatism and Other Writings*, ed. with an Introduction and Notes by Giles Gunn (New York: Penguin, 2000), 198–218, 199.
42 On this objection see Ian MacKenzie, 'Pragmatism, Rhetoric, and History', *Poetics Today* 16:2 (1995), 283–99, 286; Charles Eric Reeves, 'Deconstruction, Language, Motive: Rortian Pragmatism and the Uses of "Literature"', *The Journal of Aesthetics and Art Criticism* 44:4 (1986), 351–6, 354; Ulf Schulenberg, 'From Redescription to Writing: Rorty, Barthes, and the Idea of a Literary Culture', *New Literary History* 38:2 (2007), 371–87, 375.
43 Cf. Dieter Thomä, *Erzähle dich selbst. Lebensgeschichte als philosophisches Problem* (Frankfurt a.M.: Suhrkamp, 2007), 133, 145, 154–5; from a diagnostic perspective esp. Andreas Reckwitz, *Die Gesellschaft der Singularitäten. Zum Strukturwandel der Moderne*, 5th ed. (Berlin: Suhrkamp, 2018), chapter V.
44 See Rorty, 'Philosophy as a Kind of Writing', in *Consequences of Pragmatism*, 90–109, 92.
45 On the problem of *in-/non-comparability* see chapter 7, section 6.1.
46 Rorty, 'Introduction: Pragmatism and Philosophy', xxxvii and xi.
47 See Rorty, *Contingency, Irony and Solidarity*, 79–80.
48 This phrasing goes back to an important paper of Rorty's: 'The World Well Lost', in *Consequences of Pragmatism*, 3–18.
49 For a structural analysis cf. chapter 1.
50 See Rorty, *Contingency, Irony and Solidarity*, 80–1.

51 Cf. Thomä, *Erzähle dich selbst*, 132.
52 Unfortunately, Rorty's critique of religion neglects this aspect of revisionary comparisons. He instead sticks with the idea that the comparative regard between science and religion remains the same, and he only allows for the refutation of the idea that science is 'closer' to reality than religion. This refutation, however, already derives from the farewell to the correspondence theory of truth, but not from a different – revised – view on religion. Particularly under Rortian conditions, religions entail all ingredients for an 'ethos' of narratively trying out different selves; see Rorty, 'Religion as Conversation-stopper', in *Philosophy and Social Hope*, 168–74; idem, 'Cultural politics and the question of the existence of God', in *Philosophy as Cultural Politics*, 3–26.
53 Rorty, 'Deconstruction and Circumvention', in *Essays on Heidegger and others*, 85–106, 85–6.
54 See Rorty, 'Freud and moral reflection', esp. 146–7.
55 According to Rorty, psychoanalysis turned out to be so incompatible with alternative accounts that it could not be integrated into another framework. Hence, there was the necessity, but also the possibility, to compare different (incompatible) vocabularies. Rorty – here again following Davidson – does not stretch this aspect to a point of total incommensurability (including untranslatability) between different vocabularies; see 'The World Well Lost', 14–15.
56 Cf. Charles Taylor, *A Secular Age* (Cambridge, MA/London: Harvard University Press, 2007), 68–70.
57 See Rorty, 'Philosophy as a transitional genre', in idem, *Philosophy as Cultural Politics*, 89–104, esp. 91 and 93.
58 Rorty agrees with the critique of consequentialist and deontological moral theories by amplifying this critique as refutation of theories – including virtue ethics as theory – in general; see also Iris Murdoch, 'Against Dryness. A Polemical Sketch', in Malcolm Bradbury (ed.), *The novel today: contemporary writers on modern fiction* (London: Fontana, 1990), 16–20, 20; Annette C. Baier, 'What do Women want in a Moral Theory?' *Noûs* 19:1 (1985), 53–63, 59.
59 Cf. Thomas E. Wartenberg, 'Beyond Mere Illustration: How Films Can Be Philosophy', *The Journal of Aesthetics and Art Criticism* 64:1, Special Issue: 'Thinking through Cinema: Film as Philosophy' (2006), 19–32.
60 Cf. Rorty, *Contingency, Irony and Solidarity*, 68–9.
61 On cognitivism and what has been coined as 'the wisdom of literature' see D.D. Raphael, 'Can Literature Be Moral Philosophy?' *New Literary History* 15:1, 'Literature and/as Moral Philosophy' (1983), 1–12, esp. 6; Nora Hämäläinen, *Literature and Moral Theory* (New York: Bloomsbury, 2015), ch. 1; on Rorty's position: Günter Leypoldt, 'Uses of Metaphor: Richard Rorty's Literary Criticism and the Poetics of World-Making', *New Literary History* 39:1, 'Remembering Richard Rorty' (2008), 145–163; Robert B. Pippin, 'Just Who Is It That We Have Become? Rorty's Hegelianism', *The Hedgehog Review* (2016), 84–8; on the relation between literature as example and thought experiments in arguments: Oliver Conolly and Bashar Haydar, 'Literature, Knowledge, and Value', *Philosophy and Literature* 31:1 (2007), 111–24; as critical reply: David Egan, 'Literature and Thought Experiments', *Journal for Aesthetics and Art Criticism* 74:2 (2016), 139–50.
62 See esp. Rorty, 'Der Roman als Mittel zur Erlösung aus der Selbstbezogenheit', 56–8.
63 Cf. ibid., 52 and 60.
64 See Hilary Putnam, 'A Comparison of Something with Something Else', *New Literary History* 17:1, 'Philosophy of Science and Literary Theory' (1985), 61–79, 74.

7 Against Structural Incomparability

1. A case against the compartmentalisation by the incommensurability of theories in Ludwik Fleck and, more prominently, in Thomas Kuhn and Paul Feyerabend raises, for instance, Richard Rorty, 'The World Well Lost', *The Journal of Philosophy* 69:19 (1972), 649–65, 659–60; Michael Hampe, *Die Lehren der Philosophie. Eine Kritik* (Berlin: Suhrkamp, 2014), 199–200.
2. See James Griffin, 'Are There Incommensurable Values?' *Philosophy & Public Affairs* 7:1 (1977), 39–59, 46; Joseph Raz, *The Morality of Freedom* (Oxford: Clarendon Press, 1986), 348; Ruth Chang, *Making Comparisons Count* (London/New York: Routledge, 2002), 125.
3. Cf. Ruth Chang, 'Introduction', in idem (ed.), *Incommensurability, Incomparability, and Practical Reason* (Cambridge, MA/London 1997), 1–34, esp. 8.
4. See Elizabeth Barnes, 'Ontic Vagueness: A Guide for the Perplexed', *Noûs* 44:4 (2010), 601–27, 604 and 613.
5. In several papers Ruth Chang introduced and defended 'being on a par' as a fourth value relation; see esp. her 'The Possibility of Parity', *Ethics* 112:4 (2002), 659–88, 664; and 'Parity. An Intuitive Case', *Ratio* 29:4 (2016), 395–411, 404–5.
6. Cf. Chang, 'The Possibility of Parity', 661.
7. The notion of being 'properly basic' was coined by Alvin Plantinga; see his *Faith and Rationality* (London/Notre Dame, IN: Notre Dame University Press, 1983), 39–44.
8. See esp. Raz, *The Morality of Freedom*, chapter 13, section V.
9. 'Overall preference' means that there might be a preference for A in regard to x and a preference for B in regard to y, but no superior regard z balancing these sub-regards for a final decision.
10. Chang, 'The Possibility of Parity', 659.
11. We will come back to these positions in section 4 and 5; see for the labels used above Chang, 'The Possibility of Parity', 659–60; cf. also Michael Messerli and Kevin Reuter, 'Hard cases of comparison', *Philosophical Studies* 174 (2017), 2227–50, 2232.
12. Chang, *Making Comparisons Count*, 43.
13. See ibid., 133; idem, 'Introduction', 9 and 13; 'Are Hard Choices Cases of Incomparability?' *Philosophical Issues* 22: 'Action Theory' (2012), 106–26, 106 and 108.
14. Cf. Griffin, 'Are There Incommensurable Values?' 43.
15. Cf. Donald Regan, 'Value, Comparability, and Choice', in Chang (ed.), *Incommensurability, Incomparability, and Practical Reason*, 129–50, 132–3; this position could already be found in Ronald De Sousa, who stays, however, at a critical distance to a comparativist usage of the Moorean Good: 'So will that traditional bugbear of Utilitarianism: the clash between Justice and Utility. If a sacrifice of utilities is required, then the smallest possible sacrifice is evidently better than the larger. Yet suppose the sacrifice of two innocent individuals maximizes Utility but clashes with the demands of Justice. If no rational decision appears possible, the case is not made evidently simpler by slightly reducing the sacrifice or slightly increasing the Utilities. So the value of Justice is not just another source of utiles, evenly balanced against the sum of other utiles' ('The Good and the True', *Mind* 83 (1974), 534–551, 545).
16. See Bernard Williams and J.J.C. Smart, *Utilitarianism: For and Against* (Cambridge: Cambridge University Press, 1973), esp. 116–17.
17. See also Elizabeth Anderson, 'Practical Reason and Incommensurable Goods', in Chang (ed.), *Incommensurability, Incomparability, and Practical Reason*, 90–109, 99 and 103.

18 One could also replace the somehow biased 'better than' and 'worse than' by a variable, such as *F*er than, as John Broome suggests; see his 'Is Incommensurability Vagueness?' in Chang (ed.), *Incommensurability, Incomparability, and Practical Reason*, 67–89, 69 and *passim*.
19 See Chang, 'Introduction', 4–5.
20 See Erik Carlson, 'Parity Demystified', *Theoria* 76 (2010), 119–28, 119. It has also been claimed that only 'better than' and 'worse than' are basic and that 'equally good' can be defined by them; see Broome, 'Is Incommensurability Vagueness?' 72.
21 Chang, 'Introduction', 6; see also her *Making Comparisons Count*, 9; italics in the original text.
22 It does not follow, however, that, if A is comparable to B, non-A would be incomparable to B.
23 Please note, that in the example I transformed the incomparability talk into talking about decision and choice.
24 Again, the far more prominent locus classicus of 'incommensurability' lies in a particular account of theories and their relation to one another, see Thomas S. Kuhn, 'Commensurability, Comparability, Communicability', *Proceedings of the Biennial Meeting of the Philosophy of Science Association*, Volume Two: Symposia and Invited Papers (1982), 669–88.
25 See also James Griffin, 'Incommensurability: What's the Problem?' in Chang (ed.), *Incommensurability, Incomparability, and Practical Reason*, 35–51, 38.
26 Cf. for these distinctions Ruth Chang, 'Incommensurability (and Incomparability)', in *The International Encyclopedia of Ethics*, ed. Hugh LaFollette (Oxford: Blackwell, 2013), 2591–604, 2592–600.
27 See Hans Joas, *The Sacredness of the Person: A New Genealogy of Human Rights* (Washington D.C.: Georgetown University Press, 2012).
28 Griffin, 'Incommensurability: What's the Problem?' 37.
29 See Chang, 'Incommensurability (and Incomparability)', 2597.
30 See also Anton Leist, 'Wertepluralismus als offenes Spiel', in *Perspektivismus. Neue Beiträge aus der Erkenntnistheorie, Hermeneutik und Ethik*, ed. Hartmut von Sass (Hamburg: Meiner, 2019), 211–42.
31 Cf. Raz, *The Morality of Freedom*, 324.
32 See George Harris, 'Value Vagueness, Zones of Incomparability, and Tragedy', *American Philosophical Quarterly* 38:2 (2001), 155–76, 156.
33 See Joseph Raz, 'Incommensurability and Agency', in Chang (ed.), *Incommensurability, Incomparability, and Practical Reason*, 110–28, 111.
34 If they serve as 'reasons' at all; see R. Jay Wallace, 'How to Argue about Practical Reason', *Mind* 99:395 (1990), 355–85, 364 and 370.
35 Cf. Elijah Millgram, who states: 'Desires and ends are incommensurable when they do not contain within themselves the resources to resolve conflict between them into a judgment of relative importance or into choice' ('Incommensurability and Practical Reasoning', in Chang (ed.), *Incommensurability, Incomparability, and Practical Reason*, 151–69, 159).
36 Cf. Raz, *The Morality of Freedom*, 322.
37 Chang, 'The Possibility of Parity', 666–7.
38 This is how Messerli and Reuter (in 'Hard cases of comparison', 2230) put the matter.
39 Cf. James Griffin, *Well-Being* (Oxford: Oxford University Press, 1986), 80–1, 96–8, 104; and Derek Parfit, *Reasons and Persons* (Oxford: Oxford University Press, 1984), 431.

40 See also Chang, 'Parity. An Intuitive Case', 400 and 402.
41 Hence, even in cases of incomparability, it is possible to really pin down what the relation between *A* and *B* is *not*.
42 See, again, Raz, *The Morality of Freedom*, 324.
43 Cf. Broome, 'Is Incommensurability Vagueness?' 89.
44 I have not entered here the complicated debate on what Broome has called the 'collapsing principle' that says in its 'special version': for any x and y, if it is false that y is F*er* than x and not false that x is F*er* than y, then it is true that x is F*er* than y (see 'Is Incommensurability Vagueness?' 74). This principle has met serious criticisms; cf., for instance, Cristian Constantinescu, 'Value Incomparability and Indeterminacy', *Ethical Theory and Moral Practice* 15:1 (2012), 57–70, 66–7; idem, 'Vague Comparisons', *Ratio* 29:4 (2016), 357–77, 373.
45 See Chang, 'The Possibility of Parity', 662.
46 See again Raz, *The Morality of Freedom*, 328.
47 For a critical discussion of using this example see Martijn Boot, 'Parity, incomparability and rationally justified choice', *Philosophical Studies* 146:1 (2009), 75–92, 82; Ryan Wasserman, 'Indeterminacy, Ignorance and the Possibility of Parity', *Philosophical Perspectives* 18: 'Ethics' (2004), 391–403, 393.
48 Chang, 'The Possibility of Parity', 672–3; on the sorites-problem also Kirk Ludwig and Greg Ray, 'Vagueness and the Sorites Paradox', *Philosophical Perspectives* 16: 'Language and Mind' (2002), 419–61, 431–4; Mozaffar Qizilbash, 'The Mere Addition Paradox, Parity and Vagueness', *Philosophy and Phenomenological Research* 75:1 (2007), 129–51, esp. 137; for a convincing critic of Chang's approach based on a sorites-scenario see Luke Elson, 'Heaps and Chains: is the Chaining Argument for Parity a Sorites?' *Ethics* 124:4 (2014), 557–1, 564–7.
49 Chang discussed an interesting, somewhat 'Hegelian' objection to her own view on small improvements in saying that, sometimes, these improvements are not merely linear, but could also trigger a new qualitative value. For example, if one adds money to the account of an initially poor man, he does not only turn to be rich, eventually, but might also enter a new class having political, economical or social access to things that had previously been sealed to him; see 'The Possibility of Parity', 668.
50 Chang, 'Parity. An Intuitive Case', 404.
51 See ibid., 410; also Carlson, 'Parity Demystified', 124.
52 Cf. Chang, *Making Comparisons Count*, 142 and 168.
53 Moreover, Chang also wants to demarcate parity from Broome's indeterminacy and vagueness; cf. 'The Possibility of Parity', 680 and 682–3. While I think there is actually a difference, I also think it is located somewhere else than Chang suggests: indeterminacy and vagueness are not on the same relational level as parity or the trichotomy-relations are, but they are possible reasons for cases Chang calls being on a par.
54 I will leave open the question what 'logical independence' really comes to, for instance, whether 'parity' could be defined by the traditional relational predicates. Chang holds, rightly I think, that even this possibility of x being definable by other predicates does not undermine x's distinct character. Take, for example colours: red is non-green, non-blue, . . ., and yet a distinct colour; see Ruth Chang, 'Parity, Interval Value, and Choice', *Ethics* 115:2 (2005), 331–50, 334–7.
55 Cf. Chang, 'The Possibility of Parity', 682.
56 *Pace* Joshua Gert, who tries to show that all examples used by Chang are eventually explainable by the traditional trichotomy – without committing himself to deny the

possibility of parity or to generally refute the trichotomy thesis; see his 'Value and Parity', *Ethics* 114:3 (2004), 492–510, esp. 492.

57 See Chang, 'Parity, Interval Value, and Choice', 333; for a critical account Boot, 'Parity, incomparability and rationally justified choice', 86. There are also attempts to decouple rational choices from comparability in holding that it is sufficient that the chosen alternative is *not worse than* other alternatives, which means: only being negatively related to the alternatives and, therefore, still incomparable and yet rationally choosable based on a principle called 'maximization'; see Nien-He Hsieh, 'Is Incomparability a Problem for Anyone?' *Economics and Philosophy* 23 (2007), 65–80, esp. 65 and 67.
58 See Parfit, *Reasons and Persons*, 431.
59 Cf. Ruth Chang, 'Parity, Imprecise Comparability, and the Repugnant Conclusion', *Theoria* 82 (2016), 182–215, section 7.
60 On the other side of the comparative spectrum is what has been called 'strict incomparability'. By that, cases are in view in which literally no incentive is thinkable or intelligible that could turn the strictly incomparable into a comparable item. This is particularly decisive when talking about incentives of high value (quality) since their value is negatively correlated with the amount (quantity): the higher a value's quality the lower the quantitative required to trigger comparability. Its strict form disclaims scenarios based on the dynamics just sketched; see Messerli and Reuter, 'Hard cases of comparison', 2233–4.
61 See, for 'incommensurability,' Chang, 'Introduction', 1–3: idem, 'Incommensurability (and Incomparability)', 2594; a stronger notion of incommensurability is to be found in James Griffin who holds that these are not cases in which we cannot decide to rank something, but when we actually can decide that values are 'unrankable'; see his 'Incommensurability: What's the Problem?' 37.
62 See Chang, *Making Comparisons Count*, 3; idem, 'Introduction', 28.
63 Cf. *Making Comparisons Count*, xix.
64 To make this point we do not need a definition of categoriality or category. All we need in this context are evident examples in which the condition of categoriality is not met and examples in which it is not really clear whether that condition is met, as in (iii) and (ii), respectively.
65 For this claim see also Constantinescu, 'Vague Comparisons', esp. 369.
66 One can create cases implying, in fact, vagueness that, however, are dissolvable by stipulation; see again Constantinescu, 'Vague Comparisons', 363.
67 See, on the problem of analyticity, Willard van Orman Quine, 'Two dogmas of empiricism', in idem, *From a Logical Point of View. Logico-Philosophical Essays*, 2nd ed. (Cambridge, MA/London: Harvard University Press, (1953) 1980), 20–46, esp. 23.
68 Cf. Robert Sugden, 'On Modelling Vagueness – and on not Modelling Incommensurability', *Proceedings of the Aristotelian Society Supplementary* 83 (2009), 95–113, 105–10; Constantinescu, 'Vague Comparisons', 372.
69 Just as a tentative note: I cannot think of an example for cases in which we have a clear, i.e. commensurable predicate (like in (i) or (i*)) while its comparative form is not clear in this sense anymore. I assume that this case does not arise.
70 See the debate on hope as an (epistemic) virtue: Victoria McGeer, 'The Art of Good Hope', *Annals of the American Academy of Political and Social Science* 592 (2004), 100–27, 109; Aaron Cobb, 'Hope and Epistemic Virtue', in *Hope* (RPT 84), ed. Ingolf U. Dalferth and Marlene A. Block (Tübingen: Mohr Siebeck, 2016), 89–102, 100–2; Hartmut von Sass, 'Kann denn Hoffnung Tugend sein?' *Zeitschrift für philosophische Forschung* 71:1 (2017), 70–104, 96–103.

71 Cf. Harris, 'Value Vagueness, Zones of Incomparability, and Tragedy', 164.
72 See De Sousa, 'The Good and the True', 547.
73 *Pace* Constantinescu, 'Vague Comparisons', 369.
74 See Charles Taylor, 'Leading a Life', in Chang (ed.), *Incommensurability, Incomparability, and Practical Reason*, 170–83, 182–3.
75 Cf. Millgram, 'Incommensurability and Practical Reasoning', 151, 154 and 158.
76 See William James, 'The Will to Believe', in idem, *Pragmatism and Other Writings*, ed. Giles Dunn (New York: Penguin Books, 2000), 198–218, esp. 201–3.
77 See De Sousa, 'The Good and the True', 548.
78 Cf. for a similar result, but for other reasons, Regan, 'Value, Comparability, and Choice', 130.

8 On Indexical Incomparability

1 See also Ruth Chang, 'Introduction', in idem (ed.), *Incommensurability, Incomparability, and Practical Reason* (Cambridge, MA/London 1997), 17–26.
2 Joseph Raz, *The Morality of Freedom* (Oxford: Clarendon Press, 1986), 346.
3 This institutional element could also be traced back to an incomparability based on the *grammar* of the item to be compared; accordingly, comparing friendship with money implied a grammatical mistake (or rather a confusion) similar to holding bachelors to be married men; I won't, however, pursue this interpretation here.
4 See Raz, *The Morality of Freedom*, chapter 11.3.
5 Steven Lukes, 'Comparing the Incomparable: Trade-offs and Sacrifices', in Chang (ed.), *Incommensurability, Incomparability, and Practical Reason*, 184–95, 185; see also Charles Taylor, 'Leading a Life', in ibid., 170–83, 173.
6 Cf. Seana Valentine Shiffrin, 'Wrongful Life, Procreative Responsibility, and the Significance of Harm', *Legal Theory* 5 (1999), 117–48, esp. 123–4.
7 See Derek Parfit, *Reasons and Persons* (Oxford: Oxford University Press, 1984), 384–90; cf. also Jeff McMahan, 'Causing People to Exist and Saving People's Lives', *The Journal of Ethics* 17:1/2. Special Issue: 'The Benefits and Harms of Existence and Non-Existence' (2013), 5–35, 5–15. Part IV of *Reasons and Persons* and papers such as the one by McMahan are, arguably, extensive comparative studies in (population and future) ethics without thematise the comparative procedure itself.
8 Lukes, 'Comparing the Incomparable: Trade-offs and Sacrifices', 189.
9 This is a similar and similarly debatable claim as the one by Aristotle who holds that one can only be a friend if one is friends with oneself; see Julia Annas, 'Plato and Aristotle on Friendship and Altruism', *Mind* 86 (1977), 532–54, 536–41.
10 Here, one might – almost – apply the idea of constitutive incomparability to itself: as much as a particular reaction of refusing to compare a value belongs, according to Raz, to the incomparable value itself, the appreciation of the idea of constitutive incomparability is part of its structure.
11 However, one has to distinguish two scenarios here. Either one talks about *generally* privileging friendship over money, no matter what; or it is meant to value a *particular* friendship over money in a concrete situation. In the one case, one stands, as it were, in distance to both options; in the second case, one is already in a friendship while confronted by money as alternative (and danger) to that friendship. Raz is focussed on this second case whereas the objection sketched above is only relevant for the first and general scenario.

12 See Ruth Chang, *Making Comparisons Count* (London/New York: Routledge, 2002), xix and 113–15.
13 Cf. Stanley Cavell, 'The Availability of Wittgenstein's Later Philosophy', in idem, *Must we mean what we say? A Book of Essays*, 9th ed. (Cambridge: Cambridge University Press, 2000), 45–72, 62–3 and 68; see also Elizabeth Anderson, 'Practical Reason and Incommensurable Goods', in Chang (ed.), *Incommensurability, Incomparability, and Practical Reason*, 90–109, 114.

9 The Case of Normative Incomparability: Comparisons, Animals, and the Quest for Adequacy

1 John Maxwell Coetzee, *Elizabeth Costello* (New York: Penguin Books, 2003), 113; all page numbers in brackets refer to this book.
2 See Boria Sax, *Animals in the Third Reich: Pets, Scapegoats, and the Holocaust* (New York: Continuum, 2000), 156–157; Timothy M. Costelloe, 'The Invisibility of Evil: Moral Progress and the "Animal Holocaust"', *Philosophical Papers* 32:2 (2003), 109–31, 110.
3 Cf. Jacques Derrida, 'The Animal That Therefore I Am (More to Follow)', *Critical Inquiry* 28:2 (2002), 369–418, 394–5.
4 Tom Regan, *The Struggle for Animal Rights* (Clarks Summit: International Society for Animals Rights, 1987), 76–7.
5 See Peter Singer, *Animal Liberation: A New Ethics for Our Treatment of Animals* (New York: Harper Collins, 1975), 102.
6 David Sztybel, 'Can the Treatment of Animals Be Compared to the Holocaust?' *Ethics and the Environment* 11:1 (2006), 97–132, 130; cf. also 99.
7 Cf. Cora Diamond, 'Eating Meat and Eating People', in idem, *The Realistic Spirit. Wittgenstein, Philosophy, and the Mind* (Cambridge, MA/London: MIT Press, 1991), 319–34, esp. 319–20.
8 One could also claim that Costello's way of putting the matter here – namely, that it is a question of *thinking* into the existence of someone else – is terminologically inaccurate, since 'thought' is still too similar and close to reason, which she otherwise repudiates as an inadequate source for our sympathetic dealings with animals. A similar problem can be found in Wittgenstein's discussion of a particular 'way of thinking' (*Denkweise*) since what he is really after is a mode of wider expression, articulation, and even feeling. The same problem can also be found in Ludwik Fleck's notion of a 'thought style' or 'style of thinking' (*Denkstil*) because what is meant here is not restricted to thinking either, but includes preferences, habituation, taste; see Ludwig Wittgenstein, *Philosophical Investigations. Part I*, 3rd edition, eds. G.E.M. Anscombe and Rush Rhees, trans. G.E.M. Anscombe (Englewood Cliffs, NJ: Prentice Hall, 1973), 1–172, § 597 *inter alia*; on Fleck (with several references) Babette E. Babich, 'From Fleck's Denkstil to Kuhn's paradigm: Conceptual schemes and incommensurability', *International Studies in the Philosophy of Science* 17:3 (2003), 75–92, 81.
9 See Thomas Nagel, 'What it is like to be a bat?' in idem, *Mortal Questions* (Cambridge: Cambridge University Press, 1979), 165–80, esp. 169 and 172.
10 Ward E. Jones, 'Elizabeth Costello and the Biography of the Moral Philosopher', *The Journal of Aesthetics and Art Criticism* 69:2 (2011), 209–20, 214–15.

11 See Janet Martin Soskice, *Metaphor and Religious Language* (Oxford: Clarendon Press, 1985), 6 and 10–11.
12 This is, however, not to say that I think Jones is correct in characterizing Costello's claim as a metaphor. Insofar as metaphors extend the meaning of a term and, hence, are not fully reducible to a nonmetaphorical expression, it is not easy to see where the metaphorical element lies when Costello relates the fate of animals to the Holocaust. But this refutation requires more space that would, given the context here, lead us astray; see Max Black, 'Metaphor', *Proceedings of the Aristotelian Society*, New Series 55 (1954/1955), 273–94, esp. 282–3.
13 See Marjorie Garber, 'Reflections', in John Maxwell Coetzee, *The Lives of Animals* (Princeton, NJ: Princeton University Press, 1999), 73–84, 74; see also Andy Lamey, 'Sympathy and Scapegoating in J.M. Coetzee', in Anton Leist and Peter Singer (eds.), *Coetzee and Philosophy. Philosophical Perspectives on Literature* (New York: Columbia University Press, 2010), 171–92, who speaks of Costello's 'wild analogy' between the treatment of animals and the Holocaust (173).
14 Although the 'report' remains ambiguous, Peter says, 'If I review my development and its goal up to this point, I do not complain, but I am not content. [...] On the whole, at any rate, I have achieved what I wished to achieve. You shouldn't say it was not worth the effort. In any case, I don't want any human being's judgment. I only want to expand knowledge. I simply report' (Franz Kafka, 'Report for an Academy', available at: http://johnstoniatexts.x10host.com/kafka/reportforacademyhtml.html).
15 Red Peter explains, 'I do not mean this great feeling of freedom on all sides. As an ape, I perhaps recognized it, and I have met human beings who yearn for it. But as far as I am concerned, I did not demand freedom either then or today. Incidentally, among human beings people all too often are deceived by freedom. And since freedom is reckoned among the most sublime feelings, the corresponding disappointment is also among the most sublime' (ibid.).
16 See also Karen Dawn and Peter Singer, 'Converging Convictions. Coetzee and His Characters on Animals', in Leist and Singer (eds.), *Coetzee and Philosophy. Philosophical Perspectives on Literature*, 109–18, 116.
17 This is not advocating behaviourism but rather underlining an important element related to it; see Dewi Z. Phillips, 'On Really Believing', in idem, *Wittgenstein and Religion* (Basingstoke/London: Macmillan, 1993), 33–55.
18 See on Costello's (and Coetzee's) plea for vegetarianism Marianne Dekoven, 'Guest Column: Why Animals Now?' *PMLA* 124:2 (2009), 361–9, esp. 364.
19 Cf. Timothy M. Costelloe, 'The Invisibility of Evil: Moral Progress and the "Animal Holocaust"', *Philosophical Papers* 32:2 (2003), 109–31, 123.
20 Stephen Mulhall, *The Wounded Animal. J.M. Coetzee and the Difficulty of Reality in Literature and Philosophy* (Princeton: Princeton University Press, 2002), 56.
21 Jennifer Flynn calls Elizabeth Costello a 'novella' (see her 'The Lives of Animals and the Form-Content Connection', in Leist and Singer (eds.), *Coetzee and Philosophy. Philosophical Perspectives on Literature*, 315–33, 317); see also Robert Pippin, 'The Paradoxes of Power in the Early Novels of J.M. Coetzee', in ibid., 22–3.
22 This problem is discussed at some length by Stephen Mulhall who is consistent in his claim that this charge is then not only to be directed at Costello, but also at those who raise objections against her in the name of the singular character of the Holocaust; see Mulhall, *The Wounded Animal*, 70 and 72.
23 Cf. Ido Geiger, 'Writing the Lives of Animals', in Leist and Singer (eds.), *Coetzee and Philosophy. Philosophical Perspectives on Literature*, 145–69, esp. 153. There is a

historical Abraham Stern, a rather dubious figure; on this topic see Andy Lamey, 'Sympathy and Scapegoating in J.M. Coetzee', 185.

24 This has been debated in the so called 'Historian's Dispute' starting off with Ernst Nolte's 1986 newspaper article 'The Past That Will Not Pass' ('Vergangenheit, die nicht vergehen will'). In Nolte's view, the decisive event of the twentieth century had been the Russian revolution in 1917, while causally connecting the Gulags with the Nazi concentration camps; his perspective is, for example, expressed in the following passage:

> It is probable that many of these reports were exaggerated. It is certain that the 'White Terror' also committed terrible deeds, even though its program contained no analogy to the 'extermination of the bourgeoisie'. Nonetheless, the following question must seem permissible, even unavoidable: Did the National Socialists or Hitler perhaps commit an 'Asiatic' deed merely because they and their ilk considered themselves to be the potential victims of an 'Asiatic' deed? Wasn't the 'Gulag Archipelago' more original than Auschwitz? Was the Bolshevik murder of an entire class not the logical and factual *prius* of the 'racial murder' of National Socialism? Cannot Hitler's most secret deeds be explained by the fact that he had *not* forgotten the rat cage? Did Auschwitz in its root causes not originate in a past that would not pass?

Available at: https://www.staff.uni-giessen.de/~g31130/PDF/Nationalismus/ErnstNolte.pdf (the German original stems from *Frankfurter Allgemeine Zeitung*, June 6 1986); see also Stefan Berg, 'Vergleichsweise orientiert. Eine orientierungstheoretische Betrachtung des Vergleichens', Andreas Mauz and Hartmut von Sass (eds.), *Hermeneutik des Vergleichs. Strukturen, Anwendungen und Grenzen komparativer Verfahren* (Würzburg: Königshausen & Neumann, 2011), 277–303, esp. 294–99. Admittedly, this dispute deserves more attention than I am able to give it here, and, surely, it would provide alternative material to elaborate on normative incomparability.

25 Robert Nozick, 'The Holocaust', in idem, *Examined Life. Philosophical Meditations* (New York/London: A Touchstone Book, 1990), 236–42, 236.
26 Ibid., 237.
27 Ibid., 239.
28 Ibid., 238.
29 See ibid., 239 and 241; for a different account cf. Johann Frick, 'On the survival of humanity', *Canadian Journal of Philosophy* 47:2/3 (2017), 344–67, 360–2.
30 I am following here David Sztybel, 'Can the Treatment of Animals Be Compared to the Holocaust?' *Ethics and the Environment* 11:1 (2006), 97–132, esp. 107–20; Sztybel lists thirty-nine regards in four groups for a comparison between the Holocaust and the cruel treatment of animals.
31 See Costelloe, 'The Invisibility of Evil: Moral Progress and the "Animal Holocaust"', 127.
32 Sabina Lovibond, *Ethical Formation* (Cambridge, MA/London: Harvard University Press, 2002), x and 13; see also G.E.M. Anscombe, 'Modern Moral Philosophy', *Philosophy* 33:1 (1958), 1–19, esp. 14.
33 Cf. Jones, 'Elizabeth Costello and the Biography of the Moral Philosopher', 216.
34 See Mulhall, *The Wounded Animal*, 55.
35 On this general and anti-rational doubt, see Anton Leist, 'Against Society, Against History, Against Reason. Coetzee's Archaic Postmodernism', in Leist and Singer (eds.), *Coetzee and Philosophy. Philosophical Perspectives on Literature*, 195–220, 209.

36 Michael Funk Deckard and Ralph Palm, 'Irony and Belief in Elizabeth Costello', in Leist and Singer (eds.), *Coetzee and Philosophy. Philosophical Perspectives on Literature*, 335–54, 347 and 350. This also sheds light on the widely discussed relation between Coetzee and Costello. It is true that there are several biographical details that both have in common, and in that sense, they are indeed close, especially in regard to criticizing the treatment of animals. Nevertheless, all this does not allow for identifying both figures as lacking – a point underlined by Elizabeth becoming a hardliner – what Coetzee calls 'self-insight' (113); cf. Dawn and Singer, 'Converging Convictions. Coetzee and His Characters on Animals', 109–10; Martin Woessner, 'Coetzee's Critique of Reason', in Leist and Singer (eds.), *Coetzee and Philosophy. Philosophical Perspectives on Literature*, 221–45, 237; Derek Attridge, 'Coetzee's Artists; Coetzee's Art', in Graham Bradshaw and Michael Neill (eds.), *J.M. Coetzee's Austerities* (Farnham/Burlington, VT: Ashgate, 2010), 25–42, 31; Barbara Dancygier, 'Close Encounters: The Author and the Character in *Elizabeth Costello*, *Slow Man* and *Diary of a Bad Year*', in ibid., 231–52, 233.
37 Cf. Pippin, 'The Paradoxes of Power in the Early Novels of J.M. Coetzee', 38, footnote 10.
38 Cf. Agustin Fuentes, 'The Humanity of Animals and the Animality of Humans: A View from Biological Anthropology Inspired by J.M. Coetzee's *Elizabeth Costello*', *American Anthropologist* 108:1 (2006), 124–32, 129.
39 See Cf. Derrida, 'The Animal That Therefore I Am (More to Follow)', 410–12; Elizabeth Susan Anker, '"Elizabeth Costello," Embodiment, and the Limits of Rights', *New Literary History* 42:1 (2011), 169–92, 185.
40 This concerns either a set of relevant features or amounts to refuting the (ontological) human-animal divide in general, as in Bruno Latour's critique of 'modernism' or Donna Haraway's blurring the binary of human/animal by paying heed to a third party, namely cyborgs and artificial intelligence.
41 Cf. Richard Rorty stating: 'If pain were all that mattered, it would be as important to protect the rabbits from the foxes as to protect the Jews from the Nazis' (*Philosophy and Social Hope* (London: Penguin Books, 1999), 86); see also Louis Tremaine, 'The Embodied Soul: Animal Being in the Work of J.M. Coetzee', *Contemporary Literature* 44:4 (2003), 587–612.
42 A highly critical response to animal rights accounts (such as the ones by Peter Singer and Tom Regan) is given by Cora Diamond, 'Eating Meat and Eating People', in idem, *The Realistic Spirit. Wittgenstein, Philosophy, and the Mind* (Cambridge, MA/London: MIT Press, 1991), 319–34, esp. 321 and 325; a counter-critique is given by Elisa Aaltola, 'Coetzee and Alternative Animal Ethics', Leist and Singer (eds.), *Coetzee and Philosophy. Philosophical Perspectives on Literature*, 119–43, 137.
43 See Alice Crary, *Inside Ethics. On the Demands of Moral Thought* (Cambridge, MA/London: Harvard University Press, 2016), 125.
44 On this Martin Heidegger, *Being and Time*, trans. by John Macquarrie and Edward Robinson (Oxford: Basil Blackwell, 1962), §§ 74 and 76.
45 Cf. Derrida, 'The Animal That Therefore I Am (More to Follow)', 373.
46 Leist, 'Against Society, Against History, Against Reason. Coetzee's Archaic Postmodernism', 215.
47 See Dekoven, 'Guest Column: Why Animals Now?' 366.
48 Cf. Anker, '"Elizabeth Costello", Embodiment, and the Limits of Rights', 172 and 177–8.
49 See Crary, *Inside Ethics*, 227 and 229; Adriaan van Heerden, 'Disgrace, Desire, and the Dark Side of the New South Africa', in Leist and Singer (eds.), *Coetzee and Philosophy.*

Philosophical Perspectives on Literature, 43–63, esp. 60, who also highlights the South-African background and historical, i.e. Apartheid- and post-colonial context informing Coetzee's *Disgrace*.
50 Cf. Cora Diamond, 'Having a rough Story about What Moral Philosophy Is', in *The Realistic Spirit*, 367–81, 371–372; Woessner, 'Coetzee's Critique of Reason', in Leist and Singer (eds.), *Coetzee and Philosophy. Philosophical Perspectives on Literature*, 221–45, esp. 224 and 228; Alice Crary, 'J.M. Coetzee, Moral Thinker', in ibid., 247–66, 252.
51 This is Peter Singer's critique of Coetzee and his 'narrative' approach; see his 'Reflections', in Coetzee, *The Lives of Animals*, 85–91, 91.
52 See Jennifer Flynn, 'The Lives of Animals and the Form-Content Connection', in Leist and Singer (eds.), *Coetzee and Philosophy. Philosophical Perspectives on Literature*, 315–33, 328.
53 In fact, the entire chapter 6 entitled 'The Problem of Evil' is dedicated to the perils of literature; see EC, 156–82, esp. 160, 167, 173–4.
54 Thomas Nagel, 'What it is like to be a bat?'; see, for instance, this passage: 'My point, however, is not that we cannot know what it is like to be a bat. I am not raising that epistemological problem. My point is rather that even to form a conception of what it is like to be a bat (and a fortiori to know what it is like to be a bat) one must take up the bat's point of view.' (172, footnote 8).
55 The contrast between 'matters of fact' and 'matters of concern' is – slightly differently – used by Bruno Latour; see his 'Why Has Critique Run out of Steam? From Matters of Fact to Matters of Concern', *Critical Inquiry* 30:2 (2004), 225–48.

Epilogue: Living in an 'Age of Comparison'? An Interpretation with Diagnostic Intent

1 See Michael Eggers, *Zur Wissenschaftsgeschichte und Epistemologie des Vergleichs und zur Genealogie der Komparatistik* (Heidelberg: Winter, 2016), ch. 2.
2 Friedrich Nietzsche, *Human, All Too Human. A Book for Free Spirit*, trans. R.J. Hollingdale. With an Introduction by Richard Schacht (Cambridge: Cambridge University Press, 1996), § 23, 24.
3 Friedrich Nietzsche, *Untimely Meditations. Second Piece: On the Use and Abuse of History for Life*, trans. Richard T. Grey (Stanford: Stanford University Press, 1995), 62.
4 See Peter Handke, 'Theater und Film. Das Elend des Vergleichens' (1968), in idem, *Ich bin ein Bewohner des Elfenbeinturms*, 12th ed. (Frankfurt a.M.: Suhrkamp, 2005), 65–77; thanks to Andreas Mauz for drawing my attention to this text.
5 See Dirk Baecker, *Wozu Kultur?* 3rd ed. (Berlin: Kadmos, 2003), 164.
6 Andreas Reckwitz, *Die Gesellschaft der Singularitäten. Zum Strukturwandel der Moderne* (Berlin: Suhrkamp, 2017), 11, my trans.; there is a forthcoming English version to be published with Polity Press.
7 Cf. Immanuel Kant, *Critique of Judgment* B 80–1.
8 Cf. Felix Stalder, *Kultur der Digitalität* (Berlin: Suhrkamp, 2016), ch. 2, esp. the section on algorithmicity.

Bibliography

Aaltola, Elisa (2010), 'Coetzee and Alternative Animal Ethics'. in Anton Leist and Peter Singer (eds.). *Coetzee and Philosophy. Philosophical Perspectives on Literature*, 119–143, New York: Columbia University Press.
Abadie, Alberto, Alexis Diamond and Jens Hainmueller (2015), 'Comparative Politics and the Synthetic Control Method', *American Journal of Political Science* 59:2: 495–510.
Abel, Günter (2016), 'Quellen der Orientierung', in Andrea Bertino, Ekaterina Poljakova, Andreas Rupschus and Benjamin Alberts (eds.), *Zur Philosophie der Orientierung*, 147–169, Berlin/New York: De Gruyter.
Albrecht, Andrea (2015), 'Analogieschlüsse und metaphorische Extensionen in der interdisziplinären literaturwissenschaftlichen Praxis,' in Andrea Albrecht, Lutz Danneberg, Olav Krämer and Carlos Spoerhase (eds.), *Theorien, Methoden und Praktiken des Interpretierens* (linguae & litterae 49), 271–99, Berlin/Boston: De Gruyter.
Anderson, Elizabeth (1997), 'Practical Reason and Incommensurable Goods', in Ruth Chang (ed.). *Incommensurability, Incomparability, and Practical Reason*, 90–109, Cambridge, MA/London: Harvard University Press.
Anker, Elizabeth Susan (2011), "'Elizabeth Costello', Embodiment, and the Limits of Rights", *New Literary History* 42:1: 169–92.
Annas, Julia (1977), 'Plato and Aristotle on Friendship and Altruism', *Mind* 86: 532–54.
Anscombe, G.E.M. (1958), 'Modern Moral Philosophy', *Philosophy* 33:1: 1–19.
Aristotle (2011), *Nicomachean Ethics*, ed. and trans. Robert C. Bartlett and Susan D. Collins. Chicago: University of Chicago Press.
Ashby, W. Ross (1957), *Introduction into Cybernetics* (London: Chapman & Hall Ltd).
Ashcroft, Bill, Gareth Griffiths, Helen Tiffin (2002), *The Empire Writes Back. Theory and Practice in Post-Colonial Literatures*, 2nd ed. London/New York: Routledge.
Attridge, Derek (2010), 'Coetzee's Artists, Coetzee's Art,' in Graham Bradshaw and Michael Neill (eds.). *J.M. Coetzee's Austerities*, 25–42, Farnham/Burlington, VT: Ashgate.
Audi, Robert (1995), 'Acting From Virtue', *Mind* 104:415 (1995): 449–71.
Babich, Babette E. (2003), 'From Fleck's Denkstil to Kuhn's paradigm: Conceptual schemes and incommensurability,' *International Studies in the Philosophy of Science* 17:3: 75–92.
Baecker, Dirk (2003), *Wozu Kultur?* Berlin: Kadmos (2000), 3rd ed.
Baier, Annette C. (1985), 'What do Women want in a Moral Theory?' *Noûs* 19:1: 53–63.
Barnes, Elizabeth (2010), 'Ontic Vagueness: A Guide for the Perplexed', *Noûs* 44:4: 601–627.
Bartha, Paul (2016), 'Analogy and Analogical Reasoning', in Edward N. Zalta (ed.), *The Stanford Encyclopedia of Philosophy*, https://plato.stanford.edu/entries/reasoning-analogy/
Beardsley, Monroe C. (1967), 'Metaphor', in Paul Edwards (ed.), *Encyclopedia of Philosophy*, Vol. 5, 284–9, New York: Macmillan.
Berg-Schlosser, Dirk (2003), 'Vergleichende Politikwissenschaft im Vergleich – multidimensionale Verortung und mögliche Anwendungen', in Hartmut Kaelble and Jürgen

Schriewer (eds.), *Vergleich und Transfer. Komparatistik in den Sozial-, Geschichts- und Kulturwissenschaften*, 117–140, Frankfurt a.M.: Campus.

Berg, Stefan (2011), 'Vergleichsweise orientiert. Eine orientierungstheoretische Betrachtung des Vergleichens,' in Andreas Mauz and Hartmut von Sass (eds.), *Hermeneutik des Vergleichs*, 277–303, Würzburg: Königshausen & Neumann.

Berg, Stefan (2011), *Spielwerk. Orientierungshermeneutische Studien zum Verhältnis von Musik und Religion (RPT 60)*, Tübingen: Mohr Siebeck.

Bernecker, Sven (2012), 'Kant on Spatial Orientation', *European Journal of Philosophy* 24:4: 519–33.

Bertino, Andrea, Ekaterina Poljakova, Andreas Rupschus and Benjamin Alberts (eds.) (2016), *Zur Philosophie der Orientierung*, Berlin/New York: De Gruyter.

Bhatti, Anil and Dorothee Kimmich (eds.) (2015), *Ähnlichkeit. Ein kulturtheoretisches Paradigma*, Konstanz: Konstanz University Press.

Bhatti, Anil and Dorothee Kimmich (eds.) (2015), 'Einleitung', in idem (eds.), *Ähnlichkeit. Ein kulturtheoretisches Paradigma*, 7–31, Konstanz: Konstanz University Press.

Birus, Henrik (1999), 'Das Vergleichen als Grundoperation der Hermeneutik', in Henk de Berg and Matthias Prangel (eds.), *Interpretation 2000: Positionen und Kontroversen. FS Horst Steinmetz*, 95–117. Heidelberg: Winter.

Black, Max (1954/1955), 'Metaphor', *Proceedings of the Aristotelian Society*, New Series 55: 273–94.

Black, Max (1970), 'Rules and Routines,' in idem, *Margins of Precision. Essay in Logic and Language*, 41–56, Ithaca, NY/London: Cornell University Press.

Black, Max (1977), 'More about metaphor', *Dialectica* 31:3/4: 431–57.

Black, Max (1979), 'How Metaphors Work: A Reply to Donald Davidson', *Critical Inquiry* 6:1: 131–43.

Blumenberg, Hans (1996), 'Paradigmen zu einer Metaphorologie', in Anselm Haverkamp (ed.). *Theorie der Metapher*, 2nd ed., 285–315, Darmstadt: WBG.

Blumenberg, Hans ([1960] 2010), *Paradigms for a Metaphorology*, trans. Robert Savage. Ithaca, NY/London: Cornell University Press.

Blumenberg, Hans (1996), 'Ausblick auf eine Theorie der Unbegrifflichkeit', in Anselm Haverkamp (ed.), *Theorie der Metapher*, 438–54, 2nd ed., Darmstadt: WBG.

Blumenberg, Hans (1971), 'Beobachtungen an Metaphern', *Archiv für Begriffsgeschichte* 25:2: 161–214.

Blumenberg, Hans (1993), 'Light as a Metaphor for Truth: At the Preliminary Stage of Philosophical Concept Formation', in David Michael Levin (ed.), *Modernity and the Hegemony of Vision*, 30–86, Los Angeles/Berkeley: University of California Press.

Blumenberg, Hans (2007), *Zu den Sachen und zurück*, Aus dem Nachlaß hrsg. von Manfred Sommer, Frankfurt a.M.: Suhrkamp.

Boot, Martijn (2009), 'Parity, incomparability and rationally justified choice,' *Philosophical Studies* 146:1: 75–92.

Bradshaw, Graham and Michael Neill (eds.) (2010), *J.M. Coetzee's Austerities*. Farnham/Burlington, VT: Ashgate.

Brandom, Robert B. (2002), *Tales of the Mighty Dead. Historical Essays in the Metaphysics of Intentionality*, Cambridge, MA/London: Harvard University Press.

Brodsky Lacour, Claudia (1995), 'Grounds of Comparison', *World Literature Today* 69:2: 'Comparative Literature: States of the Art': 271–4.

Broome, John (1997), 'Is Incommensurability Vagueness? in Ruth Chang (ed.), *Incommensurability, Incomparability, and Practical Reason*, 67–89, Cambridge, MA/London: Harvard University Press.

Burge, Tyler (1974), 'Demonstrative Constructions, Reference, and Truth,' *The Journal of Philosophy* 71:7: 205–23.
Cahn, Michael (1991), 'Das Schwanken zwischen Abfall und Wert. Zur kulturellen Hermeneutik des Sammlers, in *Merkur* 509, online: https://www.merkur-zeitschrift.de/michael-cahn-das-schwanken-zwischen-abfall-und-wert/
Carlson, Erik (2010), 'Parity Demystified,' *Theoria* 76: 119–28.
Casanova, José (1994), *Public Religions in the Modern World*, Chicago and London: University of Chicago Press.
Cavell, Stanley (1979), *The Claim of Reason. Wittgenstein, Skepticism, Morality, and Tragedy*, Oxford/New York: Oxford University Press.
Cavell, Stanley (2000), 'The Availability of Wittgenstein's Later Philosophy,' in idem, *Must we mean what we say? A Book of Essays*, 45–72, 9th ed., Cambridge: Cambridge University Press.
Cavell, Stanley (2004), *Cities of Words*, Cambridge, MA/London: Harvard University Press.
Chang, Ruth (ed.) (1997), *Incommensurability, Incomparability, and Practical Reason*, Cambridge, MA/London: Harvard University Press.
Chang, Ruth (1997), 'Introduction', in Ruth Chang (ed.), *Incommensurability, Incomparability, and Practical Reason*, 1–34, Cambridge, MA/London: Harvard University Press.
Chang, Ruth (2002), *Making Comparisons Count*, London/New York: Routledge.
Chang, Ruth (2002), 'The Possibility of Parity', *Ethics* 112:4: 659–88.
Chang, Ruth (2005), 'Parity, Interval Value, and Choice', *Ethics* 115:2: 331–50.
Chang, Ruth (2012), 'Are Hard Choices Cases of Incomparability?' *Philosophical Issues* 22: 'Action Theory': 106–26.
Chang, Ruth (2013), 'Incommensurability (and Incomparability),' in Hugh LaFollette (ed.), *The International Encyclopedia of Ethics*, 2591–604. Oxford: Blackwell.
Chang, Ruth (2016), 'Parity, Imprecise Comparability, and the Repugnant Conclusion', *Theoria* 82: 182–215.
Chang, Ruth (2016), 'Parity. An Intuitive Case', *Ratio* 29:4: 395–411.
Chignell, Andrew (2013), 'Rational Hope, Moral Order, and the Revolution of the Will', in Eric Watkins (ed.), *Divine Order, Human Order, and the Order of Nature: Historical Perspectives*, 197–218, Oxford: Oxford University Press.
Cobb, Aaron (2016), 'Hope and Epistemic Virtue', in Ingolf U. Dalferth and Marlene A. Block (eds.), *Hope* (RPT 84), 89–102. Tübingen: Mohr Siebeck.
Cockburn, David (2002), 'Critical Notice: Rush Rhees, Wittgenstein and the possibility of discourse', *Philosophical Investigations* 25:1: 79–93.
Coetzee, John Maxwell (1999), *The Lives of Animals*, Princeton, NJ: Princeton University Press.
Coetzee, John Maxwell (1999), *Disgrace*, New York: Penguin Books.
Coetzee, John Maxwell (2003), *Elizabeth Costello*, New York: Penguin Books.
Conolly, Oliver, and Bashar Haydar (2007), 'Literature, Knowledge, and Value', *Philosophy and Literature* 31:1: 111–24.
Constantinescu, Cristian (2012), 'Value Incomparability and Indeterminacy,' *Ethical Theory and Moral Practice* 15:1: 57–70.
Constantinescu, Cristian (2016), 'Vague Comparisons', *Ratio* 29:4: 357–77.
Cooper, Neil (1995), 'Paradox lost: understanding vague predicates', *International Journal of Philosophical Studies* 3: 244–69.
Costelloe, Timothy M. (2003), 'The Invisibility of Evil: Moral Progress and the "Animal Holocaust"', *Philosophical Papers* 32:2: 109–31.

Costelloe, Timothy M. (2004), 'In every civilized community: Hume on belief and the demise of religion', *International Journal for Philosophy of Religion* 55:2: 171–85.
Cottingham, John (2006), 'What Difference Does It Make? The Nature and Significance of Theistic Belief', *Ratio* 29:4: 401–20.
Crary, Alice (2010), 'J.M. Coetzee, Moral Thinker', in Anton Leist and Peter Singer (eds.), *Coetzee and Philosophy. Philosophical Perspectives on Literature*, 247–266, New York: Columbia University Press.
Crary, Alice (2016), *Inside Ethics. On the Demands of Moral Thought*. Cambridge, MA/London: Harvard University Press.
Crouch, Colin (2004), *Post-democracy*. Cambridge: Polity Press.
Culler, Jonathan (1995), 'Comparability', *World Literature Today* 69:2: 'Comparative Literature: States of the Art': 268–70.
Dalferth, Ingolf U. (2003), *Die Wirklichkeit des Möglichen. Hermeneutische Religionsphilosophie*, Tübingen: Mohr Siebeck.
Dalferth, Ingolf U. (2005), 'Leben angesichts des Unverfügbaren. Die duale Struktur religiöser Lebensorientierung', in Werner Stegmaier (ed.), *Orientierung. Philosophische Perspektiven*, 245–66, Frankfurt a.M.: Suhrkamp.
Dalferth, Ingolf U. (2016), 'Verstehen als Orientierungspraxis. Eine hermeneutische Skizze', in Andrea Bertino et al. (eds.), *Zur Philosophie der Orientierung*, 171–84, Berlin/New York: De Gruyter.
Dancygier, Barbara (2010), 'Close Encounters: The Author and the Character in *Elizabeth Costello*, *Slow Man* and *Diary of a Bad Year*', in Graham Bradshaw and Michael Neill (eds.). *J.M. Coetzee's Austerities*, 231–52, Farnham/Burlington, VT: Ashgate.
Davidson, Donald (1978), 'What Metaphors Mean', *Critical Inquiry* 5:1, Special Issue on Metaphor: 31–47.
Dawn, Karen and Peter Singer (2010), 'Converging Convictions. Coetzee and His Characters on Animals', in Anton Leist and Peter Singer (eds.). *Coetzee and Philosophy. Philosophical Perspectives on Literature*, 109–18, New York: Columbia University Press.
De Sousa, Ronald (1974), 'The Good and the True', *Mind* 83: 534–51.
Decock, Lieven, and Igor Douven (2011), 'Similarity After Goodman', *Review of Philosophy and Psychology* 2:1: 61–75.
Decosimo, David (2010), 'Comparison and the Ubiquity of Resemblance', *Journal of the American Academy of Religion* 78:1: 226–58.
Dekoven, Marianne (2009), 'Guest Column: Why Animals Now?' *PMLA* 124:2: 361–9.
Derrida, Jacques (2002), 'The Animal That Therefore I Am (More to Follow), *Critical Inquiry* 28:2: 369–418.
Descartes, René (1996), *Meditations on First Philosophy*, trans. John Cottingham, Cambridge: Cambridge University Press.
Dewey, John ([1907] 1931), 'The Practical Character of Reality', in idem, *Philosophy and Civilisation*, 36–55, New York/London: G.P. Putnam's Sons.
Diamond, Cora (1991), *The Realistic Spirit. Wittgenstein, Philosophy, and the Mind*, Cambridge, MA/London: MIT Press.
Diamond, Cora (1991), 'Eating Meat and Eating People', in idem, *The Realistic Spirit. Wittgenstein, Philosophy, and the Mind*, 319–34, Cambridge, MA/London: MIT Press.
Diamond, Cora (1991), 'Having a rough Story about What Moral Philosophy Is', in idem, *The Realistic Spirit. Wittgenstein, Philosophy, and the Mind*, 367–381.
Dorschel, Andreas (2006), 'Einwände gegen das Vergleichen. Ein Versuch, sie zu beantworten', *Philosophisches Jahrbuch* 113:1: 177–85.

Dreyfus, Hubert L. (1991), *Being-in-the-world: A Commentary in Heidegger's* Being and Time, Division I, Cambridge, MA: MIT Press.
Eckensberger, Lutz H., and Ingrid Plath (2003), 'Möglichkeiten und Grenzen des 'variablenorientiereten' Kulturvergleichs: Von der kulturvergleichenden Psychologie zur Kulturpsychologie.' In Hartmut Kaelble and Jürgen Schriewer (eds.), *Vergleich und Transfer. Komparatistik in den Sozial-, Geschichts- und Kulturwissenschaften*, 55–98, Frankfurt a.M.: Campus.
Egan, David (2016), 'Literature and Thought Experiments', *Journal for Aesthetics and Art Criticism* 74:2: 139–50.
Eggers, Michael (v), '"Vergleichung ist ein gefährlicher Feind des Genusses." Zur Epistemologie des Vergleichs in der deutschen Ästhetik um 1800', in Ulrich Johannes Schneider (ed.), *Kulturen des Wissens im 18. Jahrhundert*, 627–35, Berlin/New York: De Gruyter.
Eggers, Michael (ed.) (2011), *Von Ähnlichkeiten und Unterschieden. Vergleich, Analogie und Klassifikation in Wissenschaft und Literatur (18./19. Jahrhundert)*, Heidelberg: Winter.
Eggers, Michael (2016), *Zur Wissenschaftsgeschichte und Epistemologie des Vergleichs und zur Genealogie der Komparatistik*, Heidelberg: Winter.
Elberfeld, Rolf (1999), 'Überlegungen zur Grundlegung "komparativer Philosophie"', *Allgemeine Zeitschrift für Philosophie* 24: 125–54.
Elson, Luke (2014), 'Heaps and Chains: is the Chaining Argument for Parity a Sorites?' *Ethics* 124:4: 557–71.
Epple, Angelika and Walter Erhart (eds.) (2015), *Die Welt beobachten. Praktiken des Vergleichens*, Frankfurt a.M./New York: Campus.
Epple, Angelika (2015), 'Doing Comparisons – Ein praxeologischer Zugang zur Geschichte der Globalisierung/en', in Angelika Epple and Walter Erhart (eds.), *Die Welt beobachten. Praktiken des Vergleichens*, 161–199, Frankfurt a.M./New York: Campus.
Erhart, Walter (2015), '"Beobachtung und Erfahrung, Sammeln und Vergleichen" – Adelbert von Chamisso und die Poetik der Weltreise im 18. und 19. Jahrhundert', in Angelika Epple and Walter Erhart (eds.). *Die Welt beobachten. Praktiken des Vergleichens*, 203–33, Frankfurt a.M./New York: Campus.
Feyerabend, Paul (1960), 'Ludwig Wittgenstein,' in *Beiheft 1 zu Wittgensteins Schriften*, 30–47. Frankfurt a.M.: Suhrkamp.
Fleck, Ludwik (1979), *Genesis and Development of a Scientific Fact*, eds. Thaddeus J. Trenn and Robert K. Merton. Foreword by Thomas S. Kuhn, Chicago/London: The University of Chicago Press.
Flynn, Jennifer (2010), 'The Lives of Animals and the Form-Content Connection', in Anton Leist and Peter Singer (eds.), *Coetzee and Philosophy. Philosophical Perspectives on Literature*, 315–33, New York: Columbia University Press.
Forgette, Richard and John W. Winkle (2006), 'Partisan Gerrymandering and the Voting Rights Act', *Social Science Quarterly* 87:1: 155–73.
Forsberg, Niklas (2019), 'Philosophy, Literature, and the Burden of Theory. Review of Toril Moi's *Revolution of the Ordinary: Literary Studies after Wittgenstein, Austin, and Cavell*', *Graduate Faculty Philosophy Journal* 39:2: 1–15.
Foucault, Michel (1982), *The Archaeology of Knowledge: and the Discourse on Language*, trans. Alan Sheridan, New York: Vintage Books, 1982.
Foucault, Michel (1989), *The Order of Things. An Archaeology of the Human Sciences*, London/New York: Routledge.

Frege, Gottlob (1997), 'On Sinn and Bedeutung', in Michael Bearney (ed.), *The Frege Reader*, Oxford: Blackwell Publishing.
Frick, Johann (2017), 'On the survival of humanity,' *Canadian Journal of Philosophy* 47:2/3: 344–67.
Fricker, Miranda (2007), *Epistemic Injustice: Power and the Ethics of Knowing*, Oxford: Oxford University Press.
Fuentes, Agustin, (2006), 'The Humanity of Animals and the Animality of Humans: A View from Biological Anthropology Inspired by J. M. Coetzee's *Elizabeth Costello*', *American Anthropologist* 108:1: 124–32.
Funk Deckard, Michael and Ralph Palm (2010), 'Irony and Belief in Elizabeth Costello', in Anton Leist and Peter Singer (eds.), *Coetzee and Philosophy. Philosophical Perspectives on Literature*, 335–54, New York: Columbia University Press.
Gadamer, Hans-Georg (2004), *Truth and Method*, 2nd and revised ed., trans. Joel Weinsheimer and Donald G. Marshall, London/New York: Continuum.
Gagné, Renaud, Simon Goldhill and Geoffrey Lloyd (eds.) (2018), *Regimes of Comparatism. Frameworks of Comparison in History, Religion and Anthropology* (Jerusalem Studies in Religion and Culture, Vol. 24), Leiden: Brill.
Galison, Peter (1984), 'Descartes's Comparisons: From the Invisible to the Visible', *Isis* 75:2: 311–26.
Garber, Marjorie (1999), 'Reflections', in John Maxwell Coetzee, *The Lives of Animals*, 73–84, Princeton, NJ: Princeton University Press.
Gasché, Rodolphe (2011), 'Das Vergnügen an Vergleichen. Über Kants Ausarbeitung der Kritik der praktischen Vernunft', in Eggers Michael (ed.). *Von Ähnlichkeiten und Unterschieden. Klassifikation in Wissenschaft und Literatur (18./19. Jahrhundert)*, 167–82, Heidelberg: Winter.
Gebauer, Gunter (2009), *Wittgensteins Anthropologisches Denken*. München: C.H. Beck.
Geertz, Clifford (1973), 'Thick Description: Toward an Interpretive Theory of Culture', in idem, *The Interpretation of Cultures: Selected Essays*, 3–30, New York: Basic Books.
Geiger, Ido (2010), 'Writing the Lives of Animals', in Anton Leist and Peter Singer (eds.), *Coetzee and Philosophy. Philosophical Perspectives on Literature*, 145–69, New York: Columbia University Press.
Gert, Joshua (2004), 'Value and Parity', *Ethics* 114:3: 492–510.
Gittleman, John L. and Hang-Kwang Luh (1992), 'On Comparing Comparative Methods', *Annual Review of Ecology and Systematics* 23: 383–404.
Gloy, Karen (2000), 'Versuch einer Logik des Analogiedenkens', in Karen Gloy and Manuel Bachmann (eds.), *Das Analogiedenken. Vorstöße in ein neues Gebiet der Rationalitätstheorie*, 298–323, Freiburg i.Br.: Alber.
Goodman, Nelson (1972), *Problems and Projects*, Indianapolis: Bobbs-Merrill.
Grave, Johannes (2015), 'Vergleichen als Praxis. Vorüberlegungen zu einer praxistheoretisch orientierten Untersuchung von Vergleichen', in Angelika Epple and Walter Erhart (eds.), *Die Welt beobachten. Praktiken des Vergleichens*, 134–59, Frankfurt a.M./New York: Campus.
Griffin, James (1977), 'Are There Incommensurable Values?' *Philosophy & Public Affairs* 7:1: 39–59.
Griffin, James (1986), *Well-Being*. Oxford: Oxford University Press.
Griffin, James (1997), 'Incommensurability: What's the Problem?' in Ruth Chang (ed.), *Incommensurability, Incomparability, and Practical Reason*, 35–51, Cambridge, MA/London: Harvard University Press.

Gutmann, Mathias (1993), 'Der Vergleich als Konstruktion – Systematische Bemerkungen zur Bestimmung entwicklungstheoretischer Ansätze in der Biologie', in Michael Weingarten and Wolfgang Friedrich Gutmann (eds.). *Geschichte und Theorie des Vergleichs in den Biowissenschaften*, 45–60, Frankfurt a.M.: Krame.

Gutmann, Mathias, and Benjamin Rathgeber (2011), 'Vergleichen und Vergleich in den Wissenschaften. Exemplarische Rekonstruktionen zu einer grundlegenden Handlungsform', in Andreas Mauz and Hartmut von Sass (eds.). *Hermeneutik des Vergleichs*, 49–73, Würzburg: Königshausen & Neumann.

Hacking, Ian (1994), 'Styles of Scientific Thinking or Reasoning: A New Analytical Tool for Historians and Philosophers of the Sciences', in Kostas Gavroglu (ed.), *Trends in the Historiography of Science*, 31–48, Dortrecht: Kluwer Academic Publishers.

Hacking, Ian (2002), *Historical Ontology*. Cambridge, MA/London: Harvard University Press.

Hacking, Ian (2002), 'The Archaeology of Michel Foucault, in Ian Hacking, *Historical Ontology*, 73–8, Cambridge, MA/London: Harvard University Press.

Hacking, Ian (2002), 'Language, Truth, and Reason', in Ian Hacking, *Historical Ontology*, 159–77, Cambridge, MA/London: Harvard University Press.

Halperin, Charles J., Robert J. Loewenberg, George Yaney, Peter Kolchin, Rowland Berthoff, David Moltke-Hansen, Forrest McDonald, Grady McWhinehy, Joan Leopold, Alette Olin Hill and Boyd H. Hill Jr (1982), 'Comparative History in Theory and Practice: A Discussion', *The American Historical Review* 87:1: 123–43.

Hämäläinen, Nora (2015), *Literature and Moral Theory*, New York: Bloomsbury.

Hampe, Michael (2014), *Die Lehren der Philosophie, Eine Kritik*. Berlin: Suhrkamp.

Handke, Peter ([1968] 2005), 'Theater und Film. Das Elend des Vergleichens, in idem, *Ich bin ein Bewohner des Elfenbeinturms*, 12th ed., 65–77. Frankfurt a.M.: Suhrkamp.

Harris, George (2001), 'Value Vagueness, Zones of Incomparability, and Tragedy', *American Philosophical Quarterly* 38:2: 155–76.

Heidegger, Martin (1962), *Being and Time*, trans. John Macquarrie and Edward Robinson. Oxford: Basil Blackwell.

Heidegger, Martin (1927), 'Phenomenology and Theology', in idem, *Pathmarks*, 39–62.

Heidegger, Martin ([1927] 2014), *Pathmarks*, ed. and trans. William McNeil, Cambridge: Cambridge University Press.

Heintz, Bettina (2010), 'Numerische Differenz. Überlegungen zu einer Soziologie des (quantitativen) Vergleichs', *Zeitschrift für Soziologie* 39:3: 162–81.

Heintz, Bettina (2016), '"Wir leben im Zeitalter der Vergleichung." Perspektiven einer Soziologie des Vergleichs', *Zeitschrift für Soziologie* 45:5: 305–23.

High, Dallas M. (1967), *Language, Persons, and Belief. Studies in Wittgenstein's Philosophical Investigations and Religious Uses of Language*, New York: Macmillan.

Hills, David (2016), 'Metaphors', in Edward N. Zalta (ed.), *The Stanford Encyclopedia of Philosophy*, https://plato.stanford.edu/entries/metaphor/

Holt, Robert T., and John E. Turner (eds.) (1970), *The Methodology of Comparative Research*, New York: The Free Press.

Holyoak, Keith J., Dedre Gentner and Boicho N. Kokinov (2001), 'Introduction', in idem (eds.), *The Analogical Mind. Perspectives from Cognitive Science*, 1–19, Cambridge, MA/London: MIT Press.

Hoyningen-Huene, Paul (1987), 'Context of Discovery and Context of Justification', *Studies in History and Philosophy of Science* 18: 501–15.

Hsieh, Nien-He (2007), 'Is Incomparability a Problem for Anyone?' *Economics and Philosophy* 23: 65–80.

Hume, David (1779), *Dialogues Concerning Natural Religion*, ed. Dorothy Coleman. Cambridge: Cambridge University Press, 2007.
Husserl, Edmund (1970), *The Crisis of European Sciences and Transcendental Philosophy* (1936/54), trans. David Carr, Evanston: Northwestern University Press.
Husserl, Edmund (1954), *Erfahrung und Urteil. Untersuchungen zur Genealogie der Logik.* Hamburg: Meiner.
James, William (2000), 'The Will to Believe' (1897), in idem, *Pragmatism and Other Writings*, ed. Giles Dunn, 198–218. New York: Penguin Books.
Janich, Peter (1993), 'Der Vergleich als Methode in den Naturwissenschaften', in Michael Weingarten and Wolfgang Friedrich Gutmann (eds.). *Geschichte und Theorie des Vergleichs in den Biowissenschaften*, 13–28. Frankfurt a.M.: Kramer.
Joas, Hans (2012), *The Sacredness of the Person: A New Genealogy of Human Rights*, Washington DC: Georgetown University Press.
Jones, Ward E. (2011), 'Elizabeth Costello and the Biography of the Moral Philosopher', *The Journal of Aesthetics and Art Criticism* 69:2: 209–20.
Jüngel, Eberhard (1983), *God as the Mystery of the World. On the Foundation of the Theology of the Crucified One in the Dispute Between Theism and Atheism*. Grand Rapids, MI/Cambridge: William B. Eerdmans Publishing.
Kaelble, Hartmut (1999), *Der historische Vergleich. Eine Einführung zum 19. und 20. Jahrhundert*. Frankfurt a.M./New York: Campus.
Kaelble, Hartmut and Jürgen Schriewer (eds.) (1999), *Diskurse und Entwicklungspfade. Der Gesellschaftsvergleich in den Geschichts- und Sozialwissenschaften*. Frankfurt a.M./New York: Campus.
Kaelble, Hartmut and Jürgen Schriewer (eds.) (2003), *Vergleich und Transfer. Komparatistik in den Sozial-, Geschichts- und Kulturwissenschaften*. Frankfurt a.M.: Campus.
Kafka, Franz, 'Report for an Academy', available at: http://johnstoniatexts.x10host.com/kafka/reportforacademyhtml.html
Kant, Immanuel ([1781/87] 1998), *Critique of Pure Reason*, eds. Paul Guyer and Allen Wood, Cambridge: Cambridge University Press.
Kant, Immanuel (1784), 'Answering the Question: What Is Enlightenment?', trans. Mary C. Smith, available from Columbia University Press at: http://www.columbia.edu/acis/ets/CCREAD/etscc/kant.html#note1
Kant, Immanuel ([1785] 2011), *Groundwork of the Metaphysics of Morals: A German-English Edition*, ed. and trans. Mary Gregor and Jens Timmermann. Cambridge: Cambridge University Press.
Kant, Immanuel ([1786] 2012) *What does it mean to orient oneself in thinking?* ed. and trans. Allen W. Wood and George di Giovanni, 1–18. Cambridge: Cambridge University Press.
Kaplan, David (1989), 'Demonstratives. An Essay on Semantics, Logic, Metaphysics, and Epistemology of Demonstratrives and other Indexicals', in Joseph Almog, John Perry, and Howard Wettstein (eds.), *Themes from Kaplan*, 481–563, Oxford: Oxford University Press.
Kaschuba, Wolfgang (2003), 'Anmerkungen zum Gesellschaftsvergleich aus ethnologischer Perspektive', in Hartmut Kaelble and Jürgen Schriewer (eds.), *Vergleich und Transfer. Komparatistik in den Sozial-, Geschichts- und Kulturwissenschaften*, 341–50, Frankfurt a.M.: Campus.
Kim, Jaegwon (1980), 'Rorty on the Possibility of Philosophy', *The Journal of Philosophy* 77:10: 588–97.

Kopperschmidt, Josef (2011), 'Vergleich und Vergleichen aus rhetorischer Sicht', in Andreas Mauz and Hartmut von Sass (eds.), *Hermeneutik des Vergleichs. Strukturen, Anwendungen und Grenzen komparativer Verfahren*, 223–42, Würzburg: Königshausen & Neumann.

Koschorke, Albrecht (2015), 'Ähnlichkeit. Valenzen eines post-kolonialen Konzepts', in Anil Bhatti and Dorothee Kimmich (eds.), *Ähnlichkeit. Ein kulturtheoretisches Paradigma*, 35–45, Konstanz: Konstanz University Press.

Kosmützky, Anna and Romy Wöhlert (2015), 'International vergleichende Forschung. Eine interdisziplinäre. Metaanalyse disziplinärer Zugänge', *SWS-Rundschau* 55:4: 279–307.

Krech, Volkhard (2011), 'Wie lassen sich religiöse Sachverhalte miteinander vergleichen? Ein religionssoziologischer Vorschlag', in Andreas Mauz and Hartmut von Sass (eds.), *Hermeneutik des Vergleichs. Strukturen, Anwendungen und Grenzen komparativer Verfahren*, 149–76, Würzburg: Königshausen & Neumann.

Kuhn, Thomas S. (1982), 'Commensurability, Comparability, Communicability', *Proceedings of the Biennial Meeting of the Philosophy of Science Association*, Volume Two: Symposia and Invited Papers: 669–88.

Laguna, Grace A. de. (1934), 'Appearance and Orientation', *The Journal of Philosophy* 31:3: 72–7.

Lamey, Andy (2010), 'Sympathy and Scapegoating in J.M. Coetzee', in Anton Leist and Peter Singer (eds.), *Coetzee and Philosophy. Philosophical Perspectives on Literature*, 171–92, New York: Columbia University Press.

Langton, Rae, (2007), 'Objective and Unconditioned Value', *The Philosophical Review* 116:2: 157–85.

Latour, Bruno, (2004), 'Why Has Critique Run out of Steam? From Matters of Fact to Matters of Concern', *Critical Inquiry* 30:2: 225–48.

Leist, Anton and Peter Singer (eds.) (2010), *Coetzee and Philosophy. Philosophical Perspectives on Literature*, New York: Columbia University Press.

Leist, Anton (2010), 'Against Society, Against History, Against Reason. Coetzee's Archaic Postmodernism', in Anton Leist and Peter Singer (eds.). *Coetzee and Philosophy. Philosophical Perspectives on Literature*, 195–220, New York: Columbia University Press.

Leist, Anton (2019), 'Wertepluralismus als offenes Spiel', in Hartmut von Sass (ed.), *Perspektivismus. Neue Beiträge aus der Erkenntnistheorie, Hermeneutik und Ethik*, 211–42, Hamburg: Meiner.

Leypoldt, Günter (2008), 'Uses of Metaphor: Richard Rorty's Literary Criticism and the Poetics of World-Making', *New Literary History* 39:1, 'Remembering Richard Rorty': 145–63.

Lijphart, Arend (1971), 'Comparative Politics and the Comparative Method', *The American Political Science Review* 65:3: 682–93.

Lorenz, Chris (1999), 'Comparative Historiography: Problems and Perspectives', *History and Theory* 38:1: 25–39.

Loriggio, Francesco (1995), 'Comparative Literature and the Genres of Interdisciplinarity', *World Literature Today* 69:2 'Comparative Literature: States of the Art': 256–62.

Lovibond, Sabina (2002), *Ethical Formation*. Cambridge, MA/London: Harvard University Press.

Luckner, Andreas (2012), *Klugheit* (Grundthemen Philosophie). Berlin/New York: De Gruyter.

Ludwig, Kirk and Greg Ray (2002), 'Vagueness and the Sorites Paradox', *Philosophical Perspectives* 16: 'Language and Mind': 419–61.

Lueken, Geert-Lueke (1997), 'On Showing in Argumentation', *Philosophical Investigations* 20:3: 205-23.
Luhmann, Niklas (1987), *Soziale Systeme. Grundriß einer allgemeinen Theorie*. Frankfurt a.M.: Suhrkamp.
Lukes, Steven (1997), 'Comparing the Incomparable: Trade-offs and Sacrifices', in Ruth Chang (ed.), *Incommensurability, Incomparability, and Practical Reason*, 184-195, Cambridge, MA/London: Harvard University Press.
Lutz, Helga, Jan-Friedrich Missfelder and Tilo Renz (eds.) (2006), *Äpfel und Birnen. Illegitimes Vergleichen in den Kulturwissenschaften*, Bielefeld: transcript.
Lutz, Helga, Jan-Friedrich Missfelder and Tilo Renz (eds.) (2006), 'Einleitung: Illegitimes Vergleichen in den Kulturwissenschaften', in idem (eds.), *Äpfel und Birnen,. Illegitimes Vergleichen in den Kulturwissenschaften*, 7-20, Bielefeld: transcript.
MacIntyre, Alasdair (1982), 'Philosophy, the "Other" Disciplines, and their Histories: A Rejoinder to Richard Rorty', *Soundings: An Interdisciplinary Journal* 65:2: 127-45.
MacKenzie, Ian (1995), 'Pragmatism, Rhetoric, and History', *Poetics Today* 16:2: 283-99.
Martis, Kenneth C. (2008), 'The Original Gerrymander', *Political Geography* 27:4: 833-9.
Martus, Steffen (2015), 'Wandernde Praktiken "after theory"? Praxeologische Perspektiven auf "Literatur/Wissenschaft"', *Internationales Archiv für Sozialgeschichte der deutschen Literatur* 40: 177-95.
Matthes, Joachim (1992), 'The Operation Called "Vergleichen"', in idem (ed.), *Zwischen den Kulturen? Die Sozialwissenschaften vor dem Problem des Kulturvergleichs*, 75-99. Göttingen: Schwartz.
Mauz, Andreas, and Hartmut von Sass (eds.) (2011), *Hermeneutik des Vergleichs. Strukturen, Anwendungen und Grenzen komparativer Verfahren*, Würzburg: Königshausen & Neumann.
McGeer, Victoria (2004), 'The Art of Good Hope', *Annals of the American Academy of Political and Social Science* 592: 100-27.
McMahan, Jeff, (2013), 'Causing People to Exist and Saving People's Lives', *The Journal of Ethics* 17:1/2. Special Issue: 'The Benefits and Harms of Existence and Non-Existence': 5-35.
McManus, Denis (2012), *Heidegger and the Measure of Truth*, Oxford: Oxford University Press.
Melas, Natalie (1995), 'Versions of Incommensurability', *World Literature Today* 69:2 'Comparative Literature: States of the Art': 275-80.
Mersch, Dieter (2004), 'Die Sprache der Materialität: Etwas zeigen und Sich-Zeigen bei Goodman und Wittgenstein', in Olaf Scholz and Jörg Steinbrenner (eds.), *Symbole, Systeme, Welten. Überlegungen zur Philosophie Nelson Goodmans*, 141-61, Heidelberg: Winter.
Messerli, Michael and Kevin Reuter (2017), 'Hard cases of comparison', *Philosophical Studies* 174: 2227-50.
Millgram, Elijah (1997), 'Incommensurability and Practical Reasoning', in Ruth Chang (ed.), *Incommensurability, Incomparability, and Practical Reason*, 151-169, Cambridge, MA/London: Harvard University Press.
Millikan, Ruth G. (1990), 'The Myth of the Essential Indexical', *Noûs* 24:5: 723-34.
Mulhall, Stephen (2002), *The Wounded Animal. J.M. Coetzee and the Difficulty of Reality in Literature and Philosophy*, Princeton: Princeton University Press.
Mulhall, Stephen (2005), *Philosophical Myths of the Fall*, Princeton/Oxford: Princeton University Press.

Müller, Herta (2003), 'Wenn wir schweigen, werden wir unangenehm – wenn wir reden, werden wir lächerlich', in idem, *Der König verneigt sich und tötet*. München: C.H. Beck.
Murdoch, Iris (1990), 'Against Dryness. A Polemical Sketch', in Malcolm Bradbury (ed.), *The Novel Today: Contemporary writers on modern fiction*, 16–20, London: Fontana.
Nagel, Thomas (1979), *Mortal Questions*, Cambridge: Cambridge University Press.
Nagel, Thomas (1979), 'What it is like to be a bat?' in Thomas Nagel, *Mortal Questions*, 165–80, Cambridge: Cambridge University Press.
Nagel, Thomas (1979), 'Subjective and Objective', in Thomas Nagel, *Mortal Questions*, 196–213.
Naroll, Raoul (1965), 'Galton's Problem: The Logic of Cross-Cultural Analysis', *Social Research* 32:4: 428–51.
Nietzsche, Friedrich (1995), *Untimely Meditations. Second Piece: On the Use and Abuse of History for Life*, trans. Richard T. Grey. Stanford: Stanford University Press.
Nietzsche, Friedrich (1996), *Human, All Too Human. A Book for Free Spirit*, trans. R.J. Hollingdale, with an Introduction by Richard Schacht, Cambridge: Cambridge University Press.
Nolte, Ernst (1986), 'Vergangenheit, die nicht vergehen will. Eine Rede, die geschrieben, aber nicht gehalten werden konnte', *Frankfurter Allgemeine Zeitung*, 6 June 1986, available at: https://www.staff.uni-giessen.de/~g31130/PDF/Nationalismus/ErnstNolte.pdf
Nozick, Robert (1990), *Examined Life. Philosophical Meditations*. New York/London: A Touchstone Book.
O'Neill, Onora (1986), 'The Power of Example', *Philosophy* 61:1: 5–29.
Oberheim, Eric and Paul Hoyningen-Huene (2016), 'The Incommensurability of Scientific Theories', in Edward N. Zalta (ed.), *The Stanford Encyclopedia of Philosophy*, https://plato.stanford.edu/archives/win2016/entries/incommensurability/
Okrent, Mark (1988), *Heidegger's Pragmatism. Understanding, Being, and the Critique of Metaphysic,* Ithaca, NY/London: Cornell University Press.
Olshewsky, Thomas M. (2003), 'Demea's Dilemmas', *British Journal for the History of Philosophy* 11:3: 473–92.
Osterhammel, Jürgen (2003), 'Transferanalyse und Vergleich im Fernverhältnis', in Hartmut Kaelble and Jürgen Schriewer (eds.), *Vergleich und Transfer. Komparatistik in den Sozial-, Geschichts- und Kulturwissenschaften*, 439–66, Frankfurt a.M.: Campus.
Ott, Konrad. (2016), 'Zum Selbst der Orientierung', in Andrea Bertino et. al. (eds.), *Zur Philosophie der Orientierung*, 115–26.
Oyen, Else (1990), 'The Imperfection of Comparisons', in idem (ed.), *Comparative Methodology. Theory and Practice in International Social Research*, 1–18, London: Sage.
Parfit, Derek (1984), *Reasons and Persons*, Oxford: Oxford University Press.
Perry, John (1979), 'The Problem of the Essential Indexical', *Noûs* 13:1: 3–21.
Phillips, Dewi Z. (1992), 'The Presumption of Theory', in idem, *Interventions in Ethics*, 61–85. Albany: Suny Press.
Phillips, Dewi Z. (1993), 'On Really Believing', in idem, *Wittgenstein and Religion*, 33–55, Basingstoke/London: Macmillan.
Phillips, Dewi Z. (2004), *Religion and Friendly Fire. Examining Assumptions in Contemporary Philosophy of Religion*, Aldershot/Burlington, VT: Ashgate.
Pippin, Robert (2010), 'The Paradoxes of Power in the Early Novels of J.M. Coetzee', in Anton Leist and Peter Singer (eds.), *Coetzee and Philosophy. Philosophical Perspectives on Literature*, 19–41, New York: Columbia University Press.
Pippin, Robert B. (2016), 'Just Who Is It That We Have Become? Rorty's Hegelianism', *The Hedgehog Review*: 84–8.

Plantinga, Alvin (1983), *Faith and Rationality*, London/Notre Dame, IN: Notre Dame University Press.
Pohlhaus Jr., Gaile (2012), 'Relational Knowing and Epistemic Injustice: Toward a Theory of Willful Hermeneutical Ignorance', *Hypatia* 27:4: 715–35.
Putnam, Hilary (1985), 'A Comparison of Something with Something Else', *New Literary History* 17:1 'Philosophy of Science and Literary Theory': 61–79.
Putnam, Ruth Anna (1985), 'Poets, Scientists, and Critics', *New Literary History* 17:1 'Philosophy of Science and Literary Theory': 17–21.
Qizilbash, Mozaffar (2007), 'The Mere Addition Paradox, Parity and Vagueness', *Philosophy and Phenomenological Research* 75:1: 129–51.
Quine, Willard van Orman ([1953] 1980), 'Two dogmas of empiricism', in idem, *From a Logical Point of View. Logico-Philosophical Essays*, 2nd ed., 20–46. Cambridge, MA / London: Harvard University Press.
Raab, Jürgen (2011), 'Wissenssoziologisches Vergleichen', in Andreas Mauz and Hartmut von Sass (eds.), *Hermeneutik des Vergleichs. Strukturen, Anwendungen und Grenzen komparativer Verfahren*, 91–113, Würzburg: Königshausen & Neumann.
Radhakrishnan, Rajagopalan (2015), 'Warum vergleichen?' in Angelika Epple and Walter Erhart (eds.), *Die Welt beobachten. Praktiken des Vergleichens*, 35–61, Frankfurt a.M./ New York: Campus.
Ragin, Charles C. (1987), *The Comparative Method. Moving Beyond Qualitative and Quantitative Strategies*, Berkeley/Los Angeles/London: University of California Press.
Raphael, D.D. (1983), 'Can Literature Be Moral Philosophy?' *New Literary History* 15:1 'Literature and/as Moral Philosophy': 1–12.
Raz, Joseph (1986), *The Morality of Freedom*, Oxford: Clarendon Press.
Raz, Joseph (1997), 'Incommensurability and Agency', in Ruth Chang (ed.), *Incommensurability, Incomparability, and Practical Reason*, 110–128, Cambridge, MA / London: Harvard University Press.
Reckwitz, Andreas (2003), 'Grundelemente einer Theorie sozialer Praktiken. Eine sozialtheoretische Perspektive', *Zeitschrift für Soziologie* 32:4: 282–301.
Reckwitz, Andreas (2018), *Die Gesellschaft der Singularitäten. Zum Strukturwandel der Moderne*, 5th ed., Berlin: Suhrkamp.
Reeves, Charles Eric (1986), 'Deconstruction, Language, Motive: Rortian Pragmatism and the Uses of "Literature"', *The Journal of Aesthetics and Art Criticism* 44:4: 351–6.
Regan, Donald (1997), 'Value, Comparability, and Choice', in Ruth Chang (ed.), *Incommensurability, Incomparability, and Practical Reason*, 129–150, Cambridge, MA / London: Harvard University Press.
Regan, Tom (1987), *The Struggle for Animal Rights*, Clarks Summit: International Society for Animals Rights.
Rhees, Rush (1998), *Wittgenstein and the Possibility of Discourse*, ed. Dewi Z. Phillips, Cambridge: Cambridge University Press.
Rheinberger, Hans-Jörg (1997), *Toward a History of Epistemic Things*, Palo Alto, CA: Stanford University Press.
Richards, Ivor A. (1936), 'Metaphor', in idem, *The Philosophy of Rhetoric*, 89–138, Oxford: Oxford University Press.
Richter, Melvin (2004), 'David Hume on Comparison. From Philosophy to Political Theory and History', in Lothar R. Waas (ed.), *Politik, Moral and Religion – Gegensätze und Ergänzungen. Festschrift Karl Graf Ballestrem*, 343–58, Berlin: De Gruyter.
Rorty, Richard (1972), 'The World Well Lost', *The Journal of Philosophy* 69:19: 649–65.

Rorty, Richard ([1979] 2009), *Philosophy and the Mirror of Nature*, with a new introduction by Michael Williams. Princeton and Oxford: Princeton University Press.

Rorty, Richard (1982), *Consequences of Pragmatism (Essays: 1972–1980)*, Minneapolis: University of Minnesota Press.

Rorty, Richard (1987), 'Unfamiliar noises I: Hesse and Davidson on metaphor', *Proceedings of the Aristotelian society*, supp. vol. 61: 283–96.

Rorty, Richard (1989), *Contingency, Irony, and Solidarity*, Cambridge: Cambridge University Press.

Rorty, Richard (1991), *Essays on Heidegger and others*, Philosophical papers, Vol. II, Cambridge: Cambridge University Press.

Rorty, Richard (1999), *Philosophy and Social Hope*, London: Penguin Books.

Rorty, Richard (2001), *Philosophie & die Zukunft. Essays*, Frankfurt a.M.: Fischer.

Rorty, Richard (2003), 'Der Roman als Mittel zur Erlösung aus der Selbstbezogenheit', in Joachim Küpper and Christoph Menke (eds.), *Dimensionen ästhetischer Erfahrung*, 49–66, Frankfurt a.M.: Suhrkamp.

Rorty, Richard (2007), *Philosophy as Cultural Politics*. Philosophical Papers, Vol. 4. Cambridge: Cambridge University Press.

Rorty, Richard (2008), 'Texts and Lumps', *New Literary History* 39:1: 53–68.

Rosefeldt, Tobias (2006), 'Kants Ich als Gegenstand', *Deutsche Zeitschrift für Philosophie* 54:2: 277–93.

Ross, Marc Howard and Elizabeth Homer (1976), 'Galton's Problem in Cross-National Research', *World Politics* 29:1: 1–28.

Saler, Benson (2001), 'Comparison: Some Suggestions for Improving the Inevitable', *Numen* 48:3: 267–75.

Savickey, Beth (2014), 'Wittgenstein and Hacker: Übersichtliche Darstellung', *Nordic Wittgenstein Review* 3:2: 99–123.

Sax, Boria (2000), *Animals in the Third Reich: Pets, Scapegoats, and the Holocaust*, New York: Continuum.

Schaub, Mirjam (2010), *Das Singuläre und das Exemplarische: Zu Logik und Praxis der Beispiele in Philosophie und Ästhetik*, Zürich/Berlin: Diaphanes.

Schenk, Günter and Andrej Krause (2001), 'Vergleich', in *Historisches Wörterbuch der Philosophie*, vol. 11, Basel: Schwabe.

Schneider, Hans Julius (1999), 'Offene Grenzen, zerfaserte Ränder: Über Arten von Beziehungen zwischen Sprachspielen,' in Wilhelm Lütterfelds and Andreas Roser (eds.), *Der Konflikt der Lebensformen in Wittgensteins Philosophie der Sprache*, 138–155, Frankfurt a.M.: Peter Lang Verlag.

Schriewer, Jürgen (1999), 'Vergleich und Erklärung zwischen Kausalität und Komplexität', in Hartmut Kaelble and Jürgen Schriewer (eds.), *Diskurse und Entwicklungspfade. Der Gesellschaftsvergleich in den Geschichts- und Sozialwissenschaften*, 53–102, Frankfurt a.M./New York: Campus.

Schriewer, Jürgen (2003), 'Problemdimensionen sozialwissenschaftlicher Komparatistik', in Hartmut Kaelble und Jürgen Schriewer (eds.), *Vergleich und Transferr. Komparatistik in den Sozial-, Geschichts- und Kulturwissenschaften*, 9–52, Frankfurt a.M.: Campus.

Schulenberg, Ulf (2007), 'From Redescription to Writing: Rorty, Barthes, and the Idea of a Literary Culture', *New Literary History* 38:2: 371–87.

Schulte, Joachim (1990), *Chor und Gesetz. Wittgenstein im Kontext*, Frankfurt a.M.: Suhrkamp.

Searle, John (1979), *Expression and Meaning. Studies in the Theory of Speech Acts*, Cambridge: Cambridge University Press.

Segal, Robert A. (2001), 'In Defense of the Comparative Method', *Numen* 48:3: 339-73.
Sewell, Jr., William H. (1967), 'Marc Bloch and the Logic of Comparative History', *History and Theory* 6:2: 208-18.
Shiffrin, Seana V. (1999), 'Wrongful Life, Procreative Responsibility, and the Significance of Harm', *Legal Theory* 5: 117-48.
Singer, Peter (1975), *Animal Liberation: A New Ethics for Our Treatment of Animals*, New York: HarperCollins.
Singer, Peter (1999), 'Reflections', in John Maxwell Coetzee, *The Lives of Animals*, 85-91, Princeton, NJ: Princeton University Press.
Soskice, Janet M. (1985), *Metaphor and Religious Language*. Oxford: Oxford University Press.
Spoerhase, Carlos and Steffen Martus (2013), 'Die Quellen der Praxis. Probleme einer historischen Praxeologie der Philologie. Einleitung', *Zeitschrift für Germanistik* 23:2: 221-25.
Spoerhase, Carlos (2018), 'Rankings: A Pre-History', *New Left Review* 114:6: 99-112.
Stalder, Felix (2016), *Kultur der Digitalität*, Berlin: Suhrkamp.
Stalnaker, Robert (1981), 'Indexical Belief', *Synthese* 49:1: 129-51.
Stanford Friedman, Susan (2015), 'Warum nicht vergleichen?' in Angelika Epple and Walter Erhart (eds.), *Die Welt beobachten. Praktiken des Vergleichens*, 63-83, Frankfurt a.M./New York: Campus.
Stegmaier, Werner (1992), '"Was heißt: Sich im Denken orientieren": Zur Möglichkeit philosophischer Weltorientierung nach Kant', *Allgemeine Zeitschrift für Philosophie* 17:1: 1-16.
Stegmaier, Werner (1994), 'Weltabkürzungskunst. Orientierung durch Zeichen', in Josef Simon (ed.), *Zeichen und Interpretation*, 119-41. Frankfurt a.M.: Suhrkamp.
Stegmaier, Werner (2005), 'Nach der Subjektivität: Selbstbezüglichkeit der Orientierung', in Ingolf U. Dalferth and Philipp Stoellger (eds.), *Krisen der Subjektivität. Problemfelder eines strittigen Paradigmas*, 179-201, Tübingen: Mohr Siebeck.
Stegmaier, Werner (2005), 'Orientierung. Einleitung', in idem (ed.), *Orientierung. Philosophische Perspektiven*, 14-50, Frankfurt a.M.: Suhrkamp.
Stegmaier, Werner (2008), *Philosophie der Orientierung*, Berlin/New York: De Gruyter.
Stegmaier, Werner (2014), 'Spielräume der Moral in Orientierungssituationen', in Stefan Berg and Hartmut von Sass (eds.), *Spielzüge. Zur Dialektik des Spiels und seinem metaphorischen Mehrwert*, 264-77, Freiburg im Br./München: Karl Alber.
Stegmaier, Werner (2015), 'Die Wirklichkeit der Orientierung. Perspektivität und Realität nach Nietzsche und Luhmann', *Nietzscheforschung* 22:1: 93-112.
Stegmaier, Werner (2016), 'Zur Philosophie der Orientierung. Fragen und Antworten', in Andrea Bertino et al. (eds.), *Zur Philosophie der Orientierung*, 375-408, Berlin/New York: De Gruyter.
Steinmetz, Willibald (2015), '"Vergleich" – eine begriffsgeschichtliche Skizze', in Angelika Epple and Walter Erhart (eds.), *Die Welt beobachten. Praktiken des Vergleichens*, 85-134, Frankfurt a.M./New York: Campus.
Stoellger, Philipp (2011), 'Unvergleichlich? Vergleich als Umgang mit dem Inkommensurablen. Ein Beitrag zur Hermeneutik der Differenz', in Andreas Mauz and Hartmut von Sass (eds.). *Hermeneutik des Vergleichs. Strukturen, Anwendungen und Grenzen komparativer Verfahren*, 321-45, Würzburg: Königshausen & Neumann.
Stoler, Ann L. (2002), *Carnal Knowledge and Imperial Power: Race and the Intimate in Colonial Rule*, Berkeley: University of California Press.
Stroumsa, Guy G. (ed.) (2018), *Comparative Studies in the Humanities*, Jerusalem: Israel Academy of Sciences and Humanities Press.

Stroumsa, Guy G. (2018), 'In Search of a New Paradigm', in idem (ed.). *Comparative Studies in the Humanities*, 7–13, Jerusalem: Israel Academy of Sciences and Humanities Press.

Strub, Christian (2011), '"Das hinreißendste Wort, über das wir verfügen, ist das Wort WIE, ganz gleichgültig, ob es ausgesprochen wird oder ungesagt bleibt." Eine These zur Geschichte der Ähnlichkeit', in Andreas Mauz and Hartmut von Sass (eds.), *Hermeneutik des Vergleichs*, 243–66, Würzburg: Königshausen & Neumann.

Stüssel, Kerstin (2015), 'Das "Zeitalter der Vergleichung" – Philologie, Ethnographie, Literatur und Medien', in Angelika Epple and Walter Erhart (eds.), *Die Welt beobachten. Praktiken des Vergleichens*, 265–283, Frankfurt a.M./New York: Campus.

Sugden, Robert (2009), 'On Modelling Vagueness – and on not Modelling Incommensurability', *Proceedings of the Aristotelian Society Supplementary* 83: 95–113.

Sully, James (1885), 'Comparison', *Mind* 10:40: 489–511.

Sztybel, David (2006), 'Can the Treatment of Animals Be Compared to the Holocaust?' *Ethics and the Environment* 11:1: 97–132.

Taylor, Charles (1997), 'Leading a Life', in Ruth Chang (ed.), *Incommensurability, Incomparability, and Practical Reason*, 170–83, Cambridge, MA/London.

Taylor, Charles (2003), 'Rorty and Philosophy', in Charles Guignon and David R. Hiley (eds.), *Richard Rorty (Contemporary Philosophy in Focus)*, 158–80, Cambridge/New York: Cambridge University Press.

Taylor, Charles (2007), *A Secular Age*. Cambridge, MA/London: Harvard University Press.

Tenbruck, Friedrich H. (1992), 'Was war der Kulturvergleich, ehe des den Kulturverglech gab?" in Joachim Matthes (ed.), *Zwischen den Kulturen? Die Sozialwissenschaften vor dem Problem des Kulturvergleichs*, 13–35, Göttingen: Otto Schartz.

Thomä, Dieter (2007), *Erzähle dich selbst. Lebensgeschichte als philosophisches Problem*. Frankfurt a.M.: Suhrkamp.

Tiles, Mary (2011), 'Is Historical Epistemology Part of the "Modernist Settlement"?' *Erkenntnis* 75:3: 525–43.

Tilly, Charles (1985), *Big Structures. Large Processes. Huge Comparisons*, New York: Sage Foundation.

Totaro, Francesco (2016), 'Orientierung, Perspektive, Wahrheit. Versuch einer Verbindung', in Andrea Bertino et al. (eds.), *Zur Philosophie der Orientierung*, 197–213, Berlin/New York: De Gruyter.

Tremaine, Louis (2003), 'The Embodied Soul: Animal Being in the Work of J. M. Coetzee', *Contemporary Literature* 44:4: 587–612.

Ullmann-Margalit, Edna and Sidney Morgenbesser (1977), 'Picking and Choosing', *Social Research* 44:4: 757–85.

van Heerden, Adriaan (2010), 'Disgrace, Desire, and the Dark Side of the New South Africa', in Anton Leist and Peter Singer (eds.), *Coetzee and Philosophy. Philosophical Perspectives on Literature*, 43–63, New York: Columbia University Press.

van Tongeren, Paul (2016), 'Der "Pflock des Augenblickes". Über die Situation und die Tugenden der Orientierung', in Andrea Bertino et al. (eds.), *Zur Philosophie der Orientierung*, 233–45, Berlin/New York: De Gruyter.

Volbers, Jörg (2018), *Die Vernunft der Erfahrung. Eine pragmatistische Kritik der Rationalität*, Hamburg: Meiner.

von Sass, Hartmut (2010), *Sprachspiele des Glaubens. Eine Studie zur kontemplativen Religionsphilosophie von Dewi Z. Phillips mit ständiger Rücksicht auf Ludwig Wittgenstein*, Tübingen: Mohr Siebeck.

von Sass, Hartmut (2010), 'Broken Mirrors – Contemplative Nowheres. Rorty and Phillips on Description, Imagination, and Literature', in Ingolf U. Dalferth and Hartmut von

Sass (eds.), *The Contemplative Spirit. Dewi Z. Phillips on Religion and the Limits of Philosophy*, 55–95, Tübingen: Mohr Siebeck.

von Sass, Hartmut (2011), 'Religion in a Private Igloo? A Critical Dialogue with Richard Rorty', *International Journal for Philosophy of Religion* 70:3: 203–16.

von Sass, Hartmut (2017), 'Kann denn Hoffnung Tugend sein?' *Zeitschrift für philosophische Forschung* 71:1: 70–104.

von Sass, Hartmut (ed.) (2019), *Perspektivismus. Neue Beiträge aus der Erkenntnistheorie, Hermeneutik und Ethik*, Hamburg: Meiner.

von Sass, Hartmut (2019), 'Beyond Hume: Demea. A Rehabilitation with Systematic Intent', *International Journal for Philosophy of Religion* 86:1: 61–84.

von Stosch, Klaus (2001), *Glaubensverantwortung in doppelter Kontingenz. Untersuchungen zur Verortung fundamentaler Theologie nach Wittgenstein*. Regensburg: Pustet.

Walker, Lawrence D. (1980), 'A Note on Historical Linguistics and Marc Bloch's Comparative Method', *History and Theory* 19:2: 154–64.

Wallace, R. Jay. (1990), 'How to Argue about Practical Reason', *Mind* 99:395: 355–85.

Wartenberg, Thomas E. (2006), 'Beyond Mere Illustration: How Films Can Be Philosophy', *The Journal of Aesthetics and Art Criticism* 64:1, Special Issue: 'Thinking through Cinema: Film as Philosophy': 19–32.

Warwick, Paul (1978), 'Galton's Problem In Comparative Political Research', *Political Methodology* 5:3: 327–46.

Wasserman, Ryan (2004), 'Indeterminacy, Ignorance and the Possibility of Parity', *Philosophical Perspectives* 18: Ethics: 391–403.

Weber, Ralph (2013), '"How to Compare?" – On the Methodological State of Comparative Philosophy', *Philosophy Compass* 8:7: 593–603.

Weber, Ralph (2014), 'Comparative Philosophy and the Tertium: Comparing What with What, and in What Respect?' *Dao* 13: 151–71.

Werner, Michael and Bénédicte Zimmermann (2002), 'Vergleich, Transfer, Verflechtung. Der Ansatz der Histoire croisée und die Herausforderung des Transnationalen', *Geschichte und Gesellschaft* 28:4: 607–36.

Werner, Michael and Bénédicte Zimmermann (2006), 'Beyond Comparison: Histoire Croisée and the Challenge of Reflexivity', *History and Theory* 45:1: 30–50.

Wettstein, Howard (2012), 'Referent and Fixing Reference', in *Prospects for Meaning. Current issues in theoretical philosophy*. Vol. 3, Berlin/New York: De Gruyter.

Whitehead, Alfred N. (1948), *Science and the Modern World. Lowell Lectures, 1925*, New York: Pelican Mentor Books.

Williams, Bernard and J.J.C. Smart (1973), *Utilitarianism: For and Against*, Cambridge: Cambridge University Press.

Winch, Peter (1972), *Ethics and Action (Studies in Ethics and the Philosophy of Religion)*, London: Routledge & Kegan Paul.

Winch, Peter (1997), 'Can We Understand Ourselves?' *Philosophical Investigations* 20:3: 193–204.

Winch, Peter (1998), 'Judgement: Proposition and Practices', *Philosophical Investigations* 21:3: 189–201.

Wittgenstein, Ludwig (1961), 'Notes on Logic', in G.H. von Wright and G.E.M. Anscombe (eds.), *Notebooks 1914–1916*, trans. G.E.M. Anscombe, 93–106, Oxford: Basil Blackwell.

Wittgenstein, Ludwig (2001), *Tractatus Logico-Philosophicus*, ed. and trans. David Pears and Brian McGuinness, London: Routledge.

Wittgenstein, Ludwig (1993), 'Remarks on Frazer's *Golden Bough*', in James C. Klagge and Alfred Nordmann (eds.), *Philosophical Occasions*, 119–55, Indianapolis/Cambridge: Hackett.
Wittgenstein, Ludwig (1958), *The Blue Book*, in Rush Rhees (ed.), *The Blue and the Brown Book*, 1–74. New York: Harper & Brothers.
Wittgenstein, Ludwig (1958), *The Brown Book*, in Rush Rhees (ed.), *The Blue and the Brown Book*, 75–185, New York: Harper & Brothers.
Wittgenstein, Ludwig (1975), *Philosophical Remarks*, ed. from his posthumous writings by Rush Rhees and trans. Raymond Hargreaves and Roger White, Oxford: Basil Blackwell.
Wittgenstein, Ludwig (1973), *Philosophical Investigations. Part I*, 3rd ed., eds. G.E.M. Anscombe and Rush Rhees, trans. G.E.M. Anscombe, 1–172, Englewood Cliffs, NJ: Prentice Hall.
Wittgenstein, Ludwig (1973), *Philosophical Investigations. Part II*, 3rd ed., eds. G.E.M. Anscombe and Rush Rhees, trans. G.E.M. Anscombe, 173–232. Englewood Cliffs, NJ: Prentice Hall.
Wittgenstein, Ludwig (1984), *Culture and Value*, ed. G.H. von Wright in collaboration with Heikki Nyman, trans. Peter Winch, Chicago: The Chicago University Press.
Wittgenstein, Ludwig (1972), *On Certainty*, eds. G.E.M. Anscombe and G.H. von Wright, trans. Denis Paul and G.E.M. Anscombe, New York/San Francisco/London: Harper & Row.
Wittgenstein, Ludwig (1967), *Zettel*, eds. G.E.M. Anscombe and G.H. von Wright, trans. G.E.M. Anscombe, Berkeley/Los Angeles: University of California Press.
Woelert, Peter (2007), 'Kant's hands, spatial orientation, and the Copernican turn', *Continental Philosophical Review* 40:1: 139–50.
Woessner, Martin (2010), 'Coetzee's Critique of Reason', in Anton Leist and Peter Singer (eds.), *Coetzee and Philosophy. Philosophical Perspectives on Literature*, 221–45, New York: Columbia University Press.
Yourgrau, Palle (2019), *Death and Nonexistence*, Oxford: Oxford University Press.
Zima, Peter V. (1992), *Komparatistik. Einführung in die Vergleichende Literaturwissenschaft*, Tübingen: Francke.
Zima, Peter V. (ed.) (2000), *Vergleichende Wissenschaften. Interdisziplinarität und Interkulturalität in den Komparatistiken*, Tübingen: Francke.
Zima, Peter V. (2000), 'Vergleich als Konstruktion. Genetische und typologische Aspekte des Vergleichs und die soziale Bedingtheit der Theorie', in idem (ed.). *Vergleichende Wissenschaften. Interdisziplinarität und Interkulturalität in den Komparatistiken*, 15–28, Tübingen: Francke.
Zima, Peter V. (2011), *Komparatistische Perspektiven. Zur Theorie der Vergleichenden Literaturwissenschaften*, Tübingen: Francke.
Zimmermann, Ruben (2007), 'Die Form bzw. Gattung der Gleichnisse', in idem et al. (eds.), *Kompendium der Gleichnisse Jesu*, 17–28, Gütersloh: Gütersloher Verlagshaus, 2007.

Index

Page numbers: Notes are given as: [page number] n. [note number]

a maiore arguments 40
abbreviated explanation 40
absolute differences 181
absolute metaphors 38–9, 74
abstraction 15, 49, 80
action-centred ethics 165, 168
active practice, orientation 87
addition, logic of 165
adequacy 151–73
Adorno, Theodor W. 56
'age of comparison' 5, 11, 21, 175–83
'agent', performative conditions 21
agent-centred ethics 165, 168
agent-centred orientation 79, 82–3
alien culture 53–4, 65, 66–9
aligning-comparing distinction 103
alterity 64
analogia attributionis 32, 34
analogia proportionalitatis 32–4, 40
analogies/analogical comparisons 32–4, 49–50, 158
    language-games 97, 102–3, 206n.25
    trichotomy thesis 136
analytical status, orientation 86
animals case study 151–73
Anscombe, G.E.M. 109, 122
anticomparativity 182
antidualist account *see* monistic account
Aquinas, Thomas 157
arbitrary comparisons 43
argumentative justification 34
Aristotelian philosophy 112, 158, 216n.9
articulations, conditional acknowledgement 116
asymmetrical comparisons 52–5, 61–2, 64–5, 97
attention-attraction 41
'authenticity revolution' 179

Baecker, Dirk 63
Baumgarten, Alexander 41
Beardsley, Monroe 36
belief/disbelief 165–8
Bentham, Jeremy 131
Black, Max 35–6
Bloom, Harold 118
Blumenberg, Hans 38–9, 96
bottom-up approaches 1, 15
Broome, John 132–5, 146

Cartesianism 113
categoriality 31, 131, 140–1, 215n.64
causal thinking 66–7
causality, typology 54–5
Cavell, Stanley 150
    Cities of Words 41
Chang, Ruth 3, 127–8, 130, 133, 135–9, 149–50
character formation 165
choice 127–9, 144–6
    see also rational choice
circularity 43, 117–18
Citizen Kane (film) 125
class concept 179–80
classical metaphysics 75, 201n.46
classification, comparing as 41
closed comparisons 47
    see also result-oriented comparisons
Coetzee, John Maxwell 153–5, 166, 168
    Disgrace 86–7, 169–70, 171
    Elizabeth Costello 10, 124, 153, 162–3, 170–1
cognitive function, comparisons 16, 39, 43
cognitive similarity 30
'collapsing principle' 214n.44
colonialism 64–5
combinational multidimensionality 144
commensurability 140, 144

communality of language 98, 207n.27
comparative constructivism 6, 23–5, 31, 42
comparative contextualism 8, 13, 25–8
comparative injustice 3, 6–8, 14, 45, 59–69, 197n.4
comparative ironism 109–22
comparative items/*relata*
   constructivism 42
   contextualism 26–7
   diachronic comparisons 51
   epistemology 59
   explorative comparisons 41
   impartial comparisons 52
   independence problem 22, 189n.26
   intentional comparisons 103
   knowledge creation 39–40
   noncomparability 141
   normative comparisons 65
   as 'objects of comparison' 96–7
   result-oriented comparisons 50
   scalability 43, 178
   structural incomparability 129
   structure of 22–4
   tertium comparationis relation 172
   unjust construction of 61, 68
comparative limits 5–6, 41–4, 182
comparative methods
   demands of 65, 69
   ontological shift 4–5
   as scientific method 16
   as set of rules 193n.80
comparative normativity 52–5, 61, 65
comparative partiality 52–3, 62
comparative perspectivism 6
comparative philosophy
   context of 3
   methodological demands 65, 69
   will to compare 63–5
comparative procedure
   'agent' 21
   analysis 7
   determination 128
   general account 2–5
   orientation 9, 89
   plurality 111
comparative purity *see* pure comparisons
comparative regards/*tertia*
   circularity 43

comparability problems 22
comparative limits 182
contextualism 26–7
emergent comparisons 48–9, 61
epistemology 59
knowledge creation 39
noncomparability 140
as 'objects of comparison' 96, 102
silencing 61–2, 65, 68
stable-emergent distinction 48–9
transforming 120
unjust construction of 61–2, 65
vocabularies 119–20, 122
see also tertia comparationis
comparative result, definitions 29
'comparative totalization' 5
comparativism
   conflicting values 2
   justified choice 128
   philosophy as 115–22
   studies in 8–9, 71–2
comparing
   aligning distinction 103
   hybrid framework 180–3
   as practice 7–8
   transition from comparisons 188n.12
comparisons
   definitions 5
   functions of 39–41
   grammar 5–6
   hybrid framework 180–3
   state of the field 2–4
   as structure 7–8
   transition to comparing 188n.12
complementarity 131, 134–5
completeness 54, 60–1
complexity/complex relations 19–21, 23, 28, 46–7
   see also multidimensional comparisons
concepts
   absolute metaphors 38
   subjectivity 82
conceptual neighbourhood 131, 138
conciseness 49
condensed explanation 40
conditional acknowledgement 116
conditions, reasonable comparisons 18–19
conflicting values 2
consciousness 83, 169

consistency 11, 23
constitutive incomparability 127, 147–50, 172, 216n.10
    see also incommensurability; indexical incomparability
constructed indexicality 85
constructed similarity 20, 25, 31
constructivism 6, 23–5, 31, 42
context-sensitive generality 7, 9
contextual elements
    complex relations 19–21
    language-games 98
    pointed comparisons 58
contextual embeddedness 28
contextual similarity 31–2, 51
contextualism 8, 13, 25–8
contrastive comparisons 49–50, 53, 64, 65, 68
correspondence theory 111–13
Costello, Elizabeth 153–73
    The House on Eccles Street 154
    The Lives of Animals 153–4
Costello, John 155, 161, 166
covering values, noncomparability 141
creativity 43
critical reflection 42
cross-cultural studies 68
cruelty 115, 117
cultural comparisons 63–4, 175–8
cultural context, alien culture 53–4, 65, 66–9

Davidson, Donald 37–8, 114, 119
de-contextualization 42, 182
de-generalizing, comparing as 40
de-regionalization 182
de-subjectivization 182
decisions
    fuzzy equality 146
    rationality of 126
deductions 42
deductive thinking 40
demonstrative acts 83–4
derivative vagueness 143
Derrida, Jacques 156, 169
Descartes, Réne 64, 92, 157, 167
description
    assets of 93–6
    comparing as mode of 100–6

plurality of 110–11, 113–15
stability of 119
descriptive philosophy 9, 91–107, 204n.2, 206n.19
descriptive purity *see* pure descriptions
desingularization 44
    see also 'nostrification'
devaluation 53, 62–3, 178
Dewey, John 121
diachronic comparisons 22, 50–2, 177
diachronic orientation 80
diachronic stability 22
dialectical method 116, 177–8
differences
    absolute 181
    alterity distinction 64
    language-games 97–8
    similarity and 50
differentiality, typology 54–5
dimensionality, typology 54
discipline-bound approaches 1, 3
disorientation 88, 89–90
divergent descriptive means 101
diversity
    problem of 131
    within games 104–5
dogmatism 91–3, 97
dynamics of comparing 104–6

embeddedness
    contextual 28
    practices 16–18, 27, 72
    theories 2
emergence, logic of 165
emergent comparisons 48–9, 61–2
emotional responsiveness 169
emphatic comparisons/comparability 36, 149
empiricism 4
enlightenment thinking 199n.11
epistemic asymmetry 54
epistemic form, 'agent' 21
epistemic function, comparisons 39
'epistemic injustice' 197n.4
'epistemic violence' 64
epistemology 59
equality
    cultural comparisons 178

incomparability and 127, 132–4, 136, 138–9, 144–6
    modernity and 175
equalization, comparing as 163
essential indexicals 202n.59
essentialism, games 106
ethical approaches
    categorization 165
    comparisons 173
    normative incomparability 152
    orientation 87
evaluation
    as devaluation 178
    incomparability and 57, 152, 172–3
Evans-Pritchard, Edward E. 66, 68
exclusion *see* devaluation
existential mode
    imaginative capacity 171
    orientation 75, 79, 118
experimental comparisons 29, 47–50, 61
explanatory abbreviation, comparing as 40
explanatory descriptions 101, 118
explicit contrastive comparisons 68
explicit precomparative judgements 53
explicit reduction, language 100
explicit *tertium* 24
explorative comparisons 36, 40–1, 47–8
    see also experimental comparisons
expressing standpoints 173
external comparison
    language-games 101
    'objects of comparison' 102–3
    orientation 85–6

factual adequacy 162, 165
factual language 100
false metaphors 38
'familiar' 53–4
family resemblances 191n.49, 205n.8
fantasy 114
feedback 203n.64
'feeling' 76–7
Feyerabend, Paul 2
fictional language 100
final vocabularies 113, 122, 209n.27
Flaubert, Gustave, *Madame Bovary* 121
Fleck, Ludwig 2
'focus' 196n.27
Fontane, Theodor, *Effi Briest* 122

formal contexts 62, 65
formal elements
    comparative contextualism 27
    constructivism 42
    see also tertia comparationis
Foucault, Michel 4, 30
free variation 47–8
freedom, deception of 218n.15
Freud, Sigmund 119
Fricker, Miranda, *Epistemic Injustice* 8
functional reductionism 100
fundamental mode, existence 79
fuzzy equality 127, 139, 144–6

Gadamer, Hans-Georg 5, 99, 206n.23
Galileo Galilei 64, 112
'Galton's Problem' 189n.26, 195n.18
games
    analogizing 97
    common features 94
    constitutive incomparability 150
    diversity 104–5
    family resemblances 191n.49
    generalizations 95
    goal definition 98
    internal comparison 102
    involvement in 99
    pure/intentional comparisons 104
    structures 106
    see also language-games
general contextualism 7, 9, 26
general theory 1, 109
generality
    context and 7, 9
    descriptive philosophy 95–6
    'practical turn' 71
generalizations
    language 94–5
    of particular 179–80, 181–2, 216n.11
generalized comparisons 1, 50
generalized structures 15
genetic comparisons 51–2
genuine vagueness 143
geographic orientation 73–4, 76, 77
gerrymandering 62
Goodman, Nelson 31
grammar 5–6, 98, 172, 216n.3
Griffin, James 133

Hacking, Ian 16
Handke, Peter 177–8, 181
'hard cases', incomparability 127
hard indeterminancy 135
Hegel, Georg Wilhelm Friedrich 116
Heidegger, Martin 26–7, 65, 83, 99, 169, 190n.36
hermeneutics of comparison 1, 104
heterogeneity, similarity and 30
heuristic analogy 34
heuristic typology 8, 14
hidden silencing 197n.6
hierarchical element, orientation 85–6
'Historian's Dispute' 219n.24
historical epistemology 59
history of comparisons 4–5
holistic approaches 10–11, 17
Holocaust lectures (Costello) 153–4, 156–64, 168, 171, 173
horizontal comparisons 111, 115
Humboldt, Alexander von 65
Hume, David 6, 16
　Dialogues 32–3
Husserl, Edmund 15, 19, 26–7, 30, 64–5
hyperbolic pointed comparisons 56

Ibsen, Henrik, *Nora* 121
identification 57
identity politics 63–4
ignorance 161, 171
imaginations 105
imaginative capacity 157, 166, 171
impartial comparisons 52–5
imprecise comparability 139, 140–1
impure comparisons 52–3, 62, 65
'inappropriate silencing' 197n.6
incommensurability 123, 125, 131–2, 144, 213n.24, 215n.61
　see also constitutive incomparability
incomparability 3–4, 9–11, 123–4
　adequacy and 151–73
　comparative methods 5
　conflicting values 2
　contextualism 28–9
　forms of 7, 57
　language-games 150, 152
　as marginalized classic 125–7
　metaphors 39
　on normative grounds 124
　pointed comparisons 57–8
　as refusal to compare 149
　scalability 129–30, 140, 163
　singularity 180, 181
　as structural breakdown 126, 129–32, 147–8, 172
incompatibility 173
incompleteness 104–6
independent *relata* problem 22, 189n.26
indeterminancy 132, 135, 139, 214n.53
indexical incomparability 9–10, 124, 147–50, 172–3
　see also constitutive incomparability
indexicality 73–90
　essential indexicals 202n.59
　orientation 73–4, 80, 82–4
　terminology 203n.63
indifference 133
individualized comparisons 50
inference, comparing as 40
institutional incomparability 147, 172, 216n.3
intentional comparisons 102, 103–4
interaction theory 35–7
interdisciplinary work 3
'interestingness' 120, 122
internal comparison
　constitutive incomparability 148
　language-games 101
　'objects of comparison' 102–3
　orientation 85–6
intracomparative injustice 197n.9
intransitivity 139
involvement
　comparison as 49
　language-games 98–9
　normative incomparability 162, 165
irony 109–22, 159

Jacobi, Friedrich 75
James, William 150
Jones, Ward 158
justice-utility clash 212n.15
justification
　description as 101
　language 95
　rational choice 146
　standard comparison 117
justified choice 127–8

Kaelble, Hartmut 3
Kafka's parables 167
Kafka's Red Peter 159–62, 166
Kant, Immanuel 6, 9, 16, 23, 41, 110
    in Costello's lectures 157, 167
    Critique of Judgment 179
    Critique of Pure Reason 76–7
    enlightenment thinking 199n.11
    incomparability 148, 181
    orientation 72, 73–90
Kaplan, David 84
Kierkegaard, Søren 109
knowledge formation 39–40, 43, 59–60, 63
Koschorke, Albrecht 30, 64
Kuhn, Thomas S. 2

language
    communal character 98, 207n.27
    descriptive philosophy 93, 105
    examples of comparison 195n.9
    generalizations 94–5
    justification 95
    metaphorization of 114–15
    phenomenology 98
    plurality of 114–15
    reality and 67, 92
    truth in 112, 114
language-games
    analogical comparisons 102–3, 206n.25
    constitutive incomparability 150
    descriptive philosophy 9, 95–6
    imaginative elements 105
    incomparability 150, 152
    as 'objects of comparison' 92–3, 96–100
    orientation 81
    problems with 207n.30
    reductive method/elements 105, 207n.31
latent precomparative judgements 53
latent *tertium comparationis* 24
levelling down 177–8, 181
    see also usurpation
liberalism, cruelty and 115, 117
limiting notions, alien culture 67–8
linguistic complexity 99–100
Linné, Carl von 41, 175
'literary criticism' 116
literary studies-philosophy convergence 111

literature
    appreciation of 120–1
    creating 116, 170
    incompatibility 173
Locke, John 6, 16
logic of addition 165
logic of emergence 165
logical irreducibility 130
Luhmann, Niklas 42, 75
Lukes, Steven 147–8

MacIntyre, Alasdair 66, 67–8, 109
maps 73–4, 79, 84–5
mass production zone 176, 177
material elements
    analogies 33–4
    comparative *relata* 42
    complex relations 19, 20–1
    contextualism 27
    ignoring/dimming 62, 65
Matthes, Joachim 53
Melville, Herman, *Billy Budd* 110
Mendelsohn, Moses 76
mental act/process, comparison as 16
metaphorology 38–9
metaphors 2, 34–9
    as comparisons 34–5
    'focus' 196n.27
    interaction theory 35–7
    irony and 114–15
    orientation as 74
    of persuasion 158
    refuting meaning 37–8, 218n.12
    semantics of 210n.32
metaphysics 75, 94, 128, 201n.46
Midgley, Mary 155
Mill, John Stuart 131
modal-reflexive element, singularization 180
modernity 175–6
monistic account, metaphors 37
monolithic structure 16–18, 21, 23, 29, 55
    contextual considerations 26
    relational aspects 45
Montesquieu 6
mood 80–1
Moorean Good 128–9, 212n.15
moral demands 60, 69, 205n.11

moral dimension, normative incomparability 152, 161, 169, 172–3
moral implications, asymmetrical comparisons 53
moral orientation 200n.18
moral theories 109–10, 120–1, 147
motivational comparisons 21
Mulhall, Stephen 162
multi-digit comparisons 56
multidimensional comparisons 24, 42
  see also complexity
multidimensionality, vagueness 143–5

Nabukov, Vladimir 110, 117, 121
Nagel, Thomas 155, 157, 171, 221n.54
narrative identity 115
narratives, plurality 120–2
'new realism' 209n.19
Nietzsche, Friedrich 41, 64, 75, 115, 118
  'age of comparison' 5, 11, 21, 176–7, 179
  Human, All Too Human 175
  Untimely Meditations 176
Nolte, Ernst 219n.24
nominalism *see* constructivism
non-substitutability 131
noncausal reading, alien culture 67
noncomparability 28, 140–2, 146
nonquantifiability 46–7
normative comparisons 52–5, 61, 65
normative incomparability 10, 28–9, 171–3
  adequacy and 151–73
  as refusal to compare 149
  structural incomparability versus 124, 171–2
  value relations 150
'nostrification' 44, 53–4, 64
novels 121–2
Nozick, Robert 163–4

objectivity 79, 83, 84, 172, 200n.18
'objects of comparison'
  descriptive philosophy 91–107
  external/internal comparisons 102–3
  language-games as 92–3, 96–100
O'Hearne, Professor 163
one-dimensionality *see* simplicity
O'Neill, Onora 109–10

ontological shift 4–5, 26
ontological similarity 20
open comparisons *see* experimental comparisons
'the order of things'
  fabrication of 4
  scientific status 5
orientation 73–90
  already oriented 87–9
  architecture of 78–89
  comparability 74, 80
  comparing as 41
  definition 78–9
  existential mode 75, 79, 118
  indexicality 73–4, 80, 82–4
  in its element 80–2
  of oneself 75–8
  respects of 9
  subjectivity 76, 78–9, 82–4, 200n.18
  tools 85
  as twofold comparison 84–7
Orwell, George 110, 121
  1984 117–18

parables 167, 195n.10
paradigms, theories embedded in 2
paradoxical structure, orientation 82
Parfit, Derek 133, 139
  Reasons and Persons 148, 194n.6
parity 126–7, 135–9, 214n.53
partial comparisons 52–3, 62
particular, generalizations of 179–80, 181–2, 216n.11
passive modes, orientation 88
performative conditions 18, 21
performative self-location 79
performativity 74, 80, 176
perspectivism 6, 81
persuasion 101, 158
phenomenology 96, 98
philosophical colonialism 64–5
philosophy
  as comparativism 115–22
  of existence 75
  literary studies convergence 111
  methodological demands 69
  moral demands 69
  of orientation 73–5
  positivist crisis 64

Pippin, Robert 168
plain equality 133, 136, 138, 139, 145
'play-off' 162
plural narratives 120–2
plural vocabularies 109–22
plurality
    of comparisons 105
    of descriptions 110–11, 113–15
    of language 114–15
    orientation 74
    problem of 131
    of values 123
Plutarch's essays 161
pointed comparisons 41, 55–8
politics-knowledge-history link 59
'population ethics' 194n.6
positive value relations 130, 134
possibilities, extending 168–71
post-comparative decision-making 146
post-post-colonial discourse 64
postmetaphysical philosophy 96
power dynamics 59, 60, 63
practical turn 13–44, 71
practices
    contextualism and 8
    definitions 16
    embeddedness 16–18, 27, 72
pragmatic/praxeological approaches 16–17, 19, 26–7, 30
precise comparability 140–1
precomparative injustice 197n.9
preconditions, reasonable comparisons 18–19
predicates
    vagueness 142–3, 145
    virtues 135, 142–4
preferences 103
'prejudices' 97, 206n.23
'present-at-hand' 26
'primitive language-games' 100
'primitive society' 66
private-public dualism 113, 119
procedural incomparability 128
productive effect, involving comparisons 49
protective function, description 105
'protocomparatistic' preconditions 18
psychoanalysis 119–20

pure comparisons 52–5, 62, 91, 103–4, 208n.37
pure descriptions 91, 101–2, 206n.20, 208n.37
pure indexicals 83–4
pure reason 76, 77

qualitative differences 138
quantifiability 43–4, 46–7

radical silencing 197n.6
rational choice 126–9, 132, 136, 139, 145–6
rationalism 68, 159, 167
rationality
    alien culture 68
    causal thinking 66–7
    of choices 127
    of decisions 126
    orientation 77
Raz, Joseph 132–6, 146, 147–50
'ready-at-hand' 26
reality
    language mirroring 67
    orientation 73–4, 84–5
    philosophical injustice to 92
reason 40, 76–7, 159, 167, 168
reasonable comparisons 18–30
receptivity, orientation 9, 80, 88, 89
Reckwitz, Andreas 179–80, 181
reductionism
    language 99–100, 105
    language-games 207n.31
    orientation 81, 86
    quantifying comparisons 43–4
    scalable *relata* 178
reflexibility 131, 138
reflexivity 180
Regan, Tom 155, 156
regulating linguistic structures 96
Reichenbach, Hans 16
relata/comparative items
    constructivism 42
    contextualism 26–7
    diachronic comparisons 51
    epistemology 59
    explorative comparisons 41
    impartial comparisons 52
    independence problem 22, 189n.26

intentional comparisons 103
knowledge creation 39–40
noncomparability 141
normative comparisons 65
as 'objects of comparison' 96–7
result-oriented comparisons 50
scalability 43, 178
structure 22–4
tertium comparationis relation 172
unjust construction of 61, 68
relational form, 'agent' 21
relational fuzziness 135
relational knowledge 43
relations
    logical irreducibility 130
    typology 45, 48
relativism, games 106
religion
    defeat of 118
    philosophy of 32–3
    refutation of 211n.52
reorientation 88
representation, vocabularies 115
result-oriented comparisons 29, 47–8, 49–50, 69
'retrospective reconstructions' 40
revisions, vocabularies 118
Richards, Ivor 36
romantic era 175
Rorty, Richard 9, 72, 95, 109–22
    Contingency, Irony and Solidarity 113
rough equality 133–4, 136, 138, 139
Rousseau, Jean-Jacques 6
rules of games 98, 99

scalability 129–30, 140, 163, 177
scalable *relata* 43, 129–30, 178
scalable *tertia* 46
scepticism 167–8
Schopenhauer, Arthur 64, 119
Schriewer, Jürgen 3
scientific hypotheses 66
scientific method, comparison as 5, 16
scientific theories 2
selectivity 81, 86
self-contained comparisons 49
self-extension, vocabularies 119–20
self-fulfilling conditions 19

self-orienting subject 83
self-sufficiency 42
semantic stability 22
semantic vagueness 144
semantics of metaphors 210n.32
sentences 112
'sharedness' 169–70
Shklar, Judith 115
short prioritizing 62–3
silencing 61–2, 65, 68, 197n.6
similarity
    asymmetrical comparisons 64
    comparisons exposing 4, 49–50
    constructed 20, 25
    contextual 51
    differences and 30–2, 50
similes 37–8
simplicity 24, 27, 42, 46–7
simulated impartiality 62–3
simulated result-oriented comparisons 69
Singer, Isaac Bashevis 156
Singer, Peter 153, 155
singularity 163, 178–80, 181
singularization
    elements of 180
    generalization and 182
    incomparability 181
small improvement thesis 133, 137
social practice, comparison as 180
Socratic philosophy 94
soft indeterminancy 135
sorites problem 137
spatial orientation 74, 76–7, 80, 84–5, 87
stable comparisons 48–50, 54, 119
standard comparison 117
Stegmaier, Werner 78–81, 83, 87
Stern, Abraham 163–4, 168, 171, 172–3
'strict incomparability' 215n.60
strong incommensurability 131
structural comparability 152
structural differences, typology 45
structural incomparability 7, 9–10, 28–9, 129–32
    arguments against 125–46
    explaining away 139–46, 147
    language-games 152

normative incomparability versus 124, 171–2
  as refusal to compare 149
structural relativism 106
structure of comparisons 5–6, 13–44, 45, 55
subcomparisons, impact of 194n.5
subject dependence 49
subject involvement 49
subjectivity 76, 78–9, 82–4, 172, 200n.18
sublimity 123, 175, 179
substantial incomparability 128
substitution theory 35
Sully, James 5–6
symmetry principle 31
sympathetic imagination 157, 166, 171
synchronic comparisons 22, 50–2, 177
synchronic orientation 80
Sztybel, David 156

Taylor, Charles 145
temporal aspects
  diachronic comparisons 51
  orientation 74, 80, 85–6
  typology 54–5
tertia comparationis 8, 13, 24–5
  complex relations 19, 21, 46–7
  incomparability 164
  normative comparisons 65
  'objects of comparison' 97
  pointed comparisons 56
  relata and 172
  simple-complex relations 46–7
  vocabularies 118
tertia/comparative regards
  circularity 43
  comparability problems 22
  comparative limits 182
  contextualism 26–7
  emergent comparisons 48–9, 61
  epistemology 59
  knowledge creation 39
  noncomparability 140
  as 'objects of comparison' 96, 102
  silencing 61–2, 65, 68
  stable-emergent distinction 48–9
  transforming 120
  unjust construction of 61–2, 65
  vocabularies 119–20, 122

theories
  accessibility 109–10
  embedded in paradigms 2
  scope of 109–10
'thick descriptions' 208n.37
'thought styles' 175, 217n.8
top-down approaches 1, 15
transcendental attributes, orientation 76
transcendental subject 82
transfer research 189n.26
transformation 105, 120
transitivity 131, 133, 138, 139
trichotomy thesis 19, 126, 130, 132, 134–9, 144
true demonstratives 83–4
trumping 131
truth 38, 111–13, 114, 135
typological comparisons 51–2
typology of comparisons 8, 14, 45–58, 60–1

ubiquity of comparison 182
uncertainty principle 30
unidimentional chaining argument 136–7
uniqueness 151, 163, 179
usurpation 53, 63, 69
utilitarianism 128–9, 212n.15

vagueness 47–9, 132–3, 135, 138–9, 141–5, 214n.53
value relations 130, 134, 150
values
  conflicting values 2
  noncomparability 141
  plurality of 123
variety reduction 177
vertical alignments 115
vertical match, vocabularies 111
virtue ethics 165
virtues
  disorientation 90
  impartial comparisons 53
  predicates 135, 142–4
  vocabularies 109–22, 209n.27

weak description 205n.18, 206n.19
weak incommensurability 131
Welles, Orson 125

wild comparisons 196n.29
Winch, Peter 14, 60, 66–9, 110
'winner take all/most' logic 181
Wittgenstein, Ludwig 9, 41, 66, 72, 109–10, 113–14, 117
   Blue Book 93, 97, 99
   descriptive philosophy 91–107
   Investigations 92, 100–1, 104
   Philosophical Investigations 191n.49, 195n.9, 204n.2
   writings, abbreviations 203n.1
'world' standpoint 80, 88

Zima, Peter 23

www.ingramcontent.com/pod-product-compliance
Lightning Source LLC
Chambersburg PA
CBHW062133300426
44115CB00012BA/1904